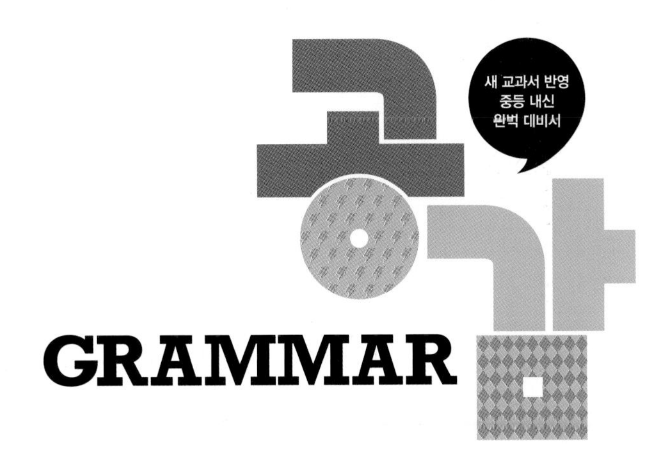

공감 GRAMMAR

Level 1

Grammar 공감 Level 1

지은이 넥서스영어교육연구소
펴낸이 임상진
펴낸곳 (주)넥서스

출판신고 1992년 4월 3일 제311-2002-2호 ⑭
10880 경기도 파주시 지목로 5
Tel (02)330-5500 Fax (02)330-5555

ISBN 978-89-6790-844-7 54740
978-89-6790-843-0 (SET)

※집필에 도움을 주신 분
:김현진 선생님, 정혜영 선생님, 임현주 선생님, 임재원 선생님, 오선행 선생님

공감 GRAMMAR

넥서스영어교육연구소 지음

NEXUS Edu

Get high scores

2,500여 개의 전국 중학교 기출 문제를 분석하여 반영한 review test를 제공함으로써 내신 성적을 향상시켜 줍니다.

Obtain a wide vocabulary

풍부한 어휘 리스트를 제공, 기본적인 어휘 실력을 향상시켜 줍니다.

Nurture your English skills

최신 개정 교과서를 분석 반영한 문법 설명을 수록, 2,500여 개에 달하는 전국 중학교 최신 기출 문제를 분석하여 반영한 문제를 수록, 중등 과정에서 알아야 하는 풍부한 어휘를 제공함으로써 종합적인 영어 실력을 향상시켜 줍니다.

Get writing skills

서술형 평가 코너를 따로 수록해 새로운 교수 평가 방법에 대비할 수 있게 해 줍니다.

Get speaking skills

영어 회화로도 활용 가능한 예문을 제공하여 영어 말하기 능력을 향상시켜 줍니다.

Acquire good English sense

2,000여 개의 충분한 연습 문제를 풀어보게 해줌으로써 문법 감각을 습득시켜 줍니다.

Master the essentials of grammar

최신 교과서를 분석하여 반영한 문법 설명으로, 내신에 필수 불가결한 문법을 학습하게 해 줍니다.

Features

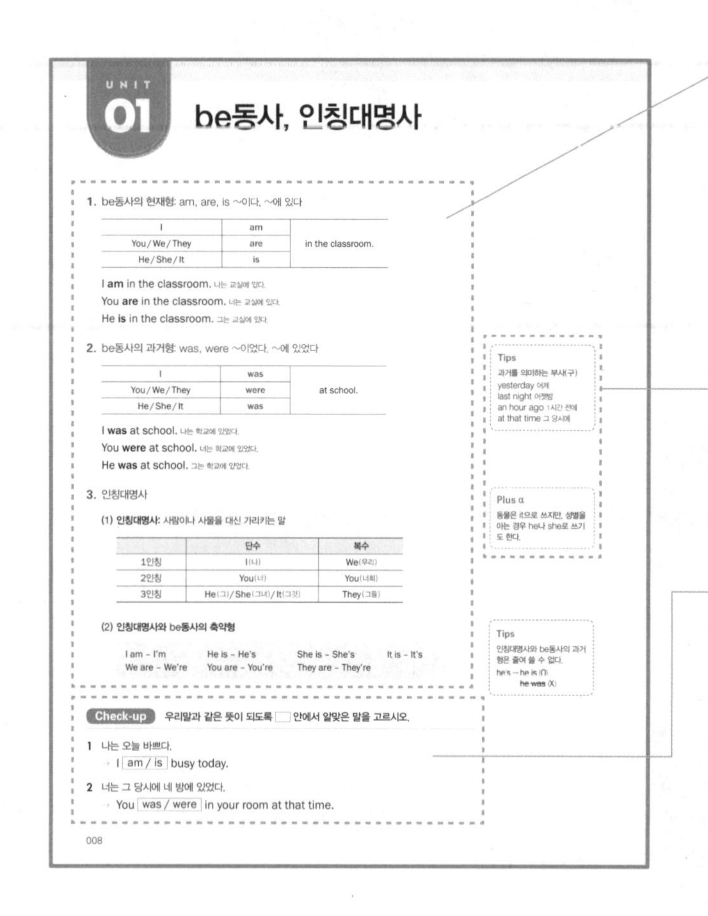

UNIT 01 be동사, 인칭대명사

1. be동사의 현재형: am, are, is ~이다, ~에 있다

I	am	in the classroom.
You / We / They	are	
He / She / It	is	

I **am** in the classroom. 나는 교실에 있다.
You **are** in the classroom. 너는 교실에 있다.
He **is** in the classroom. 그는 교실에 있다.

2. be동사의 과거형: was, were ~이었다, ~에 있었다

I	was	at school.
You / We / They	were	
He / She / It	was	

I **was** at school. 나는 학교에 있었다.
You **were** at school. 너는 학교에 있었다.
He **was** at school. 그는 학교에 있었다.

3. 인칭대명사

(1) 인칭대명사: 사람이나 사물을 대신 가리키는 말

	단수	복수
1인칭	I(나)	We(우리)
2인칭	You(너)	You(너희)
3인칭	He(그) / She(그녀) / It(그것)	They(그들)

(2) 인칭대명사와 be동사의 축약형

I am - I'm　He is - He's　She is - She's　It is - It's
We are - We're　You are - You're　They are - They're

Tips
과거를 의미하는 부사(구)
yesterday 어제
last night 어젯밤
an hour ago 1시간 전에
at that time 그 당시에

Plus α
동물은 it으로 쓰지만, 성별을 아는 경우 he나 she로 쓰기도 한다.

Tips
인칭대명사와 be동사의 과거형은 줄여 쓸 수 없다.
he's → he is (O)
he was (X)

Check-up 우리말과 같은 뜻이 되도록 ☐ 안에서 알맞은 말을 고르시오.

1 나는 오늘 바쁘다.
→ I [am / is] busy today.

2 너는 그 당시에 네 방에 있었다.
→ You [was / were] in your room at that time.

008

핵심 문법 정리

내신에 꼭 필요한 핵심 문법 사항들을 알기 쉽게 단계별로 설명하였습니다. 실용적인 예문과 간결하고 정확한 문법 설명을 제시하여 대표 예문만 봐도 문법의 개념을 이해할 수 있습니다. 시험에 꼭 나오는 문법 내용이 자연스럽게 반복되어 충분한 학습 효과를 볼 수 있습니다.

Plus α & Tips

핵심 문법 사항 이외에 추가로 심화 문법 사항과 학생들이 특히 주의해야 할 사항을 정리하였습니다.

Check-up

학습한 핵심 문법을 올바로 이해하였는지 바로 확인할 수 있는 문제로, 핵심 문법 사항만 숙지하였다면 누구나 쉽고 재미있게 풀 수 있는 기본 문제들로 구성하였습니다.

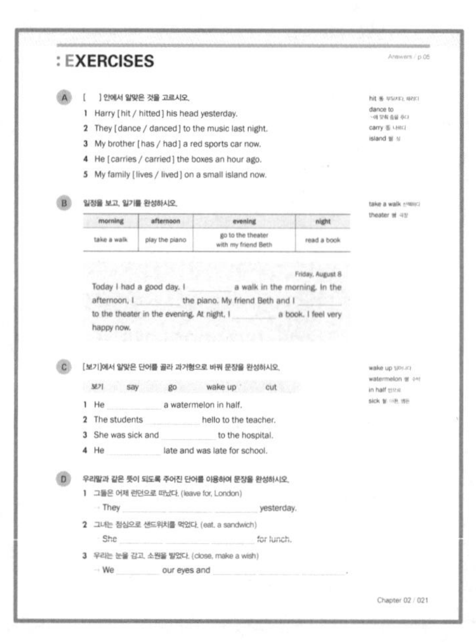

: EXERCISES　Answers / p.05

A [ ] 안에서 알맞은 것을 고르시오.
1 Harry [hit / hitted] his head yesterday.
2 They [dance / danced] to the music last night.
3 My brother [has / had] a red sports car now.
4 He [carries / carried] the boxes an hour ago.
5 My family [lives / lived] on a small island now.

B 일정을 보고, 일기를 완성하시오.

morning	afternoon	evening	night
take a walk	play the piano	go to the theater with my friend Beth	read a book

Friday, August 8
Today I had a good day. I ______ a walk in the morning. In the afternoon, I ______ the piano. My friend Beth and I ______ to the theater in the evening. At night, I ______ a book. I feel very happy now.

C [보기]에서 알맞은 단어를 골라 과거형으로 바꿔 문장을 완성하시오.
보기　say　go　wake up　cut
1 He ______ a watermelon in half.
2 The students ______ hello to the teacher.
3 She was sick and ______ to the hospital.
4 He ______ late and was late for school.

D 우리말과 같은 뜻이 되도록 주어진 단어를 이용하여 문장을 완성하시오.
1 그들은 어제 런던으로 떠났다. (leave for, London)
→ They ______ ______ ______ yesterday.
2 그녀는 점심으로 샌드위치를 먹었다. (eat, a sandwich)
→ She ______ ______ ______ for lunch.
3 우리는 눈을 감고, 소원을 빌었다. (close, make a wish)
→ We ______ our eyes and ______ ______ ______.

hit 동 부딪치다, 때리다
dance to ~에 맞춰 춤을 추다
carry 동 나르다
island 명 섬
take a walk 산책하다
theater 명 극장
wake up 일어나다
watermelon 명 수박
in half 반으로
sick 형 아픈, 병든

Chapter 02 / 021

Exercises

해당 Unit에서 학습한 문법 사항을 다양한 유형의 주관식 문제를 통해 완벽하게 정리할 수 있도록 하였습니다. 단순 암기한 내용을 가지고 푸는 것이 아니라 직접 응용해서 써 보고 생각해 볼 수 있도록 구성하였습니다.

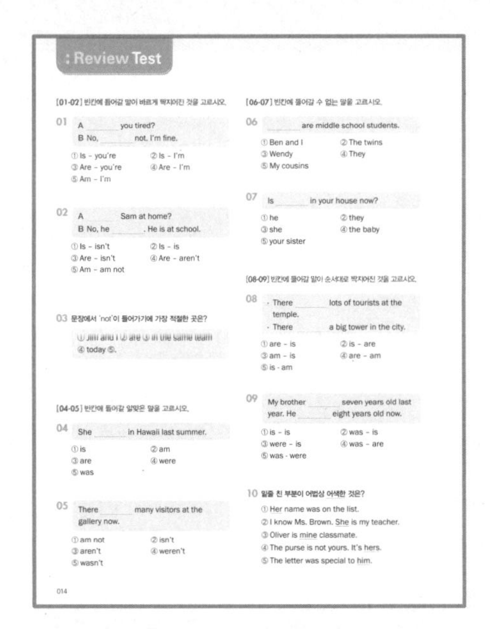

: Review Test

[01-02] 빈칸에 들어갈 말이 바르게 짝지어진 것을 고르시오.

01 A ______ you tired?
B No, ______ not. I'm fine.
① Is - you're ② Is - I'm
③ Are - you're ④ Are - I'm
⑤ Am - I'm

02 A ______ Sam at home?
B No, he ______. He is at school.
① Is - isn't ② Is - is
③ Are - isn't ④ Are - aren't
⑤ Am - am not

03 문장에서 'not'이 들어가기에 가장 적절한 곳은?
① Jim and I ② are ③ in the same team ④ today ⑤.

[04-05] 빈칸에 들어갈 알맞은 말을 고르시오.

04 She ______ in Hawaii last summer.
① is ② am
③ are ④ were
⑤ was

05 There ______ many visitors at the gallery now.
① am not ② isn't
③ aren't ④ weren't
⑤ wasn't

[06-07] 빈칸에 들어갈 수 없는 말을 고르시오.

06 ______ are middle school students.
① Ben and I ② The twins
③ Wendy ④ They
⑤ My cousins

07 Is ______ in your house now?
① he ② they
③ she ④ the baby
⑤ your sister

[08-09] 빈칸에 들어갈 말이 순서대로 짝지어진 것을 고르시오.

08 · There ______ lots of tourists at the temple.
· There ______ a big tower in the city.
① are - is ② is - are
③ am - is ④ are - am
⑤ is - am

09 My brother ______ seven years old last year. He ______ eight years old now.
① is - is ② was - is
③ were - is ④ was - are
⑤ was - were

10 밑줄 친 부분이 어법상 어색한 것은?
① Her name was on the list.
② I know Ms. Brown. She is my teacher.
③ Oliver is mine classmate.
④ The purse is not yours. It's hers.
⑤ The letter was special to him.

014

Review Test

해당 Chapter에서 학습한 내용을 통합형 문제 유형을 통해서 다시 한 번 정리할 수 있도록 하였습니다. 실제 학교 시험과 동일한 유형의 문제들로 구성하여 내신을 완벽하게 대비할 수 있습니다. 스스로 자신의 취약한 부분을 점검하며 문법에 대한 자신감을 기를 수 있습니다.

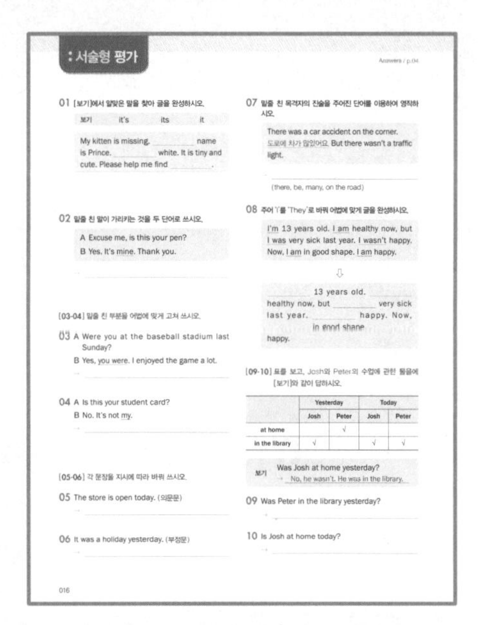

: 서술형 평가

Answers / p.04

01 [보기]에서 알맞은 말을 찾아 글을 완성하시오.
보기 it's its it
My kitten is missing. ______ name is Prince. ______ white. It is tiny and cute. Please help me find ______.

02 밑줄 친 말이 가리키는 것을 두 단어로 쓰시오.
A Excuse me, is this your pen?
B Yes. It's mine. Thank you.
→

[03-04] 밑줄 친 부분을 어법에 맞게 고쳐 쓰시오.

03 A Were you at the baseball stadium last Sunday?
B Yes, you were. I enjoyed the game a lot.
→

04 A Is this your student card?
B No. It's not my.
→

[05-06] 각 문장을 지시에 따라 바꿔 쓰시오.

05 The store is open today. (의문문)
→

06 It was a holiday yesterday. (부정문)
→

07 밑줄 친 목격자의 진술을 주어진 단어를 이용하여 영작하시오.
There was a car accident on the corner. 도로에 차가 많았어요. But there wasn't a traffic light.
→
(there, be, many, on the road)

08 주어 'I'를 'They'로 바꿔 어법에 맞게 글을 완성하시오.
I'm 13 years old. I am healthy now, but I was very sick last year. I wasn't happy. Now, I am in good shape. I am happy.
⇩
______ 13 years old. ______ healthy now, but ______ very sick last year. ______ happy. Now, ______ in good shape ______ happy.

[09-10] 표를 보고, Josh와 Peter의 수업에 관한 물음에 [보기]와 같이 답하시오.

	Yesterday		Today	
	Josh	Peter	Josh	Peter
at home		√		
in the library	√		√	√

보기 Was Josh at home yesterday?
→ No, he wasn't. He was in the library.

09 Was Peter in the library yesterday?
→

10 Is Josh at home today?
→

016

서술형 평가

최신 교수 평가 방법에 대비할 수 있도록 서술형 평가 코너를 따로 마련하였습니다. 학교 내신 시험에 자주 나오는 유형의 서술형 문제를 통해서 어떤 문제가 나와도 대비할 수 있도록 하였으며 학생들의 사고력과 창의력도 길러줍니다.

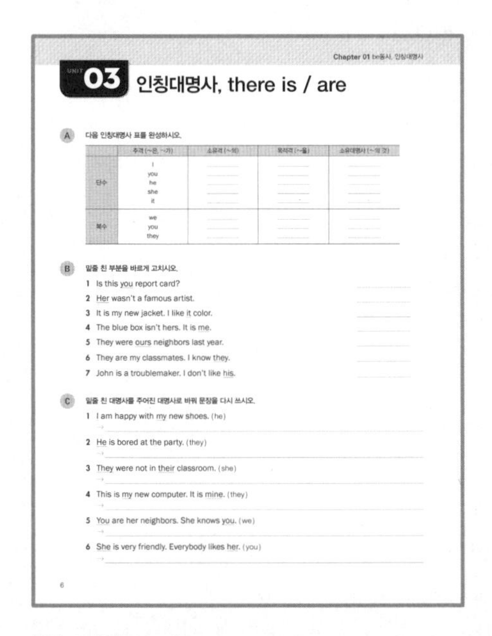

Chapter 01 be동사, 인칭대명사

UNIT 03 인칭대명사, there is / are

A 다음 인칭대명사 표를 완성하시오.

	주격 (~은, ~가)	소유격 (~의)	목적격 (~을)	소유대명사 (~의 것)
단수	I you he she it			
복수	we you they			

B 밑줄 친 부분을 바르게 고치시오.
1 Is this you report card?
2 Her wasn't a famous artist.
3 It is my new jacket. I like it color.
4 The blue box isn't hers. It is me.
5 They were ours neighbors last year.
6 They are my classmates. I know they.
7 John is a troublemaker. I don't like his.

C 밑줄 친 대명사를 주어진 대명사로 바꿔 문장을 다시 쓰시오.
1 I am happy with my new shoes. (he)
→
2 He is bored at the party. (they)
→
3 They were not in their classroom. (she)
→
4 This is my new computer. It is mine. (they)
→
5 You are her neighbors. She knows you. (we)
→
6 She is very friendly. Everybody likes her. (you)
→

6

Workbook (서술형 대비)

본책에서 학습한 내용을 다양한 서술형 문제를 통해서 핵심 문법 사항을 충분히 연습할 수 있도록 하였습니다. 숙제나 자습을 통해 문법 사항을 최종 정리하며 복습할 수 있는 좋은 기회가 될 수 있습니다.

C
1 am으로 답했으므로 현재로 물어야 함
A 너는 축구를 잘 하니?
B 응, 그래. 나는 매일 축구 연습을 해.
2 weren't로 답했으므로 과거로 물어야 함
A 그들이 회의에 늦었니?
B 아니, 그렇지 않았어. 그들은 제시간에 왔어.
3 wasn't로 답했으므로 과거로 물어야 함
A 수학 시험은 어려웠니?
B 아니, 그렇지 않았어. 쉬웠어.

UNIT 03

Check-up P. 012
1 my 2 are

1 '나의 노트북 컴퓨터'라는 의미이므로 my가 적절
2 「There are + 복수 명사(two puppies)」

: EXERCISES P. 013
A 1 Is 2 Are 3 are 4 was 5 weren't
B 1 our 2 They 3 Her 4 yours 5 me
C 1 her, hers 2 They, them 3 He, His
D 1 is, hers 2 There, is, a, calendar 3 There, was, a, speech, contest

A
1 「Is there + 단수 명사(a problem)?」
문제가 있나요?
2 「Are there + 복수 명사(books)?」
책장에 책들이 있나요?
3 「There are + 복수 명사(some kids)」
운동장에 몇 명의 아이들이 있다.
4 「There was + 단수 명사(a terrible storm)」
지난밤에 끔찍한 폭풍이 있었다.
5 「There weren't + 복수 명사(any teachers)」
그 당시 학교에 교사들이 한 명도 없었다.

B
1 '우리의 영어 선생님'이라는 뜻이므로 us가 아니라 our가 적절
그 남자는 우리의 영어 선생님이다.
2 '그들은'이라는 의미이므로 Their가 아니라 They가 적절
그들은 일본에서 온 학생들이다.
3 '그녀의 이름'이라는 의미이므로 Hers가 아니라 Her가 적절
그녀는 나의 이웃이다. 그녀의 이름은 Helen이다.
4 '너의 것'이라는 의미이므로 you가 아니라 yours가 적절
파란색 재킷은 내 것이고 빨간색 재킷은 너의 것이다.
5 '나를'이라는 의미이므로 I가 아니라 me가 적절
그와 나는 같은 반이다. 그는 나를 매우 잘 안다.

C
1 Nancy는 여성 3인칭 단수, her, hers으로 바꿔 쓸 수 있음
이것은 Nancy의 그림이다. 저것 또한 Nancy의 것이다.
→ 이것은 그녀의 그림이다. 저것 또한 그녀의 것이다.
2 Jess and Mike는 3인칭 복수, They, them으로 쓸 수 있음
Jess와 Mike는 재미있다. 모두 Jess와 Mike를 좋아한다.
→ 그들은 재미있다. 모두가 그들을 좋아한다.
3 Brian은 남성 3인칭 단수, He, His로 바꿔 쓸 수 있음
Brian은 나의 가장 친한 친구이다. Brian의 취미는 독서이다.
→ 그는 나의 가장 친한 친구이다. 그의 취미는 독서이다.

: Review Test P. 014

01 ④	02 ①	03 ③	04 ⑤	05 ③
06 ③	07 ②	08 ①	09 ②	10 ③
11 ①	12 ②	13 ⑤	14 ①	15 ④

01 you와 함께 쓰는 be동사는 Are, '아니, 나는 그렇지 않아'라고 대답해야 하므로 I'm이 적절
A 너 피곤하니? B 아니, 그렇지 않아. 나는 괜찮아.
02 Sam은 3인칭 단수, 3인칭 단수와 함께 쓰는 be동사는 Is. No가 왔으므로 isn't가 적절
A Sam은 집에 있니? B 아니, 없어. 그는 학교에 있어.
03 be동사의 부정문: 「주어 + be동사(are) + not」
Jim과 나는 오늘 같은 팀이다 / 같은 팀이 아니다.
04 「She + was + 과거 부사구(last summer)」
그녀는 작년 여름에 하와이에 있었다.
05 「There aren't + 복수 명사(many visitors) + 현재 부사(now)」
지금 화랑에는 방문객이 많지 않다.
06 「We / You / 3인칭 복수 + are」, Ben and I, The twins, They, My cousins는 3인칭 복수. Wendy는 3인칭 단수
Ben과 나는/쌍둥이는/그들은/내 사촌들은 중학교 학생들이다.
07 「Is + 3인칭 단수~?」, he, she, the baby, your sister는 3인칭 단수. they는 3인칭 복수
그는/그녀는/아기는/네 여동생은 지금 너의 집에 있니?
08 「There are + 복수 명사(lots of tourists)」, 「There is + 단수 명사(a big tower)」
· 그 사원에 많은 관광객이 있다.
· 그 도시에 큰 탑이 하나 있다.

03

정답 및 해설

기존의 어렵고 복잡한 설명에서 벗어나 간결하고 정확한 설명을 통해서 해설집만 보고도 핵심 문법 정리를 한눈에 할 수 있도록 하였습니다.

Contents

Chapter 1

be동사, 인칭대명사

UNIT 01

be동사, 인칭대명사

1. be동사의 현재형: am, are, is ~이다, ~에 있다

I	am	in the classroom.
You / We / They	are	
He / She / It	is	

I **am** in the classroom. 나는 교실에 있다.

You **are** in the classroom. 너는 교실에 있다.

He **is** in the classroom. 그는 교실에 있다.

2. be동사의 과거형: was, were ~이었다, ~에 있었다

I	was	at school.
You / We / They	were	
He / She / It	was	

I **was** at school. 나는 학교에 있었다.

You **were** at school. 너는 학교에 있었다.

He **was** at school. 그는 학교에 있었다.

Tips
과거를 의미하는 부사(구)
yesterday 어제
last night 어젯밤
an hour ago 1시간 전에
at that time 그 당시에

3. 인칭대명사

(1) **인칭대명사:** 사람이나 사물을 대신 가리키는 말

	단수	복수
1인칭	I(나)	We(우리)
2인칭	You(너)	You(너희)
3인칭	He(그)/She(그녀)/It(그것)	They(그들)

Plus α
동물은 it으로 쓰지만, 성별을 아는 경우 he나 she로 쓰기도 한다.

(2) **인칭대명사와 be동사의 축약형**

I am - I'm　　He is - He's　　She is - She's　　It is - It's
We are - We're　　You are - You're　　They are - They're

Tips
인칭대명사와 be동사의 과거형은 줄여 쓸 수 없다.
he's → he is (O)
~~he was~~ (X)

Check-up 우리말과 같은 뜻이 되도록 [ ] 안에서 알맞은 말을 고르시오.

1 나는 오늘 바쁘다.
→ I [am / is] busy today.

2 너는 그 당시에 네 방에 있었다.
→ You [was / were] in your room at that time.

: EXERCISES

Answers / p.02

A [ ] 안에서 알맞은 것을 고르시오.

1 He [am / are / is] from Australia.
2 I [am / are / is] a new student here.
3 They [am / are / is] proud of their son.
4 She [am / are / is] my English teacher.
5 You [am / are / is] a good soccer player.

Australia 명 호주
be proud of ~을 자랑스러워하다
soccer player 축구 선수

B 밑줄 친 부분을 줄여 쓰시오.

1 It is my backpack. → ______________
2 You are a good cook. → ______________
3 He is at the shopping mall. → ______________
4 We are ready for the exam. → ______________
5 I am a member of the soccer team. → ______________

backpack 명 배낭
cook 명 요리사
be ready for ~ 할 준비가 되다

C be동사의 과거형을 이용하여 문장을 완성하시오.

1 It __________ a sad story.
2 They __________ rivals at the game.
3 I __________ late for school yesterday.
4 He __________ my homeroom teacher last year.
5 John and Peter __________ in the hallway a minute ago.

rival 명 경쟁자
be late for ~에 늦다
homeroom teacher 담임
hallway 명 복도

D 우리말과 같은 뜻이 되도록 주어진 단어를 이용하여 문장을 완성하시오.

1 그는 거울 앞에 있다. (be)
→ __________ __________ in front of the mirror.

2 그것은 흥미로운 책이다. (be)
→ __________ __________ an interesting book.

3 그들은 지금 정원에 있다. (be)
→ __________ __________ in the garden now.

4 우리는 목이 마르고 배가 고팠다. (be)
→ __________ __________ thirsty and hungry.

5 나는 작년에 초등학생이었다. (be)
→ __________ __________ an elementary school student last year.

UNIT 02

be동사의 부정문, 의문문

1. be동사의 부정문

(1) **be동사 현재형의 부정문:** 「am/are/is+not」 ~이 아니다, ~에 없다

I	**am not**	in the kitchen.
You/We/They	**are not**	
He/She/It	**is not**	

She **is not** in the kitchen. 그녀는 부엌에 없다.

(2) **be동사 과거형의 부정문:** 「was/were+not」 ~이 아니었다, ~에 없었다

I/He/She/It	**was not**	in the backyard.
You/We/They	**were not**	

They **were not** in the backyard. 그들은 뒷마당에 없었다.

Tips

1 be동사와 not은 줄여 쓸 수 있다.
is not - isn't
are not - aren't
was not - wasn't
were not - weren't
2 am not은 줄여 쓸 수 없다.
~~amn't~~ (X)

2. be동사의 의문문

(1) **be동사 현재형의 의문문:** 「Am/Are/Is+주어 ~?」 ~인가요?, ~에 있나요?

Am	I	late?	- Yes, you are.	- No, you aren't.
Are	you/we/they		- Yes, I am. - Yes, we/they are.	- No, I'm not. - No, we/they aren't.
Is	he/she/it		- Yes, he/she/it is.	- No, he/she/it isn't.

A **Am I** late? 제가 늦은 건가요?

B Yes, you are./No, you aren't. 네, 그래요. / 아니요, 그렇지 않아요.

(2) **be동사 과거형의 의문문:** 「Was/Were+주어 ~?」 ~였나요?, ~에 있었나요?

Was	I/he/she/it	all right?	- Yes, you were. - Yes, he/she/it was.	- No, you weren't. - No, he/she/it wasn't.
Were	you/we/they		- Yes, I was. - Yes, we/they were.	- No, I wasn't. - No, we/they weren't.

A **Were you** all right? 당신은 괜찮았나요?

B Yes, I was./No, I wasn't. 네, 그랬어요. /아니요, 안 그랬어요.

Tips

Yes로 대답할 때 주어와 be동사는 줄여 쓸 수 없다.
Are you at home?
- Yes, **I am.** (O)
- ~~Yes, I'm.~~ (X)

Check-up 우리말과 같은 뜻이 되도록 [ ] 안에서 알맞은 말을 고르시오.

1 그들은 형제가 아니다.
→ They [aren't / isn't] brothers.

2 그녀가 네 여동생이니?
→ [Are / Is] she your sister?

: EXERCISES

Answers / p.02

A [ ] 안에서 알맞은 것을 고르시오.

1 My friend [isn't / aren't] a liar.
2 [Was / Were] your diary on the desk?
3 [Is / Are] Mr. Lyons your math teacher?
4 My parents and I [am not / aren't] in London.
5 [Are / Is] these colored pencils in the can yours?

liar 명 거짓말쟁이
diary 명 다이어리, 일기장
colored pencil 색연필

B 밑줄 친 부분을 어법에 맞게 고쳐 쓰시오. [문장의 의미를 변경하지 말 것]

1 Were you free now?
2 I amn't the top student in my class.
3 Is Jamie in the hospital last Sunday?
4 Are your school far away from home?
5 My little brother not was afraid of ghosts.

free 형 한가한
far away 멀리
be afraid of ~을 두려워하다
ghost 명 귀신, 유령

C 주어진 말과 be동사를 이용하여 대화를 완성하시오.

1 A ________ ________ good at soccer? (you)
B Yes, I am. I practice soccer every day.

2 A ________ ________ late for the meeting? (they)
B No, they weren't. They were on time.

3 A ________ ________ ________ ________ difficult? (the math test)
B No, it wasn't. It was easy.

be good at ~을 잘하다
practice 동 연습하다
meeting 명 회의
on time 제시간에

D 우리말과 같은 뜻이 되도록 주어진 단어를 이용하여 문장을 완성하시오.

1 너는 오늘 아침에 네 방에 있었니? (you, be)
→ ________ ________ in your room this morning?

2 그 음악가들은 브라질 출신이 아니다. (the musicians, be)
→ ________ ________ ________ ________ from Brazil.

3 A 그 공책은 너의 것이니? (the notebook, be)
B 응, 그래. (it, be)
→ A ________ ________ ________ yours?
B Yes, ________ ________.

UNIT 03 인칭대명사, There is/are

1. 인칭대명사: 사람이나 사물을 대신 가리키는 말

	주격(~은, ~가)	소유격(~의)	목적격(~을)	소유대명사(~의 것)
단수	I you he she it	my your his her its	me you him her it	mine yours his hers -
복수	we you they	our your their	us you them	ours yours theirs

(1) **주격**(~은, ~는, ~이, ~가): 주로 동사 앞에 쓰여 주어(행위의 주체) 역할을 한다.

Cathy and Sue are pretty. **They** are twins. Cathy와 Sue는 예쁘다. 그들은 쌍둥이이다.

(2) **소유격**(~의): 명사 앞에 쓰여 소유 관계를 나타낸다.

His family is from China. 그의 가족은 중국에서 왔다.

(3) **목적격**(~을, ~를, ~에게): 주로 동사와 전치사 뒤에 쓰여 목적어(동작의 대상) 역할을 한다.

Charles likes **her** very much. Charles는 그녀를 매우 많이 좋아한다.

Tom's mother is proud of **him**. Tom의 어머니는 그를 자랑스러워한다.

(4) **소유대명사**(~의 것): 「소유격+명사」를 대신한다.

This umbrella is **mine**. 이 우산은 내 것이다.
=my umbrella

> **Plus α**
> 고유명사(사람, 사물의 이름)의 소유격, 소유대명사는 「고유명사+'s」로 나타낸다.
> This is **Cindy's bag.**
> 이것은 Cindy의 가방이다.
> This bag is **Cindy's**.
> =Cindy's bag
> 이 가방은 Cindy의 것이다.

2. There is/There are

(1) 「There is/was+**단수 명사**」 ~가 있다, ~가 있었다

There is a car outside. 밖에 차가 한 대 있다.

There was an old tree in the village. 마을에 오래된 나무가 한 그루 있었다.

(2) 「There are/were+**복수 명사**」 ~들이 있다, ~들이 있었다

There are many stars in the sky. 하늘에 많은 별들이 있다.

There were a lot of people on the street. 거리에 많은 사람들이 있었다.

> **Plus α**
> 장소 부사로 쓰인 there는 '그곳에'라고 해석하지만, '~이 있다(there is/are)'라는 의미로 쓰인 there는 '그곳에'라고 해석하지 않는다.
> I was **there** last night.
> 나는 어젯밤에 그곳에 있었다.
> **There is** a man on the corner.
> 모퉁이에 한 남자가 있다.

Check-up 우리말과 같은 뜻이 되도록 [ ] 안에서 알맞은 말을 고르시오.

1 저것은 나의 노트북 컴퓨터가 아니다.
→ That is not [my / mine] laptop computer.

2 상자 안에 강아지 두 마리가 있다.
→ There [are / is] two puppies in the box.

: EXERCISES

Answers / p.03

A [ ] 안에서 알맞은 것을 고르시오.

1 [Is / Are] there a problem?

2 [Is / Are] there books on the shelf?

3 There [is / are] some kids in the playground.

4 There [was / were] a terrible storm last night.

5 There [wasn't / weren't] any teachers at the school at that time.

shelf 명 선반, 책꽂이
playground 명 운동장, 놀이터
terrible 형 심한, 끔찍한
storm 명 폭풍

B 밑줄 친 부분을 어법에 맞게 고쳐 쓰시오.

1 The man is <u>us</u> English teacher.

2 <u>Their</u> are students from Japan.

3 She is my neighbor. <u>Hers</u> name is Helen.

4 The blue jacket is mine, and the red jacket is <u>you</u>.

5 He and I are in the same class. He knows <u>I</u> very well.

neighbor 명 이웃
jacket 명 재킷

C 밑줄 친 부분을 알맞은 인칭대명사로 바꿔 쓰시오.

1 This is <u>Nancy's</u> painting. That is also <u>Nancy's</u>.
→ This is __________ painting. That is also __________.

2 <u>Jess and Mike</u> are very funny. Everybody likes <u>Jess and Mike</u>.
→ __________ are very funny. Everybody likes __________.

3 <u>Brian</u> is my best friend. <u>Brian's</u> hobby is reading books.
→ __________ is my best friend. __________ hobby is reading books.

painting 명 그림
funny 형 웃기는, 재미있는

D 우리말과 같은 뜻이 되도록 주어진 단어를 이용하여 문장을 완성하시오.

1 그 노란색 필통은 그녀의 것이다. (be, she)
→ The yellow pencil case __________ __________.

2 책상 위에 달력이 하나 있다. (there, be, a calendar)
→ __________ __________ __________ __________ on the desk.

3 어제 학교에서 말하기 대회가 있었다. (there, be, a speech contest)
→ __________ __________ __________ __________ __________
in the school yesterday.

: Review Test

[01-02] 빈칸에 들어갈 말이 바르게 짝지어진 것을 고르시오.

01

A ________ you tired?
B No, ________ not. I'm fine.

① Is – you're
② Is – I'm
③ Are – you're
④ Are – I'm
⑤ Am – I'm

02

A ________ Sam at home?
B No, he ________. He is at school.

① Is – isn't
② Is – is
③ Are – isn't
④ Are – aren't
⑤ Am – am not

03 문장에서 'not'이 들어가기에 가장 적절한 곳은?

① Jim and I ② are ③ in the same team ④ today ⑤.

[04-05] 빈칸에 들어갈 알맞은 말을 고르시오.

04

She ________ in Hawaii last summer.

① is
② am
③ are
④ were
⑤ was

05

There ________ many visitors at the gallery now.

① am not
② isn't
③ aren't
④ weren't
⑤ wasn't

[06-07] 빈칸에 들어갈 수 없는 말을 고르시오.

06

________ are middle school students.

① Ben and I
② The twins
③ Wendy
④ They
⑤ My cousins

07

Is ________ in your house now?

① he
② they
③ she
④ the baby
⑤ your sister

[08-09] 빈칸에 들어갈 말이 순서대로 짝지어진 것을 고르시오.

08

· There ________ lots of tourists at the temple.
· There ________ a big tower in the city.

① are – is
② is – are
③ am – is
④ are – am
⑤ is - am

09

My brother ________ seven years old last year. He ________ eight years old now.

① is – is
② was – is
③ were – is
④ was – are
⑤ was - were

10 밑줄 친 부분이 어법상 어색한 것은?

① Her name was on the list.
② I know Ms. Brown. She is my teacher.
③ Oliver is mine classmate.
④ The purse is not yours. It's hers.
⑤ The letter was special to him.

11 빈칸에 들어갈 말이 바르게 짝지어진 것은?

Harry is my best friend. ________ is from the U.K. ________ hobby is playing soccer. He and I are in the same soccer team. I like ________ very much.

① He - His - him
② His - He - his
③ His - His - his
④ His - He - him
⑤ He - His - his

[12-13] 대화의 빈칸에 들어갈 알맞은 말을 고르시오.

12

A Were you busy yesterday?
B ________________. I was free all day.

① Yes, I was.
② No, I wasn't.
③ Yes, I wasn't.
④ Yes, you were.
⑤ No, you weren't.

13

A Is there a post office near here?
B ________________. It is on the corner.

① Yes, there was.
② No, there wasn't.
③ Yes, there are.
④ No, there isn't.
⑤ Yes, there is.

[14-15] 글을 읽고, 물음에 답하시오.

(A) 우리 가족은 다섯 명이다: my father, my mother, my twin brothers, and me. My parents are teachers. My twin brothers are nine years old. They are playful. ___ⓐ___ favorite game is hide-and-seek. They are cute. I love ___ⓑ___ a lot.

14 빈칸 ⓐ와 ⓑ에 들어갈 말이 바르게 짝지어진 것은?

	ⓐ		ⓑ
①	Their	-	them
②	They	-	them
③	Their	-	theirs
④	They	-	theirs
⑤	Them	-	their

15 밑줄 친 (A)의 우리말을 영어로 바르게 옮긴 것은?

① There is five people in my family
② There was five people in my family
③ There were five people in my family
④ There are five people in my family
⑤ There is five people there in my family

: 서술형 평가

Answers / p.04

01 [보기]에서 알맞은 말을 찾아 글을 완성하시오.

보기	it's	its	it

My kitten is missing. ________ name is Prince. ________ white. It is tiny and cute. Please help me find ________.

02 밑줄 친 말이 가리키는 것을 두 단어로 쓰시오.

A Excuse me, is this your pen?
B Yes. It's mine. Thank you.

→ ________________

[03-04] 밑줄 친 부분을 어법에 맞게 고쳐 쓰시오.

03 A Were you at the baseball stadium last Sunday?
B Yes, you were. I enjoyed the game a lot.

→ ________________

04 A Is this your student card?
B No. It's not my.

→ ________________

[05-06] 각 문장을 지시에 따라 바꿔 쓰시오.

05 The store is open today. (의문문)

→ ________________

06 It was a holiday yesterday. (부정문)

→ ________________

07 밑줄 친 목격자의 진술을 주어진 단어를 이용하여 영작하시오.

There was a car accident on the corner. 도로에 차가 많았어요. But there wasn't a traffic light.

→ ________________
(there, be, many, on the road)

08 주어 'I'를 'They'로 바꿔 어법에 맞게 글을 완성하시오.

I'm 13 years old. I am healthy now, but I was very sick last year. I wasn't happy. Now, I am in good shape. I am happy.

⇩

________ 13 years old. ________ healthy now, but ________ very sick last year. ________ happy. Now, ________ in good shape. ________ happy.

[09-10] 표를 보고, Josh와 Peter의 수업에 관한 물음에 [보기]와 같이 답하시오.

	Yesterday		Today	
	Josh	Peter	Josh	Peter
at home		√		
in the library	√		√	√

보기 Was Josh at home yesterday?
→ No, he wasn't. He was in the library.

09 Was Peter in the library yesterday?

→ ________________

10 Is Josh at home today?

→ ________________

Chapter 2

일반동사

일반동사의 의미와 형태

☆ **일반동사**: be동사와 조동사를 제외한 동사로, 주어의 동작이나 상태를 나타낸다.

be동사	am / are / is ~이다, ~에 있다 was / were ~이었다, ~에 있었다
조동사	can ~할 수 있다 will ~할 것이다 may ~ 일 것이다 등
일반동사	sing 노래하다 live 살다 run 달리다 climb 오르다 like 좋아하다 want 원하다 등

1. 일반동사의 현재형: 「1·2인칭 단·복수/3인칭 복수+동사원형」, 「3인칭 단수+동사원형+(e)s」로 쓰며, 현재의 사실이나 습관 등을 나타낼 때 사용한다.

I / You / We / They	sing	a song every morning.
He / She / It	sings	

We **sing** a song every morning. 우리는 매일 아침 노래를 부른다.

She **sings** a song every morning. 그녀는 매일 아침 노래를 부른다.

2. 3인칭 단수 현재형 만드는 법

대부분의 동사	+ -s	open - opens	sit - sits	like - likes
o, x, s(s), sh, ch로 끝나는 동사	+ -es	wash - washes catch - catches	do - does fix - fixes	cross - crosses
「자음+y」로 끝나는 동사	y → -ies	study - studies	try - tries	worry - worries
불규칙 동사		have - has		

He **teaches** English. 그는 영어를 가르친다.

My uncle **has** a camper van. 우리 삼촌은 캠핑카를 소유하고 있다.

Check-up 우리말과 같은 뜻이 되도록 □ 안에서 알맞은 말을 고르시오.

1 아기가 온종일 운다.
→ The baby [crys / cries] all day.

2 그들은 학교에서 영어를 배운다.
→ They [learn / learns] English at school.

3 그는 저녁 식사 전에 손을 씻는다.
→ He [washs / washes] his hands before dinner.

: EXERCISES

Answers / p.05

A [ ] 안에서 알맞은 것을 고르시오.

1 The birds [fly / flies] south.

2 I [pray / prays] for my grandma.

3 Andy [speak / speaks] English well.

4 She [watch / watches] TV after dinner.

5 Ron and Mary [wash / washes] the dishes.

fly 동 날다, 날아가다
south 부 남쪽으로
pray for ~를 위해 기도하다
wash the dishes 설거지를 하다

B 주어진 동사의 현재형을 이용하여 문장을 완성하시오.

1 My brother __________ a cold. (have)

2 Kathy __________ pizza very much. (love)

3 He __________ his brother's computer. (fix)

4 Jerry and Ian __________ shopping together. (go)

5 My parents __________ about my future. (worry)

have a cold 감기에 걸리다
fix 동 고치다
go shopping 쇼핑하러 가다
worry about ~에 대해 걱정하다
future 명 미래, 장래

C Andy와 Sarah의 일정을 보고, 글을 완성하시오. [현재 시제를 사용할 것]

	Friday	Saturday	Sunday
Andy	study English	play soccer	take care of his brother
Sarah	draw pictures	go hiking	clean the house

1 On Friday, Andy __________ English, and Sarah __________ pictures.

2 On Saturday, Andy __________ soccer, and Sarah __________ hiking.

3 On Sunday, Andy __________ care of his brother, and Sarah __________ the house.

take care of ~를 돌보다
draw 동 그리다
go hiking 하이킹을 가다, 도보 여행을 가다

D 우리말과 같은 뜻이 되도록 주어진 단어를 이용하여 문장을 완성하시오.

1 우리 학교는 9시에 시작한다. (my school, start)

→ __________ __________ __________ at 9 o'clock.

2 그는 매일 아침 체육관에서 운동을 한다. (exercise)

→ Every morning, __________ __________ at the gym.

3 Ron과 그의 동생은 수요일마다 체스를 둔다. (Ron and his brother, play)

→ __________ __________ __________ __________ __________ chess on Wednesdays.

일반동사의 과거형

1. 일반동사의 과거형: 주어의 인칭이나 수에 관계없이 쓰며, 규칙 변화 동사와 불규칙 변화 동사가 있다. 주로 last ~, ~ago 등 과거를 나타내는 표현과 함께 쓴다.

2. 규칙 변화

대부분의 동사	+ -ed	call - called　clean - cleaned　watch - watched
-e로 끝나는 동사	+ -d	live - lived　move - moved　like - liked
「자음+y」로 끝나는 동사	-y → -ied	try - tried　hurry - hurried　carry - carried
「단모음+단자음」으로 끝나는 동사	자음을 한 번 더 쓰고+-ed	pop - popped　stop - stopped drop - dropped　mop - mopped

He **called** me last night. 그가 지난밤에 나에게 전화를 했다.

She **dropped** her wallet. 그녀가 지갑을 떨어뜨렸다.

3. 불규칙 변화

현재형과 과거형이 같은 동사	cut - cut hurt - hurt	cost - cost set - set	put - put read[ri:d] - read[red]	hit - hit
불규칙 변화 동사	begin - began break - broke buy - bought bring - brought catch - caught come - came do - did drink - drank eat - ate feel - felt find - found	fly - flew get - got give - gave go - went grow - grew have - had hear - heard keep - kept know - knew leave - left lend - lent	lose - lost make - made meet - met ride - rode run - ran see - saw send - sent sing - sang sit - sat sleep - slept speak - spoke	spend - spent stand - stood steal - stole take - took teach - taught tell - told think - thought wake - woke wear - wore win - won write - wrote

He **came** to my house last night. 그가 지난밤에 우리 집에 왔다.

She **put** her hat on the desk. 그녀가 책상 위에 모자를 놓았다.

Tips

read는 현재형과 과거형의 형태가 같지만 발음이 다르다. 현재형은 [ri:d], 과거형은 [red]로 발음한다.

Check-up 우리말과 같은 뜻이 되도록 ☐ 안에서 알맞은 말을 고르시오.

1 우리는 지난주에 축구 경기에서 이겼다.
→ We [wined / won] the soccer game last week.

2 그는 몇 분 전에 바닥을 쓸었다.
→ He [moped / mopped] the floor a few minutes ago.

3 그 남자는 서둘러 집으로 갔다.
→ The man [hurried / hurryed] home.

: EXERCISES

A [ ] 안에서 알맞은 것을 고르시오.

1 Harry [hit / hitted] his head yesterday.
2 They [dance / danced] to the music last night.
3 My brother [has / had] a red sports car now.
4 He [carries / carried] the boxes an hour ago.
5 My family [lives / lived] on a small island now.

hit ⓓ 부딪치다, 때리다
dance to ~에 맞춰 춤을 추다
carry ⓓ 나르다
island ⓝ 섬

B 일정을 보고, 일기를 완성하시오.

morning	afternoon	evening	night
take a walk	play the piano	go to the theater with my friend Beth	read a book

Friday, August 8

Today I had a good day. I ________ a walk in the morning. In the afternoon, I ________ the piano. My friend Beth and I ________ to the theater in the evening. At night, I ________ a book. I feel very happy now.

take a walk 산책하다
theater ⓝ 극장

C [보기]에서 알맞은 단어를 골라 과거형으로 바꿔 문장을 완성하시오.

보기 say go wake up cut

1 He ________ a watermelon in half.
2 The students ________ hello to the teacher.
3 She was sick and ________ to the hospital.
4 He ________ late and was late for school.

wake up 일어나다
watermelon ⓝ 수박
in half 반으로
sick ⓐ 아픈, 병든

D 우리말과 같은 뜻이 되도록 주어진 단어를 이용하여 문장을 완성하시오.

1 그들은 어제 런던으로 떠났다. (leave for, London)
→ They ________ ________ ________ yesterday.

2 그녀는 점심으로 샌드위치를 먹었다. (eat, a sandwich)
→ She ________ ________ ________ for lunch.

3 우리는 눈을 감고, 소원을 빌었다. (close, make a wish)
→ We ________ our eyes and ________ ________ ________.

UNIT 03

일반동사의 부정문

1. 일반동사 현재형의 부정문: 「주어+don't/doesn't+동사원형」 ~하지 않는다

I / You / We / They	do not [don't]	feel	good.
He / She / It	does not [doesn't]		

I **do not [don't] feel** good. 나는 기분이 좋지 않다.

He **does not [doesn't] feel** good. 그는 기분이 좋지 않다.

We **live** around here. 우리는 이 근처에 산다.
➡ We **do not [don't] live** around here. 우리는 이 근처에 살지 않는다.

She **has** a sister. 그녀는 여동생이 있다.
➡ She **does not [doesn't] have** a sister. 그녀는 여동생이 없다.

Tips
영어 회화에서는 축약형을 주로 쓴다.
do not ➡ don't
does not ➡ doesn't
did not ➡ didn't

2. 일반동사 과거형의 부정문: 「didn't+동사원형」 ~하지 않았다

☆ 과거형의 부정문은 주어의 인칭이나 수에 관계없이 didn't[did not]를 사용한다.

We **didn't go** to the bookstore. 우리는 서점에 가지 않았다.

He **didn't ride** a bike yesterday. 그는 어제 자전거를 타지 않았다.

I **walked** fast. 나는 빠르게 걸었다.
➡ I **didn't walk** fast. 나는 빠르게 걷지 않았다.

She **called** you this morning. 그녀가 오늘 아침에 너에게 전화를 했다.
➡ She **didn't call** you this morning. 그녀는 오늘 아침에 너에게 전화를 걸지 않았다.

Check-up 우리말과 같은 뜻이 되도록 [ ] 안에서 알맞은 말을 고르시오.

1 그녀는 일기를 쓰지 않는다.
→ She [don't / doesn't] keep a diary.

2 그녀는 아이스크림을 좋아하지 않는다.
→ She doesn't [like / likes] ice cream.

3 그들은 지금 도시에 살지 않는다.
→ They [don't / doesn't] live in the city now.

4 나는 요즘 텔레비전을 보지 않는다.
→ I [don't / doesn't] watch TV nowadays.

5 그는 지난주에 그 경기를 보지 않았다.
→ He didn't [watch / watches] the game last week.

6 우리 형은 요즘 체육관에 가지 않는다.
→ My brother [doesn't / isn't] go to the gym these days.

: EXERCISES

Answers / p.06

A [ ] 안에서 알맞은 것을 고르시오.

1 I [don't / doesn't] eat breakfast these days.
2 Susan [don't / doesn't] understand the lesson.
3 We [doesn't / didn't] visit the museum last month.
4 Jenny [doesn't / didn't] stay in the dormitory last year.
5 Tony likes rock music, but he [don't / doesn't] like classical music.

lesson 명 수업
visit 동 방문하다
museum 명 박물관, 미술관
stay 동 머무르다
dormitory 명 기숙사
classical music 클래식 음악

B 주어진 동사의 현재형을 이용하여 문장을 완성하시오. [축약형으로 쓸 것]

1 She ____________ a lie. (not, tell)
2 John ____________ glasses. (not, wear)
3 I ____________ early in the morning. (not, get up)
4 They ____________ computer games. (not, like)
5 We ____________ board games after school. (not, play)

tell a lie 거짓말을 하다
glasses 명 안경
get up 일어나다

C 주어진 문장을 부정문으로 고쳐 쓰시오. [축약형으로 쓸 것]

1 I had pizza for dinner.
→ ______________________ for dinner.
2 It rained hard this morning.
→ ______________________ this morning.
3 Sandra invited Chris to her birthday party.
→ ______________________ to her birthday party.

rain 동 비가 오다
hard 형 어려운, 딱딱한 부 세차게, 맹렬히; 열심히
invite 동 초대하다

D 우리말과 같은 뜻이 되도록 주어진 단어를 이용하여 문장을 완성하시오.

1 나는 지난밤에 잠을 잘 못 잤다. (sleep, well)
→ ______ ______ ______ ______ last night.
2 Jack은 이 건물에서 일하지 않는다. (work)
→ ______ ______ ______ in this building.
3 학생들은 토요일에는 교복을 입지 않는다. (wear, school uniforms)
→ Students ______ ______ ______ ______ on Saturday.

일반동사의 의문문

1. 일반동사 현재형의 의문문: 「Do/Does+주어+동사원형~?」 ~하나요?

Do	I / we / they	look	OK?	- Yes, you / they do. - No, you / they don't.
Do	you	like	sweets?	- Yes, I / we do. - No, I / we don't.
Does	he / she / it	look	OK?	- Yes, he / she / it does. - No, he / she / it doesn't.

A **Do we look** OK? 우리 괜찮아 보이니?
B Yes, you do. / No, you don't. 응, 그래./아니, 안 그래.
A **Do you like** sweets? 단것을 좋아하니?
B Yes, I do. / No, I don't. 응, 그래./아니, 안 그래.
A **Does he look** OK? 그는 괜찮아 보이니?
B Yes, he does. / No, he doesn't. 응, 그래./아니, 안 그래.

2. 일반동사 과거형의 의문문: 「Did+주어+동사원형~?」 ~했나요?

☆ 과거형의 의문문은 주어에 관계없이 Did를 사용한다.

A **Did** you **see** the movie on TV last night? 너 어젯밤에 텔레비전에서 그 영화를 봤니?
B Yes, I did. / No, I didn't. 응, 봤어./아니, 안 봤어.
A **Did** he **pass** the test? 그가 그 시험에 통과했니?
B Yes, he did. / No, he didn't. 응, 했어./아니, 못 했어.

Plus α

일반동사로 쓰인 do는 해석하지만, 일반동사의 부정문과 의문문을 만드는 do는 해석하지 않는다.
I **do** my homework before dinner. [일반동사 do] 나는 저녁 먹기 전에 숙제를 한다.
I **do**n't have a smartphone. [부정문을 만드는 do] 나는 스마트폰이 없다.
Do you have a cat? [의문문을 만드는 do] 너는 고양이를 기르니?

Check-up 우리말과 같은 뜻이 되도록 [ ] 안에서 알맞은 말을 고르시오.

1 어젯밤에 비가 왔니?
→ [Does / Did] it rain last night?

2 너 지금 시간 있니?
→ [Do / Does] you have time now?

3 너 남자 형제와 여자 형제가 있니?
→ [Are / Do] you have brothers and sisters?

4 너의 할머니는 너와 함께 사니?
→ [Do / Does] your grandmother live with you?

: EXERCISES

Answers / p.06

A 주어진 동사의 현재형을 이용하여 의문문을 완성하시오.

1 ________ you ________ my help? (need)
2 ________ your sister ________ Jessica? (know)
3 ________ Kelly ________ a shower at night? (take)
4 ________ he ________ jogging every morning? (go)

help 명 도움
take a shower 샤워를 하다
go jogging 조깅을 하다

B 주어진 동사를 이용하여 대화를 완성하시오.

1 A ________ Molly ________ last night? (cry)
B No, she didn't.

2 A ________ you ________ in the city? (live)
B No, I don't. I live in the countryside.

3 A ________ the story ________ a happy ending? (have)
B No, it doesn't. It's a sad story.

4 A ________ you ________ dinner for your mother? (cook)
B Yes, I did. She was very happy about that.

countryside 명 시골, 지방
happy ending 행복한 결말, 해피 엔딩
cook 동 요리하다

C 주어진 동사와 시제를 이용하여 대화를 완성하시오.

1 A ________ she ________ her nails? (bite, 현재)
B Yes, ________ ________.

2 A ________ they ________ my phone number? (know, 현재)
B No, ________ ________.

3 A ________ you ________ the full moon last night? (see, 과거)
B Yes, ________ ________. I saw many stars, too.

nail 명 손톱
bite 동 물다
full moon 보름달

D 우리말과 같은 뜻이 되도록 주어진 단어를 이용하여 문장을 완성하시오.

1 너는 내 이름을 기억하니? (remember)
→ ________ ________ ________ my name?

2 겨울에 눈이 많이 오나요? (snow, a lot)
→ ________ it ________ ________ ________ in winter?

3 그가 실수로 그 거울을 깼나요? (break, the mirror)
→ ________ ________ ________ ________ ________ by mistake?

: Review Test

[01-02] 빈칸에 들어갈 알맞은 말을 고르시오.

01

James is a teacher. He ________ math at school now.

① teach ② teachs
③ teaches ④ taught
⑤ teaching

02

Jane and I ________ to the same elementary school last year.

① go ② goes
③ goed ④ went
⑤ going

03 빈칸에 들어갈 수 없는 말은?

He walked in the rain ____________.

① last night ② next week
③ yesterday ④ two days ago
⑤ this morning

[04-05] 대화의 빈칸에 들어갈 말이 바르게 짝지어진 것을 고르시오.

04

A ________ you finish your homework?
B Yes, I did. I ________ it an hour ago.

① Do – finish ② Do – finished
③ Did – finish ④ Did – finishes
⑤ Did – finished

05

A Does Sally ________ at night?
B No, she doesn't. She ________ during the day.

① study – study ② study – studies
③ studies – study ④ study – studied
⑤ studies – studied

[06-07] 밑줄 친 부분이 어법상 어색한 것을 고르시오.

06

① Ronnie wakes up early in the morning.
② We use dictionaries in class.
③ Tess and Dan borrows books from the library.
④ Janice watches baseball games on TV.
⑤ My brother and I learn Taekwondo.

07

① My dad went to bed at 11 pm yesterday.
② Tim put his bag on his bed one hour ago.
③ I left my umbrella on the school bus.
④ He studied hard for the finals.
⑤ My mother cutted an apple with a knife.

[08-09] 밑줄 친 ❶~❺ 중 어법상 어색한 것을 고르시오.

08

My mom is a homemaker. Every morning, she ❶ does the laundry. After the laundry, she ❷ mops the floor. She ❸ cooks three meals a day but ❹ don't wash the dishes. My brother and I ❺ do the dishes.

09

Mom Did you have an English class today?
Minki Yes, I did. I ❶ took the morning class.
Mom Did you talk a lot in class?
Minki No, I ❷ didn't talk a lot. I ❸ read an English book and ❹ wrote a book report.
Mom Did you ❺ had fun?
Minki Yes. I had fun in class.

10 주어진 문장을 부정문으로 바르게 고친 것은?

Dad took a nap in the living room.

① Dad didn't took a nap in the living room.
② Dad didn't take a nap in the living room.
③ Dad doesn't took a nap in the living room.
④ Dad doesn't takes a nap in the living room.
⑤ Dad don't take a nap in the living room.

11 주어진 문장을 의문문으로 바르게 고친 것은?

① He drinks orange juice every morning.
→ Do he drink orange juice every morning?
② She left school at 5 o'clock.
→ Did she left school at 5 o'clock?
③ They eat lunch in the cafeteria.
→ Does they eat lunch in the cafeteria?
④ James plays the piano after school.
→ Does James play the piano after school?
⑤ He bought a new computer yesterday.
→ Did he buys a new computer yesterday?

12 다음 대화 중 가장 자연스러운 것은?

① A Do you know his email address?
B No, you don't. Let me ask him.
② A Did they feel sick after dinner?
B Yes, they do. They went to the hospital.
③ A Does she sing well?
B Yes, she doesn't. She's a great singer.
④ A Did you talk to the teacher?
B No, I didn't. He wasn't in the office.
⑤ A Do you cut your finger?
B Yes, I did. It hurt a lot.

13 다음 중 어법상 올바른 문장은?

① Did the bus arrive at 2 o'clock?
② They doesn't play tennis last weekend.
③ Do you come home late yesterday?
④ He don't like salty food.
⑤ Did you saw the concert last night?

[14-15] 글을 읽고, 물음에 답하시오.

I have a cousin. His name is John. He lives in Hawaii. I ___ⓐ___ him every summer. Last summer, my cousin and I went to the beach. I didn't swim because (A) 나는 수영복을 가져오지 않았다. We ___ⓑ___ some seashells. We also ___ⓒ___ a sandcastle. We had a great time together.

14 빈칸 ⓐ, ⓑ, ⓒ에 들어갈 말이 바르게 짝지어진 것은?

	ⓐ		ⓑ		ⓒ
①	visit	-	collect	-	make
②	visit	-	collected	-	make
③	visit	-	collected	-	made
④	visited	-	collect	-	made
⑤	visited	-	collect	-	make

15 밑줄 친 (A)의 우리말을 영어로 바르게 옮긴 것은?

① I don't bring my swimsuit
② I don't brought my swimsuit
③ I didn't bring my swimsuit
④ I brought not my swimsuit
⑤ I didn't brought my swimsuit

: 서술형 평가

Answers / p.08

01 주어진 동사를 이용하여 조건에 맞게 글을 완성하시오.

Tom ________ (like) basketball very much. He ________ (play) basketball after school. Tom sometimes ________ (try) a dunk shot. He is a good basketball player.

조건 현재 시제를 사용할 것

[02-03] 주어진 문장을 부정문으로 바꿔 쓰시오.

02 She carries a big bag.

→ ________________

03 I understand Chinese.

→ ________________

[04-05] 학급일지를 읽고, 어법상 어색한 부분을 바르게 고쳐 쓰시오.

- Peter bringed a frog to the classroom.
- Matt didn't came to school.

04 Peter ________________.

05 Matt ________________.

[06-07] [보기]와 같이 문장을 바꿔 쓰시오.

보기 He went to the library. (park)
→ He didn't go to the library. He went to the park.

06 He cut the bread. (ham)

→ ________________

07 She took the bus. (train)

→ ________________

08 표를 보고, 나와 Sam의 학교생활을 비교하는 글을 완성하시오.

	I	Sam
walk to school	O	X
go to school by bus	X	O
study hard in class	X	O
have many friends	O	O

Sam and I go to the same school. I walk to school. I don't go to school by bus. I ________ hard in class. I have many friends. Sam ________ to school. He ________ to school by bus. He ________ hard in class. He ________ many friends.

[09-10] 체육수업 활동에 대한 표를 보고, 밑줄 친 우리말을 영작하시오.

play with a ball	do push-ups
X	O

A We had a PE class this morning.
B **09** 너희들은 공놀이를 했니?
A No, we didn't.
B Then, did you do push-ups?
A **10** 응, 그랬어.

09 ________________ with a ball?

10 ________________

Chapter 3

명사, 관사

셀 수 있는 명사

☆ 명사는 사람, 동물, 사물, 장소 등을 나타내는 말로, 셀 수 있는 명사와 셀 수 없는 명사로 나뉜다.
☆ 셀 수 있는 명사가 한 개일 때는 a(n)을 붙이고, 여러 개일 때는 복수형으로 쓴다.

1. 명사의 복수형 규칙 변화

대부분의 명사	+ -s	girl – girls pen – pens friend – friends
s, x, sh, ch로 끝나는 명사	+ -es	bus – buses box – boxes brush – brushes
「자음+y」로 끝나는 명사	y → -ies	city – cities party – parties hobby – hobbies
「모음+y」로 끝나는 명사	+ -s	day – days toy – toys monkey – monkeys
「모음+o」로 끝나는 명사	+ -s	zoo – zoos radio – radios kangaroo – kangaroos
「자음+o」로 끝나는 명사	+ -es	potato – potatoes tomato – tomatoes 예외) photo – photos, piano – pianos
f(e)로 끝나는 명사	f(e) → -ves	leaf – leaves knife – knives 예외) roof – roofs, chief – chiefs, belief – beliefs

There are two **churches** in town. 마을에는 두 개의 교회가 있다.
My **hobbies** are playing soccer and reading **books.** 나의 취미는 축구와 독서이다.

2. 명사의 복수형 불규칙 변화

foot – **feet** goose – **geese** tooth – **teeth** man – **men**
ox – **oxen** deer – **deer** woman – **women** child – **children**
mouse – **mice** sheep – **sheep** person – **people**

Women and **children** were in the building. 여자들과 아이들이 그 건물 안에 있었다.
The **sheep** were afraid of **mice.** 그 양들은 쥐들을 무서워했다.

Plus α

1 many는 '많은'이라는 뜻으로 셀 수 있는 명사의 복수형과 함께 쓰고, a lot of[lots of]로 바꿔 쓸 수 있다.
We saw **many[a lot of / lots of]** animals on the farm.
우리는 농장에서 많은 동물을 봤다.

2 한 쌍으로 이루어진 물건은 대부분 복수로 쓰고, 개수를 셀 때는 a pair of, two pairs of를 사용한다.
e.g.) socks, pants, jeans, glasses, shoes, scissors
He bought **a pair of** socks.
그는 양말 한 켤레를 샀다.
He bought **two pairs of** socks.
그는 양말 두 켤레를 샀다.

Check-up 우리말과 같은 뜻이 되도록 ☐ 안에서 알맞은 말을 고르시오.

1 도시에 많은 건물들이 있다.
→ There are many [building / buildings] in the city.

2 그 아이들이 카메라를 향해 미소 지었다.
→ The [childs / children] smiled at the camera.

3 그녀는 병원에서 아기들을 돌본다.
→ She takes care of [babies / babys] in the hospital.

4 탁자 위에 물 두 잔이 있다.
→ There are two [glass / glasses] of water on the table.

: EXERCISES

Answers / p.08

A 주어진 단어를 복수형으로 바꿔 문장을 완성하시오.

1 There are three __________ in the park. (bench)

2 Many __________ go camping these days. (person)

3 Five __________ chased the __________. (wolf, deer)

4 __________ bit carrots with their __________. (donkey, tooth)

go camping 캠핑 가다
chase ⓢ 쫓다
bite ⓢ 씹다
carrot ⓜ 당근

B 밑줄 친 부분을 바르게 고쳐 쓰시오.

1 He traveled in many <u>countrys</u>.

2 The plant has many flowers and <u>leafs</u>.

3 There are a lot of <u>student</u> in the library.

4 The shepherd has fifteen <u>sheeps</u> on the farm.

travel ⓢ 여행하다
plant ⓜ 식물
shepherd ⓜ 양치기

C 우리말과 같은 뜻이 되도록 [보기]에서 알맞은 것을 골라 어법에 맞게 바꿔 문장을 완성하시오.

보기	lady	mouse	foot	deer

1 그들은 발을 씻었다.
→ They cleaned their __________.

2 나는 숲에서 사슴 두 마리를 보았다.
→ I saw two __________ in the forest.

3 일반적으로 사람들은 쥐들을 매우 싫어한다.
→ People usually hate __________.

4 신사, 숙녀 여러분, 쇼에 오신 것을 환영합니다.
→ __________ and gentlemen, welcome to the show.

D 우리말과 같은 뜻이 되도록 주어진 단어를 이용하여 문장을 완성하시오.

1 그녀는 공원에서 친구들과 많은 사진을 찍었다. (photo)
→ She took __________ __________ with her friends in the park.

2 나는 양말 다섯 켤레를 여행 가방 안에 넣었다. (a pair of, sock)
→ I put __________ __________ __________ __________ in my suitcase.

3 문 앞에 많은 사람들이 있었다. (person)
→ There are __________ __________ __________ __________ in front of the door.

셀 수 없는 명사

1. 셀 수 없는 명사의 종류: 일반적으로 물질 명사, 추상 명사, 고유 명사는 셀 수 없고, 셀 수 없는 명사 앞에는 a(n)를 붙일 수 없다.

물질 명사	일정한 형태가 없는 물질을 나타내는 명사	air milk	salt juice	sugar paper	water money
추상 명사	눈에 보이지 않는 추상적인 개념을 나타내는 명사	love liberty	peace luck	hope life	advice happiness
고유 명사	사람, 장소, 사물 등의 고유한 이름을 나타내는 명사	Mary Newton	Korea Eiffel	New York Sunday	Seoul July

I need some fresh **air.** 나는 신선한 공기가 좀 필요해요.
People love **peace.** 사람들은 평화를 사랑한다.
Seoul is the capital of **Korea.** 서울은 한국의 수도이다.

Plus α

1 paper, rice, money 등은 셀 수 없는 명사이다.
2 furniture, homework, mail처럼 종류가 여러 개인 것을 합쳐 부르는 명사도 셀 수 없는 명사이다.
3 much는 '많은'이라는 뜻으로 셀 수 없는 명사와 함께 쓰고, a lot of[lots of]로 바꿔 쓸 수 있다.
We don't have **much[a lot of / lots of]** time.
우리는 시간이 많지 않다.

Tips

셀 수 없는 명사는 단수 취급하며 항상 단수형으로 쓴다.
There are **two bottles of water.**
두 병의 물이 있다.
There are ~~two waters~~. (X)

2. 물질 명사 세는 방법: 물질 명사는 셀 수 없으므로 단위나 용기를 사용하여 양을 나타낸다.

a glass of ~ 한 잔의	a cup of ~ 한 컵의	a piece of ~ 한 조각의	a slice of ~ 한 장의
a bowl of ~ 한 그릇의	a loaf of ~ 한 덩어리의	a bottle of ~ 한 병의	

She gave me **a cup of coffee.** 그녀가 나에게 커피 한 잔을 주었다.
I bought **three loaves of bread.** 나는 빵 세 덩어리를 샀다.
I put **two slices of cheese** on the bread. 나는 빵 위에 치즈 두 장을 놓았다.
He had **a bowl of cereal** for breakfast. 그는 아침 식사로 시리얼 한 그릇을 먹었다.
The boy drank **two glasses of milk.** 그 소년은 우유를 두 잔 마셨다.

Check-up 우리말과 같은 뜻이 되도록 [ ] 안에서 알맞은 말을 고르시오.

1 그녀는 여름에 물을 많이 마신다.
→ She drinks a lot of [water / waters] in summer.

2 그는 주스 세 병을 샀다.
→ He bought three [bottle / bottles] of juice.

3 나는 저녁 식사로 닭고기 수프를 한 그릇 먹었다.
→ I had a [bowl / slice] of chicken soup for dinner.

: EXERCISES

Answers / p.09

A [ ] 안에 제시된 명사를 찾아 동그라미 하시오.

1 [추상명사] I wish you good luck.

2 [고유명사] Annie cleans her room.

3 [물질명사] He passed me the salt.

4 [물질명사] My mother cooked the meat.

5 [추상명사] I have great respect for my parents.

pass 동 건네주다
respect 명 존경

B [보기]에서 알맞은 단어를 골라 어법에 맞게 바꿔 문장을 완성하시오.

보기	advice	homework	sugar	slice

1 He has a lot of ______________ today.

2 May I have some ______________ in my coffee?

3 She had three ______________ of pizza for dinner.

4 Can you give me a piece of ______________ on this problem?

advice 명 조언, 충고
homework 명 숙제

C 우리말과 같은 뜻이 되도록 주어진 표현을 이용하여 문장을 완성하시오.

1 그녀는 오늘 아침에 커피를 두 잔 마셨다. (a cup of, coffee)
→ She drank ______________________________ this morning.

2 나는 점심으로 밥을 두 공기 먹었다. (a bowl of, rice)
→ I ate ______________________________ for lunch.

3 내 여동생과 나는 저녁 식사 후에 케이크 세 조각을 먹었다. (a piece of, cake)
→ My sister and I had ______________________________ after dinner.

4 그는 샌드위치에 햄을 두 장 넣었다. (a slice of, ham)
→ He put ______________________________ in the sandwich.

D 우리말과 같은 뜻이 되도록 주어진 단어를 배열하시오.

1 나는 돈이 많지 않다. (money, don't, much, have)
→ I ______________________________.

2 그녀는 가게에서 물 두 병을 샀다. (water, two, of, bought, bottles)
→ She ______________________________ in the store.

3 바구니에 빵이 일곱 덩어리 있다. (seven, are, bread, loaves, there, of)
→ ______________________________ in the basket.

UNIT 03

관사

1. 부정관사(a, an): 셀 수 있는 명사의 단수형 앞에 쓰고, 바로 뒤에 나오는 발음이 자음이면 a를, 모음이면 an을 쓴다.

(1) 특별히 정해지지 않은 막연한 하나

Do you have **a car**? 너는 차가 있니?

(2) 하나의(=one)

Please wait for **a minute** or two. 일, 이분만 기다려 주세요.

(3) ~마다

She drinks water once **an hour.** 그녀는 한 시간에 한 번씩 물을 마신다.

2. 정관사(the)

(1) 이미 언급했거나 알고 있는 특정한 것

He bought a car. **The car** is black. 그는 자동차를 샀다. 그 차는 검은색이다.

Can you pass me **the sugar**? 설탕 좀 건네주겠니?

(2) 세상에 하나뿐인 것

the sun, the moon, the earth 등

(3) 기타 표현: 악기, 매체, 서수, 형용사의 최상급 앞 등

play **the piano**, **the Internet**, **the radio**, watch **the movies**, **the first** player, **the smartest** girl 등 ☆ 예외) watch TV

3. 관사를 쓰지 않는 경우

(1) 식사 이름, 운동 경기, 학과목, 언어

eat **breakfast[lunch, dinner]**, play **soccer[baseball]**, study **math[English]** 등

(2) 「by+교통, 통신 수단」

by **bus**, by **taxi**, by **train**, by **subway**, by **email**, by **mail** 등

(3) 본래의 목적으로 쓰인 장소

go to **school** 공부하러 가다 go to **bed** 잠자러 가다 go to **college** 대학에 다니다

Tips

1 첫 글자가 모음이지만 자음으로 발음되는 단어 앞에는 a를 쓴다.
a university, **a** uniform

2 첫 글자가 자음이지만 모음으로 발음되는 단어 앞에는 an을 쓴다.
an hour, **an** MP3

3 명사가 수식어의 꾸밈을 받아서 가리키는 대상이 분명해진 경우 the를 쓴다.
The girl on the bench is my niece.
벤치에 앉아 있는 소녀가 내 조카이다.

Plus α

식사 이름 앞에 꾸미는 말이 온 경우 관사를 쓴다.
We had **a big** lunch yesterday.
우리는 어제 점심을 푸짐하게 먹었다.

Check-up 우리말과 같은 뜻이 되도록 [ ] 안에서 알맞은 말을 고르시오.

1 나는 지난주에 시험을 보았다.
→ I took [a / an] exam last week.

2 그들은 한 달에 한 번 도서관을 방문한다.
→ They visit the library once [a / an] month.

3 그는 자전거를 가지고 있다. 그 자전거는 빨간색이다.
→ He has a bike. [A / The] bike is red.

: EXERCISES

Answers / p.09

A [ ] 안에서 알맞은 것을 고르시오.

1 Do you have [a / an] pen?

2 She wears [a / an] uniform at work.

3 We have exams twice [a / the] year.

4 They take a break once [an / the] hour.

5 There is [a / an] supermarket on the corner.

wear 동 입다
uniform 명 제복, 유니폼
at work 직장에서
take a break 휴식을 취하다
on the corner 모퉁이에

B 빈칸에 a, an, X 중 알맞은 것을 써 넣으시오. [X는 필요 없는 경우임]

1 It was ________ great dinner. Thank you.

2 I brush my teeth three times ________ day.

3 My father bought me ________ MP3 player.

4 He is ________ honest man. He never lies.

5 My sister and I play ________ badminton every Saturday.

brush one's teeth 양치질하다
honest 형 정직한
lie 동 거짓말하다
badminton 명 배드민턴

C 빈칸에 the와 X 중 알맞은 것을 써 넣으시오. [X는 필요 없는 경우임]

1 He came here by ________ train.

2 Would you open ________ window for me?

3 We go to ________ school from Monday to Friday.

4 I sat in ________ sun and read a book.

5 Mary played ________ guitar at the school festival.

window 명 창문
guitar 명 기타
school festival 학교 축제

D 우리말과 같은 뜻이 되도록 주어진 단어를 이용하여 문장을 완성하시오.

1 1년은 365일이다. (day, year)
→ There are 365 __________ in __________ __________.

2 나는 11시에 잠자리에 든다. (bed)
→ We __________ __________ __________ at 11 pm.

3 그들은 작년에 세계 일주를 했다. (around, world)
→ They traveled __________ __________ __________ last year.

4 그녀는 1시간 동안 산책을 했다. (for, hour)
→ She took a walk __________ __________ __________.

: Review Test

[01-03] 빈칸에 들어갈 말이 순서대로 짝지어진 것을 고르시오.

01

Henry has ________ old bike.
________ old bike is in the yard.

① an - A ② the - A
③ the - An ④ a - An
⑤ an - The

02

Jessica plays ________ piano very well. She practices ________ piano for three hours ________ day.

① the - the - a ② the - the - the
③ the - a - the ④ a - the - a
⑤ a - a - the

03

I like my school life. I don't have ________ homework, and I have ________ friends.

① a lot of - much ② much - many
③ much - much ④ many - much
⑤ many - a lot of

[04-05] 대화의 빈칸에 들어갈 수 없는 말을 고르시오.

04

A What did you buy at the mall?
B I bought a pair of ________.

① gloves ② glass
③ sneakers ④ jeans
⑤ scissors

05

A What's wrong?
B I don't have much ________.

① money ② information
③ sugar ④ teeth
⑤ time

[06-07] 다음 중 어법상 올바른 것을 고르시오.

06
① Leafs turn brown in fall.
② I have many classes today.
③ There are five benchs in the park.
④ He didn't wash his foots last night.
⑤ The babys played with toys.

07
① I need two slice of cheese.
② She had cup of coffee this morning.
③ They want four glasses of milks.
④ He brought three pieces of paper.
⑤ We drank two bottle of juice.

08 빈칸에 the를 쓸 수 없는 것은?

① Molly looked at ______ moon through the window.
② People buy many things on ______ Internet these days.
③ Please, come in and close ______ door.
④ Janet plays ______ tennis with her sister.
⑤ Sandy has a cat. ______ cat is very cute.

09 다음 10개의 문장 중, 어법상 올바른 문장의 개수는?

· She has a broken teeth.
· We saw many sheeps.
· My brother loves cheeses.
· Men and women are equal.
· James plays the soccer after school.
· I bought two pair of jeans yesterday.
· Emily plays piano very well.
· I sent you a picture by email.
· She has three childs.
· I love yellow leaves.

① 0개 ② 1개 ③ 2개 ④ 3개 ⑤ 4개

10 빈칸에 들어갈 수 없는 말은?

There are ________ on the table.

① tomatoes ② dishes
③ a slice of pizza ④ eggs
⑤ two glasses of juice

[11-12] 밑줄 친 ❶~❺ 중 어법상 어색한 것을 고르시오.

11

It was ❶ a beautiful day. Kate and Danny went to the beach ❷ by bus. ❸ The sun was high in the sky. They played beach volleyball for ❹ a hour. They had sandwiches for lunch. In the evening, Kate ❺ played the guitar, and Danny sang a song. They had a lot of fun together.

12

Cindy and her ❶ children went shopping today. They bought ❷ two tomatos, ❸ three onions, two carrots and ❹ a bottle of olive oil. Cindy made tomato soup. Her children ate ❺ three bowls of tomato soup for dinner. They loved her tomato soup.

13 우리말을 영어로 바르게 옮긴 것은?

그는 샌드위치 두 개와 커피 두 잔을 주문했다.

① He ordered two sandwich and two coffee.
② He ordered two sandwich and two coffees.
③ He ordered two sandwiches and two cups of coffee.
④ He ordered two sandwichs and two cups of coffees.
⑤ He ordered two sandwiches and two coffee.

[14-15] 글을 읽고, 물음에 답하시오.

John Hi, Emma. Why were you late for school today?
Emma I usually take ❶ a bus to school at 8:00, but I missed ❷ the bus this morning. So, I had to take the next bus.
John Oh, that's why. Why don't you ride a bike ❸ to school? I usually come to school ❹ by the bike.
Emma That's a good idea. By the way, aren't you hungry?
John Yes. I'm so hungry. What do you want to eat?
Emma I'll have a hamburger and ❺ a bottle of cold water. How about you?
John I'll have (A) 피자 두 조각과 콜라 한 잔.

14 밑줄 친 ❶~❺ 중 어법상 어색한 것은?

15 밑줄 친 (A)를 바르게 영작한 것은?

① two pizzas and a coke
② two slice of pizza and a glass of coke
③ two slices of pizzas and a glass of coke
④ two slice of pizza and a glass of a coke
⑤ two slices of pizza and a glass of coke

: 서술형 평가

Answers / p.11

[01-02] 우리말과 같은 뜻이 되도록 주어진 단어를 이용하여 문장을 완성하시오.

01 농장에 사슴 열 마리가 있다. (deer)

→ There are ________ ________ on the farm.

02 그들은 어제 지하실에서 두 마리의 쥐를 보았다. (mouse)

→ They saw ________ ________ in the basement yesterday.

[03-04] 어법상 어색한 부분을 찾아 바르게 고쳐 쓰시오.

03 She has nice white tooths.

→ ____________________

04 I need a pair of pant.

→ ____________________

05 [보기]에서 알맞은 단위를 골라 우리말과 같은 뜻이 되도록 문장을 완성하시오.

보기	bottle	cup	bowl

(1) 그녀는 오늘 점심 식사 후에 차를 한 잔 마셨다.

→ She drank ____________________ after lunch.

(2) 저에게 물 세 병을 건네주세요.

→ Pass me ____________________.

(3) 그녀는 채소로 샐러드 두 그릇을 만들었다.

→ She made ____________________ with vegetables.

[06-07] 밑줄 친 부분을 괄호 안의 지시대로 바꿔 문장을 다시 쓰시오.

06 There was <u>a woman</u> in the room. (세 명의 여자들)

→ ____________________

07 There are <u>three pairs of scissors</u> in the box. (가위 한 개)

→ ____________________

[08-09] 우리말과 같은 뜻이 되도록 주어진 단어를 배열하시오.

08 그는 일주일에 5일 학교에 간다.
(goes to, days, a, five, week, school)

→ He ____________________.

09 나는 보통 지하철을 타고 학교에 가지만, 오늘은 버스를 탔다.
(go to, took, bus, school, subway, a, by, usually)

→ I ____________________, but today I ____________________.

10 Peter가 엄마에게 보낸 편지를 읽고, 밑줄 친 ❶~❻ 중 어법상 어색한 것을 두 개 찾아 바르게 고치시오.

> Hi Mom!
>
> Today was my first day of camp. ❶ <u>The sky was clear and blue.</u> ❷ <u>We played the soccer before breakfast.</u> In the afternoon, we swam in the river. ❸ <u>We also crossed the river by boat.</u> ❹ <u>We had a barbecue for dinner.</u> ❺ <u>After dinner, we had a mini concert.</u> ❻ <u>I played drums.</u> We had so much fun.
>
> *Your son, Peter*

(1) ____________________

(2) ____________________

Chapter 4

대명사

UNIT 01 **this, that, it**
UNIT 02 **one, the other, some, any**
UNIT 03 **재귀대명사**

UNIT 01

this, that, it

1. 지시대명사: 사람이나 사물을 대신 가리키는 말

	가까이 있는 대상		멀리 있는 대상	
단수	this	이것, 이 사람, 이 ~	that	저것, 저 사람, 저 ~
복수	these	이것들, 이 사람들, 이 ~들	those	저것들, 저 사람들, 저 ~들

This is my friend, Jacky. 이 사람은 내 친구 Jacky야.

These are my sisters, Tracy and Britney. 이 아이들은 내 동생 Tracy와 Britney야.

That is my grandmother. 저 분이 우리 할머니야.

Those are my grandparents. 저 분들은 우리 조부모님이야.

Tips

1 지시대명사 vs. 지시형용사
this(these)와 that(those)이 단독으로 쓰이면 지시대명사이고, 명사를 수식하면 지시형용사이다.
This is my favorite book.
[지시대명사] 이것은 내가 가장 좋아하는 책이다.
This book is very funny.
[지시형용사] 이 책은 매우 재밌다.

2 「that is」는 that's로 줄여 쓸 수 있지만, this, these, those와 is는 줄여 쓸 수 없다.

Plus α

1 사람을 소개하거나 전화 통화를 할 때 this[these]를 사용한다.
James, **this** is my classmate, Teddy. James, 이쪽은 우리 반 친구 Teddy야.
A Hello. Who is **this**? 여보세요, 누구시죠?
B Hello. **This** is Matt. 여보세요, 저는 Matt입니다.

2 지시대명사가 동·식물이나 사물을 지칭하는 경우, it이나 they를 사용해서 대답한다.
A Is **this** your book? 이것이 너의 책이니?
B No. **It**'s Sally's. 아니요, 그것은 Sally의 거예요.

2. 비인칭주어(it): 시간, 요일, 날짜, 날씨, 계절, 거리, 명암 등을 나타낼 때 주어로 쓰는 말로 '그것'이라고 해석하지 않는다.

It's 8 o'clock now. [시간] 지금은 정각 여덟 시야.

It's Friday today. [요일] 오늘은 금요일이야.

It's March 13th today. [날짜] 오늘은 3월 13일이야.

It's cloudy and windy. [날씨] 구름이 끼고 바람이 불어.

It's about 700 meters. [거리] 약 700미터예요.

It's already dark outside. [명암] 밖이 벌써 어두워요.

Tips

비인칭주어 it vs. 인칭대명사 it
It's already autumn.
[비인칭주어: 계절] 벌써 가을이야.
It's my computer.
[인칭대명사: '그것']
그것은 내 컴퓨터야.

Check-up 우리말과 같은 뜻이 되도록 [ ] 안에서 알맞은 말을 고르시오.

1 기차로 30분 걸린다.
→ [It / That] takes half an hour by train.

2 저 사람은 내 남동생이다.
→ [It / That] is my brother.

: EXERCISES

Answers / p.11

A [ ] 안에서 알맞은 것을 고르시오.

1 Is [this / these] girl your cousin?

2 [This / These] earrings are not expensive.

3 These are my shoes. [That / Those] are yours.

4 [That / Those] are my friends, Tom and Terry.

5 [That / Those] picture in the album looks nice.

cousin 명 사촌
earring 명 귀고리
expensive 형 비싼

B 주어진 단어와 비인칭주어를 이용하여 대화를 완성하시오. [가능하면 축약형으로 쓸 것]

1 A What day is it today? B ______________ (Friday)

2 A What time is it now? B ______________ (7:30)

3 A What's the date today? B ______________ (May 7th)

4 A How was the weather yesterday? B ______________ (sunny)

May 명 5월
weather 명 날씨
sunny 형 화창한

C [보기]에서 알맞은 단어를 골라 문장을 완성하시오. [한 번씩만 사용할 것]

보기 this these that it

1 __________ is Monday today.

2 This is my notebook. Is __________ yours?

3 Look at __________ clothes. They are very beautiful.

4 Let me introduce my classmate. __________ is Anthony.

look at ~을 보다
clothes 명 의류, 옷
introduce 동 소개하다
classmate 명 급우, 반 친구

D 우리말과 같은 뜻이 되도록 주어진 단어를 이용하여 문장을 완성하시오.

1 나는 저 카메라를 정말 좋아한다. (camera)
→ I like __________ __________ a lot.

2 나는 지난주에 이 안경을 샀다. (glasses)
→ I bought __________ __________ last week.

3 어제는 내 생일이었다. (my birthday)
→ __________ __________ __________ __________ yesterday.

4 여기서 시청까지는 20분 정도 걸린다. (take, about, 20, minutes)
→ __________ __________ __________ __________ __________
from here to the city hall.

one, the other, some, any

1. one: 앞서 언급한 명사와 같은 종류의 불특정한 하나를 나타낼 때 사용하며, 복수일 때는 ones를 사용한다.

This skirt is too small for me. Do you have a larger **one**? (one = a skirt)
이 치마는 나에게 너무 작아요. 더 큰 것이 있나요?

I'll buy new **shoes**. How about these white **ones**? (ones = shoes)
나는 새 신발을 살 거야. 이 흰색 신발 어때?

> **Tips**
> 앞서 언급된 바로 그것을 가리킬 때는 it을 쓴다.
> I cannot find **my pen**. Did you take **it**?
> [it = my pen] 펜을 찾을 수가 없어. 네가 그것을 가져갔니?

2. 「one ~, the other …」 (둘 중에서) 하나는 ~, 나머지 하나는 …
「one ~, the others …」 (세 개 이상 중에서) 하나는 ~, 나머지 모두는 …

I have two backpacks. **One** is black, and **the other** is yellow.
나는 배낭이 두 개 있다. 하나는 검은색이고 나머지 하나는 노란색이다.

Suji has four dresses. **One** is long, and **the others** are short.
수지는 원피스가 네 벌 있다. 하나는 길고 나머지는 모두 짧다.

> **Plus α**
> 1 「one ~, another …, the other」 (세 개 중) 하나는 ~, 다른 하나는 …, 나머지 하나는 ~
> There are three cats in the box. **One** is black, **another** is white, and **the other** is striped.
> 상자 속에 고양이가 세 마리 있다. 한 마리는 검은색, 다른 한 마리는 흰색, 나머지 한 마리는 줄무늬이다.
> 2 another: '하나 더, 또 다른 하나'라는 의미로, 같은 종류의 또 다른 하나를 나타낸다.
> This cup is dirty. Can you bring me **another**? 이 컵은 더러워요. 다른 컵을 가져다주시겠어요?

3. some, any 약간(의), 몇 개(의)

(1) some: 주로 긍정문, 권유문에 쓰인다.
I have **some** money in my pocket. 나는 주머니에 돈을 좀 가지고 있다.
Would you like **some** coffee? 커피 좀 드릴까요?
I baked cookies. Would you like **some**? 쿠키를 구웠어요. 몇 개 드실래요?

(2) any: 주로 부정문과 의문문에 쓰인다.
I don't have **any** money. 나는 돈이 하나도 없다.
Is there **any** question? 질문 있나요?
I wanted milk, but there wasn't **any**. 나는 우유를 마시고 싶었지만, 하나도 없었다.

Check-up 우리말과 같은 뜻이 되도록 ☐ 안에서 알맞은 말을 고르시오.

1 이것이 네 공책이니? 내가 그것을 빌려도 될까?
→ Is this your notebook? Can I borrow [one / it]?

2 이 버스는 만원이야. 다음 버스를 기다리자.
→ This bus is full. Let's wait for the next [one / it].

: EXERCISES

Answers / p.12

A [ ] 안에서 알맞은 것을 고르시오.

scarf 명 스카프, 목도리
playground 명 운동장

1 Joe has two scarves. One is red, and [another / the other] is blue.
2 Clare has two cats. [One / It] is white, and the other is brown.
3 Look! There are [any / some] children in the playground.
4 We don't have [any / some] bread at home.

B [보기]에서 알맞은 단어를 골라 문장을 완성하시오.

lose 동 잃어버리다
fit 동 (옷 등이) 맞다, 어울리다

보기 the other ones it one

1 I lost my bag. I need to buy a new ________________.
2 This coat doesn't fit me. I will not buy ________________.
3 My glasses are too old. I want new ________________.
4 Mary has two brothers. One is tall, and ________________ is short.

C 빈칸에 some이나 any 중 알맞은 것을 써 넣으시오.

borrow 동 빌리다
special 형 특별한

1 A Would you like __________ tea?
B Yes, please.
2 A What do you need for the pie?
B I need __________ apples.
3 A May I borrow a pen?
B I'm sorry. I don't have __________ pens.
4 A Do you have __________ plans for the holiday?
B No. Nothing special.

D 우리말과 같은 뜻이 되도록 주어진 단어를 배열하시오.

1 Teresa는 쿠키를 몇개 먹었다. (cookies, some, ate)
→ Teresa ________________________________.
2 그들은 고기를 전혀 먹지 않는다. (eat, meat, don't, any)
→ They ________________________________.
3 나는 우산을 잃어버렸어. 하나 살 거야. (one, buy, will)
→ I lost my umbrella. I ________________________________.
4 나는 아이스크림콘을 두 개 샀다. 하나는 바닐라이고, 나머지 하나는 초콜릿이다.
(is, chocolate, the other, vanilla, is, one)
→ I bought two ice cream cones. ________________________,
and ________________________.

UNIT 03

재귀대명사

단 · 복수	인칭	주격	소유격	목적격	소유대명사	재귀대명사
단수	1인칭	I	my	me	mine	myself
	2인칭	you	your	you	yours	yourself
	3인칭	he	his	him	his	himself
		she	her	her	hers	herself
		it	its	it	-	itself
복수	1인칭	we	our	us	ours	ourselves
	2인칭	you	your	you	yours	yourselves
	3인칭	they	their	them	theirs	themselves

1. 주어 · 목적어를 강조하는 재귀대명사

He (**himself**) returned the book to Emma. [주어 강조] 그가 직접 Emma에게 그 책을 돌려주었다.

We want to meet the singer (**himself**). [목적어 강조] 우리는 그 가수를 직접 만나기를 원한다.

> **Tips**
> 주어나 목적어를 강조하는 재귀대명사는 생략할 수 있다.

2. 주어와 목적어가 같을 때 목적어 자리에 쓰는 재귀대명사

Mr. Brown watched **himself** in the mirror. Brown 씨는 거울 속의 자신을 바라보았다.

Cats usually clean **themselves.** 고양이는 대개 스스로를 깨끗이 한다.

3. 전치사의 목적어로 쓰인 재귀대명사

Kate is talking to **herself.** Kate는 혼잣말을 하고 있다.

Michael must be proud of **himself.** Michael은 분명 스스로를 자랑스러워 할 거야.

> **Tips**
> 동사나 전치사의 목적어로 사용된 재귀대명사는 생략할 수 없다.

4. 재귀대명사를 포함하는 관용표현

by oneself 스스로, 혼자서
help yourself to ~을 마음껏 먹다
between ourselves 우리끼리 이야기이지만
make oneself at home 편하게 지내다
talk to oneself 혼잣말하다
enjoy oneself 즐거운 시간을 보내다

A child can't enter the theater **by himself.** 어린이는 공연장에 혼자 들어갈 수 없습니다.

Welcome! Please **make yourself at home.** 환영합니다! 편하게 지내세요.

Check-up 우리말과 같은 뜻이 되도록 [ ] 안에서 알맞은 말을 고르시오.

1 이 케이크 맛있어요. 당신이 직접 만들었나요?
→ This cake is tasty. Did you make it [you / yourself]?

2 나는 나 스스로 방 청소를 해야 한다.
→ I have to clean my room by [me / myself].

: EXERCISES

Answers / p.12

A [ ] 안에서 알맞은 것을 고르시오.

1 Watch out! You could hurt [yourself / myself].
2 Let them introduce [yourselves / themselves].
3 He lives alone. He has to look after [himself / yourself].
4 Please, make [yourselves / ourselves] at home during the stay.

Watch out! 조심해!
hurt 동 ~을 다치게 하다
introduce 동 ~을 소개하다
stay 명 머무름, 체류

B 밑줄 친 재귀대명사가 강조하는 말을 찾아 쓰시오.

1 Did Susan herself build the house?
2 Don't worry. I will talk to David myself.
3 I saw Angelina Jolie herself in the park.
4 Students wanted to meet the teacher himself.

build 동 (건물을) 짓다
talk to ~에게 이야기하다

C [보기]에서 알맞은 재귀대명사를 골라 문장을 완성하시오.

보기 themselves yourself myself herself

1 I don't like to look at ______________ in the mirror.
2 Rachel ______________ drew the picture on the wall.
3 They blamed ______________ for the accident.
4 Good job! You should be proud of ______________.

look at ~을 보다
blame 동 ~을 탓하다, 비난하다
accident 명 사고
be proud of ~을 자랑스러워 하다

D 우리말과 같은 뜻이 되도록 재귀대명사와 주어진 단어를 이용하여 문장을 완성하시오.

1 그는 콘서트에서 매우 즐거운 시간을 보냈다. (enjoy)
→ He __________ __________ a lot at the concert.

2 아무에게도 말하지 마. 이건 우리끼리 이야기야. (between)
→ Don't tell anybody. It's __________ __________.

3 케이크를 마음껏 드세요. (help)
→ Please __________ __________ __________ the cakes.

4 네 숙제는 너 스스로 해야 한다. (do one's homework)
→ You should __________ __________ __________ __________ __________.

: Review Test

[01-03] 빈칸에 들어갈 알맞은 말을 고르시오.

01

My suitcase is broken. I need to buy a new ________.

① it ② that ③ one
④ another ⑤ them

02

There are 25 students in the class. Today only five of them came to school. ________ didn't come.

① One ② Some ③ Another
④ The other ⑤ The others

03

Do you have a cell phone? Can I borrow ________?

① one ② some ③ it
④ the other ⑤ the others

04 빈칸에 들어갈 말이 바르게 짝지어진 것은?

I have two sisters. ________ is a teacher, and ________ is a doctor.

① One - other ② One - the other
③ Other - another ④ Other - the other
⑤ Another - other

05 밑줄 친 It의 쓰임이 나머지와 다른 하나는?

① It is Sunday today.
② It is my backpack.
③ It will be sunny tomorrow.
④ It is December sixth.
⑤ It takes about five minutes.

06 대화의 빈칸에 들어갈 말이 바르게 짝지어진 것은?

A Mom, I'm so hungry.
B Would you like ________ bread?
A Yes, please. And do we have milk?
B I'm sorry. We don't have ________.

① a - any ② some - any
③ some - some ④ some - other
⑤ any - any

07 빈칸에 공통으로 들어갈 알맞은 말은?

· She painted a picture of ________.
· Mother Teresa went to India by ________.

① myself ② yourself ③ himself
④ herself ⑤ themselves

08 대화의 빈칸에 공통으로 들어갈 알맞은 말은?

· A Hello. ________ is Monica. May I speak to Eric, please?
  B He's not home. Do you want to leave a message?
· A ________ is my girlfriend, Brenda.
  B Glad to see you.

① He ② She ③ It
④ This ⑤ That

09 밑줄 친 this의 쓰임이 [보기]와 같은 것은?

보기 This book is exciting.

① This is my friend, Jay.
② Is this your cell phone?
③ This color is my favorite.
④ This is a present for you.
⑤ Can I take this?

10 밑줄 친 yourself의 쓰임이 [보기]와 같은 것은?

보기 Did you really make it yourself?

① Please make yourself at home.
② You need to talk to him yourself.
③ Did you hurt yourself at the camp?
④ Did you enjoy yourself at the picnic?
⑤ Help yourself to the snacks.

11 다음 대화 중 자연스럽지 않은 것은?

① A What time is it now?
B It's two o'clock.
② A What day is it today?
B It's Friday.
③ A How much is the book?
B It's 12,000 won.
④ A What's the weather like today?
B This is windy and cloudy.
⑤ A How far is it from here to the airport?
B It takes an hour by car.

[12-13] 다음 중 어법상 어색한 것을 고르시오.

12 ① I can't find my bag. Did you see one?
② He taught himself English.
③ I don't like this color. Do you have a different one?
④ It's already ten o'clock. I should go to sleep.
⑤ I have two uncles. One lives in Korea, and the other lives in America.

13 ① That plane flies to England.
② It takes about 10 minutes on foot.
③ This glasses are mine.
④ John fixed the toy himself.
⑤ How long does it take from here to the train station?

[14-15] 글을 읽고, 물음에 답하시오.

Here is my shopping list for Christmas gifts. I'm going to buy a necklace for Mom. She already has ___ⓐ___ but ___ⓑ___ is too old. For Dad, I'll buy a pair of training shoes. He can wear them and go jogging. And I plan to buy a gift for ⓒ myself: a new dress. It is really exciting!

14 빈칸에 들어갈 말이 바르게 짝지어진 것은?

	ⓐ		ⓑ
①	one	–	one
②	one	–	the other
③	it	–	the other
④	it	–	one
⑤	one	–	it

15 밑줄 친 ⓒ와 쓰임이 같은 것은?

① I ran into James himself.
② Sarah herself took the photo.
③ You yourself should solve the problem.
④ He doesn't like to talk about himself.
⑤ Anne prepared her lunch herself.

: 서술형 평가

Answers / p.14

01 빈칸에 공통으로 들어갈 알맞은 말을 쓰시오.

- ________ is a wonderful city.
- ________ was warm yesterday.

[02-04] 우리말과 같은 뜻이 되도록 빈칸에 알맞은 말을 쓰시오.

02 이 신발은 여성용이고 저 신발이 남성용입니다.

→ ________ shoes are for women, and ________ shoes are for men.

03 나는 펜은 몇 개 있지만, 연필은 하나도 없어.

→ I have ________ pens, but I don't have ________ pencils.

04 Jasmine은 두 개의 악기를 가지고 있다. 하나는 피아노이고, 나머지 하나는 플루트이다.

→ Jasmine has two musical instruments. ________ is a piano, and ________ is a flute.

[05-06] 우리말과 같은 뜻이 되도록 주어진 단어를 이용하여 문장을 완성하시오.

05 저것들은 정말 맛있는 쿠키이다. (that)

→ ________ ________ really delicious cookies.

06 그들은 수영장에서 정말 즐거운 시간을 보냈다. (enjoy)

→ They ________ ________ very much at the pool.

07 두 문장이 같은 뜻이 되도록 빈칸에 알맞은 말을 써넣으시오.

This is my favorite color.

→ ________ ________ is my favorite.

[08-09] 대화의 빈칸에 알맞은 재귀대명사를 써넣으시오.

08 A Is he angry with me?

B Not at all. He is just angry with ________.

09 A What's wrong with you?

B I hurt ________ last night.

10 그림을 보고, 대화를 완성하시오.

1:15
Nov. 11 Sun
Sunny / 28°C
1:15 pm

조건 it을 사용하여 완전한 문장으로 쓸 것, 축약형으로 쓸 것

(1) A What time is it now?

B ________________

(2) A What's the date today?

B ________________

(3) A What day is it today?

B ________________

(4) A How's the weather today?

B ________________

Chapter 5

시제

현재 시제, 과거 시제

1. 현재 시제: 불변의 진리, 속담 및 격언, 현재의 사실이나 상태, 습관, 반복적인 동작을 나타낼 때 사용한다.

☆주로 now, every day, every Monday, on Mondays, once a week[month, year] 등의 현재를 나타내는 어구와 함께 쓰인다.

My mom **is** a nurse. [현재의 사실] 우리 엄마는 간호사이다.

She **looks** tired now. [현재의 상태] 그녀는 지금 피곤해 보인다.

I **eat** cereal and milk for breakfast every morning. [습관]
나는 매일 아침식사로 시리얼과 우유를 먹는다.

The moon **goes** around the earth. [불변의 진리] 달은 지구 주위를 돈다.

Walls **have** ears. [속담] 벽에도 귀가 있다. (낮말은 새가 듣고 밤말은 쥐가 듣는다.)

Tips

every Monday는 '매주 월요일'이란 뜻으로 on Mondays와 바꿔 쓸 수 있다.

Plus α

영화, 공연 및 열차 출발 시간 등과 같이 이미 확정된 일정은 현재 시제로 쓸 수 있다.

The movie **starts** in five minutes.
그 영화는 5분 후에 시작할 것이다.

2. 과거 시제: 과거에 이미 끝난 동작이나 상태, 역사적 사실을 나타낼 때 사용한다.

☆주로 yesterday, before, ago, last week[month, year] 등의 과거를 나타내는 어구와 함께 쓰인다.

He **was** busy yesterday. [과거의 상태] 그는 어제 바빴다.

I **took** a shower last night. [과거의 동작] 나는 어젯밤에 샤워를 했다.

The Wright brothers **invented** the airplane in 1903. [역사적 사실]
Wright 형제가 1903년에 비행기를 발명했다.

Check-up 우리말과 같은 뜻이 되도록 [ ] 안에서 알맞은 말을 고르시오.

1 그들은 매년 겨울 스키를 타러 간다.
→ They [go / went] skiing every winter.

2 나는 아침에 샤워를 한다.
→ I [take / took] a shower in the morning.

3 그는 어제 저녁 식사로 피자를 먹었다.
→ He [eats / ate] pizza for dinner yesterday.

4 그녀는 2시간 전에 숙제를 끝마쳤다.
→ She [finishes / finished] her homework two hours ago.

: EXERCISES

Answers / p.14

A [ ] 안에서 알맞은 것을 고르시오.

1 The sun [rises / rose] in the east.

2 Dan and I [are / were] classmates last year.

3 He [moves / moved] to Canada three years ago.

4 I woke up early this morning. I [feel / felt] tired now.

rise ⓢ (해, 달이) 뜨다
classmate ⓜ 반 친구
move to ~로 이사하다, 이동하다
wake up 일어나다

B 주어진 단어를 어법에 맞게 바꿔 문장을 완성하시오.

1 It __________ heavily last night. (rain)

2 The Korean War __________ in 1953. (end)

3 Banks in Korea __________ on weekends. (close)

4 Sandy __________ the school bus ten minutes ago. (miss)

heavily ⓑ 세차게
end ⓢ 끝나다
on weekends 주말마다
miss ⓢ 놓치다

C 표의 내용과 일치하도록 빈칸에 알맞은 말을 쓰시오.

Last Year	Now
elementary school student	middle school student
wear casual clothes	wear a uniform
finish school at 3 o'clock	finish school at 4 o'clock

I __________ an elementary school student last year. I __________ a middle school student now. I __________ casual clothes last year. I __________ a uniform now. Last year, I __________ school at 3 o'clock. Now, I __________ school at 4 o'clock.

wear ⓢ 입다
casual clothes ⓜ 평상복
uniform ⓜ 교복, 제복

D 우리말과 같은 뜻이 되도록 주어진 단어를 이용하여 문장을 완성하시오.

1 나는 어제 시험을 봤다. (take, an exam)
→ I __________ __________ __________ __________.

2 그들은 매년 나무를 심는다. (plant, trees)
→ They __________ __________ __________ __________.

3 Jack은 지난 일요일에 영어를 공부했다. (study, English)
→ Jack __________ __________ __________ __________.

UNIT 02 진행 시제

1. 진행 시제: 특정한 시점에서 진행 중인 일을 나타낼 때 사용한다.

☆동사의 -ing형 만들기

대부분의 동사	동사원형+ing	go - going stand - standing	play - playing talk - talking
-e로 끝나는 동사	e를 삭제+ing	make - making use - using	smile - smiling write - writing
-ie로 끝나는 동사	ie를 y로 고치고+ing	die - dying	lie - lying
단모음+단자음으로 끝나는 동사	동사원형+마지막 자음+ing	put - putting sit - sitting	run - running stop - stopping

(1) **현재진행:** 「am/are/is+-ing」 ~하고 있다 [현재 시점에 진행되고 있는 동작]

I **am reading** a book. 나는 책을 읽고 있다.

He **is listening** to music now. 그는 지금 음악을 듣고 있다.

They **are riding** a bike at the park. 그들은 공원에서 자전거를 타고 있다.

(2) **과거진행:** 「was/were+-ing」 ~하고 있었다 [과거의 한 시점에 진행되고 있는 동작]

I **was eating** lunch with my friend then. 나는 그때 친구와 점심을 먹고 있었다.

We **were walking** on the street at that time. 우리는 그 당시에 거리를 걷고 있었다.

> **Tips**
>
> 1 소유나 상태를 나타내는 동사는 진행 시제로 쓸 수 없다.
>
> I **have** a car. (O)
> 나는 차를 소유하고 있다.
>
> I ~~am having~~ a car. (X)
>
> 2 '먹다'의 의미로 쓰인 have는 진행 시제로 쓸 수 있다.
>
> They **are having** lunch at the cafeteria.
> 그들은 구내식당에서 점심을 먹고 있다.

> **Plus α**
>
> 현재진행은 최근에 일어나고 있는 일 혹은 가까운 미래에 일어날 일 등을 나타내기도 한다
>
> **He's visiting** us **tonight.**
> 그는 오늘 밤에 우리를 방문할 것이다.
>
> **I'm taking** four subjects **this semester.**
> 나는 이번 학기에 4과목을 듣고 있다.

2. 진행 시제의 부정문과 의문문

(1) **부정문:** 「be동사+not+-ing」 ~하고 있지 않다, ~하고 있지 않았다

She **is not [isn't] wearing** a hat. 그녀는 모자를 쓰고 있지 않다.

They **were not [weren't] using** computers. 그들은 컴퓨터를 사용하고 있지 않았다.

(2) **의문문:** 「be동사+주어+-ing ~?」 ~하고 있니?, ~하고 있었니?

A **Is** your sister **sitting** on a chair? 너의 여동생은 의자에 앉아 있니?

B Yes, she is. / No, she isn't. 응, 그래. / 아니, 그렇지 않아.

A **Were** they **lying** on the grass? 그들은 잔디에 누워 있었니?

B Yes, they were. / No, they weren't. 응, 그랬어. / 아니, 그렇지 않았어.

Check-up 우리말과 같은 뜻이 되도록 [ ] 안에서 알맞은 말을 고르시오.

1 너 지금 울고 있니?

→ [Are / Were] you crying now?

2 Tom은 그때 자신의 방을 청소하고 있었다.

→ Tom [is cleaning / was cleaning] his room at that time.

: EXERCISES

Answers / p.15

A [ ] 안에서 알맞은 것을 고르시오.

1 [Were / Are] you listening to him then?

2 Sandy [is / was] swimming in the pool now.

3 I [am / was] meeting my friends at that time.

4 [Was / Is] she having breakfast at seven o'clock yesterday?

5 Emily and Tom [aren't / weren't] doing their homework now.

listen to ~을 듣다
pool 명 수영장
do one's homework 숙제를 하다

B 주어진 동사를 –ing형으로 바꿔 문장을 완성하시오.

1 Sally's plants are __________ now. (die)

2 Matt was __________ a nap at that time. (take)

3 John is __________ coffee right now. (drink)

4 My sister was __________ some cookies last night. (bake)

5 People were __________ at the park this morning. (jog)

plant 명 식물
die 동 죽다
take a nap 낮잠 자다
bake 동 굽다
jog 동 조깅을 하다

C 주어진 동사를 이용하여 대화를 완성하시오.

1 A Is your mother __________ dinner? (make)
B No, she isn't. She is __________ a newspaper. (read)

2 A Was Sam __________ at Fred' house at that time? (stay)
B No, he wasn't. He was __________ a movie at the theater. (watch)

3 A __________ you __________ the dishes then? (wash)
B No, I wasn't. I __________ __________ __________ the garbage. (take out)

stay 동 머물다
wash the dishes 설거지하다
garbage 명 쓰레기
take out ~을 가지고 나가다

D 우리말과 같은 뜻이 되도록 주어진 단어를 이용하여 문장을 완성하시오.

1 Andy는 지금 코트를 찾고 있다. (look for)
→ Andy __________ __________ __________ his coat now.

2 그때 많은 사람들이 버스 정류장에 서 있었다. (stand)
→ Many people __________ __________ at the bus stop then.

3 그는 그 당시에 선생님의 말을 듣고 있지 않았다. (listen to)
→ He __________ __________ __________ the teacher at that time.

: Review Test

[01-03] 빈칸에 들어갈 알맞은 말을 고르시오.

01 The game ________ 30 minutes ago.

① start ② starts
③ started ④ starting
⑤ is starting

02 We ________ dinner at 7:30 every day.

① eat ② eats
③ was eating ④ eating
⑤ is eating

03 She ________ the piano for the contest now.

① is practicing ② are practicing
③ was practicing ④ were practicing
⑤ practiced

[04-05] 대화의 빈칸에 들어갈 알맞은 말을 고르시오.

04 A What did you do last weekend?
B I ________ care of my sister.

① takes ② took
③ am taking ④ are taking
⑤ were taking

05 A Are you playing computer games now?
B No, I'm not. I ________ an email to my mom.

① sends ② sent
③ am sending ④ are sending
⑤ was sending

[06-07] 빈칸에 들어갈 수 없는 것을 고르시오.

06 David visited his grandparents ________.

① an hour ago ② last night
③ this morning ④ right now
⑤ last summer

07 They exercise at the gym ________.

① last Sunday ② every day
③ once a week ④ on Sundays
⑤ every Sunday

[08-09] 다음 중 어법상 어색한 것을 고르시오.

08
① Are they having lunch now?
② Sue is riding not her bike.
③ They were walking home at that time.
④ Were you cleaning the floor then?
⑤ She is working at the hospital now.

09
① Water boils at 100°C.
② We went shopping last weekend.
③ The train leaves at 9 o'clock.
④ World War II breaks out in 1939.
⑤ He came home an hour ago.

10 밑줄 ❶~❺ 중 어법상 <u>어색한</u> 것은?

A man was walking across the old bridge. He ❶ stepped carefully onto the bridge. Suddenly, he ❷ slipped and ❸ falled into the water. He ❹ cried for help, but there ❺ was no one around.

11 우리말을 영어로 바르게 옮긴 것은?

그들은 지금 전화 통화를 하고 있다.

① They were talking on the phone now.
② They was talking on the phone now.
③ They are talking on the phone now.
④ They talked on the phone now.
⑤ They talking on the phone now.

12 대화의 빈칸에 들어갈 말이 순서대로 짝지어진 것은?

A ________ you playing tennis on the court then?
B No, I wasn't. I ________ swimming in the pool.

① Are, am ② Were, was
③ Were, am ④ Are, was
⑤ Was, were

13 질문에 대한 응답으로 가장 알맞은 것은?

A Are you reading a novel?
B ________ I'm reading a comic book.

① Yes, I am. ② No, I'm not.
③ Yes, I'm not. ④ Yes, I do.
⑤ No, I don't.

[14-15] 대화를 읽고, 물음에 답하시오.

Officer What happened?
Witness The driver hit an old man and ran away.
Officer Was it a man or a woman?
Witness It was a man.
Officer What were you doing <u>그 당시에</u>?
Witness I ___ⓐ___ jogging in the park.
Officer Which way did he go?
Witness He ___ⓑ___ that way.

14 빈칸 ⓐ와 ⓑ에 들어갈 말이 바르게 짝지어진 것은?

	ⓐ		ⓑ
①	am	-	goes
②	am	-	went
③	were	-	was going
④	was	-	goes
⑤	was	-	went

15 밑줄 친 우리말을 영어로 바르게 옮긴 것은?

① right now ② these days
③ at times ④ at that time
⑤ long ago

: 서술형 평가

Answers / p.16

01 밑줄 친 우리말과 같은 뜻이 되도록 주어진 단어를 이용하여 대화를 완성하시오.

A Where are you going now?
B <u>나는 도서관에 가고 있어.</u> I want to borrow some books.

→ I ____________ to the library. (go)

02 밑줄 친 ❶과 ❷를 어법에 맞게 고쳐 쓰시오.

A What did you do last weekend?
B I ❶ (visit) my grandpa's farm.
A Oh, really? Where does your grandpa live?
B He ❷ (live) in Daegu.

❶ ________ ❷ ________

[03-05] 질문을 읽고, 응답을 완성하시오.

03 A Was it snowing heavily at that time?
B Yes, ________ ________.

04 A Did the telephone ring a minute ago?
B No, ________ ________. I didn't hear anything.

05 A Are you an elementary school student?
B ________, ________ ________.
I am a middle school student.

[06-07] 우리말과 같은 뜻이 되도록 주어진 단어를 배열하시오.

06 Frank는 매주 일요일에 교회에 간다.
(church, to, on Sundays, goes)

→ Frank ____________________.

07 나는 그때 시험공부를 하고 있지 않았다.
(studying, was, for the exam, not, then)

→ I ____________________.

08 글을 읽고, 어법상 <u>어색한</u> 문장을 <u>두 개</u> 찾아 고쳐 쓰시오.

Last summer, I went camping with my friends. Michael set up the tent. John maked a bonfire. Andy cooked dinner. I play the guitar. We had a lot of fun.

(1) ____________________

(2) ____________________

[09-10] 표를 보고, Sarah와 Mandy가 어제 한 일에 대한 질문에 답하시오.

	3:00 - 4:00	6:30 - 7:00	9:00 - 11:00
Sarah	watch TV	have dinner	do her homework
Mandy	feed her dog	have dinner	read a book

09 What were Sarah and Mandy doing at 6:45?
→ They ________ ________ ________ at 6:45.

10 Was Mandy doing her homework at 10:00?
→ No, ________ ________.
She ________ ________ ________ ________.

Chapter 6

조동사

UNIT 01

can, may

☆ 조동사는 동사에 미래, 추측, 가능, 허가, 부탁 등의 의미를 보충해 주는 말이다. 인칭이나 수에 따라 형태가 변하지 않고, 조동사 뒤에는 항상 동사원형이 온다.

1. 「can+동사원형」

(1) **능력, 가능** ~할 수 있다 (=be able to)

Kyle **can speak** English well. Kyle은 영어를 잘할 수 있다.

➡ Kyle **is able to speak** English well.

☆ **부정문**: 「cannot[can't]+동사원형」, 「be동사+not able to+동사원형」

I **cannot[can't] play** the drums. 나는 드럼을 연주할 수 없다.

➡ I **am not able to play** the drums.

☆ **의문문**: 「can+주어+동사원형 ~?」

A **Can** you **drive** a car? 너는 운전할 수 있니?

B Yes, I can. / No, I can't. 응, 할 수 있어./아니, 할 수 없어.

☆ **과거형**: 「could (not)+동사원형」, 「be동사의 과거형+(not) able to+동사원형」

Nate **could [was able to] read** at three. Nate는 세 살 때 글을 읽을 수 있었다.

Jack **could not [was not able to] read** at eight. Jack은 여덟 살 때 글을 읽을 수 없었다.

(2) **허락, 허가** ~해도 좋다 (=may)

A **Can [May]** I **borrow** your notebook? 내가 너의 공책을 빌릴 수 있을까?

B Here you are. You **can [may] borrow** it. 여기 있어. 너는 그것을 빌려도 돼.

2. 「may+동사원형」

(1) **추측** ~일지도 모른다

He **may be** in the library. 그는 도서관에 있을지도 모른다.

Take your jacket. It **may be** cold at night. 재킷을 가져가렴. 밤에 추울 수도 있어.

☆ **부정문**: 「may not+동사원형」

He **may not come** today. 그는 오늘 오지 않을 수도 있어.

(2) **허락, 허가** ~해도 된다 (can보다 정중한 표현)

A **May** I **use** your cell phone? 제가 당신의 휴대 전화를 사용해도 될까요?

B Yes, you may. / No, you may not. 네, 그래요. /아니요, 안 돼요.

Plus α

1 can't be ~일 리가 없다 [강한 추측]

It **can't be** true.
그것은 사실일 리가 없어.

2 can의 미래 표현: 「will be able to+동사원형」

Sarah **will be able to** ride a bike next year.
Sarah는 내년에는 자전거를 탈 수 있을 것이다.

3 may보다 약한 추측을 의미할 때는 might를 사용한다.

I'm not sure, but they **might** go skiing this weekend.
확신할 순 없지만 그들은 이번 주말에 스키를 타러 갈지도 몰라.

Tips

요청, 부탁, 허가에 대한 답변

승낙
- Yes, you may[can].
- Of course.
- Sure.
- No problem.

거절
- No, you may not[can't].
- Sorry, you can't.
- I'm afraid not.

Check-up 우리말과 같은 뜻이 되도록 [ ] 안에서 알맞은 말을 고르시오.

1 Rick은 한 손으로 그 상자를 들어 올릴 수 있다.
→ Rick can [lift / lifts] the box with one hand.

2 밤 동안 눈이 내릴지도 모른다.
→ It may [snow / snowing] during the night.

: EXERCISES

Answers / p.16

A [ ] 안에서 알맞은 것을 고르시오.

1 It may [is / be] true.
2 Can you [are / be] my friend?
3 She can't [play / plays] the violin.
4 Rachel [can / is] able to draw well.
5 They may [go / going] to the amusement park tomorrow.

violin ⓜ 바이올린
draw ⓢ 그림을 그리다
amusement park 놀이공원

B 밑줄 친 부분에 유의하여 해석을 완성하시오.

1 Can I come in?
→ 내가 ____________________?
2 Lena can swim in the sea.
→ Lena는 바다에서 ____________________.
3 He may be late today.
→ 그는 오늘 ____________________.
4 We couldn't go to the movies.
→ 우리는 영화를 보러 ____________________.

C can 또는 can't와 주어진 동사를 이용하여 문장을 완성하시오.

1 I need that book. You __________ it. (take)
2 Did you see my cell phone? I __________ it. (find)
3 Michael is so smart. He __________ and write very well. (read)
4 I was absent from school yesterday. __________ I __________ your notebook? (borrow)

take ⓢ 가져가다
be absent from ~에 결석하다
borrow ⓢ 빌리다

D 우리말과 같은 뜻이 되도록 주어진 단어를 이용하여 문장을 완성하시오.

1 Julia는 스페인 어를 유창하게 구사할 수 있다. (speak)
→ Julia ______ ______ Spanish fluently.
2 그는 내 이름을 기억하지 못할지도 몰라. (remember)
→ He ______ ______ ______ my name.
3 내 우산을 가져가도 돼. 나는 하나 더 있어. (take)
→ You ______ ______ my umbrella. I have another one.
4 시험 시간에 사전을 사용해도 되나요? (use)
→ ______ ______ ______ my dictionary during the test?

UNIT 02 must, have to, should

1. 「must+동사원형」

(1) 필요, 의무 ~해야 한다 (=have to)

Every bike rider **must [has to] wear** a helmet.
오토바이를 타는 사람은 모두 헬멧을 착용해야 합니다.

☆**부정문:** 「must not [mustn't]+동사원형」 ~하면 안 된다 [금지]

You **must not park** here. 여기에 주차하면 안 됩니다.

We **mustn't shout** in the library. 우리는 도서관에서 소리 지르면 안 된다.

> **Plus α**
> 의무를 나타내는 의문문: 「Must+주어+동사원형 ~?」, 「Do[Does]+주어+have to+동사원형 ~?」
> **Must** I **tell** him the news?
> → **Do** I **have to tell** him the news? 제가 그에게 그 소식에 대해 말해야 하나요?

(2) 강한 추측 ~임이 틀림없다

I saw Gail in the hospital. She **must be** sick.
나는 병원에서 Gail을 봤어. 그녀는 아픈 것이 틀림없어.

> **Plus α**
> 1 must의 과거는 had to로 나타낸다
> I **had to** take six subjects last year.
> 나는 작년에 여섯 과목을 들어야 했다.
> 2 부정적인 강한 추측에는 can't를 사용하며, '~일 리가 없다'라는 뜻이다.
> Jim is at the park. He **can't be** sick.
> Jim은 공원에 있어. 그는 아플 리가 없어.

2. 「have to+동사원형」 ~해야 한다 (=must) [필요, 의무]

Every passenger **has to [must] wear** a seat belt. 모든 승객은 안전벨트를 매야 합니다.

☆**부정문:** 「don't have to+동사원형」 ~할 필요가 없다 [불필요]

We **don't have to go** to school on weekends. 우리는 주말에는 학교에 갈 필요가 없다.

3. 「should+동사원형」 ~해야 한다, ~하는 것이 좋겠다 [의무, 충고, 제안]

You **should work** out every day. 너는 매일 운동을 해야 한다.

☆**부정문:** 「should not [shouldn't]」 ~하지 말아야 한다

You **shouldn't eat** sweets. They are bad for your teeth.
너는 단것을 먹지 말아야 한다. 그것은 치아에 나쁘다.

> **Plus α**
> should 의문문:
> 「Should+주어+동사원형 ~?」
> **Should** I **go** with him?
> 내가 그와 함께 가야 할까?

Check-up ☐ 안에서 밑줄 친 must가 의미하는 것을 고르시오.

1 Daniel didn't sleep last night. He must be tired.
→ 임이 틀림없다 / 해야 한다

2 All students must be at school by 9:00. Don't be late!
→ 임이 틀림없다 / 해야 한다

: EXERCISES

Answers / p.17

A [ ] 안에서 알맞은 것을 고르시오.

1 You should [are / be] quiet in the museum.
2 Tom ate a lot a minute ago. He must [is / be] full.
3 The exam is at 9:30. You must [be not / not be] late.
4 We have [go / to go] home now. It will get dark soon.
5 We [must not / don't have to] hurry. We have enough time.

a minute ago 조금 전에
full 형 배가 부른, 가득 찬
get dark (날이) 어두워지다
hurry 동 서두르다

B have to를 이용하여 문장을 완성하시오.

1 You must follow the rules.
→ You ______________________ the rules.
2 He must listen to his parents.
→ He ______________________ his parents.
3 They must respect their teachers.
→ They ______________________ their teachers.

follow 동 따르다
rule 명 규칙
respect 동 존경하다

C should 또는 shouldn't와 주어진 단어를 이용하여 충고를 의미하는 문장을 완성하시오.

1 You are late. You ______________________. (hurry)
2 You look tired. You ______________________. (take a rest)
3 The kitchen is dirty. You ______________________. (wash the dishes)
4 You have a heavy cold. You ______________________. (go out)
5 He wants to lose weight. He ______________________. (eat fast food)

take a rest 휴식을 취하다
wash the dishes 설거지하다
heavy 형 심한, 무거운
go out 외출하다
lose weight 체중이 줄다

D [보기]에서 조동사를 골라 우리말과 같은 뜻이 되도록 주어진 단어를 이용하여 문장을 완성하시오.

보기	must	must not	don't have to

1 그는 교복을 입어야 한다. (wear)
→ He ______________________ a school uniform.
2 학생들은 수업 중에 전화를 사용하면 안 된다. (use)
→ Students ______________________ their cell phones in class.
3 너의 개에 대해서 걱정할 필요 없어. 내가 그것을 돌봐 줄게. (worry about)
→ You ______________________ your dog. I'll take care of it.

UNIT 03

will, be going to

1. 「will+동사원형」 ~할 것이다 [예측], ~하겠다 [의지]

Get some sleep. You **will feel** better. 잠을 좀 자도록 해. 기분이 나아질 거야.

I **will be** right back. 금방 돌아올게.

☆ **부정문**: 「will not [won't]+동사원형」

It **will not [won't] take** long. 오래 걸리진 않을 거야.

I'm sorry. I **won't be** late again. 미안해. 다시는 늦지 않을게.

☆ **의문문**: 「Will+주어+동사원형 ~?」

A **Will** you **go** to the library today? 오늘 도서관에 갈거니?

B Yes, I **will**. / No, I **won't**. 응, 그럴 거야./아니, 안 그럴 거야.

> **Tips**
>
> 1 「Will you ~?」는 '~해 줄래?'라는 뜻으로 상대방에게 도움을 요청하거나 부탁할 때 쓴다.
> **Will you** give me a drink? 마실 것을 좀 줄래?
>
> 2 「Would you ~?」는 「Will you ~?」보다 더 정중한 표현이다.
> **Would you** give me a drink? 마실 것을 좀 주시겠어요?
>
> 3 「would like to+동사원형」 ~하고 싶다
> I **would like to drink** some water. 물을 좀 마시고 싶어요.

2. 「be going to+동사원형」 ~할 것이다, ~할 예정이다 [예정, 계획]

Take your umbrella. It'**s going to rain** later. 우산을 가져가렴. 이따가 비가 올 거야.

Tonight Betty **is going to study** all night. Betty는 오늘밤에 밤새도록 공부할 예정이다.

☆ **부정문**: 「be동사+not going to+동사원형」

She **is not going to call** you today. 그녀는 오늘 네게 전화하지 않을 거야.

I'**m not going to visit** my grandmother on Sunday.
나는 일요일에 할머니를 방문하지 않을 예정이다.

☆ **의문문** 「Be동사+주어+going to+동사원형 ~?」

A **Are** you **going to talk** to him? 그에게 말할 거니?

B Yes, I **am**. / No, I'**m not**. 응, 그럴 거야. / 아니, 안 그럴 거야.

Check-up 우리말과 같은 뜻이 되도록 [ ] 안에서 알맞은 말을 고르시오.

1 나는 10시 정각까지 돌아올 거야.
→ I [am / will] be back by 10 o'clock.

2 내일은 화창할 것입니다.
→ It [is / will] going to be sunny tomorrow.

: EXERCISES

Answers / p.17

A [ ] 안에서 알맞은 것을 고르시오.

1 Will he [comes / come] home early tonight?
2 [Is / Will] Kate get a haircut tomorrow?
3 I [am not / won't] going to join the club.
4 Joshua will [is / be] a famous writer one day.
5 Ted is going to [help / helps] me to clean my house.

get a haircut 머리카락을 자르다
join ⓓ 가입하다
famous ⓗ 유명한
writer ⓜ 작가

B will과 주어진 동사를 이용하여 문장을 완성하시오.

1 It's so cold here. I ______________ the window. (close)
2 Kelly is always on time. She ______________ late. (not, be)
3 Let's eat something now. We ______________ time later. (not, have)
4 ____________ you ____________ your new dress tomorrow? (wear)
5 Don't worry. I ______________ anybody your secret. (not, tell)

on time 제시간에
have time 시간이 있다
later ⓑ 후에, 나중에
secret ⓜ 비밀

C be going to와 주어진 단어를 이용하여 문장을 완성하시오.

1 __________ it ____________________ tomorrow? (rain)
2 __________ you ____________________ at the party? (sing)
3 They ____________________________ piano lessons. (not, take)
4 Larry ____________________________ cereal for breakfast. (eat)
5 I ____________________________ these pants. They look pretty. (buy)

lesson ⓜ 수업
cereal ⓜ 시리얼

D 우리말과 같은 뜻이 되도록 주어진 단어를 이용하여 문장을 완성하시오.

1 나는 같은 실수를 반복하지 않을 것이다. (make)
→ I __________ __________ the same mistake again.

2 너는 다음 주 파티에 올 거니? (come)
→ __________ you __________ to the party next week?

3 나는 주말에 야구를 할 거야. (play)
→ I __________ __________ __________ __________ baseball this weekend.

4 월요일에는 Rita가 연설을 하기로 예정되어 있다. (give a speech)
→ Rita __________ __________ __________ __________ __________ __________ on Monday.

: Review Test

[01-02] 빈칸에 들어갈 알맞은 말을 고르시오.

01

John ________ to Europe next spring.

① go ② went
③ will go ④ were going
⑤ will goes

02

The deadline is at the end of next month, so you ________ finish the report today.

① should ② had to
③ must ④ don't have to
⑤ have to

03 빈칸에 공통으로 들어갈 알맞은 말은?

· Kim was sick, so she ________ go to school.
· I didn't practice hard, so I ________ win the competition.

① could ② must
③ couldn't ④ shouldn't
⑤ had to

[04-05] 대화의 빈칸에 들어갈 알맞은 말을 고르시오.

04

A Let's go to the movies tomorrow.
B Sorry, I ________ go with you. I have something to do.

① can ② must
③ have to ④ can't
⑤ don't have to

05

A Good afternoon. ________ I see your passport?
B Sure. Here you are.

① Have to ② May
③ Must ④ Am
⑤ Should

06 다음 중 어법상 어색한 것은?

① Can they wear jeans at work?
② Could you open the window for me?
③ Will Eddie invites me to his party?
④ Jessica couldn't do her homework last night.
⑤ He's going to give her a birthday present.

07 밑줄 친 조동사와 쓰임이 [보기]와 같은 것은?

보기 Students must be at school by 8:00.

① Sue owns many buildings. She must be rich.
② James studied all night. He must be tired.
③ The baby is crying now. He must be hungry.
④ He helped the woman. He must be kind.
⑤ Let's finish the project tonight. We must hand it in tomorrow.

08 밑줄 친 조동사와 쓰임이 나머지와 다른 하나는?

① Can you swim in the sea?
② It's so cold. Can I borrow your coat?
③ I can read and write in English.
④ Can they solve this problem?
⑤ He can run very fast.

09 다음 대화 중 자연스럽지 않은 것은?

① A Do I have to go to the meeting?
B No, you can't.
② A May I talk to Mr. Yang?
B Yes, this is he speaking.
③ A Are you going to eat out tonight?
B Yes, we will.
④ A Will you send him a thank-you card?
B Of course.
⑤ A Can we meet at the station?
B Okay. I'll see you there.

10 짝지어진 두 문장의 의미가 같지 않은 것은?

① I can repair the computer.
→ I am able to repair the computer.

② May I see your ID?
→ Can I see your ID?

③ She will take a taxi.
→ She is going to take a taxi.

④ Will you pass me the paper?
→ Can you pass me the paper?

⑤ You don't have to go home now.
→ You must not go home now.

11 우리말을 영어로 옮긴 것 중 바르지 않은 것은?

① 다시는 수업에 지각해서는 안 돼.
→ You must not be late for class again.

② 여기서는 우회전을 할 수 없습니다.
→ You can't turn right here.

③ 히터를 좀 켜 주겠니?
→ Should you turn on the heater?

④ 그는 오늘 밤에 숙제를 끝내야만 한다.
→ He has to finish his homework tonight.

⑤ 나는 지난 토요일에 그녀를 만날 수 없었다.
→ I wasn't able to meet her last Saturday.

12 [보기]의 문장과 의미가 같은 것은?

보기 Passengers must stay in their seats during landing.

① Passengers can stay in their seats during landing.

② Passengers may stay in their seats during landing.

③ Passengers will stay in their seats during landing.

④ Passengers are going to stay in their seats during landing.

⑤ Passengers have to stay in their seats during landing.

13 대화의 빈칸에 들어갈 말이 바르게 짝지어진 것은?

A Did you watch the weather forecast? ________ I take an umbrella?

B No, you ________. It's not going to rain today.

① May – can't
② May – will not
③ Should – can't
④ Should – will not
⑤ Should – don't have to

[14-15] 대화를 읽고, 물음에 답하시오.

A Why were you absent from the meeting?

B I'm sorry I ___ⓐ___ there. Yesterday, my son broke his leg, and I ___ⓑ___ him to the hospital.

A Oh, I'm sorry to hear that. So, how is he?

B He's okay. But he has to have his leg in a cast for a month.

A He ___ⓒ___ sad.

B Yeah. He really loves soccer, but (A) 그는 축구를 하지 말아야 해요.

14 빈칸 ⓐ, ⓑ, ⓒ에 들어갈 말이 바르게 짝지어진 것은?

	ⓐ	ⓑ	ⓒ
①	can't be	– must take	– has to be
②	couldn't be	– had to take	– must be
③	can't be	– had to take	– must be
④	couldn't be	– must take	– must be
⑤	couldn't be	– must take	– has to be

15 밑줄 친 (A)를 바르게 영작한 것은?

① he can't play soccer
② he won't play soccer
③ he may not play soccer
④ he shouldn't play soccer
⑤ he doesn't have to play soccer

: 서술형 평가

Answers / p.19

[01-02] 표지판을 보고 [보기]와 같이 must 또는 must not을 이용하여 문장을 완성하시오.

보기 You __must not smoke__ here. (smoke)

01 STOP You ______________ at this sign. (stop)

02 You ______________ in the river. (swim)

03 빈칸에 알맞은 말을 넣어 대화를 완성하시오.

A ________ ________ borrow your math book?

B Sure, you can.

A When do I ________ ________ return it to you?

B Next week, please.

04 빈칸에 should 또는 shouldn't 중 알맞은 말을 넣어 환경 보호 수칙을 완성하시오.

To protect our natural environment:

· You ____________ litter.

· You ____________ turn off the lights.

· You ____________ waste water.

· You ____________ save energy.

05 대화를 읽고, 빈칸에 공통으로 들어갈 말을 쓰시오.

A Hello, Pizza House. How ______ I help you?

B I would like to order a pizza. Super supreme, regular size.

A OK. ______ you give me your address, please?

B It's 12 Main Street. How long will it take?

A We ______ deliver it in thirty minutes.

[06-07] 대화를 읽고, 물음에 답하시오.

A Did you see Brian?

B No. But he may be in the library.

A ❶ 그가 거기에 있을 리가 없어. I was just there and couldn't find him.

B You can call him. I'm not sure, but ❷ he may has his phone.

A Okay. I will do that.

06 밑줄 친 ❶과 같은 뜻이 되도록 문장을 완성하시오.

→ He ______________________________.

07 밑줄 친 ❷에서 어법상 어색한 곳을 찾아 고쳐 쓰시오.

→ ______________________________

[08-10] 표를 보고, [보기]와 같이 문장을 완성하시오.

Name	ride a horse	speak Chinese	play the guitar
Philip	X	O	
Susan		X	O
Tony	X	O	
Danny	X		O

보기 Philip __can't ride a horse__, but he __can speak Chinese__.

08 Susan ______________________, but she ______________________.

09 Tony ______________________, but he ______________________.

10 Danny ______________________, but he ______________________.

Chapter 7

여러 가지 문장

who, what, which

1. who 누구, whom 누구를, whose 누구의

A **Who** is she? 그녀는 누구니?
B She is my twin sister. 그녀는 나의 쌍둥이 여동생이야.
A **Who(m)** did you meet yesterday? 어제 누구를 만났니?
B I met my friend, Terry. 내 친구 Terry를 만났어.
A **Whose** notebook is this? 이것은 누구의 공책이야?
B It's mine. 그것은 내 것이야.

2. what 무엇, 무슨

A **What** is this? 이것은 무엇이니?
B It's my new smartphone. 그것은 나의 새 스마트폰이야.
A **What** did you study in school today? 너는 오늘 학교에서 무슨 공부를 했니?
B I studied Korean history. 한국 역사를 공부했어요.
A **What** subject do you like? 너는 무슨 과목을 좋아하니?
B I like English. 영어를 좋아해.

3. which 어느 (것), 어떤 (것): 정해진 대상 가운데 선택을 요구하는 질문을 할 때 사용한다.

A **Which** is yours, this one or that one? 이것과 저것 중 어느 것이 네 것이니?
B That one is mine. 저것이요.
A **Which** flavor do you want, cherry or green tea? 너는 체리와 녹차 중에 어떤 맛을 원하니?
B I want cherry flavor. 난 체리 맛을 원해요.

Plus α
1 정해진 대상 중에서 고를 때는 which를, 정해진 대상이 없이 고를 때는 what을 쓴다.
Which color do you like, red or blue? 빨강과 파랑 중 너는 어떤 색을 좋아하니?
What color do you like? 너는 무슨 색을 좋아하니?
2 의문사 what과 which는 단독으로 쓰기도 하고, 명사와 함께 쓰기도 한다.
What is it? 그것은 무엇이니?
What color is your hat? 네 모자는 어떤 색이니?

Tips
1 회화체에서는 목적격 자리에 whom 대신 주로 who를 쓴다.
2 의문사 의문문은 정보를 묻는 의문문이므로 yes, no로 답할 수 없다.
A **Who** took this picture? 누가 이 사진을 찍었니?
B I did. (O) 내가 찍었어.
~~Yes, I did.~~ (X)
~~No, I didn't.~~ (X)

Plus α
의문사가 주어로 쓰이면 3인칭 단수 취급한다.
Who has a cell phone? 누가 휴대 전화를 가지고 있니?

Check-up 우리말과 같은 뜻이 되도록 [ ] 안에서 알맞은 말을 고르시오.

1 너의 형의 이름은 무엇이니?
→ [Who / What] is your brother's name?

2 이 길과 저 길 중 어떤 길이 더 빠르니?
→ [What / Which] way is faster, this way or that way?

Answers / p.19

: EXERCISES

A [ ] 안에서 알맞은 것을 고르시오.

stage 명 무대
prefer 동 선호하다
swimming 명 수영
hiking 명 등산
bowling 명 볼링

1 A [Who / Which] is that girl on the stage?
  B She is my daughter.

2 A [What / Which] do you prefer, swimming or hiking?
  B I like hiking better.

3 A [Who / What] do you want to do tonight?
  B I want to go bowling.

4 A [Who / Which] is your best friend?
  B My best friend is Alex.

B 주어진 질문에 알맞은 대답을 찾아 연결하시오.

hat 명 모자
sell 동 팔다

1 What does your father do? • (a) Those red ones are mine.
2 Who is the woman with a hat? • (b) She is my mother.
3 Which shoes are yours? • (c) Tom was.
4 What did you do last night? • (d) He makes and sells bread.
5 Who was at the party? • (e) I went to a concert.

C [보기]에서 알맞은 의문사를 골라 문장을 완성하시오.

in the future 장차, 미래에
favorite 형 가장 좋아하는
painter 명 화가
choice 명 선택

보기	Who	What	Which

1 ________ do you want to be in the future?
2 ________ is your favorite painter?
3 ________ one is your choice, the small one or the big one?

D 우리말과 같은 뜻이 되도록 주어진 단어를 이용하여 문장을 완성하시오.

1 네가 가장 좋아하는 과일은 무엇이니? (your favorite fruit, be)
→ ________ ________ ________ ________ ________?

2 저기에 있는 그 여자는 누구니? (the woman, be)
→ ________ ________ ________ ________ over there?

3 딸기와 초콜릿 중 어떤 케이크를 더 좋아하니? (cake, like)
→ ________ ________ ________ ________ ________
better, strawberry or chocolate?

when, where, why, how

1. When 언제

A **When** is your birthday? 네 생일은 언제니?

B It's the 13th of May. 5월 13일이야.

2. Where 어디(에)

A **Where** do penguins live? 펭귄은 어디에 사나요?

B They live in the Southern Hemisphere. 그들은 남반구에 삽니다.

3. Why 왜

A **Why** are you here? 너는 왜 여기에 있니?

B I'm here to meet you. 널 만나러 왔어.

A **Why** did you go to the cafeteria? 너는 왜 매점에 갔니?

B Because I wanted to have a sandwich. 나는 샌드위치가 먹고 싶었어.

> **Tips**
> 의문사 why를 이용한 질문에는 because로 답하는 경우가 많다.
> A **Why** do you like dogs?
> 너는 왜 개를 좋아하니?
> B **Because** they are friendly.
> 그들은 우호적이니까.

4. How

(1) How 어떻게, 어떤

A **How** did you get here? 여기 어떻게 오셨어요?

B I came here by train. 기차를 타고 왔어요.

A **How** was your trip? 여행은 어떠셨나요?

B It was great. 굉장했어요.

(2) 「how+**형용사/부사**」 얼마나 ~한[~하게]

how old 몇 살	how far 얼마나 먼	how long 얼마나 긴/오래
how tall 얼마나 큰	how often 얼마나 자주	

How long does it take to get to school? 학교까지 얼마나 오래 걸리나요?

How often do you go to the library? 넌 도서관에 얼마나 자주 가니?

(3) 「how many+**셀 수 있는 명사의 복수형**」 얼마나 많은 수의 ~

「how much+**셀 수 없는 명사**」 얼마나 많은 양의 ~

How many sisters do you have? 너는 여자 형제가 몇 명이니?

How much money do you have? 너는 돈이 얼마나 있니?

Check-up 우리말과 같은 뜻이 되도록 [ ] 안에서 알맞은 말을 고르시오.

1 제가 역에 어떻게 갈 수 있나요?

→ [Where / How] can I get to the station?

2 어버이날이 언제인가요?

→ [When / Why] is Parents' Day?

: EXERCISES

Answers / p.20

A [ ] 안에서 알맞은 것을 고르시오.

by bicycle 자전거로
hurt 동 다치다
Germany 명 독일

1 A [Where / When] is your phone? B It's on the desk.
2 A [Why / How] do you go to school? B I go to school by bicycle.
3 A [Where / Why] are you crying? B Because I hurt my leg.
4 A [When / How] will you go to Germany? B Next September.

B [보기]에서 알맞은 의문사를 골라 문장을 완성하시오. [한 번씩만 쓸 것]

subway station 지하철 역
join 동 ~에 가입하다

보기 When Where Why How

1 A __________ did you meet her?
B Yesterday.
2 A __________ often does the bus come?
B Every ten minutes.
3 A __________ can I find the subway station?
B I'll show you the way.
4 A __________ did you join the reading club?
B Because I like reading books.

C 「How+형용사/부사」를 이용하여 대화를 완성하시오.

the Great Wall 만리장성
go to the movies 영화 보러 가다
hamburger 명 햄버거

1 A ____________ boys are there in your class? B Fifteen boys.
2 A ____________ is the Great Wall? B Over 6,400 km.
3 A ____________ do you go to the movies? B Once a month.
4 A ____________ is your sister? B She's 13 years old.
5 A ____________ is the hamburger? B It's 3,000 won.

D 우리말과 같은 뜻이 되도록 주어진 단어를 이용하여 문장을 완성하시오.

1 서점은 어디에 있습니까? (the bookstore)
→ ________ ________ ________ ________?
2 뉴욕의 날씨는 어떻습니까? (the weather)
→ ________ ________ ________ ________ in New York?
3 너는 어제 왜 수업에 늦었니? (late, for)
→ ________ ________ ________ ________ ________ class yesterday?

UNIT 03 부가의문문, 부정의문문, 선택의문문

1. 부가의문문과 응답: 상대방의 의사를 확인하거나 동의를 구하기 위해 평서문 뒤에 덧붙이는 짧은 의문문이다.

(1) 부가의문문 만들기

① 긍정은 부정으로, 부정은 긍정으로 바꾼다.

They **are** great singers, **aren't** they? 그들은 훌륭한 가수야, 그렇지 않니?

② be동사, 조동사는 그대로, 일반동사는 do, does, did를 사용한다.

You **don't** like spinach, **do** you? 너 시금치 안 좋아하지, 그렇지?

Edward **can** speak English, **can't** he? Edward는 영어를 할 수 있어, 그렇지 않니?

③ 주어는 대명사를 사용한다.

Diana looks young, doesn't **she**? Diana는 어려 보여, 그렇지 않니?

(2) **부가의문문의 응답:** 질문에 대한 대답이 긍정이면 yes로, 부정이면 no로 답한다.

A They are at home, **aren't they**? 그들은 집에 있지, 그렇지 않니?

B **Yes, they are. / No, they aren't.** 응, 집에 있어./아니, 집에 있지 않아.

2. 부정의문문과 응답: 부정의문문은 '~하지 않니?'라는 뜻으로 동사의 부정형으로 시작한다. 응답은 긍정일 때는 yes로, 부정일 때는 no로 한다.

A **Isn't** he tall? 그는 키가 안 크니?

B **Yes, he is. / No, he isn't.** 아니, 커. / 응, 안 커.

A **Doesn't** he like reading books? 그는 독서하는 것을 안 좋아하니?

B **Yes, he does. / No, he doesn't.** 아니, 좋아해./응, 안 좋아해.

3. 선택의문문과 응답: 선택의문문은 정해진 대상 중에서 선택을 요구하는 의문문으로 or를 사용한다. yes 또는 no로 대답할 수 없다.

A Is she your sister **or** your girlfriend? 그녀는 네 여동생이니 아니면 여자 친구니?

B **She is my sister.** 그녀는 내 여동생이야.

A **Which** do you like better, pizza **or** hamburger? 너는 피자와 햄버거 중 어느 것이 더 좋니?

B **I like pizza better.** 나는 피자가 더 좋아.

> **Tips**
> 부가의문문과 부정의문문은 항상 축약형으로 쓴다

> **Plus α**
> 1 명령문의 부가의문문: 「명령문, will you?」
> Don't make a noise, **will you**?
> 시끄럽게 하지 마, 그럴 거지?
> 2 제안문의 부가의문문: 「제안문, shall we?」
> Let's go camping, **shall we**?
> 캠핑 가자, 그럴래?

Check-up 우리말과 같은 뜻이 되도록 [ ] 안에서 알맞은 말을 고르시오.

1 우리 늦지 않았지, 그렇지?
→ We are not late, [are / aren't] we?

2 그것은 너의 것이니 아니면 네 남동생의 것이니?
→ Is it yours [and / or] your brother's?

: EXERCISES

Answers / p.21

A [ ] 안에서 알맞은 것을 고르시오.

1 You like jazz music, [do / don't] you?
2 He was very happy, [was / wasn't] he?
3 She opened the window, [didn't / doesn't] she?
4 You will call your sister, [don't / won't] you?

jazz 명 〈음악〉 재즈
call 동 부르다, ~에게 전화를 걸다

B 빈칸에 알맞은 말을 넣어 부가의문문을 완성하시오.

1 Fred can't swim at all, __________ __________?
2 Liz is your girlfriend, __________ __________?
3 They didn't go on a field trip, __________ __________?
4 Bob and Ted went to a concert last night, __________ __________?

not ~ at all 전혀 ~ 아니다
go on a field trip 현장 학습을 가다

C [보기]와 같이 부정의문문으로 바꿔 쓰시오.

보기 She is lovely. → Isn't she lovely?

1 You love him.
→ ______________________________
2 The bank opens at 10.
→ ______________________________
3 He is your best friend.
→ ______________________________
4 You can hear my voice.
→ ______________________________

bank 명 은행
open 동 열다, 개업하다
hear 동 듣다
voice 명 목소리

C 우리말과 같은 뜻이 되도록 주어진 단어를 배열하시오.

1 그것은 돌고래니, 아니면 고래니? (it, a dolphin, a whale, or, is)
→ ______________________________
2 그는 파란색을 좋아하지 않아, 그렇지? (doesn't, blue, like, does, he, he)
→ ______________________________
3 너는 재즈 음악과 힙합 음악 중에 어느 것을 더 좋아하니?
(jazz music, hip-hop music, like better, which, you, do, or)
→ ______________________________
4 너의 남동생은 지금 학교에 있지 않니? (now, your brother, at school, isn't)
→ ______________________________

감탄문

1. What 감탄문: 「What(+a/an)+형용사+명사(+주어+동사)!」

What a smart boy (you are)! 너는 정말 똑똑한 아이구나!
⬅ You are a very smart boy.

What an exciting story (it is)! 그것은 정말 신나는 이야기구나!
⬅ It is a really exciting story.

What strange weather (it is)! 날씨가 정말 이상하구나!
⬅ It is very strange weather.

What expensive pictures (they are)! 그것들은 정말 비싼 그림이구나!
⬅ They are really expensive pictures.

> **Tips**
> 부정관사(a/an)는 뒤에 나오는 명사에 의해 결정된다. 셀 수 있는 명사 앞에는 a/an이 나오고, 복수 명사나 셀 수 없는 명사 앞에는 a/an이 오지 않는다.

2. How 감탄문: 「How+형용사/부사(+주어+동사)!」

How pretty (she is)! 그녀는 정말 예쁘구나!
⬅ She is very pretty.

How interesting (the movie is)! 그 영화는 정말 재미있구나!
⬅ The movie is really interesting.

How fast (the cheetah runs)! 치타는 참으로 빠르게 달리는구나!
⬅ The cheetah runs very fast.

How hard (they study)! 그들은 참 열심히 공부하는구나!
⬅ They study really hard.

> **Tips**
> 1 감탄문에서는 주어와 동사를 이미 알고 있으므로 주어, 동사를 생략하는 경우가 많다.
> 2 How 감탄문 vs. How 의문문
> • How 감탄문: 「How+형용사+주어+동사!」
> How tall **you are**! 너는 정말 키가 크구나!
> • How 의문문: 「How+형용사+동사+주어?」
> How tall **are you**? 너는 키가 몇이니?

Check-up 우리말과 같은 뜻이 되도록 ☐ 안에서 알맞은 말을 고르시오.

1 그 책은 정말 무겁구나! → [What / How] heavy the book is!

2 그녀는 정말 아름다운 여인이구나! → [What / How] a beautiful lady she is!

3 너는 정말 말을 빨리 할 수 있구나! → [What / How] fast you can speak!

4 그들은 정말 귀여운 아기들이구나! → [What / How] cute babies they are!

: EXERCISES

Answers / p.21

A [ ] 안에서 알맞은 것을 고르시오.

1 [What / How] pretty dolls you have!

2 [What / How] tall the fashion model is!

3 [What / How] a beautiful voice she has!

4 [What / How] difficult the puzzle is!

doll 명 인형
fashion model 패션 모델
voice 명 목소리

B 빈칸에 What과 How 중 알맞은 말을 넣어 감탄문을 완성하시오.

1 ________ clean the beach is!

2 ________ a slim smartphone you have!

3 ________ beautiful houses!

4 ________ great the concert was!

clean 형 깨끗한
beach 명 해변
slim 형 얇은, 가느다란
smartphone 명 스마트폰

C 주어진 문장을 감탄문으로 바꿔 쓰시오.

1 Samantha is a very sweet girl.
→ What ______________________________!

2 The screen is really wide.
→ How ______________________________!

3 The castle is really beautiful.
→ How ______________________________!

4 They are very intelligent students.
→ What ______________________________!

sweet 형 다정한
wide 형 넓은
castle 명 성, 성곽
intelligent 형 지적인

D 우리말과 같은 뜻이 되도록 주어진 단어를 배열하시오.

1 정말 긴 여행이었어! (a, trip, long, was, it, what)
→ ______________________________

2 그 소녀는 정말 친절하구나! (the girl, kind, how, is)
→ ______________________________

3 너는 정말 좋은 생각을 가졌구나! (great, you, idea, what, have, a)
→ ______________________________

4 그 파스타는 정말 맛있었어! (the pasta, delicious, how, was)
→ ______________________________

명령문, 제안문

1. 명령문

(1) **긍정명령문:「동사원형 ~.」** ~ 해라

Be quiet in the library. 도서관에서는 조용히 해라.

Go straight and **turn** left. 곧장 가서 왼쪽으로 도시오.

(2) **부정명령문:**「Don't+**동사원형 ~.**」~하지 마라

Don't be late again. 다시는 늦지 마라.

Don't go out too late. 너무 늦게 밖에 나가지 마라.

> **Tips**
> 좀 더 공손하게 표현하고 싶을 때는 앞이나 뒤에 please를 붙인다.
> **Please** be quiet.
> Be quiet, **please.**
> 조용히 해 주세요.

Plus α

- 「명령문, and」 ~해라. 그러면 …할 것이다
  Do your best, **and** you'll get good grades. 최선을 다해라. 그러면 좋은 성적을 얻을 것이다.
  ➡ **If** you **do** your best, you'll get good grades.
- 「명령문, or」 ~해라. 그렇지 않으면 ~할 것이다
  Speak loudly, **or** she won't hear you. 크게 말해라. 그렇지 않으면 그녀는 네 소리를 듣지 못할 것이다.
  ➡ **If** you **don't speak** loudly, she won't hear you.

2. 제안문

(1)「Let's+**동사원형 ~.**」~하자

Let's meet at the theater. 영화관에서 만나자.

Let's have a cup of coffee. 커피 한 잔 하자.

(2)「Let's not+**동사원형 ~.**」~하지 말자

Let's not eat fast food. 패스트푸드를 먹지 말자.

Let's not talk about it. 그것에 대해서는 이야기하지 말자.

Plus α

「Why don't we[you]+동사원형 ~?」=「How[What] about -ing ~?」~하는 게 어때?
Why don't we go for a walk? = **How[What] about going** for a walk? 산책 가는 게 어때?

Check-up 우리말과 같은 뜻이 되도록 ☐ 안에서 알맞은 말을 고르시오.

1 너 이미 늦었어. 서둘러.
→ You're already late. [Hurry / Don't hurry] up!

2 밖에 비가 오고 있어. 우비를 가져가자.
→ It's raining outside. [Let's / Let's not] take our raincoats.

: EXERCISES

Answers / p.22

A [ ] 안에서 알맞은 것을 고르시오.

1 You look tired. [Take / Takes] a rest.
2 Happy birthday! Let's [have / has] a party.
3 The baby is sleeping. [Don't talk / Talk not] loudly.
4 The weather is nice. [Let's / Let's not] take a walk.
5 It's still hot. [Don't let / Let's not] turn off the air conditioner.

take a rest 휴식을 취하다
loudly 부 시끄럽게
take a walk 산책을 하다
turn off ~을 끄다
air conditioner 에어컨

B 주어진 단어를 이용하여 명령문을 완성하시오.

1 ____________ quiet in the theater. (be)
2 ____________ late for class again. (not, be)
3 ____________ your hands before you eat. (wash)
4 ____________ at night. It's dangerous. (not, swim)
5 There are so many people here. ____________ in line, please. (stand)

theater 명 극장
be late for ~에 늦다
wash one's hands ~의 손을 씻다
stand in line 줄을 서다

C [보기]에서 알맞은 동사를 골라 의미에 맞게 바꿔 비행기에서 지켜야 할 규칙을 완성하시오.

보기 fasten walk around turn off make bring

Attention, please.
1 ______________________ heavy baggage on board.
2 ______________________ your seat belt.
3 ______________________ when the sign is on.
4 ______________________ loud noise.
5 ______________________ your cell phone.

fasten 동 매다, ~을 단단히 고정시키다
walk around 걸어서 돌아다니다
Attention, please. 안내 말씀 드리겠습니다. 귀 기울여 주십시오.
baggage 명 짐
on board 비행기에 탑승하여
seat belt 명 안전 벨트
sign 명 표시등
be on 사용 중이다, 작동 중이다

D 우리말과 같은 뜻이 되도록 주어진 단어를 배열하시오.

1 미술품을 만지지 마시오. (the paintings, touch, don't)
→ ______________________

2 우리 매점에서 간식을 좀 사 먹자. (at the cafeteria, snacks, have, let's, some)
→ ______________________

3 반 친구들에게 친절하게 대해라. (your classmates, kind, be, to)
→ ______________________

: Review Test

[01-03] 대화의 빈칸에 들어갈 알맞은 말을 고르시오.

01

A ________ did you buy that sandwich?
B At the store near my house.

① What ② Why
③ Where ④ When
⑤ Which

02

A ________ is your father doing now?
B He is taking a nap.

① Which ② Why
③ Where ④ When
⑤ What

03

A ________ didn't you come yesterday?
B Because I caught a cold.

① What ② Why
③ Where ④ When
⑤ Which

[04-05] 빈칸에 공통으로 들어갈 알맞은 말을 고르시오.

04

· ________ color is your bag, black or white?
· ________ do you like, soccer or baseball?

① How ② Why
③ Which ④ Where
⑤ What

05

· ________ did you get here?
· ________ much is the watch?

① How ② Why
③ Which ④ Where
⑤ What

[06-07] 빈칸에 들어갈 알맞은 말을 고르시오.

06

You sent me an email, ________?

① aren't you ② weren't you
③ didn't you ④ did you
⑤ don't you

07

Daniel can't buy that car, ________?

① doesn't he ② does Daniel
③ can't he ④ can he
⑤ does he

[08-09] 빈칸에 들어갈 말이 나머지와 다른 하나를 고르시오.

08

① ________ clever he is!
② ________ beautiful you are!
③ ________ heavy these boxes are!
④ ________ difficult the question is!
⑤ ________ tiny shoes they are!

09

① ________ subject do you like?
② ________ tall is your brother?
③ ________ much are these boots?
④ ________ long does it take to go there?
⑤ ________ often do you wash your hands?

[10-11] 다음 중 어법상 어색한 것을 고르시오.

10 ① You have a test today, do you?
② Tom doesn't have a sister, does he?
③ She wrote these letters, didn't she?
④ The movie wasn't very good, was it?
⑤ The package will arrive tomorrow, won't it?

11 ① What great books you have!
② How simple the problem is!
③ How smart the dolphins are!
④ What delicious the chocolate is!
⑤ What an elegant restaurant it is!

[12-13] 우리말을 영어로 바르게 옮긴 것을 고르시오.

12 우리 아버지에게 말하지 않을 거지, 그렇지?

① You won't tell my dad, won't you?
② You won't tell my dad, did you?
③ You won't tell my dad, will you?
④ You will tell my dad, aren't you?
⑤ You won't tell my dad, do you?

13 너와 Ben은 참 좋은 우정을 나눴구나!

① How good friendship you and Ben have!
② How a good friendship you and Ben have!
③ What you and Ben have a good friendship!
④ What a good friendship you and Ben have!
⑤ What a good friendship have you and Ben!

[14-15] 대화를 읽고, 물음에 답하시오.

A __ⓐ__ lovely weather! Let's go on a picnic.
B Well, I would love to, but I can't.
A __ⓑ__ ?
B I have to go to the library. I have an exam.
A __ⓒ__ is your exam?
B This Friday.
A I see. Then __ⓓ__ don't we go to the library together?
B (A) 넌 정말 진정한 친구로구나!

14 빈칸 ⓐ~ⓓ에 들어갈 말이 바르게 짝지어진 것은?

	ⓐ		ⓑ		ⓒ		ⓓ
①	What	–	Why	–	Why	–	how
②	How	–	Why	–	When	–	how
③	What	–	Which	–	When	–	how
④	How	–	Which	–	Why	–	why
⑤	What	–	Why	–	When	–	why

15 밑줄 친 (A)를 바르게 영작한 것은?

① How a true friend you are!
② What a true friend you are!
③ How true your friend is!
④ What a true friend are you!
⑤ How true friend you are!

Answers / p.23

[01-02] 그림을 보고, 주어진 단어를 이용하여 명령문을 완성하시오.

01

__________ the paintings on the wall. (touch)

02

__________ when the light turns green. (turn, right)

[03-05] [보기]에서 알맞은 말을 골라 대화를 완성하시오.

보기 how long how often how much

03 A __________ do you visit your grandparents?

B I visit them once a week.

04 A __________ is this black skirt?

B It's $20.

05 A __________ is the movie?

B It's two hours long.

06 대화를 읽고, 주어진 단어를 이용하여 밑줄 친 우리말을 바르게 영작하시오.

A It's your birthday. What do you want to do?

B <u>우리 외식하자.</u> I want to eat Italian food.

→ __________ (eat out)

07 빈칸에 알맞은 부가의문문을 써 넣으시오.

(1) The grocery store opens on Sunday, __________?

(2) You can't carry all the boxes, __________?

(3) Ms. Johns is your homeroom teacher, __________?

[08-09] 주어진 단어를 알맞게 배열하여 대화를 완성하시오.

08 A You look great. __________!
(a, beautiful, what, coat)

B Thanks a lot. It was a birthday gift from my mom.

09 A It was a great concert. The singer really did a good job.

B I agree. __________!
(his songs, amazing, were, how)

10 설문지를 읽고, 어법상 <u>어색한</u> 문장을 <u>두 개</u> 찾아 고쳐 쓰시오.

Write about YOU!

1. What is your name?
2. How old are you?
3. How much brothers and sisters do you have?
4. What subject do you like?
5. What do you like better, summer or winter?

→ __________

→ __________

Chapter 8

to부정사, 동명사

to부정사의 명사적 쓰임

☆ 「to+동사원형」: to부정사라고 부르며, 문장에서 명사, 형용사, 부사처럼 쓰인다.

☆ 명사적 쓰임: to부정사는 문장에서 명사처럼 주어, 목적어, 보어 역할을 한다.

> **Tips**
> to부정사 주어는 단수 취급한다.
> **To ride** a bike is fun.
> 자전거를 타는 것은 재미있다.

1. 주어 역할 ~하기는, ~하는 것은

To go there alone is dangerous. 거기에 혼자 가는 것은 위험하다.

☆to부정사가 주어로 올 경우, 대개 주어 대신 It을 쓰고, to부정사를 뒤로 보낸다. It을 '가주어', to부정사를 '진주어'라고 부른다.

To pass the exam is difficult. 그 시험에 통과하는 것은 어렵다.

➡ **It** is difficult **to pass the exam**.
가주어 진주어

2. 보어 역할 ~하는 것(이다)

His hobby is **to collect** stamps. [his hobby=to collect stamps] 그의 취미는 우표를 수집하는 것이다.

Her dream is **to become** a movie director. [her dream=to become a movie director] 그녀의 꿈은 영화감독이 되는 것이다.

My goal is **to win** first prize. [my goal=to win first prize] 나의 목표는 일등상을 받는 것이다.

3. 목적어 역할 ~하기를, 하는 것을

☆to부정사를 목적어로 취하는 동사: ask, decide, expect, hope, learn, plan, promise, refuse, want, wish, would like 등

I want **to do** my best. 나는 최선을 다하기를 원한다.

Mr. Collins asked **to see** you. Collins 씨가 당신을 만나기를 요청했습니다.

4. 「의문사+to부정사」: 명사처럼 주어, 목적어, 보어로 사용된다.

「what+to부정사」 무엇을 ~할지	「how+to부정사」 어떻게 ~할지, ~하는 방법
「where+to부정사」 어디서/어디로 ~할지	「when+to부정사」 언제 ~할지

Please tell me **what to do.** 나에게 무엇을 해야 할지 말해 줘.

We can't decide **where to stay.** 어디에 머무를지 결정할 수가 없어.

Check-up 우리말과 같은 뜻이 되도록 [ ] 안에서 알맞은 말을 고르시오.

1 훌륭한 요리사가 되는 것은 쉽지 않다.
→ [It / That] is not easy to be a great chef.

2 나는 불고기를 어떻게 요리하는지 모른다.
→ I don't know [how / when] to cook bulgogi.

3 그는 여름에 수영을 배우기로 계획했다.
→ He planned [learn / to learn] to swim in summer.

: EXERCISES

Answers / p.24

A [ ] 안에서 알맞은 것을 고르시오.

1 Nancy wants [buy / to buy] a new car.
2 His job is [to write / to writes] novels.
3 He refused [join / to join] your football club.
4 It is hard [to get up / to getting up] early.
5 My dream is [be / to be] an animal doctor.

novel 명 소설
refuse 동 거절하다
join 동 가입하다
football 명 미식 축구
get up 일어나다
animal doctor 수의사

B 주어진 동사를 알맞은 형태로 바꾸어 문장을 완성하시오.

1 He refused __________ a doctor. (see)
2 Jessica wants __________ here. (stay)
3 I hope __________ a new bicycle. (buy)
4 He decided __________ new languages. (learn)
5 We are planning __________ the soccer game. (watch)

stay 동 머무르다
bicycle 명 자전거
decide 동 결정하다
language 명 언어

C [보기]에서 알맞은 동사를 골라 주어진 우리말과 같은 뜻이 되도록 to부정사로 바꿔 문장을 완성하시오.

보기	finish	shop	leave

1 우리는 오늘 밤에 떠나기로 결정했다.
→ We decided ____________________ tonight.
2 나의 계획은 두 시까지 일을 끝내는 것이다.
→ My plan is ____________________ the work by 2 o'clock.
3 온라인으로 물건을 구매하는 것은 어렵지 않다.
→ It is not difficult ____________________ online.

D 우리말과 같은 뜻이 되도록 주어진 단어를 이용하여 문장을 완성하시오.

1 축구를 하는 것은 재미있다. (play, soccer)
→ It is fun __________ __________ __________.
2 나는 내년에 해외에서 공부하기를 희망한다. (study, abroad)
→ I hope __________ __________ __________ next year.
3 나는 오늘 무엇을 입어야 할지 모르겠다. (wear)
→ I don't know __________ __________ __________ today.

UNIT 02

to부정사의 형용사적, 부사적 쓰임

1. 형용사적 쓰임 (~할): to부정사는 형용사처럼 (대)명사를 수식하는 역할을 하고, 이때 to부정사는 (대)명사 뒤에 온다.

I have enough money **to spend.** 나는 쓸 돈이 충분하다.

Did you bring a book **to read?** 읽을 책을 가져왔니?

You have nothing **to worry** about. 넌 걱정할 것 하나도 없어.

Plus α

「-thing/-one/-body + 형용사 + to부정사」 vs. 「형용사+일반명사+to부정사」

I need someone **kind** to help me. 나는 나를 도와줄 친절한 누군가가 필요하다.

I need a **kind** friend to help me. 나는 나를 도와줄 친절한 친구가 필요하다.

Tips

1 형용사는 일반적으로 명사 앞에서 명사를 수식한다.
I saw **blue** stone.
나는 파란 돌을 보았다.

2 -thing/-one/-body 등으로 끝나는 명사는 형용사가 명사 뒤에 온다.
I saw something **blue**.
나는 파란 무엇인가를 보았다.

2. 부사적 쓰임: to부정사는 부사처럼 형용사, 부사 등을 수식하고, 특히, 목적, 판단의 근거, 감정의 원인, 결과 등의 의미로 해석된다.

(1) **목적** (~하기 위해, ~하려고)

He's going to the market **to buy** some food. 그는 약간의 음식을 사기 위해 시장에 가고 있다.

I will go to the gym **to lose** weight. 나는 살을 빼기 위해 체육관에 갈 것이다.

(2) **판단의 근거** (~하다니), **감정의 원인** (~해서)

You are so kind **to help** me. [판단의 근거] 나를 도와주다니 당신은 매우 친절하군요.

I'm glad **to meet** you. [감정의 원인] 당신을 만나서 기뻐요.

(3) **결과** (~해서 …하다)

He grew up **to be** a famous movie star. 그는 자라서 유명한 영화배우가 되었다.

She lived **to be** ninety years old. 그녀는 아흔 살까지 살았다.

(4) **형용사 수식**

This book is easy **to read.** 이 책은 읽기 쉽다.

The question is difficult **to answer.** 그 질문은 대답하기 어렵다.

Tips

목적을 나타내는 to부정사는 「in order to부정사」로 바꿔 쓸 수 있다.

I'm here **to say** hello.
= in order to say
나는 안부를 전하려고 여기 왔어.

Plus α

1 「too+형용사/부사+to부정사」
너무 ~해서 …할 수 없다
She was **too tired to work** out.
그녀는 너무 피곤해서 운동을 할 수 없었다.

2 「형용사/부사+enough+to부정사」
~할 만큼 충분히 …하다
She is **smart enough to solve** this puzzle.
그녀는 이 퍼즐을 풀 만큼 충분히 똑똑하다.

Check-up 우리말과 같은 뜻이 되도록 [ ] 안에서 알맞은 말을 고르시오.

1 그녀는 너를 만나러 여기에 왔다.
→ She came here [meet / to meet] you.

2 나는 오늘 할 일이 있다.
→ I have [to do something / something to do] today.

: EXERCISES

Answers / p.24

A 굵은 글씨로 된 명사를 수식하는 말을 찾아 밑줄을 그으시오.

invite 동 초대하다
magazine 명 잡지

1 I have **something** to say.
2 I need **some time** to sleep.
3 We have **many friends** to invite.
4 He brought **some apples** to eat.
5 He bought **a magazine** to read.

B [보기]처럼 밑줄 친 부분을 해석하시오.

보기 I'm happy to see you. → 너를 보게 되어 기뻐.

1 Ben is silly to believe it. → 그것을 ______ Ben은 어리석구나.
2 She was happy to pass the exam. → 그녀는 시험에 ______ 기뻤다.
3 I'm very glad to meet your mother. → 너의 어머니를 ______ 영광이야.
4 He went to the library to read books. → 그는 책을 ______ 도서관에 갔다.

C 두 문장의 뜻이 통하도록 to부정사를 이용하여 문장을 완성하시오.

market 명 가게
tie 명 넥타이 동 ~을 묶다

1 He will go to the concert. He is happy.
→ He is happy ______ to the concert.
2 She went to the market. She bought some milk.
→ She went to the market ______ some milk.
3 I have a tie. I will give it to my father.
→ I have a tie ______ to my father.
4 She wanted to be a teacher. So she studied hard.
→ She studied hard ______ a teacher.

D 우리말과 같은 뜻이 되도록 주어진 단어를 이용하여 문장을 완성하시오.

1 나는 버스를 잡으려고 열심히 뛰었다. (catch, the bus)
→ I ran hard ______ ______ ______ ______.
2 런던에는 가볼 만한 곳이 많다. (visit, many places)
→ London has ______ ______ ______ ______.
3 Simpson 씨는 그 사진을 보고 깜짝 놀랐다. (see, the picture)
→ Mr. Simpson was surprised ______ ______ ______
______.

동명사의 쓰임

☆ 동명사는 「동사원형+-ing」 형태로 명사처럼 문장에서 주어, 목적어, 보어 역할을 한다.

Tips
동명사 주어는 단수 취급한다.
Riding a horse is fun.
말을 타는 것은 재미있다.

1. 주어 역할 ~하는 것은, ~하기는

Using smartphones is not difficult. 스마트폰을 사용하는 것은 어렵지 않다.

Climbing the mountain was a great experience. 등산은 좋은 경험이었다.

Reading books is helpful for me. 책을 읽는 것은 나에게 유익하다.

2. 목적어 역할 ~하는 것을, ~하기를

☆동명사를 목적어로 취하는 동사: avoid, deny, dislike, enjoy, finish, give up, keep, mind, practice, put off, quit, stop, suggest 등

Mom enjoys **talking** on the phone. 엄마는 전화 통화를 즐기신다.

Tommy likes **visiting** museums. Tommy는 박물관에 가는 것을 좋아한다.

She finished **doing** her homework. 그녀는 숙제 하는 것을 마쳤다.

Plus α
동명사는 전치사의 목적어로도 사용된다.
Thank you for **coming.** 와 주셔서 감사합니다.
Dave was happy about **winning** the contest. Dave는 대회에서 우승해서 기뻤다.
I'm looking forward to **meeting** you. 만나 뵙기를 고대하고 있습니다.

3. 보어 역할 ~하기, 하는 것(이다)

My job is **teaching** Korean. 나의 직업은 한국어를 가르치는 것이다.

Jean's hobby is **drawing** cartoons. Jean의 취미는 만화를 그리는 것이다.

His goal is **finishing** the work by 7. 그의 목표는 일곱 시까지 그 일을 마치는 것이다.

Check-up 우리말과 같은 뜻이 되도록 [ ] 안에서 알맞은 말을 고르시오.

1 그녀는 계속 미소를 지었다.
→ She kept [smiling / to smile].

2 일본어를 배우는 것은 재미있다.
→ [Learn / Learning] Japanese is fun.

3 그의 직업은 가난한 사람들을 도와주는 것이다.
→ His job is [help / helping] poor people.

: EXERCISES

Answers / p.25

A [ ] 안에서 알맞은 것을 고르시오.

1 [Ride / Riding] a bicycle is exciting.
2 I love [talking / to talking] to my sister.
3 My sister enjoys [bake / baking] cookies.
4 Steve's goal is [loses / losing] 5 kilograms.

ride ⓢ (탈 것을) 타다
bake ⓢ (빵 등을) 굽다
goal ⓜ 목표

B [보기]에서 알맞은 것을 골라 동명사로 바꿔 문장을 완성하시오.

보기	cook	join	miss	buy

1 I'm afraid of ______________ the train.
2 I enjoyed ______________ Italian food.
3 She gave up ______________ new shoes.
4 They talked about ______________ the dance club.

miss ⓢ 놓치다
be afraid of ~을 두려워하다
Italian ⓗ 이탈리아의
give up 포기하다

C 밑줄 친 부분에 유의하여 문장을 해석하시오.

1 Jamie enjoys taking a walk.
→ Jamie는 ______________________________ 즐긴다.
2 My bad habit is biting my nails.
→ 나의 나쁜 습관은 ______________________________이다.
3 Jane is interested in helping people.
→ Jane은 ______________________________ 관심이 있다.
4 Studying hard is important for your future.
→ ______________________________ 너의 미래를 위해 중요하다.

D 우리말과 같은 뜻이 되도록 동명사와 주어진 단어를 이용하여 문장을 완성하시오.

1 그녀는 뮤지컬 보는 것을 좋아한다. (watch, musicals)
→ She loves ________ ________.
2 새로운 음식을 시도해 보는 건 좋은 생각이다. (try, new, food)
→ ________ ________ ________ is a good idea.
3 Alex는 직업을 바꾸는 것에 대해 생각 중이다. (change, his job)
→ Alex is thinking about ________ ________ ________.
4 내 취미는 영화배우의 사진을 모으는 것이다. (collect, photos of movie stars)
→ My hobby is ________ ________ ________ ________
________.

to부정사 vs. 동명사

1. to부정사를 목적어로 취하는 동사: ask, decide, expect, hope, learn, plan, promise, refuse, want, wish, would like 등

I want **to meet** him as soon as possible. 나는 그를 최대한 빨리 만나고 싶다.

Rick promised **to tell** me the truth. Rick은 나에게 진실을 말하겠다고 약속했다.

We are planning **to travel** to Europe. 우리는 유럽으로 여행을 가려고 계획하고 있다.

2. 동명사를 목적어로 취하는 동사: avoid, deny, dislike, enjoy, finish, give up, keep, mind, practice, put off, quit, stop, suggest 등

Rebecca finished **reading** the newspaper. Rebecca는 신문 읽던 것을 끝냈다.

Don't give up **exercising** every morning. 아침마다 운동하는 것을 포기하지 마세요.

I don't mind **speaking** in front of the class. 나는 반 학생들 앞에서 말하는 것을 꺼리지 않는다.

Plus α

1 「stop+동명사」
~하던 것을 멈추다
I **stopped talking** to her.
나는 그녀에게 말하기를 중단했다.

2 「stop+to부정사」
~하기 위해 멈추다
I **stopped to talk** to her.
나는 그녀에게 말하기 위해 멈췄다.

3. to부정사와 동명사 모두를 목적어로 취하는 동사: begin, start, love, like, hate 등

It started **raining** [**to rain**]. 비가 오기 시작했다.

Do you like **swimming** [**to swim**]? 수영 좋아하세요?

I love **chatting** [**to chat**] with my sister. 나는 언니랑 수다 떠는 것을 정말 좋아해요.

Plus α

- forget+to부정사 ~할 일을 잊다 (아직 하지 않음)
- forget+동명사 ~한 일을 잊다 (이미 했음)
- remember+to부정사 ~할 일을 기억하다 (아직 하지 않음)
- remember+동명사 ~한 일을 기억하다 (이미 했음)
- try+to부정사 ~하려고 노력하다[애쓰다]
- try+동명사 시험 삼아 (한번) ~하다

I **forgot calling** him and called him again. 나는 그에게 전화 걸었던 것을 잊고 또 전화를 걸었다.
Don't **forget to wake** me up. 나를 깨우는 것을 잊지 마.
I **remember calling** you. 나는 너에게 전화 걸었던 것을 기억한다.
Remember to carry an umbrella with you. 우산을 가져가는 걸 기억해.
I **tried to find** my bag, but I couldn't. 나는 가방을 찾으려고 애썼지만, 찾을 수 없었다.
Try calling him at home. 그의 집으로 한번 전화해 봐.

Check-up 우리말과 같은 뜻이 되도록 [ ] 안에서 알맞은 말을 모두 고르시오.

1 나는 우리 가족을 위해 요리하는 것을 즐긴다.
→ I enjoy [to cook / cooking] for my family.

2 너는 무엇을 하고 싶니?
→ What do you want [to do / doing]?

3 Mark는 해변을 따라 걷는 것을 매우 좋아한다.
→ Mark loves [to walk / walking] along the beach.

: EXERCISES

Answers / p.25

A [ ] 안에서 알맞은 것을 모두 고르시오.

1 I want [to use / using] the bathroom.
2 He hates [to cry / crying] in front of people.
3 Stella finished [to read / reading] the book.
4 I would like [to have / having] a hamburger.
5 She started [to exercise / exercising] to get healthy.

in front of ~ 앞에서
have ⓢ 먹다
get healthy 건강해지다

B 주어진 동사를 알맞은 형태로 바꿔 문장을 완성하시오.

1 We expect __________ you soon. (meet)
2 Jessica gave up __________ on a diet. (go)
3 Jack decided __________ a doctor. (become)
4 They planned __________ abroad next year. (study)
5 She enjoys __________ around the world. (travel)

expect ⓢ 예상하다, 기대하다
give up 포기하다
go on a diet 식이요법을 하다
study abroad 외국에서 공부하다
around the world 세계 곳곳에

C [보기]에서 알맞은 단어를 골라 어법에 맞게 바꿔 문장을 완성하시오.

보기	close	work	move	meet

1 I promised ______________ her tonight.
2 Do you mind ______________ the window?
3 Mr. Long decided ______________ to Canada.
4 Mr. Kim quit ______________ for the company last month.

move ⓢ 이주하다
mind ⓢ 꺼려하다
quit ⓢ 그만두다

D 우리말과 같은 뜻이 되도록 주어진 단어를 이용하여 문장을 완성하시오.

1 우리 할아버지께서는 낮잠 주무시는 걸 즐기신다. (enjoy, take a nap)
→ My grandfather __________ __________ __________ __________.

2 그 안과의사는 그녀의 눈을 검사하는 것을 마쳤다. (finish, check one's eyes)
→ The eye doctor __________ __________ __________ __________.

3 그녀는 열 시까지 돌아온다고 약속했다. (promise, come back)
→ She __________ __________ __________ __________ by 10.

4 길을 따라 쭉 걸어 내려가세요. (keep, walk down)
→ __________ __________ __________ the street.

: Review Test

[01-03] 빈칸에 들어갈 알맞은 말을 고르시오.

01 He wants ________ a great artist.

① is ② be
③ being ④ to be
⑤ will be

02 Did you finish ________ the laundry?

① do ② does
③ did ④ to do
⑤ doing

03 ________ too much sugar is not good.

① Eat ② Eats
③ Ate ④ Eating
⑤ To eating

[04-05] 빈칸에 들어갈 말이 바르게 짝지어진 것을 고르시오.

04 He enjoys ________ on weekends.
He would like ________ a journalist.

① fishing – becoming
② fishing – to become
③ fish – become
④ to fish – becoming
⑤ to fish – to become

05 My dream is ________ a guitarist.
Teddy finished ________ for the exam.

① being – study
② being – to study
③ be – study
④ to be – to study
⑤ to be – studying

06 대화의 빈칸에 들어갈 알맞은 말은?

A Do you have ________ today?
B Actually, I'm going to see a movie with my girlfriend.

① special anything to do
② do special anything
③ anything special to do
④ do anything special
⑤ special to do anything

07 대화의 빈칸에 들어갈 수 없는 말은?

A What is Kevin's hobby?
B His hobby is ________.

① to watch movies
② playing online games
③ to go shopping
④ singing in a choir
⑤ to gardening at home

08 다음 중 어법상 바른 것은?

① She plans to go to college next year.
② Run near the pool is dangerous.
③ Susan was happy see Michael.
④ Thank you for invite me to your party.
⑤ This question is too hard to answering.

09 빈칸에 들어갈 말이 바르게 짝지어진 것은?

· Anna knows ________ table tennis.
· Do you know ________ this Saturday?

① what to play – how to go
② what to play – where to go
③ how to play – where to go
④ how to play – what to go
⑤ what to play – when to go

[10-11] 다음 중 어법상 어색한 것을 고르시오.

10 ① It was hard to travel to China.
② She gave up eating fast food.
③ Would you mind to go with me?
④ They learned to swim in the pool.
⑤ I enjoyed taking care of my little brother.

11 ① Do you want to see her?
② Peter finished washing his father's car.
③ My brother loves playing the guitar.
④ Her job is to teach music at school.
⑤ She planned taking a trip to London.

[12-13] 밑줄 친 to부정사의 쓰임이 나머지와 다른 것을 고르시오.

12 ① Jenny wants to go to the concert.
② We went to the market to buy some water.
③ Robert plans to retire at 60.
④ She decided to finish the history report.
⑤ I hope to see you again soon.

13 ① My hobby is to make model cars.
② It's time to start the show.
③ I'll bring something to eat.
④ I have something important to say.
⑤ I have some money to buy the shirt.

[14-15] 글을 읽고, 물음에 답하시오.

I went to the zoo last week. There were many animals ___ⓐ___. My favorite activity was ___ⓑ___ the monkeys. They jumped around and made funny sounds. I also took many pictures with my friends. It was really fun. I want ⓒ to go there again.

14 빈칸 ⓐ와 ⓑ에 들어갈 말이 바르게 짝지어진 것은?

	ⓐ		ⓑ
①	to see	–	feed
②	see	–	to feed
③	to see	–	feeding
④	seeing	–	feeding
⑤	seeing	–	to feed

15 밑줄 친 ⓒ와 쓰임이 같은 것은?
① It's time to go to bed.
② I have lots of things to do.
③ We planned to visit our grandmother.
④ I eat healthy food to keep in shape.
⑤ Kelly grew up to be president.

Answers / p.26

[01-02] 우리말과 같은 뜻이 되도록 주어진 단어를 이용하여 문장을 완성하시오.

01 도서관에서 휴대 전화를 사용하는 것은 무례한 일이다.

→ It is rude ________ ________ your cell phone in the library. (use)

02 나는 Carrie를 다시 만나기를 고대하고 있다.

→ I'm looking forward to ________ Carrie again. (see)

[03-04] 두 문장의 의미가 통하도록 문장을 완성하시오.

03 I wanted to catch the train, so I ran hard.

→ I ran hard ________ the train.

04 I met an old friend, so I was very happy.

→ I was very happy ________ an old friend.

[05-06] 어법상 어색한 부분을 찾아 바르게 고쳐 쓰시오.

05 He wanted to winning first prize.

→ ________

06 Do you mind hold the door for me?

→ ________

[07-08] 대화를 읽고, 의미가 통하도록 문장을 완성하시오.

07 A How about meeting at four?
B That's good.

→ They plan ________ at four.

08 A Hello?
B Hello. May I talk to Alice?

→ The person wants ________ to Alice.

09 밑줄 친 우리말과 같은 뜻이 되도록 주어진 단어를 이용하여 질문에 답하시오.

Q What do you want to do in the future?

A 나는 아프리카에 있는 가난한 사람들을 위해 일하기를 원해요.

→ I ________ poor people in Africa. (want, work for)

10 표를 보고, [보기]와 같이 문장을 완성하시오.

	exercise	travel	read books
Jessica	O	O	
David		O	O
Steve	O		O

보기 Jessica enjoys exercising and traveling .

(1) David ________.

(2) Steve ________.

Chapter 9

여러 가지 동사

UNIT 01

감각동사

1. 「감각동사+형용사」: 보고, 듣고, 느끼는 등 사람의 감각을 표현하는 동사를 감각동사라고 한다.

feel ~하게 느끼다 look ~해 보이다 taste ~한 맛이 나다 smell ~한 냄새가 나다 sound ~하게 들리다

She **felt** thirsty. 그녀는 목마르다고 느꼈다.

The pizza in this restaurant **tastes** great. 이 식당의 피자는 맛이 정말 좋다.

Your voice **sounds** wonderful. 네 목소리는 멋지게 들린다.

Tips

감각동사 바로 뒤에 부사를 쓰지 않도록 주의한다.

The song sounds beautiful. (O)
그 노래가 아름답게 들린다.

The song sounds ~~beautifully~~. (X)

2. 「감각동사+like+명사」: 감각동사 뒤에 명사를 쓸 때는 전치사 like를 써야 한다.

He **felt like** a real prince. 그는 진짜 왕자가 된 것처럼 느꼈다.

She **looked like** an angel. 그녀는 천사처럼 보였다.

The perfume **smells like** roses. 그 향수는 장미 향기가 난다.

Tips

like: ~을 좋아하다 [동사], ~처럼, ~와 같이 [전치사]

I **like** music. [동사]
나는 음악을 좋아한다.

He looks **like** an actor. [전치사] 그는 배우처럼 보인다.

Plus α

1 문장의 성분

① 주어: 동작을 행하는 주체
She ran fast. 그녀는 빨리 달렸다.

② 동사: 주어의 동작이나 상태를 나타내는 말
He **drank** water. 그가 물을 마셨다.
He **became** popular. 그는 유명하게 되었다.

③ 주격보어: 주어를 보충 설명해 주는 말
She is **a doctor**. 그녀는 의사다.
The candies smell **sweet**. 사탕은 단 냄새가 난다.

④ 목적어: 동사가 나타내는 동작의 대상이 되는 말
I study **English**. 나는 영어를 공부한다.

⑤ 목적격보어: 목적어를 보충 설명해 주는 말
My grandma calls me **Puppy**.
우리 할머니는 나를 '강아지'라고 부른다.
Rain makes me **sad**. 비는 나를 슬프게 한다.

2 문장의 구조

① 목적어나 보어가 필요 없는 동사: go, run, sleep 등
The baby **slept**. 그 아기는 잠을 잤다.

② 주격보어가 필요한 동사: be, become, feel, look, taste, smell, sound 등
He **became** a teacher. 그는 교사가 되었다.
I **feel** hungry. 나는 배가 고프다.

③ 목적어가 필요한 동사: love, want, like, have 등
I **like** fruit. 나는 과일을 좋아한다.

④ 목적어가 두 개 필요한 동사: give, tell, show 등
He **gave** me a book. 그가 나에게 책을 주었다.

⑤ 목적어와 목적격보어가 필요한 동사: keep, make, call, find 등
The present **made** me happy.
그 선물이 나를 행복하게 했다.

Check-up 우리말과 같은 뜻이 되도록 [ ] 안에서 알맞은 말을 고르시오.

1 그 과일은 이상하게 생겼다.
→ The fruit looks [strange / strangely].

2 그 과일은 별처럼 생겼다.
→ The fruit [looks / looks like] a star.

: EXERCISES

Answers / p.27

A [ ] 안에서 알맞은 것을 고르시오.

1 I felt [excited / excitedly] today.

2 This milk tastes [fresh / freshly].

3 The soup smells [great / greatly].

4 The sweater looks [warm / warmly].

5 The game sounds [interesting / interestingly].

excited ⓗ 신난, 들뜬
fresh ⓗ 신선한
warm ⓗ 따뜻한

B [보기]에서 알맞은 말을 골라 문장을 완성하시오.

[1-2] 보기 sounds sounds like

1 The song ________________ familiar.

2 The song ________________ her favorite song.

[3-4] 보기 look look like

3 You ________________ your father.

4 You ________________ really handsome in this picture.

familiar ⓗ 익숙한
favorite ⓗ 가장 좋아하는

C 밑줄 친 부분에서 어법상 어색한 것을 찾아 바르게 고쳐 쓰시오.

1 The tea tastes sweetly.

2 The soap smells chocolate.

3 It's still hot. It feels summer.

4 His singing sounds beautifully.

tea ⓜ 차
soap ⓜ 비누

D 우리말과 같은 뜻이 되도록 주어진 단어를 이용하여 문장을 완성하시오.

1 나는 기분이 좋지 않아. (feel, good)
→ I ________ ________ ________.

2 두부에서 나쁜 냄새가 난다. (smell, bad)
→ The tofu ________ ________.

3 그녀의 목소리는 천사같이 들린다. (sound, an angel's)
→ Her voice ________ ________ ________ ________.

4 그는 친절한 사람처럼 보였다. (look, a friendly person)
→ He ________ ________ ________ ________ ________.

UNIT 02

수여동사

1. 「수여동사+간접목적어+직접목적어」: '~에게(간접목적어) …을(직접목적어) 해주다'라는 의미를 갖는 동사를 수여동사라고 한다.

give ~에게 …를 주다	send ~에게 …를 보내 주다	teach ~에게 …를 가르쳐 주다
show ~에게 …를 보여 주다	buy ~에게 …를 사 주다	make ~에게 …를 만들어 주다
lend ~에게 …를 빌려 주다	tell ~에게 …를 말해 주다	bring ~에게 …를 가져다주다

I **gave** my brother a wallet. 나는 오빠에게 지갑을 주었다.

I will **send** you a card. 내가 너에게 카드를 보내 줄게.

Betty **teaches** students French. Betty는 학생들에게 불어를 가르친다.

He **bought** his wife a ring. 그는 아내에게 반지를 사 주었다.

2. 「수여동사+직접목적어+to[for/of]+간접목적어」: 직접목적어가 간접목적어 앞에 오면 간접목적어 앞에 전치사를 써야 한다.

(1) **to를 쓰는 동사:** give, send, pass, lend, bring, show, tell, write, teach 등

My grandmother **gave** me her necklace. 나의 할머니가 나에게 목걸이를 주었다.

➡ My grandmother **gave** her necklace **to** me.

(2) **for를 쓰는 동사:** make, cook, buy, get, build 등

My mom **made** me a cheesecake. 나의 엄마가 나에게 치즈 케이크를 만들어 주었다.

➡ My mom **made** a cheesecake **for** me.

(3) **of를 쓰는 동사:** ask 등

May I **ask** you a favor? 당신에게 부탁을 하나 해도 될까요?

➡ May I **ask** a favor **of** you?

Check-up 우리말과 같은 뜻이 되도록 [ ] 안에서 알맞은 말을 고르시오.

1 그녀가 나에게 자신의 사진을 보여 주었다.
→ She showed [me her pictures / her pictures me].

2 나는 할머니에게 편지를 보냈다.
→ I sent a letter [to / of] my grandmother.

3 그가 나에게 인형을 주었다.
→ He gave [a doll to me / to me a doll].

: EXERCISES

Answers / p.28

A [ ] 안에서 알맞은 것을 고르시오.

1 My teacher bought ice cream [to / for / of] his students.
2 Anne sometimes asks personal questions [me / of me].
3 I won't tell [your secret anybody / your secret to anybody].
4 My best friend sent [me a birthday gift / a birthday gift me] yesterday.

personal question 사적인 질문
secret 명 비밀
anybody 명 아무도

B [보기]에서 알맞은 단어를 골라 문장을 완성하시오. [한 번씩만 쓸 것]

보기 to for of

1 Ken is building a house ________ his parents.
2 The interviewers asked many questions ________ me.
3 Sidney often writes emails ________ her grandparents.

interviewer 명 면접관, 인터뷰에서 질문하는 사람
often 부 종종

C 두 문장이 같은 뜻이 되도록 [보기]와 같이 문장을 완성하시오.

보기 He told me the truth. → He told the truth to me.

1 My father got me opera tickets.
→ My father got ________________________.
2 An old man asked me directions.
→ An old man asked ________________________.
3 A kind girl showed us the way to the station.
→ A kind girl showed ________________________.

truth 명 진실
opera 명 오페라
direction 명 길, 방향

D 우리말과 같은 뜻이 되도록 주어진 단어를 이용하여 문장을 완성하시오.

1 나는 그에게 이름을 물어보았다. (ask, his name)
→ I ______ ______ ______ ______.
2 저에게 당신의 표를 보여 주세요. (show, your ticket)
→ Please ______ ______ ______ ______.
3 Bill은 나에게 자신의 책들을 빌려 준다. (lend, his books)
→ Bill ______ ______ ______ ______ ______.
4 Chris는 아들에게 한국음식을 만들어 주었다. (make, his son, Korean food)
→ Chris ______ ______ ______ ______ ______ ______.

목적격보어가 필요한 동사

☆ 「동사+목적어+목적격보어」: 목적어와 목적격보어를 필요로 하는 동사가 있다. 목적격보어는 목적어의 상태나 성질을 보충 설명해 주는 말이며, 목적격보어 자리에는 명사, 형용사, to부정사, 동사원형 등이 온다.

1. 「동사+목적어+명사」: make, call, name 등

Her confidence **made** her the winner. 그녀의 자신감이 그녀를 우승자로 만들었다.

I'm Elizabeth Hurley. You can **call** me Liz. 난 Elizabeth Hurley라고 해. Liz라고 불러줘.

They **named** the baby May. 그들은 그 아기를 May라고 이름 지었다.

2. 「동사+목적어+형용사」: keep, make, find 등

The workers must **keep** their desks clean. 직원들은 책상을 깨끗하게 유지해야 한다.

The students **made** the teacher angry. 학생들이 선생님을 화나게 만들었다.

I **found** the book boring. 나는 그 책이 지루하다는 것을 알았다.

3. 「동사+목적어+to부정사」: want, expect, tell, order, advise, ask 등

We **want** you to be happy. 우리는 네가 행복하길 원해.

They **expect** him to come back home early. 그들은 그가 집에 일찍 돌아오길 기대한다.

The teacher **ordered** Fred to clean the blackboard. 선생님은 Fred에게 칠판을 지우라고 했다.

Plus α 「지각동사/사역동사+목적어+동사원형」

1 사역동사: '~에게 …하도록 하다[시키다]'라는 의미의 동사

e.g.) let, make, have

He **made** me wash his car. 그가 나에게 세차를 하게 했다.

My mom doesn't **let** me play computer games. 우리 엄마는 내가 컴퓨터 게임을 하게 두지 않는다.

2 지각동사: 감각 기관을 통해 다른 사물의 행동이나 상황을 인식하여 표현하는 동사

feel 느끼다 see 보다 hear 듣다 listen to 듣다 watch 보다 smell ~하는 냄새가 나다

Did you **see** him make a speech? 그가 연설하는 것을 보았니?

I **heard** you cry last night. 나는 어젯밤에 네가 우는 소릴 들었어.

Check-up 우리말과 같은 뜻이 되도록 [ ] 안에서 알맞은 말을 고르시오.

1 나는 그 아기가 귀엽다는 것을 알게 되었다.

→ I found the baby [cute / cuteness].

2 그는 나에게 자신을 도와달라고 부탁했다.

→ He asked me [helping / to help] him.

: EXERCISES

Answers / p.28

A [ ] 안에서 알맞은 것을 고르시오.

1 I found Korean food [healthy / healthily].
2 We expected her [be / to be] on time.
3 The movie made him [a star / to being a star].
4 The hot coffee will keep you [warm / warmly].
5 My father wants us [read / to read] these books.

healthily 부 건강하게
expect 동 예상하다, 기대하다
on time 정각에, 제 시간에

B [보기]에서 알맞은 말을 골라 문장을 완성하시오.

보기	boring	tidy	happy	a liar

1 She called me ____________________.
2 He found the work ____________________.
3 Please keep your room ____________________.
4 The birthday gifts made me ____________________.

boring 형 지루한
tidy 형 깔끔한
liar 명 거짓말쟁이

C 주어진 단어를 어법에 맞게 바꿔 문장을 완성하시오.

1 My mom told me ____________ my hands. (wash)
2 Justin asked me ____________ his reading club. (join)
3 He wanted his daughter ____________ once a week. (call)
4 I expected the birds in the cage ____________ a song. (sing)
5 Most parents advise their kids ____________ lots of friends. (make)
6 The teacher ordered her students ____________ their homework. (bring)

wash one's hands 손을 씻다
reading club 독서 동아리
once a week 일주일에 한 번
cage 명 새장
advise 동 충고하다
make friends 친구를 사귀다
bring 동 가져오다

D 우리말과 같은 뜻이 되도록 주어진 단어를 이용하여 문장을 완성하시오.

1 그는 네가 파티에 오기를 원해. (want, come)
→ He __________ __________ __________ __________ to the party.

2 그 소음이 사람들을 언짢게 만들었다. (make, upset)
→ The noise __________ __________ __________.

3 그 교실을 깨끗하게 유지해 주세요. (keep, clean)
→ Please __________ __________ __________ __________.

4 우리는 그가 시험에 합격할 것으로 기대했다. (expect, pass)
→ We __________ __________ __________ __________ the exam.

: Review Test

[01-02] 빈칸에 들어갈 알맞은 말을 고르시오.

01 Her painting looks ________.

① well ② wonderfully
③ good ④ greatly
⑤ beautifully

02 Can I ask a favor ________ you?

① of ② to ③ in
④ for ⑤ at

[03-05] 빈칸에 들어갈 수 없는 말을 고르시오.

03 The pumpkin pie ________ good.

① is ② looks
③ smells ④ tastes
⑤ shows

04 His mother ________ him to do his best.

① told ② made
③ wanted ④ advised
⑤ expected

05 My aunt ________ some delicious pizza for me.

① bought ② gave
③ cooked ④ made
⑤ got

06 빈칸에 공통으로 들어갈 알맞은 말은?

· Could you pass the salt ________ me?
· Do you want me ________ come with you?

① in ② of ③ as
④ to ⑤ for

07 밑줄 친 ❶~❺ 중 어법상 바르지 않은 것은?

Reading *The Scarlet Letter* was my homework. At first, the book didn't ❶ look ❷ interesting. But later I ❸ found it very ❹ touchingly. I told my friend ❺ to read it, too.

08 빈칸에 들어갈 말이 나머지와 다른 하나는?

① I sent a postcard ______ my sister in England.
② My grandmother made a cake ______ us.
③ Mr. Kendrick will lend the truck ______ us.
④ He didn't pass the ball ______ me.
⑤ She told a secret ______ her best friend.

09 빈칸에 들어갈 말이 바르게 짝지어진 것은?

· The skirt looks ________ on her.
· James asked me ________ to the movie.
· My teacher gave some advice ________ me.

① good – to go – to
② good – to go – for
③ good – go – to
④ well – to go – for
⑤ well – go – for

[10-11] 다음 중 어법상 어색한 것을 고르시오.

10 ① It sounds silly.
② The soup smells like bad.
③ Her cookies taste wonderful.
④ Mrs. Delaware always looks cheerful.
⑤ All the people in the room felt angry.

11 ① Wanda found him friendly.
② We expected you to be honest.
③ Her mom called her Snow White.
④ They must keep their seats clean.
⑤ I asked Tom buy flowers in the market.

12 우리말을 영어로 바르게 옮긴 것을 모두 고르시오.

그가 그녀에게 연애편지를 보냈다.

① He sent her a love letter.
② He sent a love letter her.
③ He sent a love letter to her.
④ He sent a love letter for her.
⑤ He sent to her a love letter.

13 다음 중 문장 전환이 바르지 않은 것은?

① Please give me the ball.
→ Please give the ball for me.
② Mr. Cooper made us a pie.
→ Mr. Cooper made a pie for us.
③ My dad asked him many questions.
→ My dad asked many questions of him.
④ He bought her a diamond ring.
→ He bought a diamond ring for her.
⑤ I will send her some flowers.
→ I will send some flowers to her.

[14-15] 대화를 읽고, 물음에 답하시오.

A It smells ___ⓐ___! What are you doing?
B I'm making breakfast ___ⓑ___ Mom. You know it's her birthday.
A Wow. You are such a good son. Your mom will love it.
B Thank you. I hope that (A) 그것이 그녀를 행복하게 할 것이다.
A I'm sure it will.

14 빈칸 ⓐ와 ⓑ에 들어갈 말이 바르게 짝지어진 것은?

	ⓐ		ⓑ
①	good	-	to
②	good	-	of
③	good	-	for
④	well	-	to
⑤	well	-	for

15 밑줄 친 (A)를 바르게 영작한 것은?

① it will make her happy
② it will make her happily
③ it will make her happiness
④ it will make her to being happy
⑤ it will make her be happily

: 서술형 평가

Answers / p.30

[01-02] 두 문장이 같은 뜻이 되도록 전치사를 이용하여 문장을 완성하시오.

01 I will send you the document tomorrow.

→ I will ____________________ tomorrow.

02 My father bought me a pair of glasses.

→ My father ____________________ ____________________.

[03-04] 문장에서 어법상 어색한 부분을 찾아 고쳐 쓰시오.

03 Bob's parents want him be a lawyer.

→ Bob's parents ____________________.

04 The roller coaster doesn't look safely.

→ The roller coaster ____________________.

[05-06] 우리말과 같은 뜻이 되도록 주어진 단어를 배열하시오.

05 엄마가 나에게 컴퓨터를 끄라고 말씀하셨다.
(the computer, to, told, turn off, me)

→ Mom ____________________.

06 Johnson 씨가 자녀들에게 재미있는 이야기를 해주었다.
(an interesting story, her children, told)

→ Ms. Johnson ____________________.

[07-08] 대화를 읽고, 밑줄 친 우리말과 같은 뜻이 되도록 주어진 단어를 이용하여 영작하시오.

07 A <u>너 오늘 기분이 안 좋아 보여.</u> What happened?
B Actually, I lost my wallet.

→ You ____________________ today.
(upset)

08 A Wow! <u>너의 오빠는 모델처럼 보여.</u>
B Yeah, he is very tall.

→ Your brother ____________________.
(a model)

[09-10] 편지를 읽고, 물음에 답하시오.

Hi Michael,

Here are some pictures from my birthday. We went to a Korean restaurant and had a great time. The woman in the picture is my teacher. ❶ <u>She teaches me Korean every Monday and Wednesday.</u> The man next to me is the chef of the restaurant. ❷ <u>그가 우리에게 맛있는 음식을 만들어 주었어.</u> They look tasty, don't they?

09 전치사를 이용하여 밑줄 친 ❶과 같은 의미가 되도록 문장을 완성하시오.

→ ____________________ every Monday and Wednesday.

10 주어진 단어를 이용하여 밑줄 친 ❷를 영작하시오.

→ He ____________________.
(make, delicious dishes)

Chapter 10

형용사, 부사, 비교급 · 최상급

UNIT 01

형용사

1. 형용사의 쓰임

(1) **명사나 대명사를 앞이나 뒤에서 수식한다. 이때, -thing, -body, -one으로 끝나는 대명사는 항상 뒤에서 수식한다.**

You have a **beautiful** voice. 너는 아름다운 목소리를 가졌다.

I'd like to drink something **cold.** 나는 차가운 것을 좀 마시고 싶어요.

(2) **주어나 목적어를 보충 설명하는 보어 역할을 한다.**

This coffee smells **fresh.** [주격보어] 이 커피는 향이 신선하다.

The news made me **sad.** [목적격보어] 그 소식이 나를 슬프게 했다.

2. 수량형용사

의미 / 용도	많은	약간의	거의 없는	
수	many	a few	few	+ 셀 수 있는 명사의 복수형
양	much	a little	little	+ 셀 수 없는 명사
수/양	a lot of [lots of] = plenty of	some any	-	+ 둘 다

There were **many [a lot of, lots of, plenty of]** people in the store. 가게에 사람이 많았다.

I don't have **much [a lot of, lots of, plenty of]** money. 나는 돈을 많이 가지고 있지 않다.

He bought **a few** flowers for his mother. 그는 어머니를 위해 꽃을 좀 샀다.

There are **few** children in the playground. 운동장에 아이들이 거의 없다.

Here is **a little** information about me. 여기 나에 관한 약간의 정보가 있다.

We had **little** snow last year. 작년에는 눈이 거의 오지 않았다.

Give me **some** time to think about it. 그것에 대해 생각할 시간을 좀 주세요.

Would you like **some** chocolate cookies? 초콜릿 쿠키를 좀 드시겠어요?

I don't put **any** sugar in my coffee. 저는 커피에 설탕을 전혀 넣지 않아요.

Don't make **any** mistakes next time. 다음에는 어떤 실수도 하지 마.

Tips
some은 긍정문과 권유문에, any는 부정문과 의문문에 주로 사용된다.

Check-up 우리말과 같은 뜻이 되도록 [ ] 안에서 알맞은 말을 고르시오.

1 Thompson 씨는 좋은 교사이다.
→ Mr. Thompson is a [good / well] teacher.

2 우리는 파티에서 멋진 시간을 보냈다.
→ We had a [wonderful / wonderfully] time at the party.

: EXERCISES

Answers / p.30

A [ ] 안에서 알맞은 것을 고르시오.

information 명 정보
exciting 형 신 나는

1 I need [a little / a few] information about it.
2 There were [a few / a little] girls in the class.
3 We don't have [many / much] homework today.
4 He wants to do [exciting something / something exciting].

B [보기]에서 알맞은 단어를 골라 우리말과 같은 뜻이 되도록 문장을 완성하시오.

보기	scary	interesting	tired	warm

1 이 재킷이 널 따뜻하게 유지해 줄 거야.
→ This jacket will keep you ______________.

2 그녀는 오늘 아침에 정말 피곤해 보였다.
→ She looked really ______________ this morning.

3 Michelle은 무서운 영화를 좋아하지 않는다.
→ Michelle doesn't like ______________ movies.

4 나는 신문에서 흥미로운 이야기를 읽었다.
→ I read a(n) ______________ story in the newspaper.

C [보기]에서 알맞은 말을 골라 문장을 완성하시오. [한 번씩만 쓸 것]

refrigerator 명 냉장고
cupboard 명 찬장
lonely 형 외로운
still 부 여전히
solve 동 풀다, 해결하다

보기	a little	little	a few	few

1 There's __________ milk in the refrigerator. You can have it.
2 There's __________ coffee in the cupboard. I need to buy some.
3 He feels so lonely. He has __________ friends in the new school.
4 I still have __________ questions to solve. Please give me some more time.

D 우리말과 같은 뜻이 되도록 주어진 단어를 이용하여 문장을 완성하시오.

1 동물원에 많은 동물이 있다. (animal)
→ There are __________ __________ in the zoo.

2 서둘러요! 우리는 시간이 많지 않아요. (time)
→ Hurry up! We don't have __________ __________.

3 그 대회에는 많은 참가자가 있었다. (participants)
→ There were __________ __________ __________ __________ in the competition.

부사

1. 부사의 쓰임: 동사, 형용사, 다른 부사, 문장 전체를 수식한다.

Ron **kindly** lent me some money. Ron은 친절하게도 나에게 약간의 돈을 빌려 주었다.

Your father is a **really** good actor. 너의 아버지는 정말 훌륭한 배우이다.

She solved the problem **very** easily. 그녀는 그 문제를 아주 쉽게 풀었다.

Luckily, I was able to catch the train. 다행히도, 나는 그 기차를 탈 수 있었다.

2. 부사의 형태와 의미

대부분의 형용사: 형용사+-ly	nice - nicely	quick - quickly	careful - carefully
y로 끝나는 형용사: y → i + -ly	easy - easily	happy - happily	lucky - luckily
le로 끝나는 형용사: e → y	simple - simply	terrible - terribly	possible - possibly
형용사와 형태가 같은 부사	fast 빠른 - **fast** 빨리 late 늦은 - **late** 늦게 near 가까운 - **near** 근처에	early 이른 - **early** 일찍 high 높은 - **high** 높게 hard 열심히 하는 - **hard** 열심히	
부사+ly가 다른 뜻을 가지는 부사	late 늦게 - **lately** 최근에 near 가까이 - **nearly** 거의	high 높게 - **highly** 매우 hard 열심히 - **hardly** 거의 ~하지 않는	

Mrs. Long had a really **late** lunch today. [형용사] Long 씨는 오늘 매우 늦은 점심을 먹었다.

You shouldn't get up **late** on weekdays. [부사] 너는 주중에 늦게 일어나면 안 된다.

Tips

형용사 good의 부사는 well이다.

Don't worry. You're doing a **good** job.
걱정 마. 넌 잘하고 있어.

Don't worry. You're doing **well**.
걱정 마. 넌 잘하고 있어.

Plus α

의미가 다양해서 혼동하기 쉬운 형용사와 부사

well 형 건강한 부 잘

pretty 형 예쁜 부 상당히, 꽤

hard 형 열심히 하는, 딱딱한, 어려운 부 열심히

3. 빈도부사: 같은 일이 반복되는 정도를 나타내며, be동사나 조동사 뒤, 일반동사 앞에 쓴다.

100% ... 0%

always – usually – often – sometimes – hardly, rarely, seldom – never

Keith is **always** on time. Keith는 항상 시간을 지킨다.

I **usually** have cereal for breakfast. 나는 보통 아침으로 시리얼을 먹는다.

Check-up 우리말과 같은 뜻이 되도록 ☐ 안에서 알맞은 말을 고르시오.

1 다음 질문을 주의 깊게 들으시오.
→ Listen [careful / carefully] to the following question.

2 밖에 비가 많이 오고 있다. .
→ It's raining [heavy / heavily] outside.

3 나는 편안한 의자를 샀다.
→ I bought a [comfortable / comfortably] chair.

: EXERCISES

Answers / p.31

A [ ] 안에서 알맞은 것을 고르시오.

1 We live in a [safe / safely] neighborhood.
2 I hurt my leg. I can't jump [high / highly].
3 The princess lived [happy / happily] ever after.
4 He [takes often / often takes] a walk along the river.

safely 부 안전하게
neighborhood 명 근처, 이웃
hurt 동 다치다
ever after 그 후로
take a walk 산책하다
along 전 ~을 따라서

B [보기]와 같이 밑줄 친 부사가 수식하는 말을 찾아 표시하시오.

보기 I will come home early today.

1 Please drive safely.
2 Finally, she passed the test.
3 She tried to speak very slowly.
4 He is really good at math.

pass 동 통과하다
try 동 ~하려고 노력하다
be good at ~을 잘하다
math 명 수학

C [ ] 안에 주어진 단어를 알맞은 곳에 써 넣으시오.

1 [good, well] Den drives very ________. He is a ________ driver.
2 [quiet, quietly] Karen is very ________. She always talks ________.
3 [fast, fast] Jim is a ________ runner. He can run very ________.
4 [happy, happily] He is a ________ kid. Look! He is playing ________.

quiet 형 조용한
fast 형 빠른 부 빠르게
runner 명 달리는 사람

D 우리말과 같은 뜻이 되도록 주어진 단어를 이용하여 문장을 완성하시오.

1 Lydia는 결코 고기를 먹지 않는다. (eat, never)
→ Lydia ________ ________ meat.
2 Sue는 매우 유명한 가수가 되었다. (popular, highly)
→ Sue became ________ ________ ________ ________.
3 그는 항상 매우 빨리 걷는다. (walk, very, fast)
→ He ________ ________ ________ ________.

UNIT 03

비교급 · 최상급

1. 비교급/최상급 형태

대부분	+ -er / -est	old – older – oldest	hard – harder – hardest
-e로 끝날 때	+ -r / -st	nice – nicer – nicest	wise – wiser – wisest
단모음 + 단자음	자음 반복 + -er / -est	hot – hotter – hottest	big – bigger – biggest
-y로 끝날 때	y → i + -er / -est	easy – easier – easiest	early – earlier – earliest
(2음절, 3음절) -ous, -ful, -ive, (부사) -ly	more + 원급 / most + 원급	famous – **more famous** – **most famous** beautiful – **more beautiful** – **most beautiful** easily – **more easily** – **most easily**	

불규칙	
late 늦은 [시간] **later** – **latest**	good 좋은, well 건강한 – **better** – **best**
[순서] **latter** – **last**	bad 나쁜, ill 아픈, badly 나쁘게 – **worse** – **worst**
old 늙은 [시간] **older** – **oldest**	much, many 많은 – **more** – **most**
[순서] **elder** – **eldest**	little 적은 – **less** – **least**

2. 비교 표현

(1) 「as+**원급**+as」 ~만큼 …한[하게]

Susan is **as tall as** Ron. Susan은 Ron만큼 키가 크다.

Greg drives **as carefully as** Carl does. Greg은 Carl만큼 조심해서 운전한다.

☆ 「not as[so]+원급+as」 ~만큼 …하지 않은[않게]

Your bag is not **as big as** mine. 네 가방은 내 가방만큼 크지 않다.

Simon cannot run **as fast as** Jake can. Simon은 Jake만큼 빠르게 달릴 수 없다.

(2) 「**비교급**+than」 ~보다 …한[하게]

Your room is **cleaner than** mine. 네 방은 내 방보다 깨끗하다.

Phillip studies **harder than** Robin does. Phillip은 Robin보다 열심히 공부한다.

(3) 「the+**최상급**」 가장 ~한[하게]

Paul is **the tallest** in my class. Paul은 우리 반에서 가장 키가 크다.

Mt. Everest is **the highest** mountain in the world. 에베레스트는 세계에서 가장 높은 산이다.

Cheetahs are **the fastest** of all animals. 치타는 모든 동물 중에서 가장 빠르다.

Plus α

비교급을 강조하는 부사: even, much, a lot, still, far 훨씬 ~한

This ring is **a lot** more expensive than that one.
이 반지가 저것보다 훨씬 더 비싸다.

Pam cooks **much** better than I do.
Pam이 나보다 요리를 훨씬 더 잘한다.

Tips

「one of the+최상급+ 복수명사」 가장 ~한 … 중 하나

May is **one of the smartest students** in my school.
May는 우리 학교에서 가장 똑똑한 학생 중 한 명이다.

Check-up 우리말과 같은 뜻이 되도록 [ ] 안에서 알맞은 말을 고르시오.

1 Amy는 나보다 똑똑하다.
→ Amy is [smarter / more smart] than I am.

2 이 책은 저 책보다 흥미롭다.
→ This book is [interestinger / more interesting] than that one.

: EXERCISES

Answers / p.31

A [ ] 안에서 알맞은 것을 고르시오.

1 I can't cook as [better / well] as my mom can.
2 Alison is [famous / more famous] than her brother.
3 Sirius is the [brighter / brightest] star in the night sky.
4 He was the [more / most] handsome actor in the movie.

famous ⓗ 유명한
Sirius ⓜ 〈천문〉 시리우스 (가장 밝은 별)
bright ⓗ 밝은

B 주어진 단어를 이용하여 문장을 완성하시오.

1 This scarf is ________ than mine. (long)
2 John's voice is as ________ as Ted's. (loud)
3 I drink ________ coffee than Andy does. (much)
4 What is the ________ country in the world? (large)

scarf ⓜ 스카프
voice ⓜ 목소리
loud ⓗ 소리가 큰

C 주어진 단어의 비교급과 최상급을 이용하여 문장을 완성하시오.

1 [early] Harold got up ________ than Bob, but Mac got up the ________ of all.
2 [tall] Wendy is ________ than Mia, but Samuel is the ________ student in my class.
3 [well] My mom cooks ________ than I do, but my dad cooks the ________ in my family.
4 [big] The museum is ________ than the bank, but the tower is the ________ in this city.

get up 일어나다
museum ⓜ 박물관
tower ⓜ 타워, 탑

D 우리말과 같은 뜻이 되도록 주어진 단어를 이용하여 문장을 완성하시오.

1 비행기가 자동차보다 빠르다. (fast)
→ Planes are ________ ________ cars.

2 이 문제는 저 문제보다 어렵다. (difficult)
→ This question is ________ ________ ________ that one.

3 세계에서 가장 높은 폭포는 무엇입니까? (high, waterfall)
→ What is ________ ________ ________ in the world?

4 Andrew의 스마트폰은 내 것만큼이나 새 것이다. (new)
→ Andrew's smartphone is ________ ________ ________ mine.

: Review Test

[01-02] 빈칸에 들어갈 가장 알맞은 말을 고르시오.

01

Would you like ________ hot water?

① a few ② any
③ many ④ few
⑤ some

02

My friend Jane plays the violin ________ than I do.

① good ② well
③ best ④ better
⑤ bad

03 빈칸에 들어갈 수 없는 말은?

There were ________ people at the park.

① lots of ② a lot of
③ many ④ much
⑤ plenty of

04 [보기]의 밑줄 친 부분과 바꿔 쓸 수 있는 것은?

보기 The teacher asked <u>some</u> questions of the students.

① any ② much
③ a few ④ little
⑤ a little

05 빈칸에 공통으로 들어갈 가장 알맞은 말은?

· Do you have ________ ideas?
· Thanks, but I don't need ________ help.

① any ② many
③ a few ④ a little
⑤ some

[06-07] 빈칸에 들어갈 말이 나머지와 <u>다른</u> 것을 고르시오.

06
① Is there ________ problem?
② I need ________ sneakers to wear.
③ Would you like ________ hot chocolate?
④ There are ________ trees in the garden.
⑤ Let's bring ________ food for the picnic.

07
① Joshua is older ________ Michael.
② Andy is more popular ________ John.
③ My brother walks faster ________ me.
④ This hairpin is as expensive ________ that one.
⑤ Jimmy spends more money ________ his sister.

08 비교급과 최상급의 형태가 바르게 짝지어진 것은?

① well – better – best
② early – earlyer – earlyest
③ bad – badder – baddest
④ long – longger – longgest
⑤ famous – famouser – famousest

09 [보기]의 밑줄 친 부분과 같은 의미로 쓰인 것은?

보기 The interviewer asked him <u>hard</u> questions.

① Jenny is a <u>hard</u> worker.
② The stone was really <u>hard</u>.
③ Try <u>hard</u> if you have a goal.
④ The book is <u>hard</u> to understand.
⑤ She studied <u>hard</u> to pass the exam.

10 주어진 문장과 의미가 통하는 것을 두 개 고르시오.

Ron isn't as tall as Susan.

① Ron is taller than Susan.
② Susan is taller than Ron.
③ Susan isn't as tall as Ron.
④ Ron is shorter than Susan.
⑤ Susan is shorter than Ron.

11 다음 중 어법상 올바른 것은?

① I can't speak as faster as my mom.
② I got up early than yesterday.
③ Money isn't as important than health.
④ Pam and Dan are the happiest couple.
⑤ Mary is the smarter student in her class.

12 다음 중 어법상 어색한 것은?

① Sarah sometimes takes a walk.
② Jake always is late for work.
③ I will never forget your kindness.
④ My brother usually wears training shoes.
⑤ Rachel often goes hiking with her friends.

13 우리말을 영어로 바르게 옮긴 것은?

① 나는 너만큼 많이 먹진 못해.
→ I can't eat as much than you can.
② 오늘이 올해 들어 가장 추운 날이다.
→ Today is the colder day in this year.
③ 이것이 스페인으로 가는 가장 저렴한 항공권이다.
→ This is the cheapest ticket to Spain.
④ 나일 강은 세계에서 가장 긴 강이다.
→ The Nile is longer river in the world.
⑤ 그녀는 상점에서 가장 비싼 가방을 샀다.
→ She bought the expensivest bag in the shop.

[14-15] 대화를 읽고, 물음에 답하시오.

A Hello. May I help you?
B Yes. I'm looking for a present for my brother. Do you have ❶ useful something for hiking?
A Sure. How about a pair of hiking shoes? These are ❷ the best-selling shoes in the store.
B They ❸ look great. But I don't think he likes red. (A) 그는 항상 검은색 신발을 신어요.
A OK, then black will be ❹ better. What size is he?
B He's size 275 or 280.
A In that case, I recommend the ❺ bigger ones.
B Thanks. I'll take them.

14 밑줄 친 ❶~❺ 중 어법상 어색한 것은?

15 밑줄 친 (A)를 바르게 영작한 것은?

① Always he wears black shoes.
② He always wears black shoes.
③ He wears always black shoes.
④ He wears black always shoes.
⑤ He wears black shoes always.

: 서술형 평가

Answers / p.32

[01-02] 두 문장의 의미가 통하도록 문장을 완성하시오.

01 Joe is a careful driver.

→ Joe drives __________.

02 Janet is a very good violinist.

→ Janet can play the violin very __________.

[03-04] 표를 보고, 주어진 단어를 이용하여 문장을 완성하시오.

Name	Height (cm)	Weight (kg)
Andy	178	72
Peter	178	69

조건 원급 비교 또는 비교급을 이용할 것

03 Andy is ______________ Peter. (tall)

04 Andy is ______________ Peter. (heavy)

[05-06] 우리말과 같은 뜻이 되도록 주어진 단어를 이용하여 문장을 완성하시오.

05 Daniel은 전보다 더 행복해 보인다.

→ Daniel looks ________________ before. (happy)

06 러시아는 세계에서 가장 큰 나라이다.

→ Russia is ________________ in the world. (big)

07 표를 보고, [보기]와 같이 빈도부사를 이용하여 문장을 완성하시오.

	Spring	Summer	Autumn	Winter
always				cold
usually	cool		windy	
often		rain		
sometimes	rain		hot	
hardly				rain
never		snow		

보기 In spring, it is usually cool, and it sometimes rains.

(1) In summer, it ______________, and it ______________.

(2) In autumn, it ______________ windy, and it ______________ hot.

(3) In winter, it ______________ cold, and it ______________.

[08-10] 우리말과 같은 뜻이 되도록 단어를 배열하시오.

08 중국어가 영어보다 어렵다.
(English, Chinese, than, is, difficult, more)

→ ______________________

09 세계에서 가장 작은 나라는 어디인가요?
(in the world, the, where, is, country, smallest)

→ ______________________

10 나는 항상 내 여동생보다 일찍 일어난다.
(earlier, get up, my sister, I, than, always)

→ ______________________

Chapter 11

접속사

and, or, but, so

☆ 등위접속사: 문법적으로 대등한 관계인 단어와 단어, 구와 구, 절과 절을 연결하는 and, or, but과 절과 절을 연결해 주는 so가 있다.

1. and ~와, 그리고

Ronald usually eats cereal **and** milk for breakfast. [단어+단어]
Ronald는 아침으로 보통 시리얼과 우유를 먹는다.

Playing the piano **and** singing in a choir are my favorite activities. [구+구]
피아노 연주하기와 합창단에서 노래하기는 내가 가장 좋아하는 활동이다.

Crystal is 17 years old, **and** her sister is 20 years old. [절+절]
Crystal은 열일곱 살이고 그녀의 언니는 스무 살이다.

> **Tips**
> both A and B A와 B 둘 다
> **Both** my mother **and** my father were disappointed by my behavior.
> 어머니와 아버지 두 분 모두 내 행동에 대해 실망하셨다.

2. or 혹은, 또는

We are going skiing on the 3rd **or** the 7th. [단어+단어] 우리는 3일이나 7일에 스키를 타러 갈 것이다.

You can pay by credit card **or** in cash. [구+구] 신용카드나 현금으로 지불하실 수 있습니다.

Were you at home, **or** did you go to the concert last night? [절+절]
어젯밤에 집에 있었니 아니면 콘서트에 갔었니?

> **Tips**
> either A or B A나 B 둘 중 하나
> Jamie wants to buy **either** a tablet PC **or** a laptop.
> Jamie는 태블릿 PC나 노트북 중 하나를 사고 싶어 한다.

3. but 하지만, 그러나

Eggs are cheap **but** healthy. [단어+단어] 달걀은 저렴하지만 건강에 좋다.

He likes listening to music **but** doesn't like singing. [구+구]
그는 음악 듣는 것은 좋아하지만 노래 부르는 것은 좋아하지 않는다.

I want to go swimming **but** my sister wants to go hiking for the weekend. [절+절]
나는 주말에 수영하러 가기를 원하지만 내 여동생은 하이킹을 하러 가기를 원한다.

4. so ~이므로, 그래서

It was raining heavily outside, **so** I closed the window. [절+절]
밖에 비가 세차게 오고 있어서 나는 창문을 닫았다.

Jenny lost her wallet, **so** she doesn't have any money. [절+절]
Jenny는 지갑을 잃어버려서 돈이 하나도 없다.

Check-up 우리말과 같은 뜻이 되도록 [ ] 안에서 알맞은 말을 고르시오.

1 나의 조카는 귀엽고 예쁘다.
→ My niece is cute [and / or] pretty.

2 나는 차를 사고 싶지만 충분한 돈이 없다.
→ I want to buy a car, [and / but] I don't have enough money.

3 나는 목이 말라서 찬 물을 한 잔 마셨다.
→ I was thirsty, [or / so] I drank a glass of cold water.

: EXERCISES

Answers / p.33

A [ ] 안에서 알맞은 것을 고르시오.

1 Eric has brown hair [and / so] brown eyes.
2 Which do you want to eat, meat [and / or] fish?
3 Karen is kind to all, [but / so] everybody likes her.
4 My grandma drinks a lot of tea, [but / or] she doesn't drink coffee.

brown 형 갈색의
meat 명 육류
be kind to ~에게 친절하다

B [보기]에서 알맞은 말을 골라 문장을 완성하시오. [한 번씩만 사용할 것]

보기 and but or so

1 Which do you want, ice cream __________ juice?
2 My brother __________ I go to the same school.
3 Dana caught a cold, __________ she went to see a doctor.
4 Eugene can speak Japanese, __________ he can't write it.

same 형 같은
catch a cold 감기에 걸리다
see a doctor 의사에게 진료를 받다
Japanese 명 일본어

C 내용이 자연스럽게 이어지도록 접속사에 유의하여 문장을 연결하시오.

1 I am so tired • • (a) or did he go home?
2 Jane missed the train • • (b) so she was late for work.
3 Is Mark in the library • • (c) and we had a cup of tea.
4 Yesterday I met Emma • • (d) but I don't want to go to bed early.

tired 형 피곤한
miss 동 놓치다
library 명 도서관
a cup of 한 잔의 ~
go to bed 잠자리에 들다

D 우리말과 같은 뜻이 되도록 주어진 단어를 이용하여 문장을 완성하시오.

1 Jack은 키가 크고 잘 생겼다. (tall, handsome)
→ Jack is __________ __________ __________.

2 너는 지금 가도 되고 아니면 여기 있어도 돼. (stay, here)
→ You can go now __________ __________ __________.

3 Kelly는 고전음악을 좋아하지만, 록음악을 좋아하지 않는다. (rock music)
→ Kelly likes classical music __________ __________ __________ __________ __________.

4 나는 방이 매우 더워서 창문을 열었다. (open, the window)
→ The room was very hot, __________ __________ __________ __________ __________.

when, before, after, until

☆ 종속접속사: 시간, 이유, 조건, 양보 등을 의미하는 절을 이끄는 접속사이다. 종속접속사가 이끄는 절은 주절의 앞이나 뒤에 올 수 있고, 주절 앞에 올 경우 종속절 끝에 쉼표를 쓴다.

When you see him, please say hello for me.

Please say hello for me **when you see him.** 그를 보면, 내 안부를 전해줘.

1. when ~할 때

When Sarah came in, I was cooking dinner. Sarah가 들어왔을 때 난 저녁을 요리하고 있었다.

I will send you a postcard **when** I get there. 내가 그곳에 도착하면 엽서를 보낼게.

> **Plus α**
> while ~하는 동안
> **While** I was driving home, it started to rain. 운전해서 집에 오는 동안 비가 오기 시작했다.

2. before ~전에

Before they moved to Vancouver, they lived in Hong Kong.
그들은 밴쿠버로 이주하기 전에 홍콩에 살았다.

Charlie will call you **before** he visits you. Charlie가 너를 방문하기 전에 전화할 거야.

3. after ~ 후에

After I finish my report, I will go swimming. 나는 보고서를 마친 후에 수영을 하러 갈 것이다.

I drank some water **after** I rode my bike. 나는 자전거를 탄 후에 물을 약간 마셨다.

4. until ~ 때까지

We will stay here **until** he arrives. 우리는 그가 도착할 때까지 여기 있을 것이다.

Please wait **until** she finishes speaking. 그녀가 말을 끝낼 때까지 기다려 주세요.

> **Tips**
> 의문사 when vs. 접속사 when
> 1 의문사 언제
> 「when+동사+주어 ~?」
> **When** are you leaving?
> 언제 떠날 거야?
> 2 접속사 ~할 때
> 「when+주어+동사」
> **When** she saw me, I smiled at her.
> 그녀가 나를 보았을 때, 나는 그녀에게 미소를 지었다.

> **Plus α**
> 시간을 나타내는 부사절에서는 미래 시제 대신 현재 시제를 쓴다.
> I will send you a postcard **when** I get there.
> 내가 그곳에 도착하면 너에게 엽서를 보낼게
> I will send you a postcard **when** I ~~will get~~ there. (X)

Check-up 우리말과 같은 뜻이 되도록 [ ] 안에서 알맞은 말을 고르시오.

1 내가 문을 열었을 때, 그는 잠을 자고 있었다.
→ [When / Until] I opened the door, he was sleeping.

2 네가 돌아올 때까지 난 널 기다릴 거야.
→ I will wait for you [before / until] you come back.

3 우리는 영화가 시작하기 전에 그곳에 도착해야 해.
→ We should arrive there [after / before] the movie starts.

4 나는 그녀와 이야기를 나눈 후에, 기분이 나아졌다.
→ [After / Before] I talked with her, I felt better.

: EXERCISES

Answers / p.33

A

[　] 안에서 알맞은 것을 고르시오.

1 What do you usually do [until / when] you have free time?

2 [Before / Until] he entered college, he moved to New York.

3 I can go out with you [after / until] I clean my room.

4 Tim will stay home until the rain [stops / will stop].

usually 부 주로, 대개
free time 여가
enter 동 들어가다
college 명 대학교
move to ~로 이주하다
go out 외출하다

B

주어진 접속사를 이용하여 두 문장을 한 문장으로 만드시오.

1 I will call you. I will arrive in London. (when)
→ I will call you ______________________.

2 Let's eat something. The movie will start. (before)
→ Let's eat something ______________________.

3 Please wait here. I will call your name. (until)
→ Please wait here ______________________.

4 They had breakfast. And then they went out for a walk. (after)
→ ______________________, they went out for a walk.

arrive 동 도착하다
call one's name ~의 이름을 부르다
go out for a walk 산책하러 나가다

C

내용이 자연스럽게 이어지도록 접속사에 유의하여 문장을 연결하시오.

1 Wash your hands •　　• (a) when we were in London.
2 He missed his family •　　• (b) before you eat.
3 We saw several plays •　　• (c) until she finishes her meal.
4 She cannot leave the table •　　• (d) after he left home.

wash one's hands ~의 손을 씻다
several 형 몇몇의
play 명 연극
meal 명 식사
leave 동 떠나다

D

우리말과 같은 뜻이 되도록 주어진 단어를 이용하여 문장을 완성하시오.

1 그들은 영화를 보기 전에 저녁을 먹었다. (watch)
→ They had dinner ________ ________ ________ a movie.

2 그는 대학 졸업 후에 수의사가 되었다. (graduate)
→ He became a vet ________ ________ ________ from college.

3 그녀가 그를 처음 만났을 때 그녀는 열다섯 살이었다. (meet)
→ ________ ________ first ________ ________, she was 15 years old.

4 학생들은 선생님이 조용히 하라고 할 때까지 계속 이야기를 했다. (their teacher, tell)
→ Students kept talking ________ ________ ________ ________ them to be quiet.

UNIT 03

because, if, that

1. 이유, 조건을 나타내는 부사절을 이끄는 종속접속사 because, if

(1) because ~ 때문에 [이유]

Ken didn't go to school **because** he was sick. Ken은 아파서 학교에 가지 않았다.

Because it was very cold, I turned the heater on. 나는 매우 추워서 난로를 켰다.

(2) if 만일 ~라면 [조건]

If you need money, I'll lend you some. 네가 돈이 필요하면 내가 좀 빌려 줄게.

If the rain stops tomorrow, I will go hiking. 내일 비가 그치면 나는 하이킹을 갈 것이다.

> **Plus α**
>
> 조건을 나타내는 if절에서는 미래 시제 대신 현재 시제를 쓴다.
>
> I **will go** hiking **if** the rain **stops** tomorrow.
> 내일 비가 그치면 하이킹을 갈 것이다.
>
> I **will go** hiking **if** the rain ~~will stop~~ tomorrow. (X)

2. 명사절을 이끄는 종속접속사 that: that절은 '~하는 것'으로 해석하며, 문장에서 주어, 목적어, 보어 역할을 한다.

(1) that**절이 주어일 때:** 주어인 that절은 주로 「It(가주어) ~ that(진주어)」 구문으로 쓰인다.

It(가주어) is good news **that** she will come to the party(진주어). 그녀가 파티에 온다는 것은 좋은 소식이다.

It was true **that** he had the key to the house. 그가 그 집 열쇠를 가지고 있다는 것은 사실이었다.

(2) that**절이 목적어일 때:** say, think, believe, hope, tell, know 등의 동사와 함께 사용하며, 이때 that은 생략할 수 있다.

I know (**that**) exercising is good for my health. 나는 운동이 건강에 좋다는 것을 알고 있다.

I can't believe (**that**) the building was built in the 16th century.
나는 그 건물이 16세기에 지어졌다는 것을 믿을 수가 없다.

(3) that**절이 보어일 때:** that절은 주어를 보충 설명한다.

The problem is **that** you drink too much coffee. [The problem = you drink too much coffee]
문제는 네가 커피를 너무 많이 마신다는 것이다.

The truth is **that** the story is not true. [The truth = the story is not true]
진실은 그 이야기가 사실이 아니라는 것이다.

Check-up 우리말과 같은 뜻이 되도록 [ ] 안에서 알맞은 말을 고르시오.

1 David가 대회에서 우승했다는 것을 들었니?
→ Did you hear [if / that] David won the contest?

2 피아니스트가 되고 싶다면, 너는 열심히 연습해야 한다.
→ You have to practice hard [because / if] you want to be a pianist.

3 Joe는 어머니를 행복하게 해드리고 싶어서 아침 식사를 준비했다.
→ Joe prepared breakfast [because / that] he wanted to make his mother happy.

: EXERCISES

Answers / p.34

A [ ] 안에서 알맞은 것을 고르시오.

1 I believe [if / that] I can be a pilot one day.
2 [If / That] it snows tomorrow, I will stay home.
3 James had two hamburgers [because / if] he was very hungry.
4 We are studying now [because / if] we have an exam tomorrow.

pilot 명 비행기 조종사
one day 언젠가
have an exam 시험을 치다

B 주어진 접속사를 이용하여 두 문장을 한 문장으로 만드시오.

1 I didn't eat breakfast. I'm so hungry now. (because)
→ ______________________________, I'm so hungry now.
2 Many children suffer from hunger in Africa. I heard. (that)
→ I heard ______________________________.
3 You have questions. Ask me. (if)
→ Ask me ______________________________.

suffer from ~를 겪다, ~에 시달리다
hunger 명 굶주림

C 내용이 자연스럽게 이어지도록 접속사에 유의하여 문장을 연결하시오.

1 We know • • (a) if he wants to.
2 You can't play soccer • • (b) that Cindy lost a lot of weight.
3 He can go with us • • (c) because it's too dark outside.

lose weight 체중을 감량하다
dark 형 어두운
outside 부 밖에

D 우리말과 같은 뜻이 되도록 주어진 단어를 이용하여 문장을 완성하시오.

1 나와 이야기하고 싶으면 언제든 내게 전화해도 돼. (want)
→ You can call me anytime ________ ________ ________ to talk to me.
2 나는 답을 몰랐기 때문에 그녀에게 물어보았다. (know)
→ I asked her ________ ________ ________ ________ the answer.
3 나는 그가 나에게 관심이 있다고 생각하지 않는다. (be interested in)
→ I don't think ________ ________ ________ ________ ________ me.
4 그 영화가 지루했기 때문에 나는 극장에서 잠이 들었다. (be, boring)
→ ________ ________ ________ ________ ________, I fell asleep in the theater.

: Review Test

[01-02] 빈칸에 들어갈 알맞은 말을 고르시오.

01

Nathan is tired ________ he didn't sleep well last night.

① before ② after ③ but
④ so ⑤ because

02

________ you hurry, you will catch the train.

① Until ② If ③ Or
④ That ⑤ So

03 빈칸에 들어갈 말이 바르게 짝지어진 것은?

· Both Jane ______ Mary like to go skiing.
· You can either buy a computer ______ save your money in the bank.

① so – and ② so – but
③ and – or ④ and – but
⑤ but – or

[04-05] 빈칸에 공통으로 들어갈 알맞은 말을 고르시오.

04

· He finished the paper ________ he went on vacation.
· Why don't we go shopping ________ we make dinner?

① if ② before ③ because
④ that ⑤ so

05

· I believe ________ you will keep the promise.
· It's important ________ we tried our best.

① that ② after ③ but
④ if ⑤ because

06 밑줄 친 that 중 생략할 수 없는 것은?

① I don't think that she will fall in love with him.
② Everybody knows that Ken is my brother.
③ Who is that girl in a red hat with sunglasses?
④ We can't believe that she's 86 years old.
⑤ Ed said that he couldn't find his glasses.

07 다음 중 어법상 어색한 것은?

① I'd love to travel, but I don't have time.
② You won't miss the bus if you will hurry.
③ Before you leave, check your backpack again.
④ Dr. Lee read a lot of books when he was a child.
⑤ Ms. Louis came late because she was stuck in traffic.

[08-09] 두 문장을 한 문장으로 만들 때 빈칸에 들어갈 알맞은 말을 고르시오.

08

I bought my dream car. I'm so happy.
→ I'm so happy ________ I bought my dream car.

① or ② so ③ if
④ until ⑤ because

09

My father called me. I was in the bathroom.
→ ________ my father called me, I was in the bathroom.

① If ② When ③ That
④ Because ⑤ So

10 밑줄 친 when의 쓰임이 나머지와 다른 것은?

① When I got good grades, I was very happy.
② When you leave the house, please close the window.
③ When are you going to meet Brian?
④ When you grow up, what do you want to be?
⑤ Do you play with your smartphone when you are in bed?

11 다음 대화 중 어법상 어색한 것은?

① A Why didn't you come to the party last night?
B I'm sorry. I couldn't make it because I was too busy.
② A Could you close the window before it starts to rain?
B Of course.
③ A Please tell John to join the club.
B OK. I'll tell him when I'll see him.
④ A Are you planning to go somewhere during the holidays?
B Yes. I'm going to Spain and Germany.
⑤ A Did you call him, or did he call you?
B He called me.

12 대화의 빈칸에 공통으로 들어갈 알맞은 말은?

A Why are you studying ______ hard?
B I have a test tomorrow, ______ I have to study.

① because ② and ③ but
④ that ⑤ so

13 밑줄 친 that의 쓰임이 나머지와 다른 것은?

① I don't think that she made a mistake.
② I think that girl is very pretty.
③ I saw that she locked the door.
④ Do you think that she is nice?
⑤ She believes that he will come.

[14-15] 대화를 읽고, 물음에 답하시오.

A You don't look well today.
B I think that I'm catching a cold.
A Why don't you go home __ⓐ__ take a rest?
B I'd love to, __ⓑ__ I can't.
A Why?
B __ⓒ__ I have a flute lesson. (A) 만약 내가 한 번 더 수업에 빠지면 곤란을 겪게 될 거야. I already skipped several lessons.
A Oh, I'm sorry to hear that.

14 빈칸 ⓐ, ⓑ, ⓒ에 들어갈 말이 바르게 짝지어진 것은?

	ⓐ		ⓑ		ⓒ
①	and	–	but	–	Because
②	and	–	but	–	If
③	but	–	so	–	Because
④	but	–	so	–	If
⑤	and	–	but	–	If

15 밑줄 친 (A)를 영작한 것이다. 빈칸에 들어갈 말로 알맞은 것은?

I will get in trouble ______ one more time.

① when I will miss the class
② if I will miss the class
③ that I miss the class
④ that I will miss the class
⑤ if I miss the class

Answers / p.35

[01-02] 우리말과 같은 뜻이 되도록 빈칸에 알맞은 접속사를 넣어 문장을 완성하시오.

01 Susan은 식사 후에 항상 이를 닦는다.

→ Susan always brushes her teeth __________ meals.

02 Tom은 열심히 공부했지만 시험에 통과하지 못했다.

→ Tom studied hard, __________ he didn't pass the exam.

[03-05] [보기]에서 알맞은 접속사를 골라 주어진 문장과 의미가 통하도록 문장을 완성하시오.

보기 because if after

03 Eat less, and you'll lose weight.

→ ______________________________, you'll lose weight.

04 I will see you at 1 pm. I'm going to meet Mike at 3 pm.

→ I'm going to meet Mike at 3 pm __________ ______________________________.

05 The movie was very sad. I cried a lot.

→ I cried a lot ______________________________.

[06-07] 우리말과 같은 뜻이 되도록 주어진 단어를 배열하시오.

06 네가 나를 도와준 덕분에 숙제를 마칠 수 있었어. (you, me, helped, because)

→ I could finish my homework __________ ______________________________.

07 Jake는 학교에 갈 때 항상 Jessica와 함께 간다. (Jake, school, when, to, goes)

→ ______________________________, he is always with Jessica.

08 영화 감상평을 보고, [보기]와 같이 의견을 완성하시오.

Movie	*One Day*
Tom	sad
Chris	not interesting
Anna	romantic
Wendy	boring

보기 Tom I think that the movie is sad.

(1) Chris I think ______________________________.

(2) Anna I think ______________________________.

(3) Wendy I think ______________________________.

[09-10] 글을 읽고, 물음에 답하시오.

Sarah is my cousin. She and I lived in the same town until her family moved to a big city five years ago. We haven't met each other since she moved. ❶ I'm so excited. She is visiting me today. ❷ When I'll see her, I'll give her a big hug.

09 밑줄 친 ❶의 두 문장을 because를 이용하여 한 문장으로 다시 쓰시오.

→ ______________________________

10 밑줄 친 ❷에서 어법상 어색한 부분을 찾아 바르게 고쳐 쓰시오.

→ ______________________________

Chapter 12

전치사

장소를 나타내는 전치사

1. in, at, on

in	안에	장소의 내부 (도시, 국가, 탈 것, 건물 등)	**in** London, **in** Japan, **in** the car, **in** the house, **in** the pocket ...
at	~에	장소의 한 지점	**at** the door, **at** the bus stop, **at** school, **at** the airport ...
on	위에	표면에 닿은 상태 (벽, 바닥 등)	**on** the desk, **on** the table, **on** the wall, **on** the floor ...

My older sister lives **in** Paris. 우리 언니는 파리에 산다.

Brian is standing **at** the door. Brian이 출입구에 서 있다.

The picture **on** the wall is beautiful. 벽에 걸린 그림이 아름답다.

2. 기타 장소 전치사

(1) over ~ 위에 under ~ 아래에 [닿지 않은 상태]

The birds are flying **over** the building. 새들이 건물 위로 날고 있다.

A dog is lying **under** the tree. 개 한 마리가 나무 아래에 누워 있다.

(2) in front of ~ 앞에 behind ~의 뒤에

I'm standing **in front of** the theater. 나는 극장 앞에 서 있어.

Who's the girl **behind** you? 네 뒤에 있는 소녀는 누구니?

(3) next to, by, beside 옆에 near 근처에

The bakery is **next to [beside / by]** the flower shop. 그 빵집은 꽃 가게 옆에 있습니다.

Is there a bank **near** here? 이 근처에 은행이 있나요?

(4) between A and B A와 B 사이에 from A to B A에서 B까지 across from ~의 맞은편에

My office is **between** the bank **and** the post office. 내 사무실은 은행과 우체국 사이에 있다.

It takes 10 minutes **from** my house **to** my office on foot.
우리 집에서 내 사무실까지는 걸어서 10분 걸린다.

There is a grocery store **across from** my house. 우리 집 맞은편에 식료품점이 있다.

> **Plus α**
> above 위쪽에
> vs. below 아래쪽에
> Put your bag on the rack **above** your head.
> 가방을 머리 위쪽에 있는 선반에 두세요.
> Please do not write **below** this line.
> 이 선 아래로는 글을 쓰지 마시오.

Check-up 우리말과 같은 뜻이 되도록 [ ] 안에서 알맞은 말을 고르시오.

1 나는 책상에 앉아 있다. → I'm sitting [at / in] my desk.

2 책상 위에 물 한 컵이 있다. → A glass of water is [at / on] the desk.

3 컵에 우유가 약간 있다. → There is some milk [in / on] the glass.

: EXERCISES

Answers / p.36

A [ ] 안에서 알맞은 것을 고르시오.

1 The bridge is [over / under] the river.

2 My grandparents live [at / in] Busan.

3 We played beach volleyball [at / in] the beach.

4 The broadcasting company is [between / to] Powell St. and King St.

bridge 명 다리
beach volleyball 비치발리볼
beach 명 해변
broadcasting company 방송국

B [보기]에서 알맞은 전치사를 골라 우리말과 같은 뜻이 되도록 문장을 완성하시오.

보기 at on in

1 상자 안에 있는 게 뭐야? → What's ________ the box?

2 당신의 책을 책상 위에 놓으세요. → Put your book ________ the desk.

3 그가 입구에 서 있다. → He is standing ________ the door.

C 그림을 보고, [보기]에서 알맞은 전치사를 골라 문장을 완성하시오.

보기 under next to between on

1 There is a picture ________ the wall.

2 There is a bag ________ the chair.

3 A dog is lying ________ the desk.

4 There is a chair ________ the desk and the bed.

wall 명 벽
chair 명 의자
lie 동 눕다

D 우리말과 같은 뜻이 되도록 주어진 단어를 이용하여 문장을 완성하시오.

1 KTX는 서울과 부산 사이를 운행한다. (Seoul, Busan)
→ The KTX runs ________ ________ ________ ________.

2 호텔은 우체국 맞은편에 있습니다. (the post office)
→ The hotel is ________ ________ ________ ________ ________.

3 그 집 앞에 우체통이 있다. (the house)
→ There is a mailbox ________ ________ ________ ________ ________.

4 네 학교에서 기차역까지 얼마나 걸리니? (your school, the train station)
→ How long does it take ________ ________ ________ ________ ________ ________ ________?

UNIT 02

시간을 나타내는 전치사

1. at, on, in

at	구체적인 시각, 시점	at 11 o'clock, at 5:35, at noon, at midnight, at night, at lunchtime, at the end of this year ...
on	요일, 날짜, 특정한 날	on Saturday, on December 25th, on Thanksgiving Day, on my birthday ...
in	비교적 긴 시간 (월, 연도, 계절, 오전, 오후 등)	in March, in 2014, in winter, in the 19th century, in the morning, in the afternoon, in the evening ...

It often snows **at** this time of the year. 이맘때면 종종 눈이 온다.

Jay has a violin lesson **on** Thursday. Jay는 목요일에 바이올린 수업이 있다.

I want to have a party for you **on** your birthday. 나는 네 생일에 파티를 열어주고 싶어.

She gets up early **in** the morning. 그녀는 아침에 일찍 일어난다.

Plus α

1 특정 요일의 아침, 점심, 저녁 앞에는 전치사 on을 쓴다.

My family always has breakfast together **on** Sunday morning.
우리 가족은 항상 일요일 아침엔 아침 식사를 함께 한다.

2 around, about 약, 대략, 쯤

Let's meet **around** 12 pm.
오후 12시쯤에 만나자.

I got up **about** 6 am.
나는 오전 6시쯤에 일어났다.

2. 기타 시간 전치사

(1) before ~ 전에 after ~ 후에

Let's eat something **before** the show. 공연 전에 뭘 좀 먹자.

Sarah took a walk **after** dinner. Sarah는 저녁 식사 후에 산책을 했다.

(2) 「for+구체적인 숫자」, 「during+특정 기간」 ~동안

I lived in Canada **for** two years. 나는 캐나다에서 2년 동안 살았다.

Lena traveled in Spain **during** the spring break. Lena는 봄방학에 스페인을 여행했다.

(3) by ~까지 until ~까지

The book will be delivered **by** Friday. [일회성 동작이나 상태가 완료] 도서는 금요일까지 배송될 것입니다.

The cafe is open **until** 2 am. [계속되던 동작이나 상태가 완료] 그 카페는 새벽 두 시까지 문을 연다.

(4) from A to B A에서 B까지 between A and B A에서 B 사이에

He has a meeting **from** 2 pm **to** 4 pm. 그는 오후 두 시부터 네 시까지 회의가 있다.

I'm not home **between** 2 pm **and** 4 pm. 저는 오후 두 시에서 네 시 사이에는 집에 없습니다.

Tips

at Christmas vs. on Christmas Day

주로 연휴기간이나 크리스마스의 막연한 시점을 이야기 할 때는 at을 쓰고, 크리스마스 당일 날을 이야기 할 때는 on을 쓴다.

I'll see you **at** Christmas.
크리스마스에 보자.

I'll be home **on** Christmas Day.
나는 크리스마스 날 집에 있을 거야.

Check-up 우리말과 같은 뜻이 되도록 [ ] 안에서 알맞은 말을 고르시오.

1 밤에는 추울 거예요.
→ It will be cold [at / in] night.

2 귀하의 항공편은 11월 11일에 출발합니다.
→ Your flight leaves [in / on] November 11th.

3 내 남동생은 1월에 태어났다.
→ My brother was born [in / on] January.

: EXERCISES

Answers / p.36

A [ ] 안에서 알맞은 것을 고르시오.

1 I have an appointment [at / in] seven.
2 The workshop will be [at / on] May 13th.
3 Mandy went to the dentist [at / on] Saturday.
4 The professor has two classes [in / on] the afternoon.

have an appointment 약속이 있다
workshop 명 워크숍
go to the dentist 치과에 가다
professor 명 교수

B at, on, in 중 알맞은 전치사를 골라 문장을 완성하시오.

1 Is the clinic closed __________ Sundays?
2 You have a reservation __________ three o'clock.
3 I love the color of the mountains __________ autumn.

clinic 명 병원
closed 형 닫힌, 휴업한
reservation 명 예약
autumn 명 가을

C [보기]에서 알맞은 전치사를 골라 문장을 완성하시오. [중복 사용 가능]

[1-3] 보기 during for

1 Larry will study in Germany __________ a year.
2 I drew this picture __________ the winter vacation.
3 Somebody broke the window __________ the night.

[4-6] 보기 by until

4 I will stay here __________ March.
5 You should finish your paper __________ Monday.
6 Luke studied in the library __________ midnight.

Germany 명 독일
draw 동 그리다
winter vacation 겨울 방학
paper 명 과제, 보고서
midnight 명 자정

D 우리말과 같은 뜻이 되도록 주어진 단어를 이용하여 문장을 완성하시오.

1 나는 7시에서 8시 사이에 저녁을 먹는다. (seven, eight)
→ I have dinner __________ __________ __________ __________.

2 Bob은 여기서 2000년부터 2004년까지 일했다. (2000, 2004)
→ Bob worked here __________ __________ __________ __________.

3 그 가게는 금요일마다 열한 시 이후에 문을 연다. (eleven, Fridays)
→ The store opens __________ __________ __________ __________.

4 나는 아침에 정각 9시 전에 학교에 도착해야 한다. (nine o'clock, the morning)
→ I have to be at school __________ __________ __________
__________ __________ __________.

UNIT 03

기타 전치사

1. by

(1) 「by+교통수단, 방법」 ~로 (by bus, by car, by train, by plane, by mail)

Many people go to work **by** subway. 많은 사람들이 지하철로 출근한다.

Kelly sent me a card **by** email. Kelly는 이메일로 나에게 카드를 보냈다.

(2) 「by+사람」 ~에 의해

Those shoes were made **by** a master. 그 신발은 장인에 의해 만들어졌다.

Pride and Prejudice was written **by** Jane Austen.
『오만과 편견』은 Jane Austen에 의해 쓰였다.

2. with ~를 가지고, ~와 함께

I enjoy drawing **with** pastels. [with+사물] 나는 파스텔로 그림 그리는 것을 좋아한다.

She came here **with** her mother. [with+사람] 그녀는 어머니와 함께 여기에 왔다.

3. about ~에 대해

Don't worry **about** it. It will be fine. 그것에 대해서는 걱정하지 마. 괜찮을 거야.

Have you heard **about** Tom? Tom에 대해 들어본 적 있니?

4. like ~처럼, 같이

You look **like** your grandmother. 너는 너의 할머니처럼 생겼다.

I love seafood **like** crabs and lobsters. 나는 게와 바닷가재 같은 해산물을 정말 좋아한다.

5. for ~을 위해

My Mom made cookies **for** me. 엄마는 나를 위해 쿠키를 만들었다.

What do you want to eat **for** dinner? 저녁으로 무엇을 먹고 싶니?

6. to ~에게, ~로

Could you please pass the tissues **to** me? 제게 그 티슈 좀 건네주시겠어요?

He went **to** Paris for his vacation. 그는 휴가 차 파리로 갔다.

Tips

「전치사+대명사의 목적격」: 전치사 뒤에는 목적격을 쓴다.

Do you want to go with **me**?
나와 함께 가고 싶니?

He was going to say something to **me**.
그는 나에게 무언가를 말하려고 했다.

Plus α

1 **in** ~을 입은

The woman **in** a black dress is my mother.
검정 드레스를 입은 여성이 나의 어머니야.

2 **from** ~에서, ~로(부터)

He came **from** China.
그는 중국에서 왔다.

Paper is made **from** trees.
종이는 나무로 만들어진다.

Check-up 우리말과 같은 뜻이 되도록 [ ] 안에서 알맞은 말을 고르시오.

1 나는 검정 펜을 가지고 내 이름을 썼다.
→ I wrote down my name [by / with] a black pen.

2 이 책은 한 용감한 소년에 관한 감동적인 이야기이다.
→ This book is a touching story [about / for] a brave boy.

: EXERCISES

Answers / p.37

A [ ] 안에서 알맞은 것을 고르시오.

1 I will talk [by / to] you later.
2 My paper is [about / by] Korean history.
3 Do you usually go to school [by / with] bus?
4 Are you going to see a musical [to / with] your girlfriend?

later 부 나중에, 후에
history 명 역사
usually 부 보통, 일반적으로

B 주어진 대명사를 알맞은 형태로 바꿔 쓰시오.

1 This is my present for __________. (you)
2 The essay was written by __________. (I)
3 I'm going to travel with __________. (they)
4 What happened to __________ during the vacation? (she)

essay 명 수필, 리포트
travel 동 여행하다
happen 동 일어나다, 생기다

C [보기]에서 알맞은 전치사를 골라 문장을 완성하시오.

보기 about with for by

1 It is expensive to go there __________ taxi.
2 Tom fixed the broken frame __________ glue.
3 I bought these blue jeans __________ my daughter.
4 Do you have any questions __________ the subject?

expensive 형 비싼
fix 동 고치다
broken 형 깨진, 부서진
frame 명 액자, 틀
glue 명 접착제
subject 명 주제

D 우리말과 같은 뜻이 되도록 주어진 단어를 이용하여 문장을 완성하시오.

1 그녀가 나에게 자신의 문제에 대해서 이야기했다. (her problem)
→ She told me __________ __________ __________.

2 그는 자신의 아버지처럼 의사가 되기를 원한다. (his father)
→ He wants to be a doctor __________ __________ __________.

3 저에게 팩스로 서류를 보내 주실래요? (fax)
→ Could you send me the document __________ __________?

4 나는 어머니와 함께 이탈리아로 여행을 갔다. (Italy, my mother)
→ I went on a trip __________ __________ __________ __________ __________.

: Review Test

[01-03] 빈칸에 공통으로 들어갈 알맞은 말을 고르시오.

01

· The teacher is ________ the classroom.
· Summer vacation starts ________ July.

① in ② on ③ at
④ for ⑤ over

02

· We are waiting for a bus ________ the bus stop.
· Let's meet ________ two o'clock in the afternoon.

① in ② during ③ on
④ at ⑤ for

03

· The wedding ceremony will take place ________ April 11th.
· Look at the picture ________ the wall.

① for ② in ③ on
④ at ⑤ to

04 빈칸에 들어갈 수 없는 말은?

There is a mailbox ________ the tall building.

① by ② behind
③ next to ④ between
⑤ in front of

[05-06] 빈칸에 들어갈 말이 바르게 짝지어진 것을 고르시오.

05

· I took yoga classes ________ ten years. Now I am a yoga instructor.
· ________ the summer, I worked at the swimming pool.

① during – During ② at – By
③ for – On ④ for – During
⑤ during – For

06

· The boss will be back ________ 2 pm.
· Mr. Brown will stay here ________ next week.

① to – by ② by – until
③ until – for ④ until – during
⑤ by – on

07 밑줄 친 on의 의미가 나머지와 다른 것은?

① The concert is on May 3rd.
② I met my friends on my birthday.
③ I have an appointment on Thursday.
④ The hat on the table is a present from my father.
⑤ The restaurant is closed on Christmas Day.

08 빈칸에 들어갈 전치사가 나머지와 다른 것은?

① People eat turkey ______ Easter Sunday.
② We will graduate ______ February.
③ My sister lives ______ Australia now.
④ I like having a cup of tea ______ the morning.
⑤ There are two big speakers ______ my room.

[09-10] 다음 중 어법상 어색한 것을 고르시오.

09 ① I love the weather in spring.
② Please send this parcel by Friday.
③ James bought a book about geography.
④ I studied for the exam during two weeks.
⑤ The amusement park was full of kids on Children's Day.

10 ① A tree stands in front of my house.
② The birds are flying on the trees.
③ You should come back before dinner.
④ The movie is about music and love.
⑤ We enjoy a lot of water sports in summer.

11 빈칸에 들어갈 말이 바르게 짝지어진 것은?

This plane is flying ________ Seoul ________ Shanghai.

① from – and ② between – to
③ from – until ④ from – for
⑤ from – to

12 우리말을 영어로 옮긴 것 중 어색한 것을 두 개 고르시오.

① 우리는 이 수업 이후에 시험을 볼 것이다.
→ We will take a test after this class.

② 나는 아버지와 일요일마다 등산을 간다.
→ I go hiking with my father on Sundays.

③ 너는 내일까지 보고서를 제출해야 한다.
→ You should hand in your report by tomorrow.

④ 학생들은 자전거를 타고 학교에 간다.
→ Students go to school in bike.

⑤ Sam은 도서관 앞에 서 있었다.
→ Sam was standing in front the library.

13 빈칸에 들어갈 말이 바르게 짝지어진 것은?

A We are having a party ________ Friday. Please come.
B Oh, what time?
A It's from 6 pm ________ 11 pm.
B OK. I'll get there ________ 7 pm. See you then.

① on – to – by ② at – to – by
③ at – and – until ④ on – to – until
⑤ on – and – until

[14-15] 그림을 보고, 물음에 답하시오.

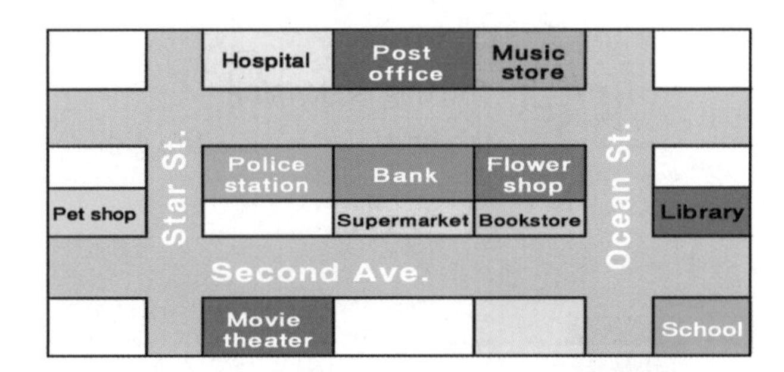

14 빈칸에 공통으로 들어갈 알맞은 말은?

• The school is ________ the library.
• The police station is ________ the hospital.

① on ② at
③ over ④ next to
⑤ across from

15 그림과 일치하지 않는 문장은?

① The bookstore is next to the supermarket.
② The supermarket is behind the bank.
③ The music store is beside the bookstore.
④ The flower shop is across from the music store.
⑤ The bank is between the police station and the flower shop.

: 서술형 평가

Answers / p.38

[01-02] 빈칸에 공통으로 들어갈 알맞은 전치사를 써 넣으시오.

01
- My birthday is ________ March.
- There is some coffee ________ the cup.

02
- ________ the night, it snowed heavily.
- Don't make a noise ________ the class.

[03-04] 그림을 보고, [보기]에서 알맞은 전치사를 골라 문장을 완성하시오. [중복 사용 가능]

보기	on	under	with

03 The dog is sleeping ________ the bed ________ the girl.

04 The girl is sitting ________ the mat ________ the tree.

[05-06] 우리말과 같은 뜻이 되도록 주어진 단어를 이용하여 문장을 완성하시오.

05 우리 버스 정류장에서 여섯 시에 만나자.
(the bus stop, six)

→ Let's meet ____________________
____________________.

06 그 중식당은 오전 10시부터 밤 9시까지 문을 연다.
(10 am, 9 pm)

→ The Chinese restaurant is open ________
____________________.

[07-08] 우리말과 같은 뜻이 되도록 주어진 단어를 배열하시오.

07 A How do you get to school?
B 나는 보통 버스를 타고 학교에 가. But sometimes I walk to school.

→ I usually ____________________.
(school, bus, go, by, to)

08 A Where is your cell phone?
B 내 생각에 집 책상 위에 두고 온 것 같아.

→ I think I left it ____________________.
(home, my desk, at, on)

[09-10] 일기를 읽고, 물음에 답하시오.

> October 13th, Saturday
> It was a tiring day. I wanted to visit the art museum ⓐ our school project. I called Sally, my classmate, and we made an appointment to meet ⓑ 3 ⓒ the afternoon. I was waiting for her ⓓ the museum, but she didn't come. (A) 나는 한 시간 동안 그녀를 기다렸지만 그녀는 네 시까지 나타나지 않았다. This wasn't the first time for her to be late. She is always late!

09 [보기]에서 빈칸 ⓐ~ⓓ에 알맞은 전치사를 고르시오.

보기	in front of	at	in	for

조건 한 번씩만 사용할 것

ⓐ ________ ⓑ ________
ⓒ ________ ⓓ ________

10 밑줄 친 (A)를 주어진 단어를 이용하여 영작하시오.

→ I waited for her ________________, but she didn't show up ________________.
(an hour, 4 pm)

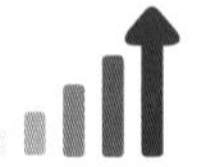

NEXUS Edu

LEVEL CHART

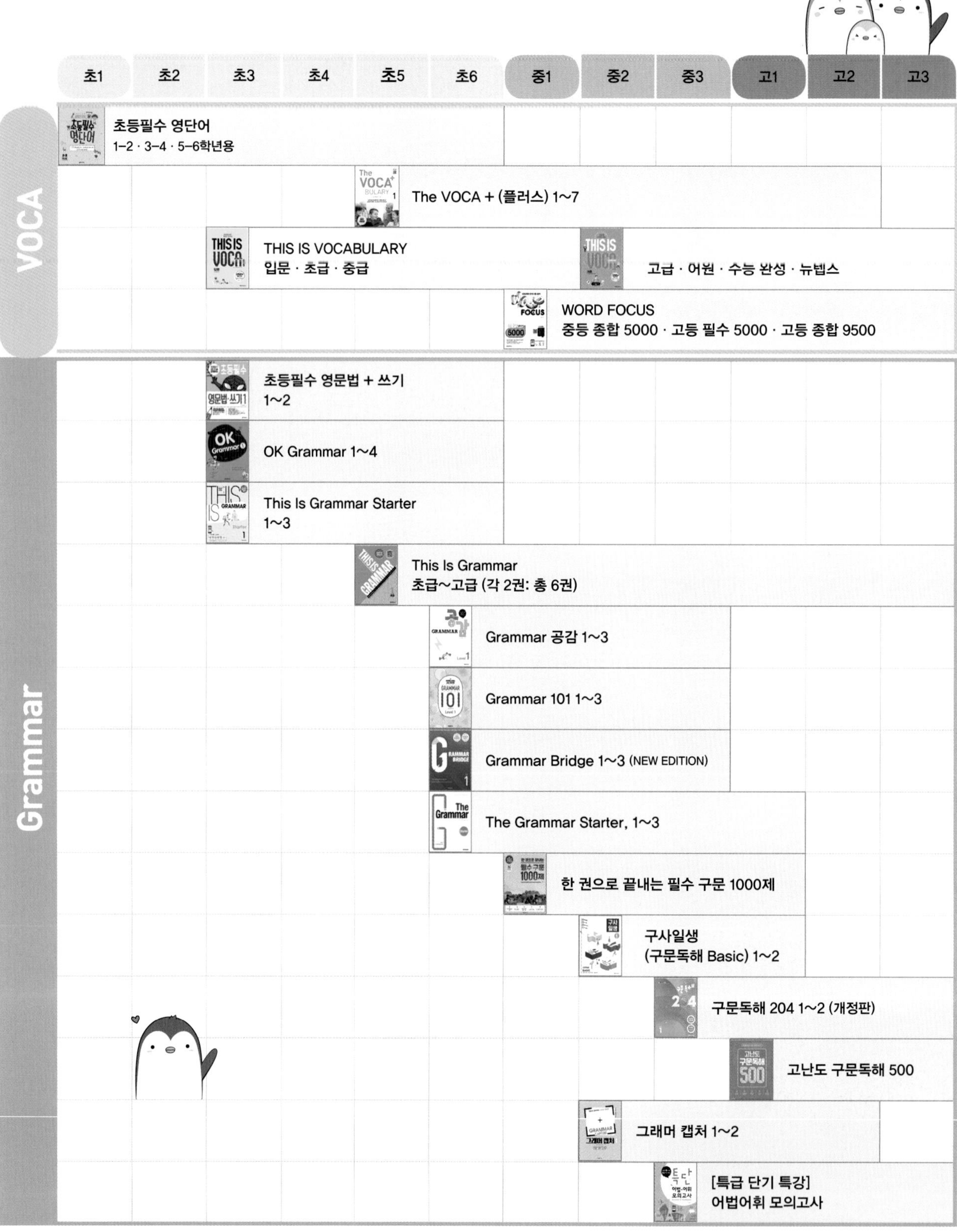

GRAMMAR

넥서스영어교육연구소 지음

Level 1

NEXUS Edu

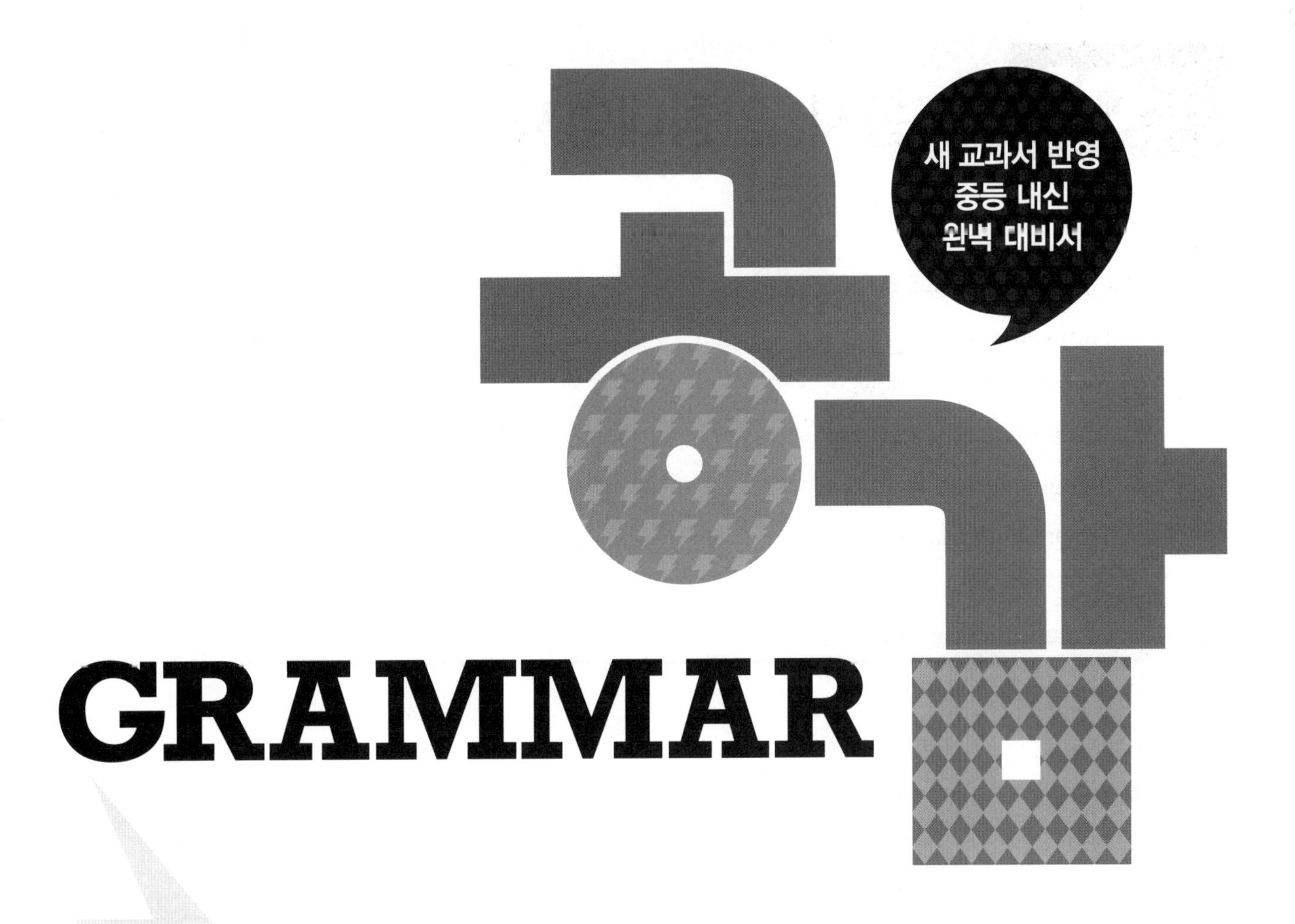

Level 1

NEXUS Edu

UNIT 01 be동사, 인칭대명사

A 밑줄 친 부분을 축약형으로 쓰시오.

1 I am very hungry. ____________
2 He is in the office now. ____________
3 You are the best players. ____________
4 It is an interesting story. ____________
5 We are in the same band. ____________

B 빈칸에 알맞은 be동사를 써 넣으시오.

[1~5] 현재 시제

1 It ____________ dark outside.
2 You ____________ so smart!
3 She ____________ my P.E. teacher.
4 We ____________ in the same grade.
5 They ____________ my friends from elementary school.

[6~10] 과거 시제

6 I ____________ tired yesterday.
7 You ____________ a good student.
8 It ____________ my favorite movie.
9 We ____________ late for the class.
10 They ____________ at school an hour ago.

C 빈칸에 알맞은 be동사를 써 넣으시오.

1 Two years ago, he ____________ in Japan, but now, he ____________ in Korea.
2 I ____________ in the playground one hour ago, but now I ____________ in the bathroom.
3 They ____________ fifteen years old last year, but this year they ____________ sixteen years old.
4 You ____________ sick last night, but today you ____________ fine.
5 She ____________ a college student three years ago, but now she ____________ a middle school teacher.

D 우리말과 같은 뜻이 되도록 주어진 단어를 이용하여 문장을 완성하시오.

1 나는 어제 온종일 집에 있었다. (at home)

→ ________ ________ ________ ________ all day yesterday.

2 우리는 현장 학습 후에 매우 피곤했다. (tired)

→ ________ ________ ________ ________ after the field trip.

3 그들은 학교에서 인기가 많다. (popular)

→ ________ ________ ________ at school.

4 너는 항상 창의적이다. (creative)

→ ________ ________ always ________.

5 오늘은 매우 더운 날이었다. (hot)

→ ________ ________ ________ ________ today.

6 너희들은 그때 놀이공원에 있었다. (at the amusement park)

→ ________ ________ ________ ________ ________ ________ then.

7 그는 지금 화장실에 있다. (in the restroom)

→ ________ ________ ________ ________ ________ now.

E 우리말과 같은 뜻이 되도록 주어진 단어를 배열하시오.

1 그녀는 유명한 재즈 가수예요. (famous, is, jazz singer, she, a)

→ ____

2 나는 지금 방 안에 있다. (in, am, my room, I)

→ ____ now.

3 그는 경기가 끝나고 배가 고프고 목이 말랐다. (hungry, was, and thirsty, he)

→ ____ after the game.

4 그것들은 아프리카에 있는 야생동물이다. (wild animals, are, in Africa, they)

→ ____

5 우리는 지난밤에 극장에 있었다. (were, the theater, we, at)

→ ____ last night.

6 너희들은 학교에서 말썽꾸러기들이다. (troublemakers, are, you)

→ ____ at school.

7 그는 내가 제일 좋아하는 학급 친구이다. (is, my favorite classmate, he)

→ ____

be동사의 부정문, 의문문

A be동사를 이용하여 부정문을 완성하시오. [가능하면 축약형을 사용할 것]

1 It ________________ my fault. It was your fault.

2 Hamburgers are fast food. They ________________ good for us.

3 You ________________ a high school student. You're a middle school student.

4 The restaurant was open yesterday, but it ________________ open today.

5 I am sleepy in class, but I ________________ sleepy at lunchtime.

6 I ________________ a good cook before, but now I am a good cook.

7 They were at the airport yesterday. They ________________ at the bus terminal.

B 주어진 단어와 be동사를 이용하여 의문문을 완성하시오.

1 A __________ __________ fat? (I)
B No, you aren't. You're thin.

2 A __________ __________ Josh's friend? (you)
B No, I'm not. I'm Tom's friend.

3 A __________ __________ __________ a vegetable? (a potato)
B Yes, it is.

4 A __________ __________ your mother? (she)
B No, she isn't. She is my aunt.

5 A __________ __________ in the playground at break time? (he)
B No, he wasn't.

6 A __________ __________ __________ on the sofa? (my books)
B No, they weren't. They were on the table.

7 A __________ __________ rainy in Tokyo yesterday? (it)
B No, it wasn't. It was sunny.

8 A __________ __________ scared during the horror movie? (you)
B Yes, I was.

C **우리말과 같은 뜻이 되도록 주어진 단어를 이용하여 문장을 완성하시오.**

1 나는 더 이상 어린 아이가 아니다. (a little child)
→ _____ _____ _____ _____ _____ anymore.

2 저곳이 사탕 가게인가요? (that)
→ a candy shop?

3 그들은 나를 보고 반가워하지 않았다. (happy)
→ _____ _____ _____ to see me.

4 그는 그 당시에 휴가 중이었나요? (on holiday)
→ _____ _____ _____ _____ at that time?

5 기말고사는 쉽지 않았다. (the final tests)
→ _____ _____ _____ _____ easy.

6 그 가방들은 지금 세일 중인가요? (the bags, on sale)
→ _____ _____ _____ _____ _____ now?

7 우리는 지금 도서관에 있지 않다. (in the library)
→ _____ _____ _____ _____ _____ now.

D **우리말과 같은 뜻이 되도록 주어진 단어를 배열하시오.**

1 이 주차장은 무료인가요? (free, is, this parking lot)
→ __________

2 그 수프는 뜨겁지 않았다. (not, hot, was, the soup)
→ __________

3 그 그림들은 비싼가요? (the paintings, are, expensive)
→ __________

4 너의 할머니는 건강하시니? (healthy, your grandma, is)
→ __________

5 Beethoven은 위대한 음악가였나요? (a great musician, Beethoven, was)
→ __________

6 나는 이 축구팀의 멤버가 아니다. (am, a member, of a soccer club, not, I)
→ __________

7 그녀는 그 당시에 배가 고프지 않았다. (was, at that time, she, hungry, not)
→ __________

인칭대명사, There is / are

A 다음 인칭대명사 표를 완성하시오.

	주격 (~은, ~가)	소유격 (~의)	목적격 (~을)	소유대명사 (~의 것)
단수	I	______	______	______
	you	______	______	______
	he	______	______	______
	she	______	______	______
	it	______	______	______
복수	we	______	______	______
	you	______	______	______
	they	______	______	______

B 밑줄 친 부분을 바르게 고치시오.

1 Is this you report card? ______
2 Her wasn't a famous artist. ______
3 It is my new jacket. I like it color. ______
4 The blue box isn't hers. It is me. ______
5 They were ours neighbors last year. ______
6 They are my classmates. I know they. ______
7 John is a troublemaker. I don't like his. ______

C 밑줄 친 대명사를 주어진 대명사로 바꿔 문장을 다시 쓰시오.

1 I am happy with my new shoes. (he)
→ ______

2 He is bored at the party. (they)
→ ______

3 They were not in their classroom. (she)
→ ______

4 This is my new computer. It is mine. (they)
→ ______

5 You are her neighbors. She knows you. (we)
→ ______

6 She is very friendly. Everybody likes her. (you)
→ ______

D **우리말과 같은 뜻이 되도록 주어진 단어를 이용하여 문장을 완성하시오. [there be 구문을 사용할 것]**

1 화장실에 거울이 하나 있다. (a mirror)
→ ________ ________ ________ ________ in the restroom.

2 너희 마을에 약국이 있니? (a drugstore)
→ ________ ________ ________ ________ in your town?

3 교실에 10명의 여자아이들이 있다. (ten girls)
→ ________ ________ ________ ________ in the classroom.

4 나의 필통에 연필 3개가 있었다. (three pencils)
→ ________ ________ ________ ________ in my pencil case.

5 너의 사물함 안에 교복이 한 벌 있니? (a uniform)
→ ________ ________ ________ ________ in your locker?

6 강당에는 학생들이 많지 않았다. (many students)
→ ________ ________ ________ ________ ________ in the auditorium.

7 내 방에는 책이 많지 않다. (many books)
→ ________ ________ ________ ________ ________ in my room.

E **우리말과 같은 뜻이 되도록 주어진 단어를 배열하시오.**

1 그의 얼굴에 상처가 있다. (a scar, there, on his face, is)
→ ________________________________

2 동굴 안에 곰 한 마리가 있었니? (there, in the cave, was, a bear)
→ ________________________________

3 저 학교에 여학생들이 있니? (at that school, there, are, girls)
→ ________________________________

4 싱크대 안에 접시들이 많이 있니? (many dishes, are, in the sink, there)
→ ________________________________

5 그 빌딩에서 화재가 나지 않았다. (a fire, there, was, in the building, not)
→ ________________________________

6 그의 지하실에 쥐가 한 마리 있다. (a mouse, in his basement, is, there)
→ ________________________________

7 오늘 아침 하늘에 무지개가 있었다. (in the sky this morning, a rainbow, was, there)
→ ________________________________

UNIT 01 일반동사의 의미와 형태

A 주어진 단어를 이용하여 현재 시제 문장을 완성하시오.

1 He __________ his bike. (fix)

2 Ants __________ six legs. (have)

3 She __________ thirsty now. (feel)

4 He __________ hard to win the game. (try)

5 Brandon __________ tennis after school. (play)

6 My brother __________ computer games. (like)

7 He __________ his face in the morning. (wash)

B 주어진 단어를 이용하여 현재 시제 문장을 완성하시오.

1 I __________ English, and my sister __________ Japanese. (speak)

2 He __________ his little brother, and I __________ my little sister. (kiss)

3 I __________ "Thank you," and then he __________ "You're welcome." (say)

4 She __________ jogging, and you __________ skateboarding every day. (go)

5 They __________ hamburgers for lunch, and he __________ pizza for lunch. (eat)

6 He __________ baseball games on TV, but I __________ the news on TV. (watch)

7 My brother and I __________ in the library, but my sister __________ at home. (study)

C 보기 에서 알맞은 것을 골라 현재 시제 문장을 완성하시오.

보기	wear	carry	do	play	have

1 She __________ a school uniform.

2 My brother __________ soccer every Sunday.

3 The kangaroo __________ its baby in its pocket.

4 My grandfather __________ a big garden.

5 Rachel and her sister __________ the laundry every day.

D **우리말과 같은 뜻이 되도록 주어진 단어를 이용하여 문장을 완성하시오.**

1 그 연은 하늘 높이 난다. (fly, high)
→ The kite __________ __________ in the sky.

2 그들은 이 동네에 산다. (live in)
→ __________ __________ __________ this neighborhood.

3 나는 매일 아침 8시에 일어난다. (get up)
→ __________ __________ __________ at 8 o'clock every morning.

4 우리는 무대에서 노래를 부른다. (sing, a song)
→ __________ __________ __________ __________ on the stage.

5 그는 강에서 그물로 고기를 잡는다. (catch, fish)
→ __________ __________ __________ in the river with a net.

6 그는 매일 식사 후 찬물을 한 잔 마신다. (drink)
→ __________ __________ a glass of cold water after meals every day.

7 그녀는 아침마다 해변에서 개를 산책시킨다. (walk one's dog)
→ __________ __________ __________ __________ on the beach every morning.

E **우리말과 같은 뜻이 되도록 주어진 단어를 배열하시오.**

1 나는 빗자루로 바닥을 쓴다. (with a broom, sweep, I, the floor)
→ ______________________________

2 그는 여자 친구를 위해 기타를 연주한다. (the guitar, plays, for his girlfriend, he)
→ ______________________________

3 그들은 자기 전에 숙제를 끝마친다. (before bedtime, they, their homework, finish)
→ ______________________________

4 그는 쉬는 시간에 만화책을 읽는다. (reads, during the break, he, comic books)
→ ______________________________

5 곰은 겨울 동안 동굴 안에서 잠을 잔다. (sleeps, during the winter, the bear, in the cave)
→ ______________________________

6 우리는 음악 시간에 악기를 연주한다. (play, we, in music class, musical instruments)
→ ______________________________

7 그는 매달 서점에서 스포츠 잡지를 산다. (sports magazines, every month, he, at the bookstore, buys)
→ ______________________________

UNIT 02 일반동사의 과거형

A 주어진 동사의 과거형을 쓰시오.

1	have	______	11	wear	______	21	begin	______
2	come	______	12	run	______	22	meet	______
3	drive	______	13	catch	______	23	feel	______
4	break	______	14	eat	______	24	cost	______
5	sit	______	15	win	______	25	take	______
6	lose	______	16	see	______	26	leave	______
7	get	______	17	hold	______	27	set	______
8	buy	______	18	hit	______	28	put	______
9	shake	______	19	swim	______	29	ride	______
10	make	______	20	cut	______	30	rise	______

B 주어진 단어를 이용하여 과거 시제 문장을 완성하시오.

1 The phone ______ a minute ago. (ring)
2 He ______ the books on the street. (drop)
3 Congratulations! You ______ a good job! (do)
4 She ______ her hairstyle yesterday. (change)
5 I ______ my friend to the party last night. (bring)

C 보기 에서 알맞은 단어를 골라 과거 시제 문장을 완성하시오.

[1–5] 보기 raise look pay stay cut

1 She ______ the carrot with a knife.
2 They ______ at home last Sunday.
3 Sam ______ his hand in science class.
4 He ______ for the movie tickets last time.
5 The principal ______ around the school.

[6–10] 보기 take hear worry listen to wear

6 We ______ about the test all night.
7 I ______ jazz music after dinner.
8 Robert ______ a mask at the festival last Friday.
9 He ______ pictures of his family at a family gathering.
10 Carolyn ______ good news from the company this morning.

D **우리말과 같은 뜻이 되도록 주어진 단어를 이용하여 문장을 완성하시오.**

1 갑자기 하늘이 어두워졌다. (become, dark)
→ Suddenly, the sky ________ ________.

2 오늘은 저녁 8시에 해가 졌다. (the sun, set)
→ Today ________ ________ ________ at 8 pm.

3 그들은 도서관에서 책을 빌렸다. (borrow, a book)
→ ________ ________ ________ ________ from the library.

4 나는 나의 어머니에게 성적표를 드렸다. (give, my mother)
→ ________ ________ ________ ________ the report card.

5 그녀는 버스 정류장에서 버스를 기다렸다. (wait for, the bus)
→ ________ ________ ________ ________ ________ at the bus stop.

6 쉬는 시간에 한 소년이 창문을 깨뜨렸다. (break, a window)
→ During the break, a boy ________ ________ ________.

7 나는 오늘 아침에 길거리에서 넘어졌다. (fall down, on the street)
→ I ________ ________ ________ ________ ________ this morning.

E **우리말과 같은 뜻이 되도록 주어진 단어를 배열하시오.**

1 우리 아빠가 신호등에서 차를 멈췄다. (his car, my dad, at the traffic light, stopped)
→ ____

2 그녀가 5분 전에 내 방문을 두드렸다. (knocked on, five minutes ago, she, my door)
→ ____

3 나의 남동생이 오늘 아침에 안경을 깨트렸다. (his glasses, this morning, broke, my brother)
→ ____

4 그들은 지난달에 다른 도시로 이사를 갔다. (another city, moved to, they, last month)
→ ____

5 그녀의 어머니가 그녀를 위해서 가방을 만들어 주었다. (a bag, made, her mother, for her)
→ ____

6 나의 햄스터가 어젯밤에 우리에서 나갔다. (its cage, my hamster, last night, got out of)
→ ____

7 우리는 오늘 음악 시간에 새로운 노래를 배웠다. (a new song, we, in music class today, learned)
→ ____

UNIT 03 일반동사의 부정문

A 주어진 동사를 이용하여 부정문을 완성하시오. [축약형으로 쓸 것]

[1~5] 현재 시제

1 We ______________ the room. (share)
2 They ______________ in the hallway. (run)
3 Your dog ______________ bad at all. (smell)
4 She ______________ about the tests all the time. (worry)
5 He ______________ his mistakes all the time. (remember)

[6–10] 과거 시제

6 I ______________ my tennis racket. (bring)
7 You ______________ my call last night. (answer)
8 He ______________ anything at the meeting. (say)
9 She ______________ tired after a two-hour walk. (feel)
10 Jeremy and Irene ______________ fun of other people. (make)

B 보기 에서 알맞은 동사를 골라 부정문을 완성하시오. [축약형으로 쓸 것]

[1–5] 현재 시제

보기 drink like wake up work know

1 I ______________________ my neighbors very well.
2 The photocopier ______________________ now.
3 Cindy ______________________ water with a meal.
4 Brenda and Christine ______________________ horror movies.
5 My brother and I ______________________ early on weekends.

[6–10] 과거 시제

보기 lose eat hear tell come

6 He ______________________ me the truth.
7 I ______________________ weight this month.
8 You ______________________ to class in time.
9 Catherine ______________________ anything from her sister.
10 They ______________________ dinner, and they were very hungry.

C 주어진 문장을 부정문으로 바꿔 쓰시오.

1 The cake tastes delicious.
→ ______________________________

2 He has curly brown hair.
→ ______________________________

3 We went on a trip last month.
→ ______________________________

4 My son believes in Santa Claus.
→ ______________________________

5 You cleaned the milk off the floor.
→ ______________________________

6 She visited her uncle in Canada.
→ ______________________________

7 I studied for the final test last week.
→ ______________________________

D 우리말과 같은 뜻이 되도록 주어진 단어를 이용하여 문장을 완성하시오.

1 너는 나에게 답장을 쓰지 않았어. (write back)
→ You ________ ________ ________ to me.

2 그들은 평일에는 텔레비전을 보지 않는다. (watch, TV)
→ They ________ ________ ________ during the week.

3 우리는 그때 선생님께 거짓말을 하지 않았다. (tell a lie)
→ We ________ ________ ________ ________ to the teacher then.

4 Taylor는 오늘 아침에 John을 만나지 않았다. (meet, John)
→ Taylor ________ ________ ________ this morning.

5 그는 건강을 위해서 단것을 먹지 않는다. (eat, sweets)
→ For his health, he ________ ________ ________.

6 그녀는 어제 시험에서 부정행위를 하지 않았다. (cheat on, the test)
→ She ________ ________ ________ ________ ________ yesterday.

7 그는 어젯밤에 컴퓨터 게임을 하지 않았다. (play, computer games)
→ He ________ ________ ________ ________ last night.

UNIT 04 일반동사의 의문문

A 주어진 단어를 이용하여 의문문을 완성하시오.

1 A ________ ________ look tired? (I)
B Yes, you do. Just a little.

2 A ________ ________ know Sarah? (you)
B No, I don't. She's a stranger to me.

3 A ________ ________ fit you? (it)
B Yes, it does. The skirt is perfect.

4 A ________ ________ like rainy days? (she)
B No, she doesn't. She likes sunny days.

5 A ________ ________ leave a message? (he)
B Yes, he did.

6 A ________ ________ ________ come to school? (your parents)
B Yes, they did.

7 A ________ ________ fail the test? (they)
B No, they didn't. They passed the test.

8 A ________ ________ solve the problem? (you)
B No, I didn't. I'll try again.

B 보기 에서 알맞은 단어를 골라 우리말과 같은 뜻이 되도록 문장을 완성하시오.

보기	play	lose	need	drive	tell

1 너 책을 또 잃어버렸니?
→ ________ ________ ________ your book again?

2 너희는 부모님에게 그 소식을 말했니?
→ ________ ________ ________ your parents the news?

3 우리가 캠핑하는 데 침낭이 필요한가요?
→ ________ ________ ________ sleeping bags for camping?

4 그는 오케스트라에서 바이올린을 연주하나요?
→ ________ ________ ________ the violin in the orchestra?

5 너희 어머니가 너를 학교까지 차로 데려다 주시니?
→ ________ ________ ________ ________ you to school?

C 주어진 단어를 이용하여 대화를 완성하시오.

1 A ________ it ________ hard yesterday? (rain)
B No, ________ ________. It was sunny.

2 A ________ she ________ animals? (raise)
B Yes, ________ ________. She raises rabbits.

3 A ________ he ________ in the countryside? (live)
B No, ________ ________. He lives in a big city.

4 A ________ we ________ enough water now? (have)
B Yes, ________ ________. Don't worry about that.

5 A ________ you ________ a strange noise last night? (hear)
B Yes, ________ ________. I was very scared.

6 A ________ they ________ their piano lessons last weekend? (start)
B No, ________ ________. They started them on Monday.

7 A ________ he ________ ________ during the class? (fall asleep)
B Yes, ________ ________. The teacher was annoyed at him.

D 우리말과 같은 뜻이 되도록 주어진 단어를 배열하시오.

1 네가 피자를 주문했니? (you, order, did, pizza)
→ ________________________________

2 그녀는 수영을 잘 하니? (swim, does, well, she)
→ ________________________________

3 그는 오늘 학교에 걸어 왔니? (walk to, did, he, school today)
→ ________________________________

4 너희는 오디션에 합격했니? (pass, you, the audition, did)
→ ________________________________

5 첫 수업은 9시에 시작하나요? (at nine o'clock, the first class, does, begin)
→ ________________________________

6 너는 도서관에서 책을 빌리니? (from the library, borrow, you, books, do)
→ ________________________________

7 그녀는 매일 아침 신문을 읽나요? (she, newspapers, read, every morning, does)
→ ________________________________

UNIT 01 셀 수 있는 명사

A 다음 명사의 복수형을 쓰시오.

1	key	______	11	foot	______	21	ox	______
2	mouse	______	12	person	______	22	sheep	______
3	tooth	______	13	zoo	______	23	woman	______
4	child	______	14	deer	______	24	radio	______
5	monkey	______	15	life	______	25	potato	______
6	man	______	16	goose	______	26	city	______
7	toy	______	17	photo	______	27	piano	______
8	roof	______	18	leaf	______	28	box	______
9	baby	______	19	boy	______	29	fox	______
10	knife	______	20	bus	______	30	church	______

B 주어진 단어를 알맞은 형태로 고쳐 쓰시오.

1 I have two older ______. (sister)

2 Snakes eat frogs and ______. (mouse)

3 The two ______ shook hands. (man)

4 He wants to help many poor ______. (child)

5 He washed many ______ after dinner. (dish)

C 우리말과 같은 뜻이 되도록 보기 에서 알맞은 단어를 골라 어법에 맞게 문장을 완성하시오.

보기 goose hobby tomato knife

1 나는 강 주위에서 많은 거위를 보았다.
→ I saw a lot of ______ near the river.

2 바구니에 토마토가 두 개 있다.
→ There are two ______ in the basket.

3 서랍 안에 다섯 개의 칼이 있다.
→ There are five ______ in the drawer.

4 나의 취미는 스카이다이빙과 윈드서핑이다.
→ My ______ are sky diving and wind surfing.

D 우리말과 같은 뜻이 되도록 주어진 단어를 이용하여 문장을 완성하시오.

1 나의 시계는 3분 느리다. (minute)
→ My watch is ________ ________ slow.

2 들판에 말들이 많이 있었다. (horse)
→ There were ________ ________ in the field.

3 그녀는 운동화 한 켤레를 샀다. (sneaker)
→ She bought ________ ________ ________ ________.

4 그녀는 사전을 두 개 가지고 있다. (dictionary)
→ She has ________ ________.

5 많은 지붕 위로 비가 떨어졌다. (roof)
→ Rain fell on ________ ________ ________ ________.

6 소방관들은 화재로부터 많은 생명을 구한다. (life)
→ Firefighters save ________ ________ from fires.

7 우리는 많은 영웅에 대한 이야기를 들었다. (hero)
→ We heard stories about ________ ________ ________.

E 우리말과 같은 뜻이 되도록 주어진 단어를 배열하시오.

1 그는 냄비에 감자 세 개를 넣었다. (three, in the pot, put, potatoes, he)
→ ________________________________

2 대도시에는 아파트들이 많다. (apartments, are, there, a lot of)
→ ________________________________ in big cities.

3 그 용감한 남자가 도둑 두 명을 잡았다. (thieves, man, caught, brave, two, the)
→ ________________________________

4 나의 선생님은 하루에 6개의 수업이 있다. (has, my teacher, a, six, classes, day)
→ ________________________________

5 그는 늑대들로부터 자신의 양들을 구했다. (from, saved, he, his sheep, the wolves)
→ ________________________________

6 공원에 많은 여자들과 남자들이 있었다. (were, women, there, and men, many)
→ ________________________________ in the park.

7 여우 세 마리와 원숭이 두 마리가 동물원에 도착했다. (arrived at, three, two, foxes, monkeys, the zoo, and)
→ ________________________________

UNIT 02 셀 수 없는 명사

A 문장을 읽고, 물질명사에는 동그라미(○), 추상명사에는 네모(□), 고유명사에는 세모(△) 표시를 하시오.

1 Is Mike at home now?

2 She bought me a cup of coffee.

3 Harry and Jane are from America.

4 He wanted advice from his teacher.

5 The puppy brought happiness to my family.

B 우리말과 같은 뜻이 되도록 보기 에서 알맞은 단어를 골라 어법에 맞게 바꿔 문장을 완성하시오.

보기 sugar money salt bottle homework

1 그녀는 많은 돈을 벌었다.
→ She made a lot of ____________.

2 우리는 설탕이 약간 필요하다
→ We need some ____________.

3 오늘은 숙제가 많다.
→ There is a lot of ____________ today.

4 수프에 너무 많은 소금을 넣지 마라.
→ Don't put too much ____________ in the soup.

5 나는 냉장고에서 물 세 병을 꺼냈다.
→ I took three ____________ of water from the refrigerator.

C 보기 에서 알맞은 말을 고르고, 주어진 표현을 이용하여 문장을 완성하시오.

[1–3] 보기 glass piece bowl

1 We need ____________________. (five, paper)

2 The kid drank ____________________. (two, milk)

3 He was very hungry and had ____________________. (three, soup)

[4–6] 보기 slice bottle cup

4 The woman drank ____________________. (two, tea)

5 My brother and I ate ____________________. (six, pizza)

6 She bought ____________________ in the store. (three, water)

D **우리말과 같은 뜻이 되도록 주어진 단어를 이용하여 문장을 완성하시오.**

1 나는 친구들을 위해 녹차 다섯 잔을 만들었다. (cup, green tea)
→ I made _____ _____ _____ _____ _____ for my friends.

2 시리얼 두 그릇이 식탁 위에 있었다. (bowl, cereal)
→ There were _____ _____ _____ on the table.

3 그녀는 빵 한 조각에 버터를 펴 발랐다. (slice, bread)
→ She spread _____ _____ _____ _____ with butter.

4 나는 샌드위치를 만들기 위해 치즈 세 장이 필요하다. (slice, cheese)
→ I need _____ _____ _____ _____ for my sandwiches.

5 우리 엄마는 레모네이드 두 잔을 내오셨다. (glass, lemonade)
→ My mom served _____ _____ _____ _____.

6 그는 다섯 켤레의 양말을 샀다. (pair, sock)
→ He bought _____ _____ _____ _____.

7 그는 따뜻한 수프 두 그릇을 빠르게 먹어 치웠다. (bowl, warm soup)
→ He finished _____ _____ _____ _____ _____ quickly.

E **우리말과 같은 뜻이 되도록 주어진 단어를 배열하시오.**

1 하루에 물을 2병 마셔라. (two, a, drink, day, water, bottles of)
→ _____________________

2 우리는 함께 빵 두 조각을 나눠 먹었다. (shared, two, bread, we, slices of)
→ _____________________ together.

3 Steve는 저녁으로 피자 세 조각을 먹었다. (three, pizza, ate, slices of)
→ Steve _____________________ for dinner.

4 그 아이는 운동 후에 우유 두 잔을 마신다. (drinks, glasses of, two, milk)
→ The kid _____________________ after exercise.

5 나는 도움 없이 다섯 점의 가구를 옮겼다. (five, furniture, pieces of, moved)
→ I _____________________ without help.

6 나는 인터넷에서 한국에 대한 정보를 찾았다. (about Korea, information, found)
→ I _____________________ on the Internet.

7 Sam은 컴퓨터에 대해서 많은 지식을 가지고 있다. (a lot of, has, about computers, knowledge)
→ Sam _____________________.

UNIT 03 관사

A 빈칸에 a, an, X 중 알맞은 것을 써 넣으시오. [X는 필요 없는 경우]

1 They are ________ great basketball players.

2 He took a nap for ________ hour yesterday.

3 She has a taekwondo class twice ________ week.

4 I'll have ________ egg sandwich for ________ breakfast.

5 My younger sister is ________ elementary school student.

B 빈칸에 a, an, the, X 중 알맞은 것을 써 넣으시오. [X는 필요 없는 경우]

1 The girl sleeps eight hours ________ day.

2 Please pass me ________ salt over there.

3 My dad plays ________ tennis once ________ week.

4 I have a bag. ________ bag is blue and big.

5 Look at the sky. ________ full moon is really big.

C 보기 에서 관사를 고르고, 우리말과 같은 뜻이 되도록 주어진 단어를 이용하여 문장을 완성하시오. [X는 필요 없는 경우]

보기	a	an	the	X

1 Sam은 중학교에 다닌다. (middle school)
→ Sam goes to ____________________.

2 우리는 버스를 타고 예배를 드리러 갔다. (bus)
→ We went to church ____________________.

3 그는 화장실을 한 시간에 한 번 이용한다. (hour)
→ He uses the restroom ____________________.

4 우리 형은 기타를 매우 잘 친다. (guitar)
→ My brother ____________________ very well.

5 우리 언니는 나에게 생일 선물로 MP3 플레이어를 주었다. (MP3 player)
→ My sister gave me ____________________ for my birthday.

D **우리말과 같은 뜻이 되도록 주어진 단어를 이용하여 문장을 완성하시오.**

1 그는 해가 너무 뜨거워서 모자를 썼다. (sun)
→ ________________ was too hot, so he wore a hat.

2 그는 중학교 영어 선생님이다. (English teacher)
→ He is ________________ in middle school.

3 우리 형은 매일 피아노를 친다. (play, piano)
→ My brother ________________ every day.

4 그녀는 어젯밤 10시에 잠자리에 들었다. (go to, bed)
→ She ________________ at ten o'clock last night.

5 우리 아빠는 선생님이시고 엄마는 예술가이시다. (teacher, artist)
→ My dad is ________________, and my mom is ________________.

6 나는 일주일에 한 번 방과 후에 친구들과 축구를 한다. (play, soccer, week)
→ I ________________ with my friends ________________ after school.

7 나의 가족은 어제 이탈리안 레스토랑에서 근사한 저녁 식사를 했다. (nice, dinner)
→ My family had ________________ at the Italian restaurant yesterday.

E **우리말과 같은 뜻이 되도록 주어진 단어를 배열하시오.**

1 그녀는 취미로 피아노를 친다. (the, as a hobby, plays, piano, she)
→ ________________

2 우리는 저녁 식사 후에 텔레비전을 시청했다. (TV, after, watched, dinner)
→ We ________________.

3 그들은 일 년에 두 번씩 휴가를 간다. (year, they, a, go on a vacation, twice)
→ ________________

4 그 학생은 도서관에서 영어 소설을 읽었다. (an, student, English novel, the, read)
→ ________________ in the library.

5 그는 야구를 하고, 자전거를 타고 집으로 갔다. (baseball, bike, went, played, home, by)
→ He ________________ and ________________.

6 나는 아침 식사로 사과 두 개와 우유 한 잔을 마셨다. (apples, glass of, a, two, milk)
→ I had ________________ and ________________ for breakfast.

7 나는 공포 영화 한 편을 보았는데 그 영화는 정말 무서웠다. (a, the, really scary, horror movie, was, movie)
→ I saw ________________ and ________________.

UNIT 01 this, that, it

A 보기 에서 알맞은 말을 골라 문장을 완성하시오. [중복 사용 가능]

[1–4]

보기 this these it

1 Mom, are ______________ mine?

2 ______________ is my sister, Ariel.

3 ______________ is very bright outside.

4 ______________ backpacks are theirs.

[5–8]

보기 that those it

5 ______________ is January first.

6 Is ______________ dog yours?

7 ______________ are my parents.

8 Are ______________ scarves your sister's?

B 주어진 단어를 이용하여 대화를 완성하시오.

1 A __________ __________ __________ __________ now? (what, time)
B It's eleven o'clock.

2 A __________ __________ __________ __________ today? (what, the date)
B It's December 17th.

3 A __________ __________ __________ __________ today? (what day)
B It's Saturday.

4 A __________ __________ __________ __________ today? (how, the weather)
B It's windy and cloudy.

5 A __________ __________ __________ __________ from here to the bookstore? (how far)
B It's about 300 meters.

6 A __________ __________ __________ __________ __________ from your house to the school? (how long, take)
B It takes about 10 minutes.

C **우리말과 같은 뜻이 되도록 주어진 단어를 이용하여 문장을 완성하시오.**

1 오늘 날씨가 어때요? (what, like)

→ ________ ________ ________ ________ ________ today?

2 이 고양이들은 아직 새끼이다. (cat)

→ ________ ________ ________ still babies.

3 저 아이들이 내 조카들이다. (kid)

→ ________ ________ ________ my nephews.

4 이 휴대 전화는 내 것이다. (cell phone)

→ ________ ________ ________ ________ mine.

5 저 여자애가 나를 쳐다보고 있다. (girl)

→ ________ ________ ________ looking at me.

6 오늘은 크리스마스이브예요. (Christmas Eve)

→ ________ ________ ________ ________ today.

7 여기에서 학교까지 한 시간쯤 걸려요. (take, about an hour)

→ ________ ________ ________ ________ ________ from here to the school.

D **우리말과 같은 뜻이 되도록 주어진 단어를 배열하시오.**

1 여기서 꽤 멀다. (quite far, it's, from here)

→ ________________________________

2 벌써 열 시가 넘었다. (already, after ten, it's)

→ ________________________________

3 이곳은 매우 따뜻하다. (very, warm, it's, here)

→ ________________________________

4 하와이는 지금 여름이다. (summer, in Hawaii, it's)

→ ________________________________

5 나는 저 남자를 잘 안다. (that, know, I, very well, man)

→ ________________________________

6 이 분은 우리 이모 Martha이다. (this, my aunt Martha, is)

→ ________________________________

7 이것들이 내가 가장 좋아하는 책들이다. (my favorite books, are, these)

→ ________________________________

UNIT 02 one, the other, some, any

A 보기 에서 알맞은 것을 골라 문장을 완성하시오. [중복 사용 가능]

[1–6]

보기	one	ones	it

1 My chair is broken. I'll buy a new __________.

2 I have a good book. I can lend __________ to you.

3 These shoes are too small! I need bigger __________.

4 I wrote down his phone number, but I can't find __________.

5 These pants are too expensive. Are there cheaper __________?

6 Somebody stole my bike. My mom will buy another __________ for me.

[7–12]

보기	one	the other	the others

7 She has three pets. __________ is a dog, and __________ are cats.

8 We ordered two dishes. __________ is pizza, and __________ is pasta.

9 I bought two skirts. __________ is for me, and __________ is for my sister.

10 There are four people in a car. __________ is a woman, and __________ are men.

11 There are six students in my class. __________ is a girl, and __________ are boys.

12 I have two sisters. __________ is thirteen years old, and __________ is twelve years old.

B 빈칸에 some과 any 중 알맞은 것을 써 넣어 문장을 완성하시오.

1 Do you have __________ aunts or uncles?

2 __________ girls are taller than boys.

3 Are there __________ bookstores around here?

4 Would you like __________ hot chocolate?

5 I don't want __________ trouble in this class.

6 There is a lot of fruit here. Please have __________.

C **우리말과 같은 뜻이 되도록 주어진 단어를 이용하여 문장을 완성하시오.**

1 뜨거운 차를 좀 마시고 싶어요. (hot, tea)
→ I would like ________ ________ ________.

2 너는 무슨 좋은 생각이라도 있니? (good, ideas)
→ Do you have ________ ________ ________?

3 내가 네 책을 잃어버렸어. 새 걸로 사줄게. (new)
→ I lost your book. I'll buy you ________ ________ ________.

4 내 우산을 찾을 수가 없어. 내가 하나 빌려도 될까? (borrow)
→ I can't find my umbrella. Can ________ ________ ________?

5 나는 이 영화를 좋아해요. 그것은 매우 재미있어요. (very funny)
→ I like this movie. ________ ________ ________ ________.

6 나는 청바지를 매우 좋아해요. 이것들이 내가 가장 좋아하는 청바지예요. (my favorite ones)
→ I love jeans. ________ ________ ________ ________ ________.

7 나는 소설책을 두 권 샀다. 한 권은 로맨스이고 나머지 한 권은 공상 과학이다. (romance, science fiction)
→ I bought two novels. ________ ________ ________, and ________ ________ ________ ________ ________.

D **우리말과 같은 뜻이 되도록 단어를 배열하시오.**

1 질문이 있니? (you, questions, any, have)
→ Do ________________________________?

2 나는 자가 한 개 필요해. 네가 하나 가지고 있니? (have, do, one, you)
→ I need a ruler. ________________________________

3 내 열쇠를 찾을 수가 없어. 내 생각에 그것을 잃어버린 것 같아. (lost, I, it)
→ I can't find my key. I think that ________________________________.

4 그가 나에게 약간의 충고를 해 주었다. (some, me, advice, gave)
→ He ________________________________.

5 모자를 사고 싶어. 온라인으로 하나 주문할거야. (order, I'll, one, online)
→ I want to buy a hat. ________________________________

6 재미있는 게임 CD를 가지고 있어. 너에게 그것을 빌려 줄게. (to, lend, you, I'll, it)
→ I have an exciting game CD. ________________________________

7 집 앞에 차가 두 대 있다. 한 대는 아버지의 것이고, 나머지 한 대는 나의 것이다.
(my father's, the other, mine, is, is, one)
→ There are two cars in front of the house. ________________________________,
and ________________________________.

UNIT 03 재귀대명사

A 주어진 대명사의 알맞은 재귀대명사를 빈칸에 쓰시오.

1 I ____________

2 we ____________

3 you (너) ____________

4 it ____________

5 he ____________

6 she ____________

7 they ____________

8 you (너희들) ____________

B 밑줄 친 단어를 강조하는 재귀대명사를 써 넣으시오.

1 I want the toy.
→ I want the toy ____________.

2 Robert baked the cakes.
→ Robert baked the cakes ____________.

3 Did Ann talk to Mr. Simpson?
→ Did Ann ____________ talk to Mr. Simpson?

4 He met Brad Pitt at the theater.
→ He met Brad Pitt ____________ at the theater.

5 You need to call your boyfriend.
→ You ____________ need to call your boyfriend.

C 보기 에서 알맞은 말을 골라 적절한 형태로 바꿔 문장을 완성하시오.

보기		
	cut oneself	by oneself
	introduce oneself	talk to oneself

1 First, let me ________________________.

2 Be careful. You can ________________________.

3 Henry ________________________ all the time. It's his habit.

4 You should finish the project ________________________.

D **우리말과 같은 뜻이 되도록 주어진 단어를 이용하여 문장을 완성하시오.**

1 그는 요리하다가 다쳤다. (hurt)
→ He ________ ________ while he was cooking.

2 여행하는 동안 즐거웠니? (enjoy)
→ Did you ________ ________ during the trip?

3 식탁 위의 피자를 마음껏 드세요. (help)
→ Please ________ ________ to the pizza on the table

4 그가 나에게 "편하게 있어."라고 말했다. (make, at home)
→ He said to me, "Please ________ ________ ________ ________."

5 조심해. 그렇지 않으면 화상을 입을 수 있어. (burn)
→ Be careful, or you will ________ ________.

6 걱정 마. 나는 내 스스로 돌볼 수 있어. (take care of)
→ Don't worry. I can ________ ________ ________ ________.

7 이건 단지 우리끼리 이야기인데, 그가 그녀를 좋아한대. (between)
→ It's just ________ ________. He likes her.

E **우리말과 같은 뜻이 되도록 주어진 단어를 배열하시오.**

1 나는 혼자 점심 식사하기 싫어요. (by, eat, myself, lunch)
→ I don't want to ________________.

2 혼잣말하는 것은 그의 습관이다. (himself, is, talking to)
→ ________________ his habit.

3 나는 네가 편하게 있기를 바라. (yourself, home, make, at)
→ I hope you ________________.

4 네 방은 네 스스로 치워야 해. (your, yourself, clean, room)
→ You ________ should ________________.

5 우리는 그 전시회를 즐겼다. (ourselves, the exhibition, at, enjoyed)
→ We ________________.

6 그녀는 지난주에 계단에서 떨어져서 다쳤다. (last week, herself, hurt)
→ She fell down the stairs and ________________.

7 4세 이하의 아동들은 혼자 풀장에 들어갈 수 없습니다. (the pool, themselves, go in, by)
→ Children under four cannot ________________.

UNIT 01 현재 시제, 과거 시제

A 주어진 동사를 이용하여 대화를 완성하시오.

1 (leave) A ________ the train ________?
B Yes, it did. It ________ an hour ago.

2 (like) A ________ you ________ math?
B No, I don't. I ________ English.

3 (be) A ________ you at the playground this morning?
B No, I wasn't. I ________ in the cafeteria.

4 (ride) A ________ she ________ a bike?
B Yes, she does. She ________ a bike every weekend.

5 (raise) A ________ he ________ animals?
B Yes, he does. He ________ pigs.

6 (live) A ________ you ________ in New York?
B No, I didn't. I ________ in L.A.

7 (read) A ________ they ________ books nowadays?
B Yes, they do. They ________ novels.

B 우리말과 같은 뜻이 되도록 주어진 동사를 알맞게 바꿔 쓰시오.

1 1년은 365일이다. (be)
→ There ________ 365 days in a year.

2 42번 버스는 중심가로 간다. (go)
→ Bus number 42 ________ downtown.

3 그녀는 매일 고양이에게 밥을 준다. (feed)
→ She ________ her cat every day.

4 Jenny는 지난달에 드라마 클럽에 가입했다. (join)
→ Jenny ________ the drama club last month.

5 우리 아버지는 2005년에 사업을 시작하셨다. (start)
→ My father ________ his business in 2005.

6 William Shakespeare가 『로미오와 줄리엣』을 썼다. (write)
→ William Shakespeare ________ *Romeo and Juliet*.

7 우리는 지난 가을에 미국에 살고 있는 친척들을 방문했다. (visit)
→ We ________ our relatives in America last fall.

C 괄호 안의 어구를 이용하여 현재는 과거로, 과거는 현재로 바꾸어 쓰시오.

1 It was hot yesterday. (today)
→ ____________________

2 Tom looked sad this morning. (now)
→ ____________________

3 We go skiing every winter. (last winter)
→ ____________________

4 We had lots of rain last year. (these days)
→ ____________________

5 She and I were very busy last month. (these days)
→ ____________________

6 She has a red car this year. (last year)
→ ____________________

7 There were many people at the gym last night. (right now)
→ ____________________

D 우리말과 같은 뜻이 되도록 주어진 단어를 이용하여 문장을 완성하시오.

1 Sally는 매일 저녁 식사를 거른다. (skip, dinner)
→ Sally ______ ______ ______ ______.

2 오늘 아침에 알람이 울리지 않았다. (not, go off)
→ The alarm ______ ______ ______ ______ ______.

3 그들은 지금 우체국에 있다. (be, at the post office)
→ They ______ ______ ______ ______ ______ ______.

4 그는 오늘 아침에 나에게 화가 나 있었다. (be angry with)
→ He ______ ______ ______ ______ ______ ______.

5 우리 엄마는 주말에 일하지 않는다. (not, work, on weekends)
→ My mom ______ ______ ______ ______.

6 James는 어제 방과 후에 축구를 했다. (play, soccer, after school)
→ James ______ ______ ______ ______ yesterday.

7 매년 봄에는 이 지역에 새들이 돌아온다. (return to, area, spring)
→ Birds ______ ______ ______ ______ ______ ______.

UNIT 02 진행 시제

A 주어진 동사의 -ing형을 쓰시오.

1 lie ______	6 sit ______	11 put ______	16 stop ______
2 ride ______	7 move ______	12 hit ______	17 die ______
3 get ______	8 make ______	13 take ______	18 have ______
4 cut ______	9 smile ______	14 swim ______	19 run ______
5 plan ______	10 drive ______	15 see ______	20 leave ______

B 주어진 단어를 사용하여 진행형 문장을 완성하시오.

[1–5] 현재 진행형

1 Jeremy ______ ______ next to his mom. (sit)

2 ______ you ______ ______ Jane now? (wait for)

3 The elevator ______ ______ at the moment. (not, work)

4 Sorry, I am busy now. I ______ ______ my homework. (do)

5 John and Emma ______ ______ on the Internet right now. (chat)

[6–10] 과거 진행형

6 The children ______ ______ on the beach. (lie)

7 I ______ ______ in the pool at that time. (swim)

8 ______ you ______ ______ me then? (look for)

9 Harry ______ ______ TV this morning. (not, watch)

10 We ______ ______ cards at ten o'clock last night. (play)

C 주어진 동사를 이용하여 대화를 완성하시오.

1 A What were you doing then?
B I ______ ______ a newspaper. (read)

2 A ______ she ______ the flowers now? (water)
B Yes, she is. She is in the garden.

3 A ______ he ______ your computer? (fix)
B Yes, he is. He knows computers well.

4 A What are you doing, Bella?
B I ______ ______ an essay. (write)

D 우리말과 같은 뜻이 되도록 주어진 동사를 이용하여 문장을 완성하시오.

1 아기는 그때 낮잠을 자고 있었다. (take, a nap)
→ The baby ________ ________ ________ ________ ________.

2 그는 지금 동화를 읽고 있나요? (read, a fairy tale)
→ Is ________ ________ ________ ________ ________ now?

3 Ben은 지금 바닥을 쓸고 있다. (mop, the floor)
→ Ben ________ ________ ________ ________ ________.

4 그 아이들은 해변에서 조개를 줍고 있었다. (collect, shells)
→ The children ________ ________ ________ at the beach.

5 우리는 올해 여행을 위해 돈을 저축하고 있다. (save, money)
→ We ________ ________ ________ for our trip this year.

6 James는 그 당시에 영화를 보고 있지 않았다. (watch, the movie)
→ James ________ ________ ________ ________ at that time.

7 Kate와 Michael은 실험실에서 함께 일을 하고 있다. (work, together)
→ Kate and Michael ________ ________ ________ in the lab.

E 우리말과 같은 뜻이 되도록 주어진 단어를 배열하시오.

1 그는 공책에 필기를 하고 있지 않다. (isn't, in his notebook, he, taking notes)
→ ____

2 Jason은 그때 청바지를 입고 있었다. (wearing, then, was, Jason, a pair of jeans)
→ ____

3 두 소년이 교실에서 말다툼을 하고 있었다. (two boys, arguing, in the classroom, were)
→ ____

4 그녀는 TV으로 일기예보를 보고 있니? (watching, a weather report, on TV, she, is)
→ ____

5 그들은 사막을 가로질러 여행을 하고 있었다. (were, across the desert, traveling, they)
→ ____

6 나는 내 휴대폰으로 게임을 하고 있지 않다. (playing, I'm, with my cell phone, not, games)
→ ____

7 그 가수들은 무대 위에서 노래를 부르고 있다. (are, the singers, a song, on the stage, singing)
→ ____

UNIT 01 can, may

A 밑줄 친 부분을 우리말로 옮기시오.

1 You can bring your friend to the party. ____________

2 Henry doesn't look well. He may be sick. ____________

3 I have two pens. You may use one of mine. ____________

4 Paul may change his major. He doesn't like it. ____________

5 Mike can run 100 meters in under 12 seconds. ____________

B 보기 에서 단어를 골라 주어진 조동사를 이용하여 문장을 완성하시오.

[1–4] can 　 보기 play　help/not　sing　drive

1 I'm very busy. I ________ ________ you now.

2 I like your voice. ________ you ________ a song for me?

3 My brother ________ ________ a car. He has a driver's license.

4 I finished my homework. ________ I ________ with my friends?

[5–8] may 　 보기 lift/not　try　borrow　be

5 I like this shirt. ________ I ________ it on?

6 I lost my notebook. ________ I ________ yours?

7 Carrie is not in school. She ________ ________ at home.

8 These boxes are too heavy. You ________ ________ ________ them.

C be able to를 이용하여 문장을 바꿔 쓰시오.

1 He can speak Korean.
→ He ________________________ Korean.

2 Can she play the piano?
→ ________ she ________________________ the piano?

3 I can't go home early today.
→ I ________________________ home early today.

4 They could dive in the sea last year.
→ They ________________________ in the sea last year.

5 He couldn't play chess well last night.
→ He ________________________ chess well last night.

D **우리말과 같은 뜻이 되도록 주어진 단어를 이용하여 문장을 완성하시오.**

1 그는 학생일 리가 없어. (be)
→ He ________ ________ ________ ________.

2 내가 창문을 좀 열어도 될까요? (open)
→ ________ ________ ________ the window?

3 그 의자를 가져 가셔도 돼요. (take)
→ You ________ ________ ________ ________.

4 Charlie는 춤을 매우 잘 출 수 있다. (dance)
→ Charlie ________ ________ ________ ________ very well.

5 너 혼자 그 문제를 해결할 수 있니? (solve)
→ ________ ________ ________ ________ ________ by yourself?

6 나는 극장에서 출구를 찾을 수 없었다. (find)
→ I ________ ________ ________ ________ an exit in the theater.

7 Simpson 씨 부부는 멕시코에 갈지도 모른다. (go)
→ Mr. and Mrs. Simpson ________ ________ ________ Mexico.

E **우리말과 같은 뜻이 되도록 주어진 단어를 배열하시오.**

1 우리 가족은 런던으로 이사 갈지도 몰라. (London, move, may, to)
→ My family ________________________________.

2 Jay는 제 시간에 나타나지 않을지도 몰라. (show up, on time, not, may)
→ Jay ________________________________.

3 Kate는 곧 직장을 구할 수 있을까? (a job, be, get, to, will, able, Kate)
→ ________________________________ soon?

4 미안하지만, 너는 그 책을 빌릴 수 없어. (the book, borrow, cannot)
→ I'm sorry, but you ________________________________.

5 제가 당신의 컴퓨터에서 이메일을 좀 확인해도 될까요? (I, my, check, May, email)
→ ________________________________ on your computer?

6 우리 오빠는 기타를 매우 잘 칠 수 있다. (very well, play, can, the guitar)
→ My brother ________________________________.

7 Nate는 그 컴퓨터를 수리할 수 없었다. (fix, was, to, the computer, able, not)
→ Nate ________________________________.

must, have to, should

A 밑줄 친 부분을 우리말로 옮기시오.

1 She <u>must clean</u> her room. ____________
2 You <u>should lock</u> the door for safety. ____________
3 Pete worked hard. He <u>must be tired</u>. ____________
4 You <u>shouldn't eat</u> too much junk food. ____________
5 You <u>must not tell a lie</u> to your parents. ____________
6 You <u>don't have to hurry</u>. You are not late. ____________

B 보기 에서 단어를 골라 주어진 조동사를 이용하여 문장을 완성하시오.

[1–4] must not 또는 don't have to

보기 drive knock run go

1 We ____________ in the library.
2 You ____________ to school. It's a holiday!
3 You ____________. Just come in, please.
4 You ____________ too fast. It is very dangerous.

[5–8] should 또는 shouldn't

보기 be see eat drink

5 I am on a diet. I ____________ fast food.
6 You don't look well. You ____________ a doctor.
7 The kid ____________ careful. The steps are very dangerous.
8 You ____________ too much coke. It's not good for your health.

C have to를 이용한 문장으로 바꿔 쓰시오.

1 She must be home by twelve o'clock.
→ She ____________.

2 Must I finish my work today?
→ ______ I ____________?

3 You must eat the vegetables on your plate.
→ You ____________.

D **우리말과 같은 뜻이 되도록 주어진 단어를 이용하여 문장을 완성하시오.**

1 제가 지금 가야 해요? (should, go)
→ ________ ________ ________ ________?

2 그 개들은 배가 고픔이 틀림없어. (must, be)
→ The dogs ________ ________ ________.

3 너는 고맙다고 말해야 한다. (should, say)
→ ________ ________ ________ thank you.

4 너는 온종일 텔레비전을 보면 안 된다. (must, watch TV)
→ You ________ ________ ________ ________ all day.

5 그들은 10시까지 집에 돌아와야 한다. (must, be back)
→ They ________ ________ ________ ________ by ten o'clock.

6 그는 그 스스로 숙제를 해야 한다. (have to, do one's homework)
→ He ________ ________ ________ ________ ________ by himself.

7 여러분은 소지품을 여기 남겨 두지 말아야 합니다. (should, leave one's belongings)
→ You ________ ________ ________ ________ ________ here.

E **우리말과 같은 뜻이 되도록 주어진 단어를 배열하시오.**

1 언젠가 한국에 꼭 한번 놀러 와야 해! (visit, Korea, should)
→ You ____ sometime!

2 빨간불에서는 멈춰야 합니다. (at, stop, must, the red light)
→ You ____.

3 너는 몇 시간씩 게임을 하면 안 된다. (play, must, computer games, not)
→ You ____ for hours.

4 수영장에서는 수영모를 착용해야 합니다. (have, wear, a swimming cap, to)
→ You ____ in the pool.

5 모든 질문에 대답할 필요는 없어. (have, answer, don't, all the questions, to)
→ You ____.

6 아이들은 낯선 사람들과 이야기하지 말아야 한다. (not, strangers, talk to, should)
→ Children ____.

7 그들이 집에 있지 않는 게 분명해. 아무도 전화를 받지 않는 걸. (at home, be, not, must)
→ They ____. No one answered the phone.

UNIT 03 will, be going to

A 주어진 조동사와 단어를 이용하여 문장을 완성하시오. [축약형으로 쓸 것]

[1–4] will

1 Don't worry. I ____________ anybody. (not, tell)

2 I'm sorry, Mom. I ____________ it again. (not, do)

3 Rachel is very tired. She ____________ to bed early tonight. (go)

4 My father is 54 years old now. He ____________ 55 years old next year. (be)

[5–8] be going to를 사용할 것

5 I ____________ her an email. (not, send)

6 It's getting so cold. It ____________ tonight. (snow)

7 It's Kelly's birthday. I ____________ a scarf for her. (buy)

8 Today is a holiday. They ____________ today. (not, work)

B 보기 에서 단어를 골라 주어진 조동사를 이용하여 대화를 완성하시오. [축약형을 사용할 것]

[1–3] will

보기 not/eat answer not/forgive

1 A The phone is ringing.
B I ____________ it.

2 A Is she really mad at him?
B Yes. She probably ____________ him easily.

3 A Does she like steak?
B No. She ____________ meat. She is a vegetarian.

[4–6] be going to

보기 come buy meet

4 A ________ you ____________ this blouse?
B No, I'm not. I don't like that color.

5 A Do you have any plans this evening?
B Yes. I ____________ my friend Charlie.

6 A ________ she ____________ home soon?
B Yes. She just called me.

C **우리말과 같은 뜻이 되도록 주어진 단어를 이용하여 문장을 완성하시오.**

1 당신은 내년에 새 차를 살 것인가요? (buy)
→ ______ ______ ______ ______ ______ ______ next year?

2 우리는 오후 6시에 런던에 도착할 예정이다. (arrive in)
→ We ______ ______ ______ ______ ______ at 6 pm.

3 Clara는 오늘 저녁에 요가를 할 예정이다. (do yoga)
→ Clara ______ ______ ______ ______ ______ this evening.

4 그녀는 이번 8월에 졸업하지 않을 것이다. (graduate)
→ She ______ ______ ______ ______ this August.

5 Edward는 이번 주말에 낚시를 갈 것이다. (go fishing)
→ Edward ______ ______ ______ this weekend.

6 우리 가족은 휴가에 뉴욕에 머물지 않을 것이다. (stay in)
→ My family ______ ______ ______ ______ ______ for the holiday.

7 그들은 오늘 밤에 그 쟁점에 대해 이야기할 예정인가요? (talk about)
→ ______ ______ ______ ______ ______ ______ the issue tonight?

D **우리말과 같은 뜻이 되도록 주어진 단어를 배열하시오.**

1 너는 저녁에 집에 있을 거니? (home, be, will, at, you)
→ ______________________________ in the evening?

2 사과를 할인 판매하는구나. 좀 사야겠어. (buy, will, some)
→ These apples are on sale. I ______________________________.

3 Harry가 나에게 다시 전화를 할까? (to, me, going, call, is, Harry)
→ ______________________________ again?

4 Lena는 금요일에 야근하지 않을 것이다. (work late, not, will)
→ Lena ______________________________ on Friday.

5 Derrick은 오늘 뮤지컬을 볼 것이다. (a musical, going, see, is, to)
→ Derrick ______________________________ today.

6 그들은 내년 봄에 결혼할 예정이니? (get married, going, are, to, they)
→ ______________________________ next spring?

7 Ashley는 우리 동아리에 가입하지 않을 거야. (to, our club, join, going, isn't)
→ Ashley ______________________________.

UNIT 01 who, what, which

A 보기 에서 알맞은 의문사를 골라 대화를 완성하시오.

보기 who what which

1 A ________ drew this picture?
B My sister did.

2 A ________ will you do this Saturday?
B I'll plant a tree.

3 A ________ do you want to drink, coffee or tea?
B Coffee, please.

B 보기 에서 알맞은 답을 골라 대화를 완성하시오.

보기
Doing jigsaw puzzles.
I think black is better.
He is my brother.
Diana did.

1 A Who is that man?
B ________________________

2 A What is your hobby?
B ________________________

3 A Who called you last night?
B ________________________

4 A I can't decide. Which do you recommend?
B ________________________

C 대화를 읽고, 의문사를 이용하여 밑줄 친 부분에 대해 묻는 질문을 완성하시오.

1 A ________________ correct, A or B?
B I think B is correct.

2 A ________________ your address?
B My address is 42 Hastings St.

3 A ________________ last weekend?
B I visited my grandparents.

4 A ________________ in the evening?
B He does his homework in the evening.

D **우리말과 같은 뜻이 되도록 주어진 단어를 이용하여 문장을 완성하시오.**

1 넌 오후에 누구를 만날 거니? (will, meet)
→ ________ ________ ________ ________ in the afternoon?

2 수영과 요가 중에서 어느 것이 더 좋아요? (like)
→ ________ ________ ________ more, swimming or yoga?

3 방 안에 있는 그 사람들은 누구니? (be, the people)
→ ________ ________ ________ ________ in the room?

4 커피와 아이스크림 중 어떤 것을 먹기를 원해? (want)
→ ________ ________ ________ ________ to have, coffee or ice cream?

5 너는 지금 무슨 과목을 공부하고 있니? (subject, study)
→ ________ ________ ________ ________ ________ now?

6 너의 어머니가 그것에 대해 뭐라고 하셨니? (your mother, say)
→ ________ ________ ________ ________ ________ about that?

7 너는 여름 방학을 위해 어떤 계획은 가지고 있어? (plans, have)
→ ________ ________ ________ ________ ________ for the summer vacation?

E **우리말과 같은 뜻이 되도록 주어진 단어를 배열하시오.**

1 너희 반의 반장이 누구니? (of your class, is, the president, who)
→ ____

2 너는 전화로 누구와 이야기를 했니? (you, on the phone, did, talk with, who)
→ ____

3 당신은 어떤 종류의 음악을 좋아하세요? (music, like, what, do, kind of, you)
→ ____

4 너는 파티에 무슨 색을 입을 거니? (will, color, for the party, you, what, wear)
→ ____

5 당신의 할아버지께서는 어떤 일을 하셨나요? (your grandfather, what, do, did)
→ ____

6 너는 영어와 불어 중 어느 것을 더 잘하니? (do, which, French, English, or, speak better, you)
→ ____

7 이쪽과 저쪽 중 그들은 어느 쪽으로 갔어요? (go, they, which, this way, way, did, that way, or)
→ ____

when, where, why, how

A 보기 에서 알맞은 의문사를 골라 대화를 완성하시오.

보기 how often where why when

1 A ______________ will you go to Europe?
B Next March.

2 A ______________ do you play baseball?
B I play baseball once a week.

3 A ______________ did you find the teddy bear?
B In my friend's house.

4 A ______________ did he call you?
B Because he wanted to tell me something.

B 보기 에서 알맞은 답을 골라 대화를 완성하시오.

보기 The first of January. In North America. Every 15 minutes. Because of heavy traffic.

1 A Where is Mexico?
B ______________________________

2 A Why was he late?
B ______________________________

3 A When is your birthday?
B ______________________________

4 A How often does the train come?
B ______________________________

C 대화를 읽고, 의문사를 이용하여 밑줄 친 부분을 묻는 질문을 완성하시오.

1 A ______________________________ him?
B She first saw him last year.

2 A ______________________________?
B Pink dolphins live in the Amazon River.

3 A ______________________________?
B The shirt was $25.

4 A ______________________________?
B I cried because the movie was so sad.

D 우리말과 같은 뜻이 되도록 주어진 단어를 이용하여 문장을 완성하시오.

1 그는 너에게 왜 화가 났니? (be)
→ ________ ________ ________ angry at you?

2 너는 시장에 어떻게 가니? (get)
→ ________ ________ ________ to the market?

3 너는 왜 그렇게 항상 바쁘니? (be)
→ ________ ________ ________ always so busy?

4 주말에는 언제 일어나세요? (get up)
→ ________ ________ ________ ________ ________ on weekends?

5 너는 어디서 네 친구들을 만났니? (meet)
→ ________ ________ ________ ________ your friends?

6 너는 얼마나 자주 손을 씻니? (wash, often)
→ ________ ________ ________ ________ ________ your hands?

7 의사 선생님과의 진료 약속은 언제니? (be, your appointment)
→ ________ ________ ________ ________ with your doctor?

E 우리말과 같은 뜻이 되도록 주어진 단어를 배열하시오.

1 우리는 왜 꿈을 꿀까? (dream, why, we, do)
→ ________________________________

2 나는 언제 너를 볼 수 있을까? (you, when, see, can, I)
→ ________________________________

3 저 빌딩은 얼마나 높니? (tall, that building, is, how)
→ ________________________________

4 그 콘서트는 언제 시작하니? (the concert, does, when, start)
→ ________________________________

5 그는 지난밤에 어디에 갔었니? (go, did, last night, he, where)
→ ________________________________

6 너는 그 책을 어디서 찾았니? (the book, you, did, find, where)
→ ________________________________

7 너는 CD를 얼마나 많이 가지고 있니? (have, do, many, how, you, CDs)
→ ________________________________

UNIT 03 부가의문문, 부정의문문, 선택의문문

A 빈칸에 알맞은 말을 넣어 부가 의문문을 완성하시오.

1 This movie is great, ______________________?
2 You weren't there, ______________________?
3 You can't drive a car, ______________________?
4 He won't be late again, ______________________?
5 You didn't order pizza, ______________________?
6 I didn't do something wrong, ______________________?
7 She is your math teacher, ______________________?
8 You did your homework, ______________________?
9 Your father doesn't like singing, ______________________?
10 You aren't going to buy a new cell phone, ______________________?

B 보기 와 같이 부정의문문을 이용하여 대화를 완성하시오.

보기
A Don't you know my name? (know)
B No. Sorry. Would you tell me, please?

1 A ______________________________ big glasses? (wear)
B Yes, he does.

2 A ______________________________ at the party last night? (be)
B Yes, they were. I saw them.

3 A ______________________________ the news? (hear)
B No, I didn't. What is it?

4 A ______________________________ an English teacher? (be)
B No. She is a photographer.

5 A ______________________________ that star? (can, see)
B Yes, I can. Wow! It's so bright.

6 A ______________________________ wonderful singers? (be)
B Yes, they are. They sing beautifully.

C 우리말과 같은 뜻이 되도록 주어진 단어를 배열하시오.

1 이 공은 너의 것이니 아니면 그녀의 것이니? (yours, hers, this ball, is, or)
→ ______________________________

2 이것과 저것 중 어느 것이 더 저렴한가요? (or, which, that, this, cheaper, is)
→ ______________________________

3 도넛과 쿠키 중 어떤 것을 원해? (donuts, cookies, want, you, which, or, do)
→ ______________________________

4 너의 언니는 의사니 아니면 선생님이니? (a doctor, a teacher, your sister, is, or)
→ ______________________________

5 커피와 차 중에서 어떤 것을 드시겠어요? (coffee, tea, which, you, would, like, or)
→ ______________________________

6 너는 학교에 버스로 가니 아니면 지하철로 가니? (you, by bus, by subway, or, school, do, go to)
→ ______________________________

7 너는 여름과 겨울 중에 어느 계절을 더 좋아하니? (summer, winter, or, you, which season, like more, do)
→ ______________________________

D 우리말과 같은 뜻이 되도록 주어진 단어를 이용하여 문장을 완성하시오.

1 다른 길을 찾을 수 있지 않니? (find)
→ ________ ________ ________ another way?

2 너 Jane의 남동생이지 않니? (be)
→ ________ ________ Jane's brother?

3 Jessica는 정말 예뻐, 그렇지 않니? (she)
→ Jessica is really pretty, ________ ________?

4 Greg은 도서관에서 공부할 거지, 그렇지 않니? (he)
→ Greg will study in the library, ________ ________?

5 복도에서는 뛰지 말도록 해, 알겠니? (you)
→ Don't run in the hallway, ________ ________?

6 그는 수영과 등산 중 어떤 것을 더 좋아하니? (like, better)
→ ________ ________ ________ ________ ________, swimming or hiking?

7 너는 쇼핑을 가고 싶니, 아니면 집에 가고 싶니? (go shopping, go home)
→ Do you want to ________ ________ ________ ________ ________?

UNIT 04 감탄문

A 보기 에서 알맞은 말을 골라 감탄문을 완성하시오.

보기 what how

1 ________ foolish I am!
2 ________ happy you look!
3 ________ a big animal it is!
4 ________ high the mountain is!
5 ________ slowly the turtle moves!
6 ________ a funny man Samuel is!
7 ________ an amazing movie it was!
8 ________ wonderful musicians they are!

B 주어진 문장을 감탄문으로 바꿔 쓰시오.

1 You cook very well.
→ How ______________________________!

2 He is a very tall guy.
→ What ______________________________!

3 She has a really nice car.
→ What ______________________________!

4 The apples are really fresh.
→ How ______________________________!

5 The news is very interesting.
→ How ______________________________!

6 You have really beautiful eyes.
→ What ______________________________!

7 You wore really expensive shoes.
→ What ______________________________!

C 우리말과 같은 뜻이 되도록 주어진 단어를 이용하여 문장을 완성하시오.

1 날이 정말 좋구나! (nice, day)
→ ________ ________ ________ ________ it is!

2 그 아기들은 정말 귀엽구나! (cute)
→ ________ ________ the babies are!

3 그 수업은 정말 지루했어! (boring)
→ ________ ________ the class was!

4 그녀의 머리는 정말 길구나! (long, hair)
→ ________ ________ ________ she has!

5 그는 정말 훌륭한 선생님이구나! (great)
→ ________ ________ ________ ________ he is!

6 그건 정말 신나는 여행이었어! (an exciting trip)
→ ________ ________ ________ ________ it was!

7 그녀는 정말 아름답게 노래를 부르는구나! (beautifully)
→ ________ ________ she sings!

D 우리말과 같은 뜻이 되도록 주어진 단어를 배열하시오.

1 너는 정말 다정하구나! (are, sweet, you, how)
→ ________________________________

2 인생은 정말 아름답구나! (life, beautiful, how, is)
→ ________________________________

3 저 코끼리는 정말 크구나! (that elephant, big, is, how)
→ ________________________________

4 정말 놀라운 이야기구나! (it, an, what, is, story, amazing)
→ ________________________________

5 너는 정말 좋은 시간을 보냈구나! (time, had, wonderful, what, you, a)
→ ________________________________

6 그들은 정말 맛있는 케이크를 파는구나! (they, cakes, what, sell, tasty)
→ ________________________________

7 그것은 정말 흥미진진한 게임이었어! (game, an, what, was, exciting, it)
→ ________________________________

UNIT 05 명령문, 제안문

A 주어진 동사를 알맞은 형태로 바꿔 명령문을 완성하시오.

1 ____________ honest. You shouldn't tell lies. (be)

2 ____________ You can do it. (not, give up)

3 ____________ straight for 100 m. You'll see it. (go)

4 ____________ at home. I will visit you tonight. (stay)

5 ____________ your cell phone in the theater. (turn off)

6 ____________ your room. Your room is too messy. (clean)

7 ____________ about that. I will take care of that. (not, worry)

8 ____________ a noise. You should be quiet in class. (not, make)

B 주어진 동사와 let's를 이용하여 제안문을 완성하시오.

1 ____________ too many sweets. (not, eat)

2 ____________ in the sun too long. (not, sit)

3 ____________ in the library. It's rude. (not, run)

4 ____________ dinner together tonight. (have)

5 ____________ some pizza. I'm hungry. (order)

6 ____________ our desks. They are dirty. (clean)

7 ____________ every day. It will be good for us. (exercise)

8 ____________ pictures in the gallery. There's a "No Photos" sign. (not, take)

C 우리말과 같은 뜻이 되도록 주어진 단어를 이용하여 문장을 완성하시오.

1 유럽으로 여행을 가자. (tako a trip)
→ ________ ________ ________ ________ to Europe.

2 정원의 꽃을 꺾지 마세요. (pick, flowers)
→ ________ ________ in the garden.

3 나가서 친구들과 놀도록 해. (go out, play)
→ ________ ________ and ________ with your friends.

4 나에게 그런 식으로 말하지 마라. (talk to)
→ ________ ________ ________ ________ like that.

5 오늘 밤에 영화를 보러 가자. (go to the movies)
→ ________ ________ ________ ________ ________ tonight.

6 이제부터 패스트푸드를 먹지 말자. (eat, fast food)
→ ________ ________ ________ ________ ________ from now on.

7 밤에 컴퓨터 게임을 하지 마라. (play, computer games)
→ ________ ________ ________ ________ at night.

D 우리말과 같은 뜻이 되도록 주어진 단어를 배열하시오.

1 박물관 앞에서 만나자. (the museum, meet, in front of, let's)
→ ____

2 케이크를 여러 조각으로 잘라 주세요. (pieces, into, the cake, cut)
→ ____

3 이번 토요일에 해변에 가자. (to the beach, go, Let's)
→ ________________________________ this Saturday.

4 길거리에 쓰레기를 버리지 말자. (trash, throw, not, let's)
→ ________________________________ on the street.

5 다시는 같은 실수를 하지 마. (the same, mistake, make, don't)
→ ________________________________ again.

6 당신의 손을 허리에 얹으세요. (your waist, your hands, put, on)
→ ____

7 수업 시간에는 휴대 전화를 사용하지 마시오. (your cell phone, use, don't)
→ ________________________________ in class.

UNIT 01 to부정사의 명사적 쓰임

A 주어진 동사를 to부정사로 바꿔 문장을 완성하시오.

1 I plan ______________ Spanish. (learn)
2 I like ______________ English books. (read)
3 ______________ coins is James' hobby. (collect)
4 It is good ______________ regularly. (exercise)
5 Her dream is ______________ a famous painter. (be)

B 보기 에서 알맞은 것을 골라 지시대로 바꿔 문장을 완성하시오.

[1-4] to부정사 보기 help eat ride learn

1 I want ______________ Japanese food.
2 It is fun ______________ roller coasters.
3 She decided ______________ taekwondo.
4 Her plan is ______________ poor children.

[5-8]「의문사 + to부정사」 보기 when/leave how/play what/do where/go

5 I learn ____________________________ hockey.
6 Please tell me ____________________________ next.
7 Did you decide ____________________________ in summer?
8 She wanted to know ____________________________ the house.

C 주어진 문장을 가주어 It를 사용한 문장으로 바꿔 쓰시오.

1 To learn Chinese is fun.
→ ________ is fun ______________________________.

2 To read this novel is exciting.
→ ________ is exciting ______________________________.

3 To cross the street here is dangerous.
→ ________ is dangerous ______________________________.

4 To find a perfect gift for her was hard.
→ ________ was hard ______________________________.

5 To keep a diary every day is a good habit.
→ ________ is a good habit ______________________________.

D **우리말과 같은 뜻이 되도록 주어진 단어를 사용하여 문장을 완성하시오.**

1 나는 며칠 쉬기를 바라. (wish, take a break)
→ I _____ _____ _____ _____ _____ for a few days.

2 너는 나와 함께 가야 할 필요가 있다. (need, go)
→ You _____ _____ _____ with me.

3 그는 너를 거기서 보기를 바란다. (hope, see, you)
→ He _____ _____ _____ _____ there.

4 친구를 사귀는 것은 신나는 일이다. (make, friends)
→ It is exciting _____ _____ _____.

5 새로운 것을 배우는 일은 재미있다. (learn, new things)
→ It is fun _____ _____ _____ _____.

6 Monica는 케이크 굽는 것을 좋아한다. (like, bake, cakes)
→ Monica _____ _____ _____ _____.

7 우리는 이번 주말에 박물관에 갈 계획이다. (plan, visit, the museum)
→ We _____ _____ _____ _____ _____ this weekend.

E **우리말과 같은 뜻이 되도록 주어진 단어를 배열하시오.**

1 말을 타는 것은 재미있다. (ride, to, fun, is, a horse)
→ It ______________________________.

2 나는 잠시 산책을 하고 싶어요. (a walk, would like, take, to)
→ I ______________________________ for a while.

3 Rachel은 영화 관람하는 것을 좋아한다. (go, to, to, likes, the movies)
→ Rachel ______________________________.

4 그들은 함께 캠핑을 가기로 결정했다. (to, they, go camping, decided)
→ ______________________________ together.

5 바다에서 수영하는 것은 위험할 수 있다. (swim, dangerous, it, can be, to)
→ ______________________________ in the sea.

6 상훈이의 꿈은 축구 선수가 되는 것입니다. (soccer player, become, is, a, to)
→ Sang-Hoon's dream ______________________________.

7 내가 좋아하는 활동은 미술관에 가는 것입니다. (to, to, is, the art gallery, go)
→ My favorite activity ______________________________.

UNIT 02 to부정사의 형용사적, 부사적 쓰임

A 보기 와 같이 우리말과 같은 뜻이 되도록 문장을 완성하시오.

> 보기 우리는 이야기할 문제가 몇 가지 있다.
> → We have some ___issues to talk about___. (talk about, issues)

1 그들은 할 일이 좀 있다.
→ They had some ______________________. (work, do)

2 나는 차를 살 돈이 없다.
→ I have no ______________________ a car. (buy, money)

3 나는 초대할 사람이 두 명 있다.
→ I have two ______________________. (invite, people)

4 먹을 빵을 몇 개 가지고 있니?
→ Do you have any ______________________? (eat, bread)

5 그녀는 읽을 잡지를 가져왔다.
→ She brought a ______________________. (read, magazine)

6 그는 입을 것이 없다.
→ He doesn't have ______________________. (wear, anything)

7 방 안에는 마실 물이 없었다.
→ There is no ______________________ in the room. (drink, water)

B 보기 와 같이 두 문장의 뜻이 통하도록 문장을 완성하시오.

> 보기 I went shopping. I bought a gift for my dad.
> → I went shopping ___to buy a gift for my dad___.

1 Jackie saw me. She was surprised.
→ Jackie was surprised ______________________.

2 He is silly. He believes Jessica's lies.
→ He is silly ______________________.

3 We are very happy. We have you here.
→ We are very happy ______________________.

4 Tony heard the bad news. So, he was very sad.
→ Tony was very sad ______________________.

5 I went to the library. I borrowed some books.
→ I went to the library ______________________.

6 They went to the riverside. They took a walk.
→ They went to the riverside ______________________.

C **우리말과 같은 뜻이 되도록 주어진 단어를 이용하여 문장을 완성하시오.**

1 나쁜 소식을 들어서 슬프네요. (sad, hear)
→ I am ________ ________ ________ the bad news.

2 나는 책을 사려고 서점에 갔다. (buy, books)
→ I went to the bookstore ________ ________ ________.

3 Tom은 새 가방을 살 돈이 없다. (money, buy)
→ Tom doesn't have ________ ________ ________ a new bag.

4 이런 말을 하게 되어 매우 유감입니다. (sorry, say)
→ I am so ________ ________ ________ this.

5 그녀는 잼을 만들려고 블루베리를 좀 샀다. (make, jam)
→ She bought some blueberries ________ ________ ________.

6 그는 그를 도와줄 많은 친구들이 있다. (many friends, help)
→ He has ________ ________ ________ ________ him.

7 나는 대학에 가기 위해 열심히 공부했다. (get into, university)
→ I studied hard ________ ________ ________ ________.

D **우리말과 같은 뜻이 되도록 주어진 단어를 배열하시오.**

1 너 나한테 할 말이 있니? (me, tell, something, to)
→ Do you have ________________________________?

2 우리는 여기 머물 시간이 없다. (to, here, stay, time)
→ We don't have ________________________________.

3 나는 내일 할 일이 좀 있어. (do, to, have, something)
→ I ________________________________ tomorrow.

4 그녀는 살을 빼기 위해 저녁을 먹지 않는다. (lose weight, to)
→ ________________________________, she doesn't eat dinner.

5 그녀는 너를 만나려고 여기에 왔다. (you, to, came here, meet)
→ She ________________________________.

6 그는 그 소식을 듣게 되어 놀랐다. (the news, hear, was, to, surprised)
→ He ________________________________.

7 나는 영어를 배우기 위해 밴쿠버에 갔다. (English, Vancouver, study, went to, to)
→ I ________________________________.

UNIT 03 동명사의 쓰임

A 주어진 단어를 동명사로 바꿔 문장을 완성하시오.

1 I'm afraid of ____________ alone. (be)

2 My father's job is ____________ cars. (sell)

3 ____________ German is really fun. (speak)

4 She loves ____________ with her friends. (chat)

B 보기 에서 알맞은 단어를 골라 어법에 맞게 바꿔 문장을 완성하시오.

보기 open look clean play

1 Tom is good at ____________ tennis.

2 Do you mind ____________ the window?

3 I enjoy ____________ at people on the street.

4 My brother and I finished ____________ our room.

C 두 문장이 같은 뜻이 되도록 to부정사를 동명사로 바꿔 문장을 완성하시오.

1 To talk with him is boring.
→ ________________________________ is boring.

2 My favorite sport is to sail.
→ My favorite sport is ________________________________.

3 Jamie's hobby is to ride horses.
→ Jamie's hobby is ________________________________.

4 To swim in the sea is a lot of fun.
→ ________________________________ is a lot of fun.

5 Hannah and Judy like to sing together.
→ Hannah and Judy like ________________________________.

D **우리말과 같은 뜻이 되도록 주어진 단어를 이용하여 문장을 완성하시오.**

1 James는 공을 잘 던진다. (be good at, throw, balls)
→ James ________ ________ ________ ________ ________.

2 우리를 초대해 주셔서 감사합니다. (for, invite, us)
→ Thank you ________ ________ ________.

3 패스트푸드를 먹는 것은 네 건강에 좋지 않아. (be, eat, fast food)
→ ________ ________ ________ ________ not good for your health.

4 나의 이번 휴가 계획은 제주도에 가는 것이다. (be, go to, Jejudo)
→ My plan for this holiday ________ ________ ________ ________.

5 참된 친구를 갖는 것은 진정한 축복이다. (be, have, a true friend)
→ ________ ________ ________ ________ ________ a real blessing.

6 Alan의 새로운 직업은 컴퓨터를 고치는 것이다. (be, fix, computers)
→ Alan's new job ________ ________ ________.

7 사람들 앞에서 말하는 것은 어렵다. (speak, in front of, people, be)
→ ________ ________ ________ ________ ________ ________ hard.

E **우리말과 같은 뜻이 되도록 주어진 단어를 배열하시오.**

1 늦어서 죄송합니다. (being late, sorry, for)
→ I'm ________________________________.

2 차 한 잔 하는 건 어때? (tea, having, how about, a cup of)
→ ________________________________

3 차를 운전하는 것은 쉽지 않다. (a car, driving, is)
→ ________________________________ not easy.

4 Samantha는 그림을 잘 그린다. (good, drawing, at, is)
→ Samantha ________________________________.

5 그의 취미는 홈 무비를 만드는 것이다. (home movies, making, is)
→ His hobby ________________________________.

6 노래를 부르는 것은 나를 행복하게 한다. (a song, makes, singing)
→ ________________________________ me happy.

7 나는 애완동물 사진 찍는 것을 즐긴다. (taking pictures, enjoy, of pets)
→ I ________________________________.

UNIT 04 to부정사 vs. 동명사

A 주어진 동사를 알맞은 형태로 바꾸어 문장을 완성하시오.

1 She quit ____________ here last week. (work)

2 Does Tom plan ____________ to America? (go)

3 They enjoyed ____________ in the sea. (swim)

4 Do you want ____________ to the radio? (listen)

5 He hopes ____________ the report tonight. (write)

6 It's time to sleep. Stop ____________ computer games. (play)

B 보기 에서 단어를 골라 어법에 맞게 바꿔 문장을 완성하시오.

[1–4] 보기 walk open get meet

1 Keep ____________ along the hallway.

2 Would you mind ____________ the door?

3 Do you expect ____________ him at the party?

4 She wishes ____________ a scholarship.

[5–8] 보기 study go eat ask

5 I gave up ____________ skiing this winter.

6 I wanted ____________ him a few questions.

7 Dave decided ____________ art in college.

8 Do you enjoy ____________ out with other people?

C 두 문장이 같은 뜻이 되도록 문장을 완성하시오.

1 The boy started to cry.
→ The boy started ______________________.

2 Suddenly, it began to rain.
→ Suddenly, it began ______________________.

3 He doesn't like to try new food.
→ He doesn't like ______________________ new food.

4 I love to listen to classical music.
→ I love ______________________ to classical music.

D **우리말과 같은 뜻이 되도록 주어진 단어를 이용하여 문장을 완성하시오.**

1 그만 말하고 내 얘기를 들어 봐. (stop, talk)
→ ______________ and listen to me.

2 Jay는 진실을 알고 싶어 한다. (want, know)
→ Jay ______________ the truth.

3 그들은 길을 따라서 계속 걸었다. (keep, walk)
→ They ______________ along the street.

4 나는 당신과 이야기해서 즐거웠습니다. (enjoy, talk)
→ I ______________ to you.

5 우리는 그를 다시 보게 되길 소망합니다. (hope, see)
→ We ______________ him again.

6 난 그를 차로 데려다 주는 것을 싫어하지 않는다. (mind, drive)
→I don't ______________ him home.

7 나는 오늘까지 그에게 이메일을 보내야 한다. (need, send)
→ I ______________ him an email by today.

E **우리말과 같은 뜻이 되도록 주어진 단어를 배열하시오.**

1 나는 고양이를 기르고 싶다. (a cat, to, want, have)
→ I ______________.

2 Jason은 뉴질랜드로 여행가기를 소망한다. (to, hopes, go on a trip)
→ Jason ______________ to New Zealand.

3 그는 그 집을 페인트칠하는 것을 끝냈다. (the house, painting, finished)
→ He ______________.

4 Jefferson은 기쁨에 겨워 뛰기 시작했다. (jumping, started, with delight)
→ Jefferson ______________.

5 소리를 좀 줄여 주시겠어요? (the volume, turning down, mind)
→ Do you ______________?

6 그는 친구들과 시간을 보내는 것을 좋아한다. (with his friends, spending time, enjoys)
→ He ______________.

7 그녀는 금요일까지 프로젝트를 끝내겠다고 약속했다. (the project, finish, promised, to)
→ She ______________ by Friday.

UNIT 01 감각동사

A 주어진 단어를 이용하여 문장을 완성하시오. [현재 시제로 쓸 것]

1 Rachel ___________ ___________. (look, sad)

2 You ___________ ___________ today. (look, nice)

3 The soup ___________ ___________. (taste, spicy)

4 The salad ___________ ___________. (taste, fresh)

5 The sweater ___________ ___________. (feel, soft)

6 The coffee ___________ ___________. (smell, great)

B 보기 에서 알맞은 단어를 골라 문장을 완성하시오.

[1–2]

보기	a strong man	strong

1 Your brother looks ______________________.

2 He looks like ______________________.

[3–4]

보기	warm	a rock star

3 He felt ______________________ in the jacket.

4 I feel like ______________________.

[5–6]

보기	so cute	babies

5 Kittens often sound like ______________________.

6 They sound ______________________.

[7–8]

보기	honey	sour

7 This drink tastes like ______________________.

8 The sauce tastes ______________________.

C **우리말과 같은 뜻이 되도록 주어진 단어를 이용하여 문장을 완성하시오.**

1 나는 친구들과 있으면 행복하다. (feel, happy)
→ ________ ________ ________ with my friends.

2 오늘 아침은 겨울처럼 느껴졌다. (feel, winter)
→ It ________ ________ ________ this morning.

3 이 음식은 닭고기 맛이 난다. (taste, chicken)
→ This food ________ ________ ________.

4 그 초콜릿 케이크는 맛이 매우 달다. (taste, sweet)
→ The chocolate cake ________ ________ ________.

5 그녀는 오늘 피곤해 보였어. (look, tired)
→ She ________ ________ ________.

6 그녀는 진짜 공주님처럼 보였다. (look, a real princess)
→ She ________ ________ ________ ________ ________.

7 네 노래가 훌륭하게 들리는 구나. (sound, wonderful)
→ Your song ________ ________.

8 너는 너의 엄마가 말하는 것처럼 들리는 구나. (sound, your mom)
→ You ________ ________ ________ ________.

D **우리말과 같은 뜻이 되도록 주어진 단어를 배열하시오.**

1 그녀는 그와 행복해 보인다. (with, happy, looks, him)
→ She ____.

2 나는 집에 혼자 있을 때 외롭다고 느낀다. (lonely, feel, I)
→ ____ when I'm home alone.

3 음, 그것은 커피 냄새가 나는 구나 (smells, coffee, it, like)
→ Um, ____.

4 그 게임은 재미있게 들린다. (interesting, sounds, the game)
→ ____

5 방에서 Jane은 매우 화가 나 보였어. (angry, Jane, looked, very)
→ ____ in her room.

UNIT 02 수여동사

A 보기 에서 알맞은 단어를 골라 문장을 완성하시오.

보기	to	for	of

1 Would you give your book ________ me?

2 Jack showed his new girlfriend ________ me.

3 He often asked silly questions ________ me.

4 My father bought a smartphone ________ me.

5 Rebecca's friend lent some money ________ her.

6 Edward sent flowers ________ me for my birthday.

7 Ted will get a wheelchair ________ his grandmother.

B 두 문장이 같은 뜻이 되도록 문장을 완성하시오.

1 He gave me some flowers.
→ He gave ____________________.

2 Helen made her cat a house.
→ Helen made ____________________.

3 Can show me the list?
→ Can you show ____________________?

4 My neighbor brought me wine.
→ My neighbor brought ____________________.

5 The professor asked her many questions.
→ The professor asked ____________________.

6 Mr. Bernard sent them a fax this morning.
→ Mr. Bernard sent ____________________ this morning.

7 She bought her husband an expensive suit.
→ She bought ____________________.

C **우리말과 같은 뜻이 되도록 주어진 단어를 이용하여 문장을 완성하시오.**

1 Jack이 지난주에 나에게 책을 빌려 주었다. (lend, a book)
→ Jack ________ ________ ________ ________ ________ last week.

2 나는 나의 어머니에게 스카프를 사 줄 것이다. (buy, a scarf)
→ I will .

3 나의 선생님이 나에게 몇 가지 질문을 했다. (ask, some questions)
→ My teacher ________ ________ ________ ________.

4 Brown 씨가 나에게 많은 정보를 주었다. (give, a lot of, information)
→ Mr. Brown ________ ________ ________ ________ ________ ________.

5 Emily는 파리에서 자신의 친구에게 우편엽서를 보냈다. (send, a postcard)
→ Emily ________ ________ ________ ________ ________ from Paris.

6 Jenny는 자신의 어머니에게 성적표를 보여 주었다. (show, her report card)
→ Jenny ________ ________ ________ ________ ________ ________ ________.

7 나의 가장 친한 친구가 나를 위해서 스웨터를 만들어 주었다. (make, a sweater)
→ My best friend ________ ________ ________ ________ ________.

D **우리말과 같은 뜻이 되도록 주어진 단어를 배열하시오.**

1 다음 주에 너한테 소포를 보낼게. (you, a package, send)
→ I will ________________________________ next week.

2 Liz는 일요일마다 나에게 영어를 가르쳐준다. (me, English, teaches)
→ Liz ________________________________ on Sundays.

3 그 경찰관은 나에게 몇 가지 질문을 했다. (questions, me, a few, asked)
→ The police officer ________________________________.

4 우리 삼촌이 우리에게 주말에 쓸 텐트를 빌려주셨다. (us, his tent, lent, to)
→ My uncle ________________________________ for the weekend.

5 우리 선생님이 우리에게 크리스마스 선물을 주었다. (to, Christmas gifts, gave, us)
→ My teacher ________________________________.

6 나는 어머니에게 커피 한 잔을 가져다주었다. (my mother, coffee, brought, a cup of)
→ I ________________________________.

7 나의 할머니가 나에게 아름다운 드레스를 만들어주었다. (me, a beautiful dress, made)
→ My grandmother ________________________________.

UNIT 03 목적격보어가 필요한 동사

A 주어진 단어를 어법에 맞게 바꿔 문장을 완성하시오.

1 I advised him ____________ her. (marry)

2 Do you want me ____________ with you? (go)

3 People in the room asked him ____________. (get out)

4 His mother told him ____________ quietly. (sit down)

5 My mom wanted me ____________ a doctor. (become)

6 My parents expected me ____________ home early. (come)

7 Mr. Person told students ____________ a book in the library. (read)

B 보기 에서 알맞은 말을 골라 우리말과 같은 뜻이 되도록 문장을 완성하시오.

보기	interesting	a bookworm	warm	calm
	cold	happy	a great swimmer	

1 요가가 나를 평온하게 만들어 준다.
→ Yoga makes me ____________.

2 냉장고는 음식을 차갑게 유지할 수 있다.
→ The refrigerator can keep food ____________.

3 그 소년은 친구들을 행복하게 만들었다.
→ The boy made his friends ____________.

4 우리 가족은 내 동생을 책벌레라고 부른다.
→ My family calls my brother ____________.

5 그는 그 영화가 흥미진진하다는 것을 알게 됐다.
→ He found the movie ____________.

6 그의 아버지는 그를 훌륭한 수영선수로 만들었다.
→ His father made him ____________.

7 Shultz 씨가 나를 위해서 그 수프를 계속 따뜻하게 했다.
→ Mrs. Shultz kept the soup ____________ for me.

C **우리말과 같은 뜻이 되도록 주어진 단어를 이용하여 문장을 완성하시오.**

1 너는 네 방을 깨끗하게 유지해야 한다. (keep, clean)
→ You should ________ ________ ________ ________.

2 나는 네가 나의 생일 파티에 오기를 원한다. (want, come)
→ I ________ ________ ________ ________ to my birthday party.

3 그녀의 부모는 그녀를 Sally라고 이름 지었다. (name, Sally)
→ Her parents ________ ________ ________.

4 그가 너에게 새로운 직업을 찾으라고 충고했니? (advise, find)
→ Did he ________ ________ ________ ________ a new job?

5 우리는 그가 일등을 할 거라고 예상하지 않았다. (expect, win)
→ We didn't ________ ________ ________ ________ first prize.

6 그녀는 그 축구 경기가 재미있다는 것을 알았다. (find, exciting)
→ She ________ ________ ________ ________ ________.

7 부모님이 나에게 매일 공부를 해야 한다고 말했다. (tell, study)
→ My parents ________ ________ ________ ________ every day.

D **우리말과 같은 뜻이 되도록 주어진 단어를 배열하시오.**

1 배심원단은 그가 유죄라고 생각했다. (him, guilty, found)
→ The jury ________________________________.

2 그들은 그 새를 도도라고 이름 지었다. (the bird, Dodo, named)
→ They ________________________________.

3 나는 그의 농담이 재미있다는 것을 알게 됐다. (found, funny, his jokes)
→ I ________________________________.

4 우리는 그가 그렇게 오래 머물 거라고 예상하지 못했다. (him, to, expect, stay)
→ We didn't ________________________________ so long.

5 그녀는 아들에게 한 시간만 게임을 하라고 했다. (to, ordered, play, her son)
→ She ________________________________ games for only an hour.

6 나의 의사가 나에게 매일 운동을 하라고 충고했다. (to, me, advised, exercise)
→ My doctor ________________________________ every day.

7 우리 엄마는 나에게 남동생을 돌보라고 말했다. (to, my brother, take care of, me, told)
→ My mom ________________________________.

UNIT 01 형용사

A 보기 에서 알맞은 말을 골라 문장을 완성하시오.

[1–4] 보기 new happy clean wrong

1 The teacher looks __________ today.

2 You should keep your desk __________.

3 Is there anything __________ with you?

4 She bought a __________ skirt last week.

[5–8] 보기 salty boring beautiful old

5 I found the book __________.

6 He threw away __________ clothes.

7 There is something __________ in this food.

8 She looked __________ in her new dress.

B 보기 에서 알맞은 말을 골라 우리말과 같은 뜻이 되도록 문장을 완성하시오.

[1–2] 보기 many much

1 나는 영화제에서 많은 배우들을 보았다.
→ I saw __________ actors at the film festival.

2 Johnson 선생님은 우리에게 숙제를 많이 내주지 않았다.
→ Mrs. Johnson didn't give us __________ homework.

[3–4] 보기 few little

3 물병에는 물이 거의 없었다.
→ There was __________ water in the bottle.

4 식당에는 손님의 거의 없었다.
→ There were __________ customers in the restaurant.

[5–6] 보기 a few a little

5 나는 친구에게 엽서를 몇 장 보냈다.
→ I sent __________ postcards to my friend.

6 여기 그 시험에 관한 정보가 약간 있어요.
→ Here's __________ information about the exam.

C **우리말과 같은 뜻이 되도록 주어진 단어를 이용하여 문장을 완성하시오.**

1 세상에는 많은 직업이 있다. (job)
→ There are __________ __________ __________ __________ in the world.

2 나는 커피에 설탕을 약간 넣어 먹어요. (sugar)
→ I have coffee with __________ __________ __________.

3 그의 지갑에는 남은 돈이 거의 없었다. (money)
→ There was __________ __________ left in his wallet.

4 그는 이 지역에 대해 아는 것이 거의 없다. (thing)
→ He knows __________ __________ about this area.

5 우리는 밤하늘에서 많은 별을 볼 수 있다. (star)
→ We can see __________ __________ in the night sky.

6 당신은 매일 물을 많이 마셔야 합니다. (water)
→ You need to drink __________ __________ __________ __________ every day.

7 나는 어제 서점에서 책을 몇 권 샀다. (book)
→ I bought __________ __________ __________ at the bookstore yesterday.

D **우리말과 같은 뜻이 되도록 주어진 단어를 알맞게 배열하시오.**

1 그 방에 의자가 몇 개 있었다. (were, a few, chairs, there)
→ ______________________________ in the room.

2 네 결정에는 잘못된 것이 없어. (wrong, nothing, is, there)
→ ______________________________ with your decision.

3 그가 그 아이들을 안전하게 지킬 것이다. (the children, keep, safe)
→ He will ______________________________.

4 위험한 일은 어떤 것도 하지 마세요. (dangerous, do, anything, don't)
→ Please ______________________________.

5 Ryan의 정원은 많은 꽃들로 정말 아름다워 보인다. (really, beautiful, looks)
→ Ryan's garden ______________________________ with many flowers.

6 그녀는 나에게 몇 가지 어려운 질문을 했다. (some, questions, asked, difficult, me)
→ She ______________________________.

7 그가 나에게 그녀에 대한 새로운 사실을 말해 주었다. (new, told, he, something, me)
→ ______________________________ about her.

UNIT 02 부사

A 주어진 형용사를 부사로 바꾸어 쓰시오.

1 quiet ___________
2 happy ___________
3 simple ___________
4 careful ___________
5 nice ___________
6 real ___________
7 main ___________
8 new ___________
9 terrible ___________
10 comfortable ___________
11 good ___________
12 fast ___________
13 heavy ___________
14 slow ___________
15 possible ___________
16 bad ___________
17 early ___________
18 special ___________
19 necessary ___________
20 lucky ___________

B 보기 에서 알맞은 말을 골라 문장을 완성하시오. [중복 사용 가능]

[1–3] 보기 late lately

1 I'm sorry I'm ___________.
2 Oh, no! I'm already running ___________!
3 I went swimming once or twice ___________.

[4–6] 보기 hard hardly

4 She ___________ eats anything after 6 pm.
5 Diane studied very ___________ for the tests.
6 I would like to buy a ___________ wooden chair.

[7–9] 보기 high highly

7 Sue is a ___________ sensitive person.
8 Charles is good at jumping. He can jump ___________.
9 Shoes with ___________ heels are not good for your body.

C 주어진 단어를 넣어 문장을 다시 쓰시오.

1 I will let you go. (never)
→ I ______________________________ you go.

2 Polly is kind to me. (always)
→ Polly ______________________________ to me.

3 My dad is at home on weekends. (usually)
→ My dad ______________________________ on weekends.

4 My mom goes to the movies with her friends. (sometimes)
→ My mom ______________________________ with her friends.

D [ ] 안에 주어진 단어를 알맞은 곳에 써 넣으시오.

1 [easy, easily] This is an __________ question. You can answer it __________.

2 [clear, clearly] Carl explains the problem very __________ with __________ examples.

3 [careless, carelessly] Robert always drives __________. He is such a __________ driver.

4 [quick, quickly] The teacher asked me to answer __________. So I gave him a __________ answer.

5 [beautiful, beautifully] Ann dressed __________ for the party. She bought the __________ dress last week.

6 [fluent / fluently] I can't speak English __________ now, but one day, I will be a __________ speaker of English.

E 우리말과 같은 뜻이 되도록 주어진 단어를 알맞게 배열하시오.

1 그는 정직하게 대답하려고 애썼다. (answer, to, honestly, tried)
→ He ______________________________.

2 나는 언제나 지하철로 출근한다. (by subway, always, work, go, to)
→ I ______________________________.

3 Maggie는 방과 후에 가끔씩 테니스를 친다. (after school, plays, sometimes, tennis)
→ Maggie ______________________________.

4 다행스럽게도 그녀가 그 어려운 문제를 해결했다. (problem, the, solved, luckily, difficult)
→ __________, she ______________________________.

UNIT 03 비교급 · 최상급

A 다음 형용사와 부사의 비교급과 최상급을 쓰시오.

1 happy ________ ________
2 serious ________ ________
3 dirty ________ ________
4 easy ________ ________
5 simple ________ ________
6 lucky ________ ________
7 good ________ ________
8 much ________ ________
9 old [나이] ________ ________
10 late [시간] ________ ________
11 expensive ________ ________
12 thin ________ ________
13 colorful ________ ________
14 hot ________ ________
15 large ________ ________
16 famous ________ ________
17 bad ________ ________
18 little ________ ________
19 old [순서] ________ ________
20 late [순서] ________ ________

B 주어진 단어를 사용하여 지시에 맞게 문장을 완성하시오.

[1–5] 비교급

1 Janet's cake is ________________ her sister's. (sweet)
2 Your suitcase looks ________________ mine. (heavy)
3 Angela drives ________________ Tom does. (carefully)
4 The silver ring costs ________________ the gold one does. (little)
5 Michael took pictures ________________ James did. (well)

[6–10] 최상급

6 Today is ________________ day of the year. (hot)
7 This is ________________ building in this city. (old)
8 Rick is ________________ player on our team. (good)
9 The lion is ________________ animal in the zoo. (strong)
10 Kate is ________________ actress in the play. (famous)

C 두 문장의 의미가 통하도록 비교급 문장을 완성하시오.

1 The moon is not as big as the earth.
→ The earth is ______________________ the moon.

2 My desk is not as clean as my sister's.
→ My sister's desk is ______________________ mine.

3 David does not eat as quickly as Peter does.
→ Peter eats ______________________ David does.

4 The apples are not as fresh as the grapes.
→ The grapes are ______________________ the apples.

5 Karen does not work as hard as Jay does.
→ Jay works ______________________ Karen does.

D 문장의 의미가 통하도록 원급 비교 문장을 완성하시오.

1 My coat was $20. My sister's coat was $20, too.
→ My coat was ______________________ my sister's. (cheap)

2 Mark is 14 years old. Sandy is 14 years old, too.
→ Mark is ______________________ Sandy. (old)

3 White Hotel is $100 a day. Green Hotel is $100 a day, too.
→ White Hotel is ______________________ Green Hotel. (expensive)

4 My new sofa is comfortable. My old sofa was comfortable, too.
→ My new sofa is ______________________ the old one. (comfortable)

5 My dog can jump one meter high. Tom's dog can jump one meter high, too.
→ My dog can jump ______________________ Tom's dog can. (high)

E 우리말과 같은 뜻이 되도록 주어진 단어를 이용하여 문장을 완성하시오.

1 네 가방은 내 것만큼 무겁다. (heavy)
→ Your bag is ________ ________ ________ mine.

2 Nancy는 자신의 여동생보다 뚱뚱하다. (fat)
→ Nancy is ________ ________ her sister.

3 Charles는 자신의 아버지보다 많이 먹는다. (much)
→ Charles eats ________ ________ his father does.

4 지하철까지 가는 가장 빠른 길을 아니? (fast, way)
→ Do you know ________ ________ ________ to the subway station?

5 요즈음 한국에서 가장 인기 있는 노래가 무엇입니까? (popular, song)
→ What is ________ ________ ________ ________ in Korea nowadays?

UNIT 01 and, or, but, so

A 보기 에서 알맞은 접속사를 골라 문장을 완성하시오. [한 번씩만 쓸 것]

[1–4]

보기 or so but and

1 Jane can play both the piano ________ the violin.

2 Rod can speak Chinese, ________ he can't write it.

3 I was very hungry, ________ I went to the cafeteria.

4 Which do you want to do, swimming ________ golfing?

[5–8]

보기 or so but and

5 I wanted to help him, ________ I couldn't.

6 The book may be on the table ________ in the drawer.

7 Connie had to wash the dishes ________ do the laundry.

8 The room was very hot, ________ they turned on the air conditioner.

B 보기 에서 알맞은 접속사를 골라 두 문장을 한 문장으로 만드시오. [한 번씩만 쓸 것]

보기 or so but and

1 Do you want to play soccer? Do you want to play baseball?
→ Do you want to play soccer ________ ________?

2 Jack is a middle school student. Gale is a middle school student, too.
→ ________ ________ ________ are middle school students.

3 I was very tired. I went to bed early.
→ I was very tired, ________ ________ ________ ________ ________ ________.

4 James told me his phone number. I can't remember it.
→ James told me his phone number, ________ ________ ________ ________ ________.

C **보기** 에서 알맞은 표현을 골라 의미가 통하도록 문장을 완성하시오.

[1–4]

보기		
	so we went on a picnic	but you didn't answer
	or send me a text message	and won first prize

1 You can call me ______________________.

2 Laura entered the competition ______________________.

3 I called you many times ______________________.

4 It was sunny and bright, ______________________.

[5–8]

보기		
	and writing children's books	but he couldn't
	so I took a taxi	or chocolate cake

5 William tried to lift the box, ______________________.

6 This morning, I missed the subway, ______________________.

7 Which do you want, strawberry cake ______________________?

8 Rita likes teaching children ______________________.

D 우리말과 같은 뜻이 되도록 주어진 단어를 이용하여 문장을 완성하시오.

1 그 수프는 새콤달콤했다. (sweet, sour)
→ The soup was ______ ______ ______.

2 나는 친구를 만나서 함께 쇼핑하러 갈 거야. (go shopping)
→ I'm going to meet my friend ______ ______ ______ with her.

3 Jack은 두통이 있었다. 그래서, 그는 약을 먹었다. (take some medicine)
→ Jack got a headache, ______ ______ ______ ______ ______.

4 영화 보는 것과 저녁을 먹는 것 중에서 어떤 것을 원해? (have dinner)
→ Which do you prefer, watching a movie ______ ______ ______?

5 네가 그녀를 만난 것이 어제니 아니면 그저께니? (yesterday, the day before yesterday)
→ Did you meet her ______ ______ ______ ______ ______ ______?

6 나는 늦게 일어났다. 그래서 학교에 지각을 했다. (be late for)
→ I woke up late, ______ ______ ______ ______ ______ ______.

7 나는 영어에서는 A학점을 받았지만 수학에서는 F학점을 받았다. (an F, in math)
→ I got an A in English ______ ______ ______ ______ ______.

UNIT 02 when, before, after, until

A 우리말과 같은 뜻이 되도록 알맞은 접속사를 넣어 써 넣으시오.

1 잠자러 가기 전에 칫솔질을 해라.
→ Brush your teeth ________ you go to bed.

2 나는 그 소식을 들었을 때 매우 행복했다.
→ I was very happy ________ I heard the news.

3 나는 언제나 샤워를 하고 나서 아침을 먹는다.
→ I always have breakfast ________ I take a shower.

4 훈련을 시작하기 전에 스트레칭을 해라.
→ Stretch your body ________ you begin training.

5 내가 사무실을 나설 때 여전히 눈이 내리고 있었다.
→ ________ I left my office, it was still snowing.

6 나는 그 영화를 볼 때까지 그 배우를 몰랐다.
→ I didn't know the actor ________ I watched the movie.

7 그 책을 다 읽은 후에 나를 도와줄래?
→ Will you help me ________ you finish reading the book?

B 주어진 접속사를 이용하여 두 문장을 한 문장으로 만드시오.

1 I go jogging. I listen to music. (when)
→ ______________________________, I listen to music.

2 Take off your shoes. You come in. (before)
→ Take off your shoes ______________________________.

3 It stopped snowing. It started raining. (after)
→ ______________________________, it started raining.

4 Carol smiled at me. I smiled back at her. (when)
→ ______________________________, I smiled back at her.

5 You can borrow the book. I finish reading it. (after)
→ You can borrow the book ______________________________.

6 I looked for the document everywhere. I found it. (until)
→ I looked for the document everywhere ______________________________.

7 The singer drank a glass of water. She sang a song. (before)
→ The singer drank a glass of water ______________________________.

C 보기 에서 알맞은 표현을 골라 의미가 통하도록 문장을 완성하시오.

[1–4]

보기		
	after she gets the message	before it gets dark
	when he was in the USA	until the dough is golden brown

1 Leo worked as lawyer ______________________.

2 She will call you ______________________.

3 Bake the bread ______________________.

4 ______________________, we should finish taking pictures.

[5–8]

보기		
	after Daniel left home	before you go back to Korea
	when winter vacation comes	until she sends me an email

5 ______________________, I will wait.

6 ______________________, his mother arrived home.

7 I want to see you ______________________.

8 ______________________, I will visit my grandparents.

D 우리말과 같은 뜻이 되도록 주어진 단어를 이용하여 문장을 완성하시오.

1 네가 밖에 나가기 전에 컴퓨터를 끄렴. (go out)
→ Turn off the computer ______ ______ ______ ______.

2 나는 저녁을 먹은 후에 설거지를 했다. (have, dinner)
→ ______ ______ ______ ______, I washed the dishes.

3 나는 대학에 입학할 때까지 가족과 함께 살았다. (go to, university)
→ I lived with my family ______ ______ ______ ______ ______.

4 우리는 파리에 살 때 루브르 박물관에 여러 번 갔었다. (live in, Paris)
→ ______ ______ ______ ______ ______, we visited the Louvre many times.

5 네가 그 DVD를 본 후에 내가 그것을 빌릴 수 있을까? (watch, the DVD)
→ ______ ______ ______ ______ ______, can I borrow it?

UNIT 03 because, if, that

A 우리말과 같은 뜻이 되도록 because, if, that 중 알맞은 접속사를 써 넣으시오.

1 네가 원하면 우리 내일 만나자.
→ Let's meet tomorrow ________ you want.

2 나는 Anna가 노래를 잘한다는 것을 몰랐다.
→ I didn't know ________ Anna sings well.

3 그는 유럽으로 여행을 갈 수 있기를 희망한다.
→ He hopes ________ he can go on a trip to Europe.

4 내일 비가 오면 나는 약속을 취소할 것이다.
→ ________ it rains tomorrow, I will cancel my appointment.

5 오늘은 공휴일이라서 은행이 문을 열지 않는다.
→ The bank doesn't open today ________ it's a national holiday.

6 Larry는 여자 친구에게 선물을 받아서 매우 기뻤다.
→ Larry was very happy ________ he got a present from his girlfriend.

B 주어진 접속사를 이용하여 한 문장을 두 문장으로 만드시오.

1 You can finish the work on time. I believe it. (that)
→ I believe ______________________________.

2 Ask your teacher. You have any questions about that. (if)
→ Ask your teacher ______________________________.

3 Christina couldn't come to the party. She was very busy. (because)
→ Christina couldn't come to the party ______________________________.

C 보기 에서 알맞은 표현을 골라 의미가 통하도록 문장을 완성하시오.

보기
because he was sick
that people always want to be happy
if you wear this suit

1 You'll look a lot better ______________________________.

2 Adam didn't go to work ______________________________.

3 It is true ______________________________.

D **우리말과 같은 뜻이 되도록 주어진 단어와 접속사를 이용하여 문장을 완성하시오.**

1 네가 원한다면 가져도 돼. (want)
→ You can have it ________ ________ ________.

2 Leo는 피곤했기 때문에 오늘 집에 일찍 갔다. (be, tired)
→ Leo went home early today ________ ________ ________ ________.

3 Jason은 자신이 영국에서 왔다고 말했다. (come from, England)
→ Jason said ________ ________ ________ ________ ________.

4 나는 그녀가 수영을 잘한다고 생각한다. (be good at)
→ I think ________ ________ ________ ________ ________ swimming.

5 나는 네 전화번호를 몰랐기 때문에 전화를 걸 수 없었어. (know, phone number)
→ I couldn't call you ________ ________ ________ ________ ________ ________ ________.

6 너희가 함께 일한다면, 너희는 그 일을 빨리 마칠 수 있을 거야. (work, together)
→ ________ ________ ________ ________, you will be able to finish the work quickly.

E **우리말과 같은 뜻이 되도록 주어진 단어를 배열하시오.**

1 그는 그 그림이 매우 멋있다고 생각한다. (nice, the picture, is, very, that)
→ He thinks ________________________________.

2 그는 또 거짓말을 해서 곤경에 처하게 되었다. (a lie, he, again, because, told)
→ He got in trouble ________________________________.

3 나는 오늘이 오빠의 생일이라는 것을 잊어버렸다. (today, my brother's birthday, is, that)
→ I forgot ________________________________.

4 교과서를 안 가져왔으면, 내 것을 같이 봐도 돼. (you, your textbook, bring, didn't, if)
→ ________________________________, you can share mine.

5 제시간에 도착하지 않으면 그들은 너를 입장시켜 주지 않을 거야. (you, on time, arrive, don't, if)
→ ________________________________, they won't let you in.

6 그녀는 나의 가장 친한 친구이니까 나는 기꺼이 그녀를 도울 것이다. (she, my best friend, is, because)
→ ________________________________, I am willing to help her.

장소를 나타내는 전치사

A 두 문장에 공통으로 들어갈 알맞은 전치사를 써 넣으시오.

1 • Mike grew up __________ a small town.
  • Jack was __________ Paris during the holiday.

2 • I'm going to meet her __________ the theater.
  • I'm planning to stay __________ home tonight.

3 • The staff put the paintings __________ the wall.
  • The lady sitting __________ the chair is Mrs. Smith.

B 그림을 보고, 보기 에서 알맞은 전치사를 골라 문장을 완성하시오.

1

보기 under over

What a nice drawing! Look at the rainbow __________ the bridge. The boat __________ the bridge looks nice.

2

보기 behind in front of

This is a picture of my family __________ our house. You can see my brother standing __________ the dog.

3

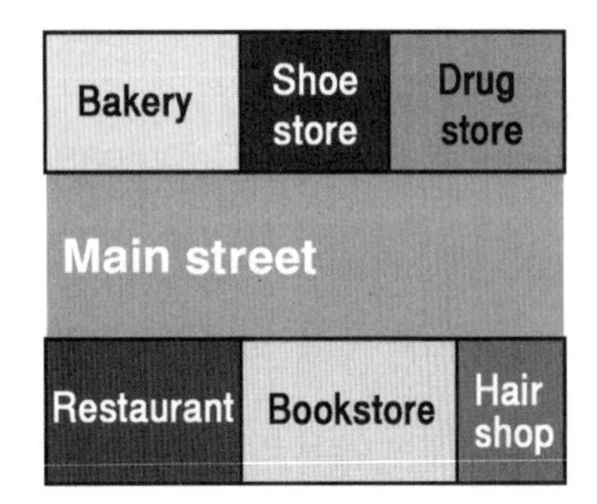

보기 next to between across from

Let me tell you about my neighborhood. There is a bookstore __________ the restaurant and the hair shop, and the shoe store is __________ the bakery. Also, my favorite restaurant is __________ the bakery.

C 우리말과 같은 뜻이 되도록 주어진 단어를 이용하여 문장을 완성하시오.

1 너 어젯밤 파티에 있었니? (the party)
→ Were you ________ ________ ________ last night?

2 네 옆에 앉아 있는 저 소녀는 누구니? (you)
→ Who is that girl sitting ________ ________ ________?

3 우리 고모는 로스앤젤레스에 산다. (Los Angeles)
→ My aunt lives ________ ________ ________.

4 Eddie는 바닥에 유리잔을 떨어뜨렸다. (the floor)
→ Eddie dropped the glass ________ ________ ________.

5 그 고양이는 담장 위로 뛰어 달아났다. (the fence)
→ The cat jumped ________ ________ ________ and ran away.

6 그 선생님 뒤에 있는 저 남자애가 전학생이야. (the teacher)
→ That boy ________ ________ ________ is the new student.

7 저기를 봐! 큰 나무 아래에 잠자는 남자가 한 명 있어. (the big tree)
→ Look at that! There is a man sleeping ________ ________ ________ ________.

D 우리말과 같은 뜻이 되도록 주어진 단어를 배열하시오.

1 조심해! 네 앞에 큰 구덩이가 있어. (front, you, in, of, a huge hole)
→ Be careful! There is ________________________________.

2 나는 그 등을 침대 옆에 놓을 거야. (the bed, the lamp, put, beside)
→ I will ________________________________.

3 우리 강아지는 내 옆에서 자는 걸 좋아한다. (me, to, next, sleeping)
→ My puppy likes ________________________________.

4 핼러윈에 나는 머리부터 발끝까지 검정색 옷을 입었다. (top, from, toe, to)
→ For Halloween, I dressed in black ________________________________.

5 우리는 도서관 맞은편에 있는 공원에서 산책을 했다. (the library, from, the park, across, at)
→ We took a walk ________________________________.

6 검정색 밴과 스포츠카 사이에 주차 공간이 있어. (the black van, the sports car, and, between)
→ There is a parking space ________________________________.

7 그들은 도심지 근처에 식당을 개업하려고 계획 중이다. (the downtown area, near, a restaurant)
→ They are planning to open ________________________________.

UNIT 02 시간을 나타내는 전치사

A 빈칸에 at, on, in 중 알맞은 전치사를 골라 문장을 완성하시오.

1 Do you have snow ________ April?
2 Let's talk about it ________ dinnertime.
3 Nowadays, I cannot sleep well ________ night.
4 Do you have special plans ________ Tuesday?
5 The workshop will be held ________ April 22nd.
6 Our school day ends ________ 5:30 in the afternoon.
7 My family usually watches TV ________ the evening.
8 I enjoy skiing and snowboarding ________ winter.
9 I'm going to meet my old friends ________ Christmas Day.

B by와 until 중 알맞은 전치사를 골라 문장을 완성하시오.

1 Maria lived in Spain ________ 2012.
2 I have to return the book ________ Saturday.
3 You should make a decision ________ tomorrow.
4 I'm going to study for the exam ________ 12 am.

C during과 for 중 알맞은 전치사를 골라 문장을 완성하시오.

1 Try to work out ________ at least 30 minutes a day.
2 I was in the hospital ________ the winter vacation.
3 It is usually snowing heavily here ________ the month of February.
4 Harry takes a ballet lesson ________ an hour on Thursdays.

D **우리말과 같은 뜻이 되도록 주어진 단어를 이용하여 문장을 완성하시오.**

1 Jennifer는 금요일까지 휴가이다. (Friday)
→ Jennifer is on holiday ________ ________.

2 그는 네 시 이후에 돌아올 거예요. (four o'clock)
→ He will be back ________ ________ ________.

3 너는 아홉 시 전에 공항에 도착해야 해. (nine)
→ You should arrive at the airport ________ ________.

4 한국의 여름은 보통 덥고 습하다. (summer)
→ In Korea, it's usually hot and humid ________ ________.

5 야구 시즌은 4월부터 10월까지이다. (April, October)
→ The baseball season is ________ ________ ________ ________.

6 미국 사람들은 추수감사절에 칠면조를 먹는다. (Thanksgiving Day)
→ Americans eat turkey ________ ________ ________.

7 회사는 크리스마스와 새해 사이에 문을 닫을 것이다. (Christmas, New Year)
→ The company will be closed ________ ________ ________ ________ ________.

E **우리말과 같은 뜻이 되도록 주어진 단어를 배열하시오.**

1 방과 후에 친구들과 축구를 할 거니? (school, soccer, play, after)
→ Are you going to ________________________________?

2 Liz는 언제나 밤 아홉 시까지 사무실에 있다. (at, nine o'clock, night, until)
→ Liz always stays at the office ________________________________.

3 그 라디오 프로그램은 오후 두 시에 시작한다. (two, the afternoon, in, at)
→ The radio show starts ________________________________.

4 그 은행은 수요일에는 여덟 시에 문을 닫는다. (8 pm, Wednesday, on, at)
→ The bank closes ________________________________.

5 나는 6월부터 8월까지 유럽 전역을 여행할 것이다. (June, August, to, from)
→ I will travel around Europe ________________________________.

6 우리는 수업 중에 15분 동안 다큐멘터리를 보았다. (for, the class, 15 minutes, during)
→ ________________, we watched a documentary film ________________.

7 나는 저녁 식사 전에 아버지의 차를 세차해야 한다. (my father's car, dinner, before, wash)
→ I have to ________________________________.

UNIT 03 기타 전치사

A 보기 에서 알맞은 전치사를 골라 문장을 완성하시오. [한 번씩만 쓸 것]

[1–4]

보기 by for with to

1 They decided to move ________ London.
2 Could you open the door ________ me?
3 We can do lots of things ________ computers.
4 How long does it take to get to your office ________ car?

[5–8]

보기 about by for with

5 Anne made some food ________ us.
6 Would you like to have dinner ________ me?
7 The tower was designed ________ Gustave Eiffel.
8 You need to think ________ the questions beforehand.

B 두 문장에 공통으로 들어갈 알맞은 전치사를 써 넣으시오.

1 · Have you heard ________ the yellow dust?
· I know that they were talking ________ me.

2 · Spanish is spoken ________ millions of people around the world.
· The students go to school ________ school bus.

3 · I'm planning to go on a trip ________ my best friend.
· Jack made a doghouse ________ his father.

4 · I went ________ the supermarket to buy some milk.
· She read a book ________ her children before they went to bed.

C 우리말과 같은 뜻이 되도록 주어진 단어를 이용하여 문장을 완성하시오.

1 네 전화번호를 Chris한테서 받았어. (Chris)
→ I got your phone number ________ ________.

2 이 향수는 장미 냄새가 난다. (smell, roses)
→ This perfume ________ ________ ________.

3 당신은 부산에 KTX를 타고 오셨나요? (Busan, the KTX)
→ Did you come ________ ________ ________ ________ ________?

4 그녀를 만나면 그 책을 줄게. (she)
→ I'll give the book ________ ________ when I meet her.

5 왕은 여왕을 위해서 그 사원을 지었다. (his queen)
→ The king built the temple ________ ________ ________.

6 Mandy는 나에게 자신의 꿈에 대해 말해 주었다. (her dream)
→ Mandy told me ________ ________ ________.

7 Jeremy는 젓가락으로 국수를 먹으려고 애썼지만, 먹을 수 없었다. (chopsticks)
→ Jeremy tried to eat noodles ________ ________, but he couldn't.

D 우리말과 같은 뜻이 되도록 주어진 단어를 배열하시오.

1 우리 언니는 붉은 색 스웨터를 입고 있다. (in, sweater, is, red, a)
→ My sister ________________________________.

2 나는 그에 관해 아무것도 모른다. (anything, him, know, about, don't)
→ I ________________________________.

3 나는 어머니를 위해 생일 선물을 샀다. (my mother, for, a birthday gift)
→ I bought ________________________________.

4 Charlie의 할아버지가 Charlie에게 선물을 보냈다. (Charlie, a present, sent, to)
→ Charlie's grandfather ________________________________.

5 Sue는 기숙사에서 룸메이트와 함께 산다. (a dormitory, a roommate, in, lives with)
→ Sue ________________________________.

6 이 식당에서는 신용카드로 지불해도 됩니다. (in, credit card, by, pay, this restaurant)
→ You can ________________________________.

7 그녀는 핼러윈에 백설공주처럼 입었다. (Snow White, like, dressed, for Halloween)
→ She ________________________________.

Memo

새 교과서 반영
중등 내신 완벽 대비서
GRAMMAR 공감

- 최신 교과서의 학습 내용을 반영한 **체계적인 문법 설명**
- 2,500여 개의 전국 중학교 기출 문제 완전 분석 후 **문법 포인트, 문제 반영**
- 공부감각을 업그레이드 시켜주는 다양한 **서술형 평가 코너 수록 및 워크북 제공**
- 놓치기 쉬운 문법 포인트를 잡아 주는 **Plus α, Tips 코너 수록**
- 말하기, 쓰기, 읽기의 실용적 쓰임을 생각한 **통합형 문법 학습**
- 2,000여 개 이상의 충분한 문제풀이를 통한 **문법 감각 향상**

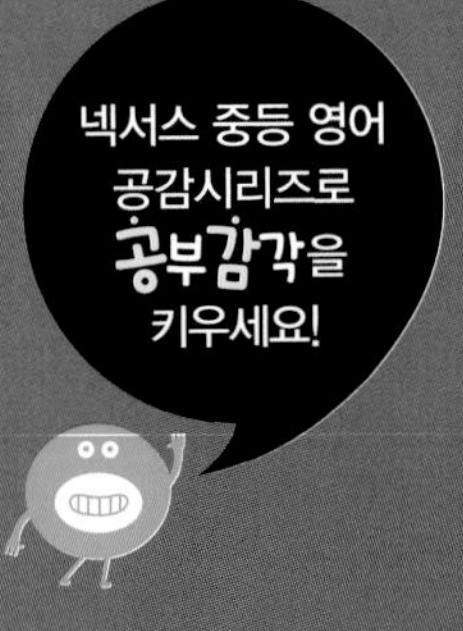

NEXUS makes your next day
www.nexusEDU.kr | 책에 대해 궁금한 사항은 넥서스에듀 홈페이지 1:1 **고객상담 게시판**을 이용하세요.

초1 | 초2 | 초3 | 초4 | 초5 | 초6 | 중1 | 중2 | 중3 | 고1 | 고2 | 고3

영역	교재	대상 학년
Writing	공감 영문법+쓰기 1~2	초4 ~ 중1
Writing	도전만점 중등내신 서술형 1~4	초6 ~ 중3
Writing	영어일기 영작패턴 1-A, B · 2-A, B	초4 ~ 중2
Writing	Smart Writing 1~2	초4 ~ 중3
Reading	Reading 101 1~3	초5 ~ 중3
Reading	Reading 공감 1~3	초5 ~ 중3
Reading	This Is Reading Starter 1~3	초5 ~ 중3
Reading	This Is Reading 전면 개정판 1~4	초6 ~ 고1
Reading	원서 술술 읽는 Smart Reading Basic 1~2	초6 ~ 중3
Reading	원서 술술 읽는 Smart Reading 1~2	중3 ~ 고2
Reading	[특급 단기 특강] 구문독해 · 독해유형	중3 ~ 고3
Reading	[앱솔루트 수능대비 영어독해 기출분석] 2019~2021학년도	고1 ~ 고3
Listening	Listening 공감 1~3	초6 ~ 중2
Listening	The Listening 1~4	초5 ~ 중2
Listening	넥서스 중학 영어듣기 모의고사 25회 1~3	초6 ~ 중2
Listening	도전! 만점 중학 영어듣기 모의고사 1~3	초6 ~ 중2
Listening	만점 적중 수능 듣기 모의고사 20회 · 35회	중3 ~ 고2
TEPS	NEW TEPS 입문편 실전 250+ 청해 · 문법 · 독해	초5 ~ 중3
TEPS	NEW TEPS 기본편 실전 300+ 청해 · 문법 · 독해	초6 ~ 고1
TEPS	NEW TEPS 실력편 실전 400+ 청해 · 문법 · 독해	중1 ~ 고2
TEPS	NEW TEPS 마스터편 실전 500+ 청해 · 문법 · 독해	중2 ~ 고3

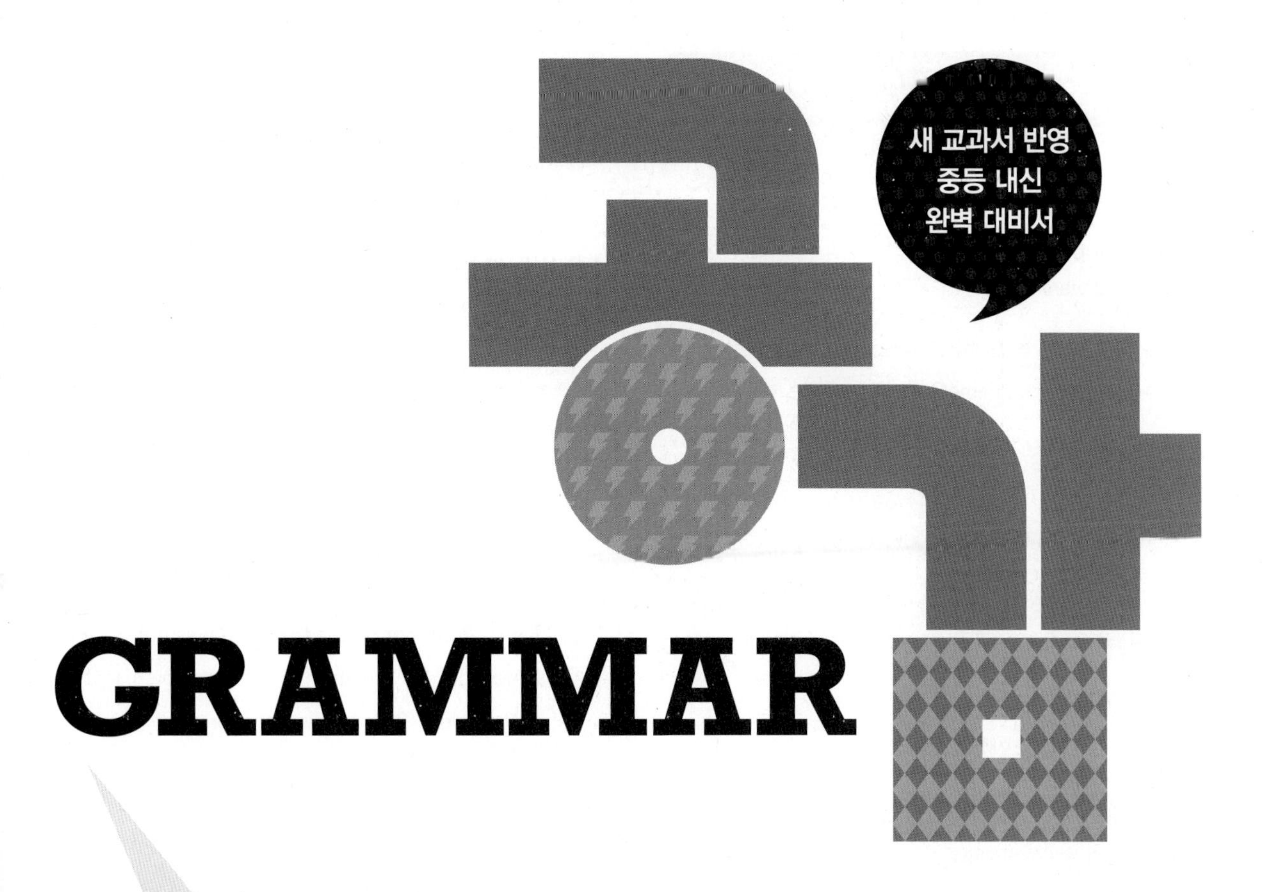

Level 1

NEXUS Edu

Chapter 01

UNIT 01

Check-up P. 008

1 am 2 were

1 주어는 I, today는 현재를 나타내는 부사

2 주어는 You, at that time은 과거를 나타내는 부사구

: EXERCISES P. 009

Ⓐ 1 is 2 am 3 are 4 is 5 are

Ⓑ 1 It's 2 You're 3 He's 4 We're 5 I'm

Ⓒ 1 was 2 were 3 was 4 was 5 were

Ⓓ 1 He, is 2 It, is 3 They, are 4 We, were 5 I, was

A

1 He와 함께 쓰는 현재형 be동사는 is
그는 호주 출신이다.

2 I와 함께 쓰는 현재형 be동사는 am
나는 여기 새로 온 학생이다.

3 They와 함께 쓰는 현재형 be동사는 are
그들은 자신의 아들을 자랑스러워한다.

4 She와 함께 쓰는 현재형 be동사는 is
그녀는 나의 영어 선생님이다.

5 You와 함께 쓰는 현재형 be동사는 are
너는 훌륭한 축구 선수이다.

B

1 그것은 나의 배낭이다.

2 너는 훌륭한 요리사이다.

3 그는 쇼핑몰에 있다.

4 우리는 시험을 볼 준비가 되어 있다.

5 나는 축구팀의 일원이다.

C

1 It과 함께 쓰는 과거형 be동사는 was
그것은 슬픈 이야기였다.

2 They와 함께 쓰는 과거형 be동사는 were
그들은 경기에서 라이벌이었다.

3 I와 함께 쓰는 과거형 be동사는 was
나는 어제 학교에 늦었다.

4 He와 함께 쓰는 과거형 be동사는 was
그는 작년에 나의 담임이었다.

5 John and Peter는 3인칭 복수, 3인칭 복수와 함께 쓰는 과거형 be동사는 were
John과 Peter는 방금 복도에 있었다.

UNIT 02

Check-up P. 010

1 aren't 2 Is

1 They와 함께 쓰는 현재형 be동사의 부정형은 aren't

2 she와 함께 쓰는 현재형 be동사는 is

: EXERCISES P. 011

Ⓐ 1 isn't 2 Was 3 Is 4 aren't 5 Are

Ⓑ 1 Are 2 am not 3 Was 4 Is 5 was not

Ⓒ 1 Are, you 2 Were, they 3 Was, the, math, test

Ⓓ 1 Were, you 2 The, musicians, are, not
3 Is, the, notebook, it, is

A

1 My friend는 3인칭 단수
내 친구는 거짓말쟁이가 아니다.

2 your diary는 3인칭 단수
너의 다이어리가 책상 위에 있었니?

3 Mr. Lyons는 3인칭 단수
Lyons 씨가 너의 수학 선생님이시니?

4 My parents and I는 1인칭 복수
나의 부모님과 나는 런던에 있지 않다.

5 these colored pencils는 3인칭 복수
그 통에 있는 이 색연필들은 너의 것이니?

B

1 now는 현재를 의미하므로 Were가 아니라 Are가 적절
너 지금 한가하니?

2 am not은 줄여 쓸 수 없음
나는 우리 반 1등이 아니다.

3 last Sunday는 과거를 의미하므로 Is가 아니라 Was가 적절
Jamie는 지난 일요일에 병원에 있었니?

4 your school은 3인칭 단수이므로 Are가 아니라 Is가 적절
너의 학교는 집에서 멀리 떨어져 있니?

5 be동사의 부정문은 「주어+be동사+not」이므로 not was가 아니라 was not이 적절
나의 남동생은 귀신을 무서워하지 않았다.

C

1 am으로 답했으므로 현재로 물어야 함
A 너는 축구를 잘 하니?
B 응, 그래. 나는 매일 축구 연습을 해.

2 weren't로 답했으므로 과거로 물어야 함
A 그들이 회의에 늦었니?
B 아니, 그렇지 않았어. 그들은 제시간에 왔어.

3 wasn't로 답했으므로 과거로 물어야 함
A 수학 시험은 어려웠니?
B 아니, 그렇지 않았어. 쉬웠어.

UNIT 03

Check-up P. 012
1 my **2** are

1 '나의 노트북 컴퓨터'라는 의미이므로 my가 적절

2 「There are + 복수 명사(two puppies)」

: EXERCISES P. 013

A **1** Is **2** Are **3** are **4** was **5** weren't
B **1** our **2** They **3** Her **4** yours **5** me
C **1** her, hers **2** They, them **3** He, His
D **1** is, hers **2** There, is, a, calendar
3 There, was, a, speech, contest

A

1 「Is there + 단수 명사(a problem)?」
문제가 있나요?

2 「Are there + 복수 명사(books)?」
책장에 책들이 있나요?

3 「There are + 복수 명사(some kids)」
운동장에 몇 명의 아이들이 있다.

4 「There was + 단수 명사(a terrible storm)」
지난밤에 엄청난 폭풍이 있었다.

5 「There weren't + 복수 명사(any teachers)」
그 당시 학교에 교사들이 한 명도 없었다.

B

1 '우리의 영어 선생님'이라는 뜻이므로 us가 아니라 our가 적절
그 남자는 우리의 영어 선생님이다.

2 '그들은'이라는 의미이므로 Their가 아니라 They가 적절
그들은 일본에서 온 학생들이다.

3 '그녀의 이름'이라는 의미이므로 Hers가 아니라 Her가 적절
그녀는 나의 이웃이다. 그녀의 이름은 Helen이다.

4 '너의 것'이라는 의미이므로 you가 아니라 yours가 적절
파란색 재킷은 내 것이고 빨간색 재킷은 너의 것이다.

5 '나를'이라는 의미이므로 I가 아니라 me가 적절
그와 나는 같은 반이나. 그는 나를 매우 잘 안다.

C

1 Nancy는 여성 3인칭 단수, her, hers으로 바꿔 쓸 수 있음
이것은 Nancy의 그림이다. 저것 또한 Nancy의 것이다.
→ 이것은 그녀의 그림이다. 저것 또한 그녀의 것이다.

2 Jess and Mike는 3인칭 복수, They, them으로 쓸 수 있음
Jess와 Mike는 재미있다. 모두 Jess와 Mike를 좋아한다.
→ 그들은 재미있다. 모두가 그들을 좋아한다.

3 Brian은 남성 3인칭 단수, He, His로 바꿔 쓸 수 있음
Brian은 나의 가장 친한 친구이다. Brian의 취미는 독서이다.
→ 그는 나의 가장 친한 친구이다. 그의 취미는 독서이다.

: Review Test P. 014

01 ④	02 ①	03 ③	04 ⑤	05 ③
06 ③	07 ②	08 ①	09 ②	10 ③
11 ①	12 ②	13 ⑤	14 ①	15 ④

01 you와 함께 쓰는 be동사는 Are, '아니, 나는 그렇지 않아'라고 대답해야 하므로 I'm이 적절
A 너 피곤하니? B 아니, 그렇지 않아. 나는 괜찮아.

02 Sam은 3인칭 단수, 3인칭 단수와 함께 쓰는 be동사는 Is, No가 왔으므로 isn't가 적절
A Sam은 집에 있니? B 아니, 없어. 그는 학교에 있어.

03 be동사의 부정문: 「주어 + be동사(are)+ not」
Jim과 나는 오늘 같은 팀이다 / 같은 팀이 아니다.

04 「She + was + 과거 부사구(last summer)」
그녀는 작년 여름에 하와이에 있었다.

05 「There aren't + 복수 명사(many visitors)+ 현재 부사(now)」
지금 화랑에는 방문객이 많지 않다.

06 「We / You / 3인칭 복수 + are」, Ben and I, The twins, They, My cousins는 3인칭 복수, Wendy는 3인칭 단수
Ben과 나는/쌍둥이는/그들은/내 사촌들은 중학교 학생들이다.

07 「Is + 3인칭 단수~?」, he, she, the baby, your sister는 3인칭 단수, they는 3인칭 복수
그는/그녀는/아기는/네 여동생은 지금 너의 집에 있니?

08 「There are + 복수 명사(lots of tourists)」, 「There is + 단수 명사(a big tower)」
• 그 사원에 많은 관광객이 있다.
• 그 도시에 큰 탑이 하나 있다.

09 「3인칭 단수(My brother)+was+과거 부사구(last year)」, 「3인칭 단수(He)+is+현재 부사(now)」
나의 남동생은 작년에 일곱 살이었다. 그는 지금 여덟 살이다.

10 ③ '나의 반 친구'라는 의미이므로 mine이 아니라 my가 적절
① 그녀의 이름이 명단에 있었다.
② 나는 Brown 씨를 안다. 그녀는 나의 선생님이다.
③ Oliver는 나의 반 친구이다.
④ 그 지갑은 당신의 것이 아니다. 그것은 그녀의 것이다.
⑤ 그 편지는 그에게 특별한 것이었다.

11 각각의 빈칸에 '그는', '그의', '그를'이라는 의미의 단어가 들어가야 하므로 He, His, him이 적절
Harry는 나의 가장 친한 친구이다. 그는 영국 출신이다. 그의 취미는 축구이다. 그와 나는 같은 축구팀에 있다. 나는 그를 매우 좋아한다.

12 you(너)로 물었으므로 I(나)로 대답해야 하고, '아니, 나는 바쁘지 않았어.'라는 의미의 답이 와야 하므로 'No, I wasn't.'가 적절, Yes 뒤에는 긍정이, No 뒤에는 부정이 와야 함
A 너 어제 바빴니?
B 아니, 안 그랬어. 나는 온종일 한가했어.

13 모퉁이에 있다고 했으므로 긍정의 응답인 'Yes, there is.'가 적절, 주어가 단수이고, 현재 시제이므로 are나 was는 올 수 없음
A 이 근처에 우체국이 있나요?
B 네, 있어요. 모퉁이에 있어요.

[14-15]
우리 가족은 아버지와 어머니, 쌍둥이 남동생들, 나 이렇게 다섯 명이다. 우리 부모님께서는 선생님이시다. 쌍둥이 남동생들은 아홉 살이다. 그들은 활발하다. 그들이 가장 좋아하는 놀이는 숨바꼭질이다. 그들은 귀엽다. 나는 그들을 매우 좋아한다.

14 ⓐ와 ⓑ에 각각 '그들의', '그들을'이라는 의미의 단어가 들어가야 하므로 ⓐ에는 Their, ⓑ에는 them이 적절

15 '우리 가족에는 다섯 명이 있다.'라는 의미의 표현으로 「There are+복수 명사+in ~」(~에 …이 있다)을 사용

: 서술형 평가 P. 016

01 Its, It's, it
02 my pen
03 I was
04 mine[my (student) card]
05 Is the store open today?
06 It wasn't[was not] a holiday yesterday.
07 There were many cars on the road.
08 They're, They are, they were, They weren't, they are, They are
09 No, he wasn't. He was at home.
10 No, he isn't. He is in the library.

01 각각의 빈칸에 '그것의', '그것은 ~이다', '그것을'이라는 의미의 단어가 들어가야 하므로 'Its', 'It's', 'It'이 적절, 문장의 첫 글자는 대문자로 시작
새끼 고양이를 잃어버렸어요. 그것의 이름은 Prince예요. 그것은 하얀색이에요. 그것은 작고 귀여워요. 제발 제가 그것을 찾도록 도와주세요.

02 소유대명사: 「소유격+명사」
A 실례합니다만, 이것은 당신의 펜인가요?
B 네. 그것은 제 것이에요. 고맙습니다.

03 'you(너)'로 물었으므로 응답으로는 you were가 아니라 I was가 적절
A 너는 지난 일요일에 야구장에 있었니?
B 네, 그랬어요. 나는 경기를 정말 재미있게 봤어요.

04 '나의 학생증'이라는 의미이므로 my가 아니라 소유대명사(mine)가 적절, mine은 my (student) card로 바꿔 쓸 수 있음
A 이것은 너의 학생증이니?
B 아니요, 그것은 제 것이 아니에요.

05 be동사의 의문문: 「be동사+주어~?」
그 가게는 오늘 문을 연다. → 그 가게는 오늘 문을 여나요?

06 be동사의 부정문: 「주어+be동사+not」
어제는 휴일이었다. → 어제는 휴일이 아니었다.

07 「There were+복수 명사(many cars)」 ~이 있었다
모퉁이에서 차 사고가 있었어요. 도로에 차들이 많았어요. 하지만 신호등이 없었어요.

08 「I+am / was / wasn't」 → 「They+are / were / weren't」
나는 열세 살이다. 나는 지금은 건강하지만, 작년에 매우 아팠다. 나는 행복하지 않았다. 이제 나는 건강하다. 나는 행복하다.
→ 그들은 열세 살이다. 그들은 지금 건강하지만, 작년에는 매우 아팠다. 그들은 행복하지 않았다. 이제 그들은 건강하다. 그들은 행복하다.

09 Peter는 어제 도서관에 있지 않았으므로, 부정의 답이 적절
Peter는 어제 도서관에 있었나요?
→ 아니요, 없었어요. 그는 집에 있었어요.

10 Josh는 오늘 집에 없으므로 부정의 답이 적절
Josh는 오늘 집에 있나요?
→ 아니요, 없어요. 그는 도서관에 있어요.

Chapter 02

UNIT 01

Check-up P. 018
1 cries **2** learn **3** washes

1 The baby는 3인칭 단수, 「자음+y → ies」

2 They는 3인칭 복수, 「3인칭 복수+동사원형」

3 He는 3인칭 단수, 「sh로 끝나는 동사+es」

: EXERCISES P. 019

Ⓐ 1 fly 2 pray 3 speaks 4 watches 5 wash

Ⓑ 1 has 2 loves 3 fixes 4 go 5 worry

Ⓒ 1 studies, draws 2 plays, goes 3 takes, cleans

Ⓓ 1 My, school, starts 2 he, exercises
3 Ron, and, his, brother, play

Ⓐ

1 「3인칭 복수(The birds)+동사원형」
그 새들은 남쪽으로 날아간다.

2 「1인칭 단수(I)+동사원형」
나는 할머니를 위해 기도한다.

3 Andy는 3인칭 단수, 「대부분의 동사+s」
Andy는 영어를 잘한다.

4 She는 3인칭 단수, 「ch로 끝나는 동사+es」
그녀는 저녁 식사 후에 텔레비전을 본다.

5 「3인칭 복수(Ron and Mary)+동사원형」
Ron과 Mary는 설거지를 한다.

Ⓑ

1 My brother(나의 남동생)는 3인칭 단수, have → has
나의 남동생은 감기에 걸려 있다.

2 Kathy는 3인칭 단수, 대부분의 동사+s
Kathy는 피자를 매우 많이 좋아한다.

3 He는 3인칭 단수, 「x로 끝나는 동사+es」
그는 남동생의 컴퓨터를 고친다.

4 「3인칭 복수(Jerry and Ian)+동사원형」
Jerry와 Ian은 함께 쇼핑을 간다.

5 「3인칭 복수(My parents)+동사원형」
우리 부모님은 나의 미래에 대해서 걱정한다.

Ⓒ

[1-3] Andy, Sarah는 3인칭 단수, 「자음+y → ies: studies」, 「대부분의 동사+s: draws, plays, takes, cleans」, 「o로 끝나는 동사+es: goes」

1 금요일에 Andy는 영어를 공부하고 Sarah는 그림을 그린다.

2 토요일에 Andy는 축구를 하고 Sarah는 하이킹을 간다.

3 일요일에 Andy는 남동생을 돌보고 Sarah는 집을 청소한다.

UNIT 02

Check-up P. 020

1 won 2 mopped 3 hurried

1 win은 불규칙 변화 동사

2 「단모음+단자음으로 끝나는 동사 → 자음을 한 번 더 쓰고+ed」

3 「자음+y → ied」

: EXERCISES P. 021

Ⓐ 1 hit 2 danced 3 has 4 carried 5 lives

Ⓑ took, played, went, read

Ⓒ 1 cut 2 said 3 went 4 woke up

Ⓓ 1 left, for, London 2 ate, a, sandwich
3 closed, made, a, wish

Ⓐ

1 hit는 불규칙 변화 동사
Harry가 어제 머리를 부딪쳤다.

2 last night은 과거를 나타내는 부사구
그들은 지난밤에 음악에 맞춰 춤을 췄다.

3 now는 현재를 나타내는 부사
우리 형은 지금 빨간 스포츠카를 소유하고 있다.

4 an hour ago는 과거를 나타내는 부사구
그는 한 시간 전에 상자들을 날랐다.

5 now는 현재를 나타내는 부사
우리 가족은 지금 작은 섬에서 살고 있다.

Ⓑ 오늘 하루 동안 일어난 일을 나타내는 글이므로 과거 시제가 적절, take의 과거형은 took, play의 과거형은 played, go의 과거형은 went, read[ri:d] 의 과거형은 read[red]
8월 8일, 금요일
오늘 나는 즐거운 하루를 보냈다. 나는 아침에 산책을 했다. 오후에는 피아노를 쳤다. 저녁에 내 친구 Beth와 나는 극장에 갔다. 밤에 나는 책을 읽었다. 지금 나는 매우 행복하다.

Ⓒ

1 cut의 과거형: cut
그는 수박을 반으로 잘랐다.

2 say의 과거형: said
그 학생들은 선생님에게 인사를 했다.

3 go의 과거형: went
그녀는 아파서 병원에 갔다.

4 wake의 과거형: woke
그는 늦게 일어나서 학교에 늦었다.

UNIT 03

Check-up P. 022
1 doesn't **2** like **3** don't **4** don't **5** watch **6** doesn't

1 「3인칭 단수(Sho) + doesn't」
2 「doesn't + 동사원형」
3 「3인칭 복수(They) + don't」
4 「1인칭 단수(I) + don't」
5 「didn't + 동사원형」
6 「3인칭 단수(My brother) + doesn't」

: EXERCISES P. 023

Ⓐ **1** don't **2** doesn't **3** didn't **4** didn't **5** doesn't
Ⓑ **1** doesn't tell **2** doesn't wear **3** don't get up **4** don't like **5** don't play
Ⓒ **1** I didn't have pizza **2** It didn't rain hard **3** Sandra didn't invite Chris
Ⓓ **1** I, didn't, sleep, well **2** Jack, doesn't, work **3** don't, wear, school, uniforms

A

1 「1인칭 단수(I) + don't」
나는 요즈음 아침 식사를 하지 않는다.

2 「3인칭 단수(Susan) + doesn't」
Susan은 그 수업을 이해하지 못한다.

3 일반동사 과거형의 부정문은 주어에 관계없이 didn't를 사용
우리는 지난달에 박물관을 방문하지 않았다.

4 일반동사 과거형의 부정문은 주어에 관계없이 didn't를 사용
Jenny는 지난해에 기숙사에 머물지 않았다.

5 「3인칭 단수(he) + doesn't」
Tony는 록 음악은 좋아하지만 클래식 음악은 좋아하지 않는다.

B

1 「3인칭 단수(She) + doesn't + 동사원형」
그녀는 거짓말을 하지 않는다.

2 「3인칭 단수(John) + doesn't + 동사원형」
John은 안경을 쓰지 않는다.

3 「1인칭 단수(I) + don't + 동사원형」
나는 아침에 일찍 일어나지 않는다.

4 「3인칭 복수(They) + don't + 동사원형」
그들은 컴퓨터 게임을 좋아하지 않는다.

5 「1인칭 복수(We) + don't + 동사원형」
우리는 방과 후에 보드게임을 하지 않는다.

C

[1-3] 일반동사 과거형의 부정문: 「didn't + 동사원형」

1 나는 저녁으로 피자를 먹었다.
→ 나는 저녁으로 피자를 먹지 않았다.

2 오늘 아침에 비가 많이 왔다.
→ 오늘 아침에 비가 많이 오지 않았다.

3 Sandra는 Chris를 자신의 생일 파티에 초대했다.
→ Sandra는 Chris를 자신의 생일 파티에 초대하지 않았다.

UNIT 04

Check-up P. 024
1 Did **2** Do **3** Do **4** Does

1 last night은 과거 부사구, 「Did + 주어 + 동사원형 ~?」
2 now는 현재 부사, 「Do + 2인칭 (you) + 동사원형 ~?」
3 일반동사 현재형의 의문문: 「Do + 2인칭(you) + 동사원형 ~?」
4 「Does + 3인칭 단수(your grandmother) + 동사원형 ~?」

: EXERCISES P. 025

Ⓐ **1** Do, need **2** Does, know **3** Does, take **4** Does, go
Ⓑ **1** Did, cry **2** Do, live **3** Does, have **4** Did, cook
Ⓒ **1** Does, bite, she, does **2** Do, know, they, don't **3** Did, see, I, did
Ⓓ **1** Do, you, remember **2** Does, snow, a, lot **3** Did, he, break, the, mirror

A

1 「Do + 2인칭(you) + 동사원형 ~?」
너는 내 도움이 필요하니?

2 「Does + 3인칭 단수(your sister) + 동사원형 ~?」
너의 여동생은 Jessica를 아니?

3 「Does + 3인칭 단수(Kelly) + 동사원형 ~?」
Kelly는 밤에 샤워를 하니?

4 「Does + 3인칭 단수(he) + 동사원형 ~?」
그는 매일 아침 조깅을 하니?

B

1 「Did + 주어 + 동사원형 ~?」
A 지난밤에 Molly가 울었니?
B 아니, 그렇지 않았어.

2 「Do + 2인칭(you) + 동사원형 ~?」
A 너는 도시에 사니?
B 아니, 그렇지 않아. 나는 시골에 살아.

3 「Does + 3인칭 단수(the story) + 동사원형 ~?」
A 그 이야기는 행복한 결말이니?
B 아니, 그렇지 않아. 슬픈 이야기야.

4 「Did + 주어 + 동사원형 ~?」
A 너는 어머니를 위해 저녁을 요리했니?
B 응, 그랬어. 그녀는 그것에 대해 매우 행복해했어.

C

1 「Does + 3인칭 단수(she) + 동사원형~?」, 응답: 「Yes, 3인칭 단수(she) + does.」
A 그녀는 손톱을 물어뜯니?
B 응, 그래.

2 「Do + 3인칭 복수(they) + 동사원형~?」, 응답: 「No, 3인칭 복수(they) + don't.」
A 그들이 내 전화번호를 알고 있니?
B 아니, 그렇지 않아.

3 「Did + 주어 + 동사원형 ~?」, 응답: 「Yes, 주어 + did.」
A 너는 어젯밤에 보름달을 봤니?
B 응, 그랬어. 나는 많은 별도 봤어.

: Review Test

P. 026

01 ③	02 ④	03 ②	04 ⑤	05 ②
06 ③	07 ⑤	08 ④	09 ⑤	10 ②
11 ④	12 ④	13 ①	14 ③	15 ③

01 now는 현재를 나타내는 부사, 「3인칭 단수(He) + teaches (ch로 끝나는 동사 + es)」
James는 선생님이다. 그는 지금 학교에서 수학을 가르친다.

02 last year는 과거를 나타내는 부사, go의 과거형은 went
Jane과 나는 작년에 같은 초등학교에 다녔다.

03 walked는 과거, next week(다음 주)은 미래 부사구
그는 어젯밤에 / 어제 / 이틀 전에 / 오늘 아침에 빗속을 걸었다.

04 'Yes, I did.'라고 대답했으므로 「Did + 주어 + 동사원형 ~?」으로 묻는 것이 적절, an hour ago는 과거를 나타내는 부사구
A 너는 숙제를 끝냈니?
B 네, 끝냈어요. 한 시간 전에 끝냈어요.

05 「Does + 3인칭 단수(Sally) + 동사원형 ~?」, 「자음 + y → ies」: studies
A Sally는 밤에 공부를 하니?
B 아니요, 그렇지 않아요. 그녀는 낮에 공부를 해요.

06 ③ 「3인칭 복수(Tess and Dan) + 동사원형」: borrows → borrow
① Ronnie는 아침에 일찍 일어난다.
② 우리는 수업 시간에 사전을 사용한다.
③ Tess와 Dan은 도서관에서 책을 빌린다.
④ Janice는 TV로 야구 경기를 본다.
⑤ 우리 형과 나는 태권도를 배운다.

07 ⑤ cut는 불규칙 변화 동사: cutted → cut
① 우리 아빠는 어제 11시에 잠자리에 드셨다.
② Tim은 한 시간 전에 자신의 가방을 침대 위에 올려놓았다.
③ 나는 스쿨버스에 우산을 두고 내렸다.
④ 그는 기말고사를 위해 열심히 공부했다.
⑤ 우리 어머니는 칼로 사과를 자르셨다.

08 ④ 「3인칭 단수(She) + doesn't」: don't → doesn't
우리 엄마는 주부이다. 엄마는 매일 아침 빨래를 한다. 빨래 후에 엄마는 바닥을 대걸레질을 한다. 엄마는 하루 세 끼 요리를 하지만, 설거지는 하지 않는다. 우리 형과 내가 설거지를 한다.

09 ⑤ 「Did + 주어 + 동사원형~?」: had → have
Mom 너 오늘 영어 수업이 있었니?
Minki 네, 있었어요. 전 아침 수업을 들었어요.
Mom 수업에서 말을 많이 했니?
Minki 아니요, 이야기를 많이 하지 않았어요. 영어 책을 읽고 감상문을 썼어요.
Mom 재미있었니?
Minki 네, 수업은 재미있었어요.

10 「주어 + didn't + 동사원형」
아빠는 거실에서 낮잠을 주무셨다/ 주무시지 않았다.

11 ① Do he → Does he ② Did she left → Did she leave ③ Does they → Do they ⑤ Did he buys → Did he buy
① 그는 매일 아침 오렌지 주스를 마신다.
→ 그는 매일 아침 오렌지 주스를 마시니?
② 그녀는 5시 정각에 학교를 떠났다.
→ 그녀가 5시 정각에 학교를 떠났니?
③ 그들은 카페테리아에서 점심을 먹는다.
→ 그들은 카페테리아에서 점심을 먹니?
④ James는 방과 후에 피아노를 친다.
→ James는 방과 후에 피아노를 치니?
⑤ 그는 어제 새 컴퓨터를 샀다.
→ 그가 어제 새 컴퓨터를 샀니?

12 ① No, you don't. → No, I don't. ② Yes, they do. → Yes, they did. ③ Yes, she doesn't. → Yes, she does. ⑤ Do → Did
① A 너 그의 이메일 주소를 아니?
B 아니, 몰라. 내가 그에게 물어볼게.
② A 그들이 저녁 식사 후에 아팠니?
B 응, 아팠어. 그들은 병원에 갔어.
③ A 그녀는 노래를 잘하니?
B 응, 그래. 그녀는 훌륭한 가수야.
④ A 선생님께 이야기했니?
B 아니, 안 했어. 교무실에 안 계셨어.
⑤ A 손가락을 베었니?
B 응 베었어. 많이 아팠어.

13 ② doesn't → didn't ③ Do → Did ④ don't → doesn't ⑤ saw → see
① 그 버스는 2시 정각에 도착했니?
② 그들은 지난 주말에 테니스를 치지 않았다.

③ 너 어제 집에 늦게 왔니?
④ 그는 짠 음식을 좋아하지 않는다.
⑤ 너 어젯밤에 콘서트를 봤니?

[14-15]
나는 사촌이 있다. 그의 이름은 John이다. 그는 하와이에 산다. 나는 매년 여름 그를 방문한다. 작년 여름, 나의 사촌과 나는 해변에 갔다. 나는 수영복을 가져 오지 않았기 때문에 수영을 하지 않았다. 우리는 조개껍데기 몇 개를 모았다. 우리는 모래성도 만들었다. 우리는 함께 즐거운 시간을 보냈다.

14 ⓐ every summer는 현재 부사구이므로 visit, ⓑ, ⓒ last summer는 과거 부사구이므로 collected, made

15 「주어 + didn't + 동사원형」

: 서술형 평가 P. 028

01 likes, plays, tries
02 She doesn't[does not] carry a big bag.
03 I don't[do not] understand Chinese.
04 brought a frog to the classroom
05 didn't come to school
06 He didn't cut the bread. He cut the ham.
07 She didn't take the bus. She took the train.
08 don't, study, doesn't, walk, goes, studies, has
09 Did you play
10 Yes, we did.

01 「대부분의 동사 + s」: likes, plays, 「자음 + y → ies」: tries
Tom은 농구를 매우 많이 좋아한다. 그는 방과 후에 농구를 한다. Tom은 가끔 덩크슛을 시도한다. 그는 훌륭한 농구 선수이다.

02 「3인칭 단수(She) + doesn't + 동사원형」
그녀는 큰 가방을 들고 다닌다.
→ 그녀는 큰 가방을 들고 다니지 않는다.

03 「1인칭(I) + don't + 동사원형」
나는 중국어를 이해한다.
→ 나는 중국어를 이해하지 못한다.

04 bringed → brought
Peter는 교실에 개구리를 가져왔다.

05 came → come
Matt는 학교에 오지 않았다.

[06-07] 「주어 + didn't + 동사원형」

06 그는 빵을 잘랐다. (햄)
→ 그는 빵을 자르지 않았다. 그는 햄을 잘랐다.

07 그녀는 버스를 탔다. (기차)
→ 그녀는 버스를 타지 않았다. 그녀는 기차를 탔다.

08 「1인칭 + don't + 동사원형」, 「3인칭 단수(Sam) + doesn't + 동사원형」, 「o로 끝나는 동사 + es」: goes, 「자음 + y → ies」: studies, have → has

Sam과 나는 같은 학교에 다닌다. 나는 학교까지 걸어간다. 나는 학교에 버스를 타고 가지 않는다. 나는 수업 시간에 열심히 공부하지 않는다. 나는 친구가 많다. Sam은 학교까지 걸어가지 않는다. 그는 버스를 타고 학교에 간다. 그는 수업 시간에 열심히 공부한다. 그에게는 많은 친구가 있다.

[09-10]
A 우리는 오늘 아침에 체육 수업을 했어.
B 너희들은 공놀이를 했니?
A 아니, 그렇지 않았어.
B 그럼, 너희들은 팔 굽혀 펴기를 했니?
A 응, 그랬어.

09 「Did + 주어 + 동사원형 ~?」

10 긍정의 응답: 「Yes, 주어 + did.」

Chapter 03

UNIT 01

Check-up P. 030
1 buildings **2** children **3** babies **4** glasses

1 「many + 복수 명사」

2 child의 복수형: children

3 「자음 + y → -ies」

4 「ss로 끝나는 명사 + es」

: EXERCISES P. 031

Ⓐ **1** benches **2** people **3** wolves, deer **4** Donkeys, teeth
Ⓑ **1** countries **2** leaves **3** students **4** sheep
Ⓒ **1** feet **2** deer **3** mice **4** Ladies
Ⓓ **1** many, photos **2** five, pairs, of, socks **3** a, lot, of, people

Ⓐ

1 「-ch로 끝나는 명사 + es」: benches
공원에 세 개의 벤치가 있다.

2 person의 복수형: people
요즘에 많은 사람들이 캠핑을 간다.

3 「f로 끝나는 명사 → -ves」: wolves, deer의 복수형: deer
다섯 마리의 늑대가 사슴들을 뒤쫓았다.

4 「대부분의 명사 + s」: Donkeys, tooth의 복수형: teeth
당나귀들이 이빨로 당근을 씹었다.

B

1 「자음 + y → ies」
그는 많은 나라를 여행했다.

2 「f로 끝나는 명사 → -ves」
그 식물에는 많은 꽃과 잎이 있다.

3 「대부분의 명사 + s」
도서관에 많은 학생이 있다.

4 sheep의 복수형: sheep
그 양치기는 농장에 열다섯 마리의 양을 가지고 있다.

UNIT 02

Check-up P. 032
1 water 2 bottles 3 bowl

1 「a lot of + 셀 수 없는 명사」

2 「three + 셀 수 있는 명사의 복수형」

3 '한 그릇'이라는 의미이므로 bowl, slice는 '한 조각'이라는 의미

: EXERCISES P. 033

A 1 luck 2 Annie 3 salt 4 meat 5 respect

B 1 homework 2 sugar 3 slices 4 advice

C 1 two cups of coffee 2 two bowls of rice
3 three pieces of cake 4 two slices of ham

D 1 don't have much money
2 bought two bottles of water
3 There are seven loaves of bread

A

1 눈에 보이지 않는 추상적인 개념의 명사: luck
당신의 행운을 빕니다.

2 사람의 고유한 이름을 나타내는 명사: Annie
Annie는 방을 청소한다.

3 형태가 일정하지 않은 명사: salt
그는 나에게 소금을 건네줬다.

4 형태가 일정하지 않은 명사: meat
우리 어머니께서는 고기를 요리하셨다.

5 눈에 보이지 않는 추상적인 개념의 명사: respect
나는 부모님을 매우 존경한다.

B

1 「a lot of + 셀 수 없는 명사」
그는 오늘 숙제가 많다.

2 「some + 셀 수 없는 명사」
제 커피에 설탕을 좀 넣을 수 있을까요?

3 「three + 셀 수 있는 명사의 복수형」
그녀는 저녁으로 피자 세 조각을 먹었다.

4 「a piece of + 셀 수 없는 명사」
이 문제에 대해 저에게 충고 한마디 해주시겠어요?

UNIT 03

Check-up P. 034
1 an 2 a 3 The

1 「an + 첫 글자가 모음인 명사(exam)」

2 「a + 첫 글자가 자음인 명사(month)」

3 「the + 이미 언급한 것(bike)」

: EXERCISES P. 035

A 1 a 2 a 3 a 4 an 5 a

B 1 a 2 a 3 an 4 an 5 X

C 1 X 2 the 3 X 4 the 5 the

D 1 days, a, year 2 go, to, bed
3 around, the, world 4 for, an, hour

A

1 「a + 첫 글자가 자음인 명사(open)」
너는 펜이 있니?

2 uniform(제복)은 첫 글자가 모음이지만 발음은 자음
그녀는 직장에서 제복을 입는다.

3 '일 년 마다'라는 의미의 a
우리는 일 년에 두 번 시험을 본다.

4 '한 시간 마다'라는 의미의 an
그들은 한 시간에 한 번 휴식을 취한다.

5 「a + 첫 글자가 자음인 명사(supermarket)」
모퉁이에 슈퍼마켓이 있다.

B

1 「a + 수식어(great) + 식사이름(dinner)」
훌륭한 저녁 식사였어요. 고맙습니다.

2 '~마다'라는 의미의 a
나는 하루에 세 번 이를 닦는다.

3 MP3는 첫 글자가 자음이지만 모음으로 발음
우리 아버지는 나에게 MP3 플레이어를 사 주셨다.

4 막연한 하나, honest는 첫 글자가 자음이지만 모음으로 발음
그는 정직한 남자이다. 그는 결코 거짓말을 하지 않는다.

5 운동경기(badminton) 앞에는 관사를 쓰지 않음
우리 누나와 나는 매주 토요일에 배드민턴을 친다.

C

1 「by + 교통수단」
그는 기차를 타고 이곳에 왔다.

2 「the + 화자와 청자가 알고 있는 것」
저를 위해 창문을 열어 주시겠어요?

3 본래의 목적으로 쓰인 장소
우리는 월요일부터 금요일까지 학교에 간다.

4 「the + 세상에 하나뿐인 것」
나는 햇빛 아래 앉아서 책을 읽었다.

5 「the + 악기 명」
Mary는 학교 축제에서 기타를 연주했다.

: Review Test

P. 036

01 ⑤	02 ①	03 ②	04 ②	05 ④
06 ②	07 ④	08 ④	09 ④	10 ③
11 ④	12 ②	13 ③	14 ④	15 ⑤

01 「an + 첫 글자가 모음인 단어(old), 막연한 하나」, 「the + 앞에서 언급한 단어(bike)」
Henry는 낡은 자전거를 하나 가지고 있다. 그 낡은 자전거는 마당에 있다.

02 「the + 악기 명(piano)」, 「the + 악기 명(piano)」, '~마다'라는 의미의 a
Jessica는 피아노를 매우 잘 연주한다. 그녀는 하루에 세 시간씩 피아노를 연습한다.

03 「much[a lot of] + 셀 수 없는 명사(homework)」, 「many[a lot of] + 셀 수 있는 명사의 복수형(friends)」
나는 학교생활을 좋아한다. 숙제가 많지 않고 친구들이 많다.

04 「a pair of + 한 쌍으로 이루어진 명사」, glass(유리)는 물질 명사
A 상점에서 무엇을 샀니?
B 나는 한 쌍의 장갑을 / 운동화를 / 청바지를 / 가위를 샀어.

05 「much + 셀 수 없는 명사」, teeth는 셀 수 있는 명사의 복수형
A 뭐가 잘못되었니?
B 나는 돈이 / 정보가 / 설탕이 / 시간이 많지 않아요.

06 ① Leafs → Leaves ③ benchs → benches ④ foots → feet ⑤ babys → babies
① 가을에는 잎이 갈색으로 변한다.
② 나는 오늘 수업이 많다.
③ 공원에 벤치가 다섯 개 있다.
④ 그는 어젯밤에 발을 씻지 않았다.
⑤ 아기들이 장난감을 가지고 놀았다.

07 ① two slice of → two slices of ② cup of → a cup of ③ milks → milk ⑤ two bottle of → two bottles of
① 나는 치즈 두 장이 필요하다.
② 그녀는 아침에 커피 한 잔을 마셨다.
③ 그들은 우유 네 잔을 원한다.
④ 그는 종이 세 장을 가져왔다.
⑤ 우리는 주스 두 병을 마셨다.

08 ① 「the + 세상에 하나뿐인 것(moon)」 ② 「the + 매체(Internet)」 ③ 「the + 화자와 청자가 알고 있는 것(door)」 ④ 운동경기 앞에 관사 없음 ⑤ 「The + 이미 언급 된 것(cat)」
① Molly는 창문을 통해 달을 쳐다보았다.
② 요즈음 사람들은 인터넷으로 많은 것을 산다.
③ 들어 와서 문을 닫아 주세요.
④ Janet은 여동생과 배드민턴을 친다.
⑤ Sandy는 고양이가 한 마리 있다. 그 고양이는 매우 귀엽다.

09 a broken teeth → a broken tooth, many sheeps → many sheep, cheeses → cheese, play the soccer → play soccer, two pair → two pairs, plays piano → plays the piano, childs → children
- 그녀는 부러진 이가 하나 있다.
- 우리는 많은 양을 보았다.
- 우리 형은 치즈를 매우 좋아한다.
- 남자들과 여자들은 동등하다.
- James는 방과 후에 축구를 한다.
- 나는 어제 청바지 두 벌을 샀다.
- Emily는 피아노를 아주 잘 친다.
- 나는 너에게 이메일로 사진 한 장을 보냈다.
- 그녀는 세 명의 아이가 있다.
- 나는 노란 나뭇잎을 좋아한다.

10 「There are + 복수 명사」, a slice of pizza는 단수 명사
탁자 위에 토마토들이 / 접시들이 / 달걀들이 / 주스 두 컵이 있다.

11 ④ a hour → an hour
화창한 날이었다. Kate와 Danny는 버스를 타고 해변에 갔다. 태양이 하늘 높이 떠 있었다. 그들은 한 시간 동안 비치발리볼을 했다. 그들은 점심으로 샌드위치를 먹었다. 저녁에 Kate는 기타를 연주했고 Danny는 노래를 불렀다. 그들은 함께 정말 즐거운 시간을 보냈다.

12 ② two tomatos → two tomatoes
오늘 Cindy와 그녀의 아이들은 쇼핑을 갔다. 그들은 두 개의 토마토, 세 개의 양파, 두 개의 당근 그리고 올리브 오일 한 병을 샀다. Cindy는 토마토 수프를 만들었다. 아이들은 저녁 식사로 토마토 수프 세 그릇을 먹었다. 그들은 토마토 수프를 아주 좋아했다.

13 「two + 셀 수 있는 명사의 복수형(sandwiches)」, 「two cups of + 셀 수 없는 명사(coffee)」

[14-15]

John 안녕, Emma. 너 오늘 왜 학교에 지각했니?
Emma 나는 보통 8시에 버스를 타고 학교에 가는데 오늘 아침에 버스를 놓쳤어. 그래서 다음 버스를 타야 했어.
John 오, 그렇게 된 거구나. 학교까지 자전거를 타고 가는 건 어때? 나는 보통 자전거를 타고 학교에 와.
Emma 좋은 생각이야. 그런데, 너 배고프지 않니?
John 응, 정말 배고파. 뭘 먹고 싶니?
Emma 햄버거와 찬 물 한 병으로 할래. 넌?
John 나는 피자 두 조각과 콜라 한 잔을 먹을래.

14 ④ by the bike → by bike

15 「two slices of + 셀 수 없는 명사(pizza)」, 「a glass of + 셀 수 없는 명사(coke)」

: 서술형 평가 P. 038

01 ten, deer
02 two, mice
03 She has nice white teeth.
04 I need a pair of pants.
05 (1) a cup of tea (2) three bottles of water
(3) two bowls of salad
06 There were three women in the room.
07 There is a pair of scissors in the box.
08 goes to school five days a week
09 usually go to school by subway, took a bus
10 (1) ② We played soccer before breakfast.
(2) ⑥ I played the drums.

03 tooths → teeth
그녀는 멋진 하얀 치아를 가지고 있다.

04 pant → pants
나는 바지 한 벌이 필요하다.

05 셀 수 없는 명사는 세는 단위로 수량을 표현: (1) 잔: cup (2) 병: bottle (3) 그릇: bowl

06 「three + 셀 수 있는 명사의 복수형(women)」
방 안에 한 명의 여자가 있었다. → 방 안에 세 명의 여자가 있었다.

07 「a pair of + 쌍으로 이루어진 명사의 복수형(scissors)」
상자 안에 가위 세 개가 있다. → 상자 안에 가위 한 개가 있다.

10 ② played the soccer → play soccer
⑥ played drums → played the drums
안녕하세요, 엄마!
오늘은 캠프 첫 날이었어요. 하늘은 맑고 파랬어요. 우리는 아침 식사 전에 축구를 했어요. 오후에는 강에서 수영을 하고 보트를 타고 강을 건너기도 했어요. 우리는 저녁 식사로 바비큐를 먹었어요. 저녁 식사 후, 우리는 작은 콘서트를 열었어요. 저는 드럼을 연주했어요. 정말 즐거웠어요.
아들, Peter로부터

Chapter 04

UNIT 01

Check-up P. 040
1 It **2** That

1 '거리'를 나타내는 비인칭주어

2 '저 사람'이라는 의미의 지시대명사

: EXERCISES P. 041

Ⓐ **1** this **2** These **3** Those **4** Those **5** That
Ⓑ **1** It's Friday. **2** It's 7:30. **3** It's May 7th.
4 It was sunny.
Ⓒ **1** It **2** that **3** these **4** This
Ⓓ **1** that, camera **2** these, glasses
3 It, was, my, birthday
4 It, takes, about, 20, minutes

A

1 「this + 단수 명사(girl)」
이 소녀가 네 사촌이니?

2 「These + 복수 명사(earrings)」
이 귀고리들은 비싸지 않다.

3 your shoes를 의미하므로 Those
이것들은 내 신발이야. 저것들이 네 것이야.

4 my friends, Tom and Terry를 의미하므로 Those
저 사람들은 내 친구인 Tom과 Terry야.

5 「That + 단수 명사(picture)」
앨범에 있는 저 사진은 멋져 보인다.

B

1 요일을 나타내는 비인칭주어 it
A 오늘은 무슨 요일이니? B 금요일이야.

2 시간을 나타내는 비인칭주어 it
A 지금 몇 시니? B 일곱 시 삼십 분이야.

3 날짜를 나타내는 비인칭주어 it
A 오늘은 며칠이니? B 5월 7일이야.

4 날씨를 나타내는 비인칭주어 it
A 어제 날씨는 어땠니? B 화창했어.

C

1 요일을 나타내는 비인칭주어 it
오늘은 월요일이다.

2 '저것'이라는 의미의 지시대명사 that
이것은 내 공책이야. 저것이 네 것이니?

3 「these + 복수 명사(clothes)」
이 옷들을 좀 봐. 아주 아름다워.

4 사람을 소개할 때 사용하는 지시대명사 this
우리 반 친구를 소개할게. 이쪽은 Anthony야.

UNIT 02

Check-up P. 042
1 it 2 one

1 앞서 언급된 바로 그것(your notebook)을 가리킬 때는 it

2 앞서 언급한 것과 같은 종류의 불특정한 하나(next bus)를 나타낼 때는 one

: EXERCISES P. 043

Ⓐ 1 the other 2 One 3 some 4 any
Ⓑ 1 one 2 it 3 ones 4 the other
Ⓒ 1 some 2 some 3 any 4 any
Ⓓ 1 ate some cookies 2 don't eat any meat
3 will buy one
4 One is vanilla, the other is chocolate

A

1 둘 중 나머지 하나는 the other
Joe는 스카프를 두 장 가지고 있다. 하나는 빨간색이고 나머지 하나는 파란색이다.

2 둘 중 첫 번째 하나는 one
Clare에게는 고양이 두 마리가 있다. 하나는 흰색이고 나머지 하나는 갈색이다.

3 긍정문에는 some
봐! 운동장에 아이들이 몇 명 있어.

4 부정문에는 any
우리는 집에 빵이 하나도 없어.

B

1 앞서 언급한 것과 같은 종류의 불특정한 하나(new bag)는 one
나는 가방을 잃어버렸어. 새 걸로 하나 사야 해.

2 앞서 언급된 바로 그것(This coat)을 가리킬 때는 it
이 외투는 나에게 맞지 않아. 나는 그것을 사지 않을 거야.

3 앞서 언급한 것과 같은 종류의 불특정한 대상(new glasses)이 복수일 때는 ones
내 안경은 너무 낡았어. 새 것을 사고 싶어.

4 둘 중 나머지 하나는 the other
Mary에게는 오빠가 둘 있다. 한 명은 크고 나머지 한 명은 작다.

C

1 권유문에는 some
A 차를 좀 드릴까요? B 네, 주세요.

2 긍정문에는 some
A 파이에 뭐가 필요하니? B 사과가 좀 필요해.

3 부정문에는 any
A 펜을 빌릴 수 있을까요? B 미안해요. 나는 펜이 하나도 없어요.

4 의문문에는 any
A 휴가에 어떤 계획이 있니? B 아니. 별로 특별한 건 없어.

UNIT 03

Check-up P. 044
1 yourself 2 myself

1 주어 you를 강조하는 yourself

2 by oneself 스스로, 혼자서

: EXERCISES P. 045

Ⓐ 1 yourself 2 themselves 3 himself 4 yourselves
Ⓑ 1 Susan 2 I 3 Angelina Jolie 4 the teacher
Ⓒ 1 myself 2 herself 3 themselves 4 yourself
Ⓓ 1 enjoyed, himself 2 between, ourselves
3 help, yourself, to
4 do, your, homework, by, yourself

A

1 주어(you)와 목적어가 동일
조심해! 다칠 수도 있어.

2 them이 스스로를 소개하는 것이므로 themselves
그들에게 자기소개를 하도록 하세요.

3 He가 스스로를 돌보는 것이므로 himself
그는 혼자 산다. 그는 스스로를 돌봐야 한다.

4 you가 스스로 집처럼 편하게 지내는 것이므로 yourselves
머무시는 동안 집에서처럼 편안하게 지내세요.

B

1 Susan이 스스로 집을 지은 것
Susan이 직접 그 집을 지었니?

2 David에게 내가 직접 말하는 것
걱정 마. 내가 David에게 직접 말할게.

3 Angelina Jolie를 직접 본 것
나는 공원에서 Angelina Jolie를 직접 봤다.

4 the teacher를 직접 만나고 싶어 하는 것
학생들은 선생님을 직접 만나고 싶어 했다.

C

1 I의 재귀대명사 myself
나는 거울에 비친 나 자신을 보는 것을 좋아하지 않는다.

2 Rachel의 재귀대명사 herself
Rachel은 벽에 걸린 그림을 직접 그렸다.

3 They의 재귀대명사 themselves
그들은 그 사건에 대해 스스로를 탓했다.

4 you의 재귀대명사 yourself
잘했어! 너는 스스로를 자랑스러워해야 해!

: Review Test P. 046

01 ③	02 ⑤	03 ③	04 ②	05 ②
06 ②	07 ④	08 ④	09 ③	10 ②
11 ④	12 ①	13 ③	14 ⑤	15 ④

01 앞서 언급한 명사와 같은 종류의 불특정한 하나(new suitcase)를 나타낼 때는 one
내 여행 가방이 부서졌어. 새 것을 하나 사야 해.

02 정해진 수 중 일정 부분을 제외한 나머지 모두는 the others
그 반에는 스물다섯 명의 학생이 있다. 오늘은 그 중 다섯 명만 학교에 왔다. 나머지는 오지 않았다.

03 앞서 언급한 명사(a cell phone)를 지칭할 때는 it
너 휴대 전화를 가지고 있니? 내가 그것을 빌릴 수 있을까?

04 두 개 중 하나는 one, 나머지 하나는 the other
나에게는 언니가 두 명 있다. 한 명은 교사이고 나머지 한 명은 의사이다.

05 ② 인칭대명사 ① ③ ④ ⑤ 요일, 날씨, 날짜, 시간을 나타내는 비인칭주어
① 오늘은 일요일이다. ② 그것은 나의 배낭이다.
③ 내일은 화창할 것이다. ④ 12월 6일이다.
⑤ 오 분 정도 걸린다.

06 권유문: some, 부정문: any
A 엄마, 나 매우 배고파요. B 빵을 좀 먹을래?
A 네. 우유도 있나요? B 미안하구나. 우유는 없단다.

07 She와 Mother Teresa의 재귀대명사 herself
• 그녀는 자신을 그렸다.
• Teresa 수녀는 혼자 인도로 갔다.

08 전화 통화에서 자신을 지칭하는 this와 사람을 소개할 때 사용하는 this
• A 여보세요. 저는 Monica예요. Eric과 통화할 수 있을까요?
B 그 애는 집에 없단다. 메시지를 남기겠니?
• A 이쪽은 내 여자 친구인 Brenda야.
B 만나서 반가워.

09 보기: 「This(지시형용사) + 명사(book)」 ③ 「This(지시형용사) + 명사(color)」 ① ② ④ ⑤ 지시대명사
[보기] 이 책은 흥미진진하다.
① 이쪽은 내 친구인 Jay야. ② 이것이 네 휴대 전화니?
③ 이 색은 내가 가장 좋아하는 거야. ④ 이것은 널 위한 선물이야.
⑤ 내가 이걸 가져도 될까?

10 보기: 주어(you)를 강조하는 재귀대명사 ② 주어(You)를 강조하는 재귀대명사 ① make oneself at home 편하게 지내다 ③ hurt oneself 다치다 ④ enjoy oneself 즐거운 시간을 보내다 ⑤ help oneself to ~을 마음껏 먹다
[보기] 정말 그것을 네가 직접 만들었니?
① 집처럼 편하게 지내세요.
② 넌 그와 직접 이야기해야 해.
③ 캠프에서 다쳤니?
④ 소풍에서 즐거운 시간을 보냈니?
⑤ 스낵을 마음껏 드세요.

11 ④ 날짜를 말할 때는 비인칭주어 it을 사용: This → It
① A 지금 몇 시죠? B 두 시 정각이에요.
② A 오늘이 무슨 요일인가요? B 금요일이에요.
③ A 그 책은 얼마죠? B 12,000원이요.
④ A 오늘 날씨가 어떤가요? B 바람이 불고 흐려요.
⑤ A 여기서 공항까지 얼마나 멀어요? B 차로 한 시간 걸려요.

12 ① one → it
① 내 가방을 찾을 수가 없어. 그것을 보았니?
② 그는 독학으로 영어를 공부했다.
③ 나는 이 색을 좋아하지 않아요. 다른 색이 있나요?
④ 벌써 열 시야. 자야겠어.
⑤ 나에게는 삼촌이 두 분 계신다. 한 분은 한국에, 나머지 한 분은 미국에 사신다.

13 ③ This → These
① 저 비행기는 영국행이다.
② 걸어서 십 분 정도 걸린다.
③ 이 안경은 내 것이다.
④ John이 직접 그 장난감을 고쳤다.
⑤ 여기서 기차역까지 얼마나 오래 걸리니?

[14-15]
이것이 나의 크리스마스 선물 쇼핑 목록이다. 엄마 선물로 목걸이를 사려고 한다. 엄마는 목걸이를 이미 하나 가지고 계시긴 하지만 그것은 너무 오래됐다. 아버지 선물로는 운동화를 한 켤레 살 것이다. 신고 조깅을 하실 수 있도록 말이다. 그리고 나는 나 자신을 위한 선물로 새 원피스를 하나 사려고 한다. 정말 신난다!

14 ⓐ 앞서 언급한 명사와 같은 종류의 불특정한 하나(necklace)를 나타내는 one, ⓑ 앞서 언급된 바로 그것(Mom's necklace)을 가리키는 it

15 ⓒ for oneself '~을 위해서'(재귀 용법) ④ talk about oneself '~에 대해 이야기하다'(재귀 용법) ① James를 강

조하는 himself ② Sarah를 강조하는 herself ③ You를 강조하는 yourself ⑤ Anne을 강조하는 herself
① 나는 James 본인을 우연히 만났다.
② Sarah가 직접 그 사진을 찍었다.
③ 네가 직접 그 문제를 풀어야 한다.
④ 그는 자신에 대해 말하는 것을 좋아하지 않는다.
⑤ Anne이 직접 점심을 준비했다.

: 서술형 평가 P. 048

01 It **02** These, those
03 some, any **04** One, the other
05 Those, are **06** enjoyed, themselves
07 This, color **08** himself
09 myself
10 (1) It's 1:15 pm. (2) It's November 11th.
(3) It's Sunday. (4) It's sunny.

01 인칭대명사 it과 날씨를 나타내는 비인칭주어 it
• 그곳은 멋진 도시구나. • 어제는 따뜻했다.

02 「These / those + 복수 명사(shoes)」

03 긍정문: 「some + 셀 수 있는 명사의 복수형(pens)」, 부정문: 「any + 셀 수 있는 명사의 복수형(pencils)」

04 둘 중 하나는 One, 나머지 하나는 the other

07 지시대명사 → 「지시형용사(This) + 명사(color)」
이것은 내가 가장 좋아하는 색이다.
→ 이 색은 내가 가장 좋아하는 것이다.

08 be angry with oneself '~에게 화가 나다', He의 재귀대명사 himself
A 그는 나에게 화났니?
B 전혀 그렇지 않아. 그는 자신에게 화가 났을 뿐이야.

09 hurt oneself '다치다', I의 재귀대명사 myself
A 무슨 일이야? B 어젯밤에 다쳤어.

10 비인칭주어 it을 사용
(1) A 지금 몇 시니? B 한 시 십오 분이야.
(2) A 오늘 며칠이야? B 11월 11일이야.
(3) A 오늘 무슨 요일이야? B 일요일이야.
(4) A 오늘 날씨는 어때? B 화창해.

Chapter 05

UNIT 01

Check-up P. 050
1 go **2** take **3** ate **4** finished

1 '타러 간다'는 의미의 현재형
2 '샤워를 한다'는 의미의 현재형
3 '먹었다'는 의미의 과거형, yesterday는 과거를 나타내는 부사
4 '끝마쳤다'는 의미의 과거형, two hours ago는 과거를 나타내는 부사구

: EXERCISES P. 051

A **1** rises **2** were **3** moved **4** feel
B **1** rained **2** ended **3** close **4** missed
C was, am, wore, wear, finished, finish
D **1** took, an, exam, yesterday
2 plant, trees, every, year
3 studied, English, last, Sunday

A

1 불변의 진리는 현재 시제 사용
태양은 동쪽에서 뜬다.

2 last year는 과거를 나타내는 부사구
Dan과 나는 작년에 반 친구였다.

3 three years ago는 과거를 나타내는 부사구
그는 삼 년 전에 캐나다로 이사를 갔다.

4 now는 현재를 나타내는 부사구
나는 오늘 아침에 일찍 일어났다. 나는 지금 피곤하다.

B

1 last night은 과거를 나타내는 부사구
지난밤에 비가 많이 왔다.

2 in 1953은 과거를 나타내는 부사구
한국 전쟁은 1953년에 끝났다.

3 은행이 주말에 문을 닫는다는 현재 사실을 의미
한국의 은행은 주말마다 문을 닫는다.

4 ten minutes ago는 과거를 나타내는 부사구
Sandy는 십 분 전에 스쿨버스를 놓쳤다.

C last year는 과거 부사구, now는 현재 부사
작년에 나는 초등학생이었다. 지금 나는 중학생이다. 나는 작년에 평상복을 입었다. 나는 이제 교복을 입는다. 작년에 나는 3시에 학교 수업이 끝났다. 지금은 4시에 학교 수업이 끝난다.

UNIT 02

Check-up P. 052
1 Are **2** was cleaning

1 now는 현재를 나타내는 부사

2 at that time은 과거를 나타내는 부사구

: EXERCISES P. 053

Ⓐ 1 Were 2 is 3 was 4 Was 5 aren't

Ⓑ 1 dying 2 taking 3 drinking 4 baking 5 jogging

Ⓒ 1 making, reading 2 staying, watching
3 Were, washing, was, taking, out

Ⓓ 1 is, looking, for 2 were, standing
3 wasn't, listening, to

A

1 then은 과거를 나타내는 부사
너는 그때 그의 말을 듣고 있었니?

2 now는 현재를 나타내는 부사
Sandy는 지금 수영장에서 수영을 하고 있다.

3 at that time은 과거를 나타내는 부사구
나는 그 당시에 친구들을 만나고 있었다.

4 at seven o'clock yesterday는 과거를 나타내는 부사구
그녀는 어제 7시 정각에 아침 식사를 하고 있었니?

5 now는 현재를 나타내는 부사
Emily와 Tom은 지금 숙제를 하고 있지 않다.

B

1 ie로 끝나는 동사: 「ie를 y로 고치고+ing」
Sally의 나무들이 지금 죽어가고 있다.

2 e로 끝나는 동사: 「e를 빼고+ing」
Matt는 그 당시에 낮잠을 자고 있었다.

3 대부분의 동사: 「동사원형+ing」
John은 지금 커피를 마시고 있다.

4 e로 끝나는 동사: 「e를 빼고+ing」
우리 누나는 어젯밤에 쿠키를 몇 개 굽고 있었다.

5 단모음+단자음으로 끝나는 동사: 「동사원형+마지막 자음+ing」
사람들은 오늘 아침에 공원에서 조깅을 하고 있었다.

C

1 「Is+3인칭 단수(your mother)+-ing ~?」
A 너희 어머니께서 저녁 식사를 만들고 계시니?
B 아니, 그렇지 않아. 신문을 읽고 계셔.

2 「Was+3인칭 단수(Sam)+-ing ~?」
A Sam은 Fred의 집에 있었니?
B 아니, 그렇지 않았어. 극장에서 영화를 보고 있었어.

3 「Were+2인칭(you)+-ing ~?」
A 너는 그때 설거지를 하고 있었니?
B 아니, 그렇지 않았어. 쓰레기를 내다 버리고 있었어.

: Review Test P. 054

01 ③	02 ①	03 ①	04 ②	05 ③
06 ④	07 ①	08 ②	09 ④	10 ③
11 ③	12 ②	13 ②	14 ⑤	15 ④

01 30 minutes ago는 과거를 나타내는 부사구
그 게임은 30분 전에 시작되었다.

02 every day는 반복적인 동작을 나타내는 부사구로 현재 시제가 적절
우리는 매일 7시 30분에 저녁을 먹는다.

03 now는 현재를 나타내는 부사
그녀는 지금 대회를 위해 피아노 연습을 하고 있다.

04 last weekend는 과거를 나타내는 부사구
A 너는 지난 주말에 무엇을 했니?
B 여동생을 돌봤어.

05 now는 현재를 나타내는 부사, 지금 이메일을 보내고 있다는 의미가 되어야 하므로 현재진행형이 적절
A 너는 지금 컴퓨터 게임을 하고 있니?
B 아니, 그렇지 않아. 나는 엄마에게 이메일을 보내고 있어.

06 visited는 과거 시제, right now는 현재를 나타내는 부사구
David는 한 시간 전에 / 지난밤에 / 오늘 아침에 / 지난여름에 조부모님을 방문했다.

07 exercise는 현재, last Sunday는 과거를 나타내는 부사구
그들은 매일 / 일주일에 한 번 / 일요일마다 / 매주 일요일에 운동을 한다.

08 ② is riding not → is not riding
① 그들은 지금 점심을 먹고 있니?
② Sue는 자전거를 타고 있지 않다.
③ 그들은 그 당시에 집으로 걸어가고 있었다.
④ 너 그때 바닥을 청소하고 있었니?
⑤ 그녀는 지금 병원에서 일하고 있다.

09 ④ breaks out → broke out
① 물은 섭씨 100도에서 끓는다.
② 우리는 지난 주말에 쇼핑을 갔다.
③ 그 기차는 9시에 떠난다.
④ 제2차 세계대전은 1939년에 일어났다.
⑤ 그는 한 시간 전에 집에 왔다.

10 ③ falled → fell
한 남자가 낡은 다리를 건너고 있었다. 그는 조심스럽게 다리 위로 발을 내디뎠다. 갑자기 미끄러져 물속으로 빠졌다. 그는 도와달라고 외쳤지만 주위에는 아무도 없었다.

11 「주어+be동사+-ing」 ~하고 있다

12 then은 과거를 나타내는 부사. 「Were you ~?」, 「I was ~」
A 너는 그때 테니스장에서 테니스를 치고 있었니?
B 아니, 그렇지 않았어. 나는 수영장에서 수영을 하고 있었어.

13 「Are you -ing~?」에 대한 응답은 Yes, I am. 또는 No, I'm not. 지금 소설을 읽고 있는 것이 아니라, 만화책을 읽고 있으므로 No, I'm not.이 적절
A 너는 소설을 읽고 있니?
B 아니, 그렇지 않아. 나는 만화책을 읽고 있어.

[14-15]
경찰관 무슨 일이 있었나요?
목격자 운전자가 노인을 치고 달아났어요.
경찰관 남자였나요, 여자였나요?
목격자 남자였어요.
경찰관 그 당시에 당신은 무엇을 하고 있었나요?
목격자 저는 공원에서 조깅을 하고 있었어요.
경찰관 그는 어느 쪽으로 갔나요?
목격자 그는 저쪽으로 갔어요.

14 과거에 일어난 일에 대해 이야기하고 있음

15 '그 당시에' at that time
① 지금 당장 ② 요즈음 ③ 때때로 ⑤ 오래 전에

: 서술형 평가 P. 056

01 am going **02** ① visited ② lives
03 it, was **04** it, didn't
05 No, I'm, not
06 goes to church on Sundays
07 was not studying for the exam then
08 (1) John made a bonfire. (2) I played the guitar.
09 were, having, dinner
10 she, wasn't, was, reading, a, book

01 「be+-ing」 ~하는 중이다
A 너 지금 어디에 가고 있니?
B 나는 도서관에 가고 있어. 책을 좀 빌리고 싶어.

02 ① last weekend는 과거를 나타내는 부사구 ② 현재 상황을 물었으므로 현재 시제로 응답
A 지난 주말에 무엇을 했니?
B 할아버지의 농장을 방문했어.
A 오, 그래? 너희 할아버지께서는 어디에 사시니?
B 대구에 살고 계셔.

03 「Was it ~」으로 물었으므로 it was로 응답
A 그 당시에 눈이 많이 내리고 있었나요?
B 네, 그랬어요.

04 the telephone은 it으로 받음
A 방금 전에 전화벨이 울렸나요?
B 아니요, 그렇지 않았어요. 저는 아무것도 듣지 못했어요.

05 나는 중학생이므로 부정의 응답이 와야 함
A 너는 초등학생이니?
B 아니요, 그렇지 않아요. 저는 중학생이에요.

08 Last summer는 과거를 나타내는 부사구
(1) maked → made (2) play → played
지난여름, 나는 친구들과 캠핑을 갔다. Michael은 텐트를 설치했다. John은 모닥불을 피웠다. Andy는 저녁을 요리했다. 나는 기타를 연주했다. 우리는 매우 즐거운 시간을 보냈다.

[09-10] 과거의 특정한 시간에 진행 중인 행동은 과거진행을 사용

09 Sarah와 Mandy는 6시 45분에 무엇을 하고 있었나요?
→ 그들은 6시 45분에 저녁을 먹고 있었어요.

10 Mandy는 10시에 숙제를 하고 있었나요?
→ 아니요, 그렇지 않았어요. 그녀는 책을 읽고 있었어요.

Chapter 06

UNIT 01

Check-up P. 058
1 lift **2** snow

1 「can+동사원형」

2 「may+동사원형」

: EXERCISES P. 059

A 1 be 2 be 3 play 4 is 5 go
B 1 들어가도 될까 2 수영을 할 수 있다 3 늦을지도 모른다 4 갈 수 없었다
C 1 can't take 2 can't find 3 can read 4 Can, borrow
D 1 can, speak 2 may, not, remember 3 may[can], take 4 Can[May], I, use

A

1 「may+동사원형」
그것은 사실일지도 몰라.

2 「Can+주어+동사원형 ~?」
내 친구가 되어 줄래?

3 「can't+동사원형」
그녀는 바이올린을 연주할 수 없다.

4 be able to ~할 수 있다
Rachel은 그림을 잘 그릴 수 있다.

5 「may + 동사원형」
그들은 내일 놀이공원에 갈지도 모른다.

C

1 가져가면 안 된다는 내용이므로 can't
나는 저 책이 필요해. 가져가면 안 돼.

2 찾을 수 없다는 내용이므로 can't
내 휴대 전화 봤니? 찾을 수가 없어.

3 읽을 수 있다는 내용이므로 can
Michael은 아주 똑똑해. 그는 읽고 쓰는 것을 매우 잘할 수 있어.

4 상대방에게 요청할 때는 「Can I + 동사원형 ~?」
나는 어제 학교에 결석했어. 네 공책을 빌려 줄래?

UNIT 02

Check-up P. 060
1 임이 틀림없다 **2** 해야 한다

1 잠을 자지 않았으므로 피곤할 것이라는 추측이 가능
Daniel은 지난밤에 잠을 자지 않았다. 그는 틀림없이 피곤할 거야.

2 문맥상 '~해야 한다'는 의무로 해석
모든 학생은 아홉 시까지 등교해 있어야 합니다. 늦지 마세요!

: EXERCISES P. 061

A **1** be **2** be **3** not be **4** to go **5** don't have to

B **1** have to follow **2** has to listen to
3 have to respect

C **1** should hurry **2** should take a rest
3 should wash the dishes **4** shouldn't go out
5 shouldn't eat fast food

D **1** must wear **2** must not use
3 don't have to worry about

A

1 「should + 동사원형」
박물관에서는 조용히 해야 한다.

2 「must + 동사원형」
Tom은 좀 전에 많이 먹었어. 그는 틀림없이 배가 부를 거야.

3 「must + not + 동사원형」
시험은 아홉 시 반이야. 늦으면 안 돼.

4 「have to + 동사원형」
우리는 지금 집에 가야 해. 곧 어두워질 거야.

5 don't have to ~할 필요 없다
서두를 필요 없어. 우린 시간이 충분히 있어.

B

1 「2인칭(You) + have to + 동사원형」
너는 규칙을 따라야 한다.

2 「3인칭 단수(He) + has to + 동사원형」
그는 부모님 말씀을 들어야 한다.

3 「3인칭 복수(They) + have to + 동사원형」
그들은 선생님들을 존경해야 한다.

C

[1-5] should ~해야 한다, 하는 것이 좋겠다,
shouldn't ~하지 않아야 한다, ~하지 않는 게 좋겠다

1 너 늦었어. 서두르는 게 좋겠어.

2 너 피곤해 보여. 좀 쉬는 게 좋겠어.

3 부엌이 더럽구나. 설거지를 하는 게 좋겠어.

4 너는 심한 감기에 걸렸잖아. 밖에 나가지 않는 게 좋겠어.

5 그는 살을 빼기를 원한다. 패스트푸드를 먹지 말아야 한다.

UNIT 03

Check-up P. 062
1 will **2** is

1 「will + 동사원형」 ~할 것이다

2 「be going to + 동사원형」 ~할 것이다

: EXERCISES P. 063

A **1** come **2** Will **3** am not **4** be **5** help

B **1** will close **2** will not[won't] be
3 will not[won't] have **4** Will, wear
5 will not[won't] tell

C **1** Is, going to rain **2** Are, going to sing
3 are not[aren't] going to take **4** is going to eat
5 am going to buy

D **1** won't, make **2** Will, come **3** am, going, to, play
4 is, going, to, give, a, speech

A

1 「Will + 주어 + 동사원형 ~?」
그가 오늘밤에 집에 일찍 올까요?

2 「Will + 주어 + 동사원형 ~?」
Kate가 내일 머리를 자를까요?

3 「be not going to + 동사원형」
나는 그 동아리에 가입하지 않을 것이다.

4 「will + 동사원형」
Joshua는 언젠가는 유명한 작가가 될 것이다.

5 「be going to + 동사원형」
Ted는 내가 집 청소하는 것을 도와줄 것이다.

[1-5] 「will + 동사원형」, 「will not[won't] + 동사원형」

1 여긴 정말 춥구나. 내가 창문을 닫을게.

2 Kelly는 항상 제시간에 와. 그녀는 늦지 않을 거야.

3 지금 뭘 좀 먹자. 나중에는 시간이 없을 거야.

4 내일 새 원피스 입을 거니?

5 걱정 마. 아무에게도 네 비밀을 말하지 않을게.

[1-5] 「be + 주어 + going to + 동사원형 ~?」,
「be (not) going to + 동사원형」

1 내일 비가 올까?

2 너 파티에서 노래를 부를 거니?

3 그들은 피아노 수업을 듣지 않을 것이다.

4 Larry는 아침으로 시리얼을 먹을 것이다.

5 나는 이 바지를 살 거야. 바지가 예뻐 보여.

: Review Test

P. 064

01 ③	02 ④	03 ③	04 ④	05 ②
06 ③	07 ⑤	08 ②	09 ①	10 ⑤
11 ③	12 ⑤	13 ⑤	14 ②	15 ④

01 next spring은 미래를 나타내는 부사구, 「will + 동사원형」
John은 내년 봄에 유럽에 갈 거야.

02 don't have to ~할 필요 없다
마감은 다음 달 말이야. 그러니까 너는 오늘 보고서를 끝낼 필요는 없어.

03 couldn't ~할 수 없었다
• Kim은 아파서 학교에 갈 수 없었다.
• 나는 열심히 연습하지 않아서 대회에서 우승할 수 없었다.

04 할 일이 있다고 했으므로 같이 갈 수 없다는 대답이 적절
A 내일 영화 보러 가자.
B 미안하지만 너와 함께 갈 수 없어. 나는 할 일이 있어.

05 허락을 구하는 May
A 안녕하세요. 제가 여권을 볼 수 있을까요?
B 그럼요. 여기 있습니다.

06 ③ invites → invite
① 그들은 회사에서 청바지를 입을 수 있나요?
② 저를 위해 창문을 좀 열어주시겠어요?
③ Eddie가 나를 파티에 초대할까?
④ Jessica는 어젯밤에 숙제를 할 수 없었다.
⑤ 그는 그녀에게 생일 선물을 줄 것이다.

07 [보기] must ~해야 한다(의무) ⑤ 의무 ① ② ③ ④ 추측
[보기] 학생들은 여덟 시까지 학교에 등교해 있어야 한다.
① Sue는 많은 건물을 소유하고 있어. 그녀는 분명 부자일 거야.
② James는 밤새 공부했어. 그는 분명 피곤할 거야.
③ 아이가 지금 울고 있어. 분명 배고플 거야.
④ 그가 저 여성을 도와줬어. 분명 친절한 사람일 거야.
⑤ 오늘 밤에 프로젝트를 끝내자. 내일 제출해야 해.

08 ② 허락, 허가 ① ③ ④ ⑤ 능력, 가능
① 넌 바다에서 수영할 수 있니?
② 정말 춥구나. 네 외투를 빌릴 수 있을까?
③ 나는 영어로 읽고 쓸 수 있다.
④ 그들이 이 문제를 풀 수 있을까?
⑤ 그는 매우 빠르게 달릴 수 있다.

09 ① 「Do + 주어 + have to + 동사원형 ~?」 ~해야 하나요?
① A 제가 회의에 가야 하나요?
B 아뇨, 그러실 수 없습니다.
② A Yang 선생님과 통화할 수 있을까요?
B 네, 접니다.
③ A 너희 오늘 밤에 외식할 거니?
B 응, 그럴 거야.
④ A 너 그에게 감사 카드를 보낼 거니?
B 당연하지.
⑤ A 우리 역에서 만나도 될까?
B 좋아. 그럼 거기서 보자.

10 ⑤ don't have to ~할 필요 없다 ≠ must not ~하지 않아야 한다 ① can = be able to ~할 수 있다 ② 「May I ~?」 = 「Can I ~?」 ~해도 될까요? ③ will = be going to ~할 것이다 ④ 「Will you ~?」 = 「Can you ~?」 ~해줄래?
① 나는 컴퓨터를 수리할 수 있다.
② 제가 당신의 신분증을 볼 수 있을까요?
③ 그녀는 택시를 탈 거야.
④ 그 종이를 건네줄래?
⑤ 너는 지금 집에 가지 않아도 돼. → 너는 지금 집에 가면 안 돼.

11 ③ 히터를 좀 켜 주겠니?: Can you turn on the heater?
③ 네가 히터를 켜야 하니?

12 [보기] must ~해야 한다(의무) ⑤ have to ~해야 한다(의무)
[보기] 착륙 시 승객은 착석해 있어야 합니다.
① 착륙 시 승객은 착석해 있을 수 있습니다.
② 착륙 시 승객은 착석해 있을지도 모릅니다.
③ 착륙 시 승객은 착석해 있을 것입니다.
④ 착륙 시 승객은 착석해 있을 것입니다.
⑤ 착륙 시 승객은 착석해 있어야 합니다.

13 「Should + 주어 + 동사원형 ~?」 ~해야 하나요?,
「don't have to + 동사원형」 ~할 필요 없다

A 너 일기예보 봤니? 내가 우산을 가져가야 할까?
B 아니, 그럴 필요 없어. 오늘 비가 오지 않을 거야.

[14-15]
A 모임에 왜 빠지셨어요?
B 참석 못해서 죄송해요. 어제 우리 아들이 다리를 다쳐서 병원에 데려가야 했어요.
A 어머나, 그거 안됐네요. 그래서 아들은 좀 어때요?
B 괜찮아요. 하지만 한 달 동안 다리에 깁스를 해야 해요.
A 애가 분명 의기소침하겠네요.
B 네. 그 아인 축구를 정말 좋아하는데 축구를 하지 말아야 해요.

14 ⓐ「couldn't + 동사원형」 ~할 수 없었다 ⓑ「had to + 동사원형」 ~했어야 했다 ⓒ「must + 동사원형」 ~임이 틀림없다

15 ④「shouldn't + 동사원형」 ~하지 않아야 한다

: 서술형 평가 P. 065

01 must stop
02 must not swim
03 Can, I, have, to
04 shouldn't, should, shouldn't, should
05 can
06 can't be there
07 has → have
08 can't speak Chinese, can play the guitar
09 can't ride a horse, can speak Chinese
10 can't ride a horse, can play the guitar

[01-02] 「must + 동사원형」 ~해야 한다, 「must not + 동사원형」 ~하지 않아야 한다
[보기] 당신은 여기서 담배를 피우면 안 됩니다.

01 당신은 이 표지판이 있는 곳에서 멈춰야 합니다.

02 당신은 강에서 수영하면 안 됩니다.

03 「Can I + 동사원형 ~?」 ~해도 될까?, 「When do I have to + 동사원형 ~?」 언제 ~해야 할까?
A 네 수학책을 빌릴 수 있을까?
B 당연하지.
A 언제 돌려줘야 하니?
B 다음 주에는 돌려줘.

04 「should + 동사원형」 ~해야 한다, 「shouldn't + 동사원형」 ~하지 않아야 한다
우리의 자연 환경을 보호하기 위해서:
• 당신은 쓰레기를 버리지 말아야 합니다.
• 당신은 불을 꺼야 합니다.
• 당신은 물을 낭비하지 않아야 합니다.
• 당신은 에너지를 절약해야 합니다.

05 「can I + 동사원형 ~?」 제가 ~할까요?, 「Can you + 동사원형 ~?」 ~해 줄래요?, 「can + 동사원형」 ~할 수 있다
A 여보세요, 피자하우스입니다. 무엇을 도와드릴까요?
B 피자를 주문하고 싶어요. 슈퍼 슈프림, 보통 크기로요.
A 알겠습니다. 주소를 알려 주시겠어요?
B 메인가 12번지예요. 얼마나 걸릴까요?
A 30분 후에 배달될 거예요.

[06-07]
A 너 Brian 봤어?
B 아니. 하지만 아마 도서관에 있을지도 몰라.
A 그는 거기에 있을 리가 없어. 내가 방금 거기 있었는데 그를 찾을 수 없었어.
B 그에게 전화를 걸어보면 되지. 확실하진 않지만, 아마 그는 전화기를 가지고 있을 거야.
A 알았어. 내가 전화해 볼게.

06 ①「can't be」 ~일 리가 없다

07 ②「may + 동사원형」

[08-10] 「can't + 동사원형」 ~할 수 없다, 「can + 동사원형」 ~할 수 있다
[보기] Philip은 말을 탈 수 없지만, 중국어를 할 수 있다.

08 Susan은 중국어를 할 수 없지만, 기타를 칠 수 있다.

09 Tony는 말을 탈 수 없지만 중국어를 할 수 있다.

10 Danny는 말을 탈 수 없지만, 기타를 칠 수 있다.

Chapter 07

UNIT 01

Check-up P. 068
1 What **2** Which

1 What 무엇

2 Which 어떤

: EXERCISES P. 069

Ⓐ **1** Who **2** Which **3** What **4** Who
Ⓑ **1** (d) **2** (b) **3** (a) **4** (e) **5** (c)
Ⓒ **1** What **2** Who **3** Which
Ⓓ **1** What, is, your, favorite, fruit
2 Who, is, the, woman
3 Which, cake, do, you, like

A

1 Who 누구
A 무대 위의 저 소녀는 누구니?
B 내 딸이야.

2 Which 어느 것
A 수영과 등산 중 어느 것을 더 좋아하니?
B 나는 등산을 더 좋아해.

3 What 무엇
A 오늘 밤에 무엇을 하고 싶니?
B 나는 볼링을 치고 싶어.

4 Who 누구
A 너의 가장 친한 친구는 누구니?
B Alex가 내 가장 친한 친구야.

B

1 What 무엇
네 아버지께서는 무슨 일을 하시니? (d) 빵을 만들어서 판매하셔.

2 Who 누구
모자를 쓰고 있는 저 여자 분은 누구니? (b) 우리 어머니셔.

3 Which 어떤
어떤 신발이 네 것이니? (a) 저 빨간색 신이 내 것이야.

4 What 무엇
어젯밤에 무엇을 했니? (e) 콘서트에 갔어.

5 Who 누가
누가 파티에 왔었니? (c) Tom이 왔었어.

C

1 What 무엇
장차 무엇이 되고 싶니?

2 Who 누구
네가 가장 좋아하는 화가는 누구니?

3 Which 어떤
작은 것과 큰 것 중 네 선택은 어떤 것이니?

UNIT 02

Check-up P. 070
1 How 2 When

1 How 어떻게

2 When 언제

: EXERCISES P. 071

A 1 Where 2 How 3 Why 4 When

B 1 When 2 How 3 Where 4 Why

C 1 How many 2 How long 3 How often
4 How old 5 How much

D 1 Where, is, the, bookstore
2 How, is, the, weather
3 Why, were, you, late, for

A

1 Where 어디에
A 네 전화기가 어디에 있어? B 책상 위에 있어.

2 How 어떻게
A 넌 학교에 어떻게 가니? B 나는 자전거를 타고 학교에 가.

3 Why 왜
A 왜 울고 있니? B 다리를 다쳤어.

4 When 언제
A 언제 독일에 갈 거니? B 다음 9월에.

B

1 When 언제
A 너는 그녀를 언제 만났니? B 어제.

2 How often 얼마나 자주
A 그 버스는 얼마나 자주 오나요? B 10분마다 와요.

3 Where 어디에
A 지하철역이 어디 있나요? B 제가 길을 안내해 드릴게요.

4 Why 왜
A 왜 독서 클럽에 가입했니? B 나는 책 읽기를 좋아하거든.

C

1 How many 얼마나 많은
A 너희 반에는 남자 애들이 몇 명이니? B 15명이야.

2 How long 얼마나 긴
A 만리장성은 얼마나 긴가요? B 6,400km가 넘어요.

3 How often 얼마나 자주
A 얼마나 자주 영화를 보러 가나요? B 한 달에 한 번이요.

4 How old 몇 살
A 네 여동생은 몇 살이니? B 열세 살이야.

5 how much (값이) 얼마, 얼마나 많은
A 그 햄버거는 얼마인가요? B 3천원이에요.

UNIT 03

Check-up P. 072

1 are **2** or

1 앞문장이 부정이면 부가의문문은 긍정

2 선택의문문의 or

: EXERCISES P. 073

Ⓐ **1** don't **2** wasn't **3** didn't **4** won't

Ⓑ **1** can, he **2** isn't, she **3** did, they **4** didn't, they

Ⓒ **1** Don't you love him?
2 Doesn't the bank open at 10?
3 Isn't he your best friend?
4 Can't you hear my voice?

Ⓓ **1** Is it a dolphin or a whale?
2 He doesn't like blue, does he?
3 Which do you like better, jazz music or hip-hop music?
4 Isn't your brother at school now?

A

1 앞문장이 긍정이면 부가의문문은 부정
너는 재즈 음악을 좋아해, 그렇지 않니?

2 앞문장이 긍정이면 부가의문문은 부정
그는 매우 행복했어, 그렇지 않니?

3 일반동사 과거형의 부가의문문은 did 동사를 이용
그녀가 창문을 열었어, 그렇지 않니?

4 will의 부가의문문은 will을 이용
너는 누나에게 전화할 거지, 그렇지 않니?

B

1 「주어+can't ~, can+대명사 주어?」
Fred는 수영을 전혀 못해, 그렇지?

2 「주어+is ~, isn't+대명사 주어?」
Liz가 네 여자 친구지, 그렇지 않니?

3 「주어+didn't ~, did+대명사 주어?」
그들은 현장 학습을 가지 않았어, 그렇지?

4 「주어+일반동사 과거형 ~, didn't+대명사 주어?」
Bob과 Ted는 어젯밤에 공연을 보러 갔어, 그렇지 않니?

C

1 「Don't+2인칭 주어(you)+동사원형 ~?」
너는 그를 사랑한다.
→ 너는 그를 사랑하지 않니?

2 「Doesn't+3인칭 단수(the bank)+동사원형 ~?」
그 은행은 열 시에 연다.
→ 그 은행은 열 시에 열지 않니?

3 「Isn't+3인칭 단수(he) ~?」
그는 너의 가장 친한 친구야.
→ 그는 너의 가장 친한 친구가 아니니?

4 「Can't+주어+동사원형 ~?」
너는 내 목소리를 들을 수 있어.
→ 너는 내 목소리를 들을 수 없니?

UNIT 04

Check-up P. 074

1 How **2** What **3** How **4** What

1 「How+형용사+주어+동사!」

2 「What+a+형용사+명사+주어+동사!」

3 「How+부사+주어+동사!」

4 「What+형용사+복수 명사+주어+동사!」

: EXERCISES P. 075

Ⓐ **1** What **2** How **3** What **4** How

Ⓑ **1** How **2** What **3** What **4** How

Ⓒ **1** a sweet girl Samantha is
2 wide the screen is
3 beautiful the castle is
4 intelligent students they are

Ⓓ **1** What a long trip it was!
2 How kind the girl is!
3 What a great idea you have!
4 How delicious the pasta was!

A

1 「What+형용사+복수 명사+주어+동사!」
너는 정말 예쁜 인형을 가지고 있구나!

2 「How+형용사+주어+동사!」
그 패션모델은 정말 키가 크구나!

3 「What+a+형용사+명사+주어+동사!」
그녀는 정말 아름다운 목소리를 가졌구나!

4 「How+형용사+주어+동사!」
그 퍼즐은 정말 어렵구나!

B

1 「How+형용사+주어+동사!」
그 해변은 정말 깨끗하구나!

2 「What + a + 형용사 + 명사 + 주어 + 동사!」
너는 정말 얇은 스마트폰을 가지고 있구나!

3 「What + 형용사 + 복수 명사!」
정말 아름다운 집들이구나!

4 「How + 형용사 + 주어 + 동사!」
그 공연은 정말 대단했어!

C

1 「What + a + 형용사 + 명사 + 주어 + 동사!」
Samantha는 매우 다정한 소녀이다.
→ Samantha는 정말 다정한 소녀구나!

2 「How + 형용사 + 주어 + 동사!」
화면이 정말 넓다.
→ 화면이 정말 넓구나!

3 「How + 형용사 + 주어 + 동사!」
그 성은 정말 아름답다.
→ 그 성은 정말 아름답구나!

4 「What + 형용사 + 복수 명사 + 주어 + 동사!」
그들은 매우 지적인 학생들이다.
→ 그들은 정말 지적인 학생들이구나!

UNIT 05

Check-up P. 076
1 Hurry 2 Let's

1 긍정명령문: 「동사원형 ~.」 ~해라

2 「Let's + 동사원형」 ~하자

: EXERCISES P. 077

A 1 Take 2 have 3 Don't talk 4 Let's 5 Let's not
B 1 Be 2 Don't be 3 Wash 4 Don't swim 5 Stand
C 1 Don't bring 2 Fasten 3 Don't walk around 4 Don't make 5 Turn off
D 1 Don't touch the paintings.
2 Let's have some snacks at the cafeteria.
3 Be kind to your classmates.

A

1 긍정명령문: 「동사원형 ~.」 ~해라
너 피곤해 보여. 좀 쉬어.

2 「Let's + 동사원형」 ~하자
생일 축하해. 파티를 열자.

3 부정명령문: 「Don't + 동사원형 ~.」 ~하지 마라
아기가 자고 있어. 크게 이야기하지 마.

4 「Let's + 동사원형」 ~하자
날씨가 좋아. 산책 가자.

5 「Let's not + 동사원형」 ~하지 말자
아직 더워. 에어컨을 끄지 말자.

B

[1-5] 긍정명령문: 「동사원형 ~.」 ~해라,
부정명령문: 「Don't + 동사원형」 ~하지 마라

1 극장에서는 조용히 해라.

2 다시는 수업에 늦지 마라.

3 먹기 전에 손을 씻어라.

4 밤에 수영하지 마. 위험해.

5 여기는 사람이 아주 많아요. 줄을 서 주세요.

C

[1-5] 긍정명령문: 「동사원형 ~.」 ~해라,
부정명령문: 「Don't + 동사원형」 ~하지 마라
승객 여러분께 알려 드립니다.
1 기내에 무거운 짐은 가져오지 말아 주세요.
2 안전벨트를 착용해 주세요.
3 안내 등이 켜졌을 때에는 돌아다니지 말아 주세요.
4 큰 소리를 내지 말아 주세요.
5 휴대 전화를 꺼 주세요.

: Review Test P. 078

01 ③	02 ⑤	03 ②	04 ③	05 ①
06 ③	07 ④	08 ⑤	09 ①	10 ①
11 ④	12 ③	13 ④	14 ⑤	15 ②

01 Where 어디에서
A 그 샌드위치를 어디에서 샀니?
B 우리 집 근처 가게에서.

02 What 무엇을
A 네 아버지께서는 지금 무엇을 하고 계시니?
B 낮잠을 주무시고 계셔.

03 Why 왜
A 너 어제는 왜 오지 않았니?
B 감기에 걸렸거든.

04 Which 어떤, 어느 것
• 검은색과 흰색 중 네 가방은 어떤 색이니?
• 너는 축구와 야구 중에 어떤 것을 좋아하니?

05 how 어떻게, how much (값이) 얼마
• 여기에 어떻게 왔나요?
• 그 시계는 얼마죠?

06 「주어 + 일반동사 과거형 ~, didn't + 대명사 주어?」
너는 나에게 이메일을 보냈어, 그렇지 않니?

07 「주어 + can't ~, can + 대명사 주어?」
Daniel은 저 차를 살 수 없어, 그렇지?

08 ⑤ 「What + 형용사 + 복수 명사 + 주어 + 동사」
① ② ③ ④ 「How + 형용사 + 주어 + 동사」
① 그는 정말 똑똑하구나!
② 너는 정말 아름답구나!
③ 이 상자들은 정말 무겁구나!
④ 그 문제는 정말 어렵구나!
⑤ 그 신발은 정말 조그맣구나!

09 ① What(무슨) 혹은 Which(어떤)가 가능 ② How tall 얼마나 큰 ③ How much (값이) 얼마 ④ How long 얼마나 오래 ⑤ How often 얼마나 자주
① 너는 어떤[무슨] 과목을 좋아하니?
② 네 오빠는 키가 몇이니?
③ 이 장화는 얼마입니까?
④ 거기 가는 데 얼마나 걸리니?
⑤ 넌 손을 얼마나 자주 씻니?

10 ① 긍정문의 부가의문문은 부정문: do you → don't you
① 너 오늘 시험이 있지, 그렇지 않니?
② Tom은 여자 형제가 없어, 그렇지?
③ 그녀가 이 편지들을 썼어, 그렇지 않니?
④ 그 영화는 아주 재미있지는 않았어, 그렇지?
⑤ 소포는 내일 도착할 거야, 그렇지 않니?

11 ④ What → How
① 너는 정말 훌륭한 책들을 가지고 있구나!
② 그 문제는 정말 간단하구나!
③ 그 돌고래들은 정말 똑똑하구나!
④ 그 초콜릿은 정말 맛있구나!
⑤ 그 식당은 정말 고급스럽구나!

12 ③ 「You won't + 동사원형 ~, will you?」

13 ④ 「What + a + 형용사 + 명사 + 주어 + 동사!」

[14-15]
A 날씨가 정말 좋구나! 소풍 가자.
B 음, 그러고 싶지만 그럴 수 없어.
A 왜?
B 난 도서관에 가야 해. 시험이 있어.
A 시험이 언젠데?
B 이번 주 금요일.
A 알겠어. 그러면 도서관에 같이 가는 건 어때?
B 넌 정말 진정한 친구로구나!

14 ⓐ 「What + 형용사 + 명사!」 ⓑ Why 왜 ⓒ When 언제
ⓓ 「Why don't we + 동사원형 ~?」 ~하는 게 어때?

15 ② 「What + a + 형용사 + 명사 + 주어 + 동사!」

: 서술형 평가 P. 080

01	Don't touch	02	Turn right
03	How often	04	How much
05	How long	06	Let's eat out.

07 (1) doesn't it (2) can you (3) isn't she
08 What a beautiful coat
09 How amazing his songs were
10 3. How many brothers and sisters do you have?
5. Which do you like better, summer or winter?

01 부정명령문: 「Don't + 동사원형 ~.」 ~하지 마라
벽에 걸린 그림을 만지지 마시오.

02 긍정명령문: 「동사원형 ~.」 ~해라
녹색 신호 시 우회전하시오.

[03-05] How long 얼마나 긴, How often 얼마나 자주, How much 얼마

03 A 너는 조부모님을 얼마나 자주 방문하니?
B 일주일에 한 번 뵈러 가.

04 A 이 검은색 치마는 얼마입니까?
B 20달러예요.

05 A 그 영화는 얼마나 길어?
B 두 시간이야.

06 「Let's + 동사원형」 ~하자
A 오늘은 네 생일이잖아. 무엇을 하고 싶니?
B 우리 외식하자. 이탈리아 음식을 먹고 싶어.

07 (1) 「3인칭 단수(The grocery store) + 일반동사의 현재형(opens), doesn't + 대명사 주어(it)」, (2) 「You can't ~, can you?」, (3) 「3인칭 단수(Ms. Johns) is ~, isn't + 대명사 주어(she)?」
(1) 그 식료품점은 일요일에 문을 열어, 그렇지 않니?
(2) 네가 그 모든 상자를 다 옮길 수는 없어, 그렇지?
(3) Johns 씨가 너의 담임 선생님이야, 그렇지 않니?

08 「What + a + 형용사 + 명사!」
A 너 멋있어 보여. 정말 아름다운 코트구나!
B 정말 고마워. 엄마에게 받은 생일 선물이야.

09 「How + 형용사 + 주어 + 동사!」
A 대단한 공연이었어. 그 가수는 정말 잘 했어.
B 맞아. 그의 노래는 정말 대단했어!

10 3. How much → How many, 5. What → Which
자신에 대해 쓰시오!
1. 이름이 무엇입니까?
2. 몇 살입니까?
3. 형제자매가 몇 명입니까?
4. 어떤 과목을 좋아합니까?
5. 여름과 겨울 중 어느 것을 좋아합니까?

Chapter 08

UNIT 01

Check-up P. 082
1 It 2 how 3 to learn

1 가주어 it, 진주어 to be a great chef
2 how to cook 어떻게 요리하는지
3 plan은 to부정사를 목적어로 취하는 동사

: EXERCISES P. 083
A 1 to buy 3 to write 2 to join 4 to get up 5 to be
B 1 to see 2 to stay 3 to buy 4 to learn 5 to watch
C 1 to leave 2 to finish 3 to shop
D 1 to, play, soccer 2 to, study, abroad
3 what, to, wear

A

1 「want + to부정사」
Nancy는 새 차를 사고 싶어 한다.
2 「to + 동사원형」
그의 직업은 소설을 쓰는 것이다.
3 「refuse + to부정사」
그가 너희 미식축구 클럽에 가입하는 것을 거절했어.
4 「to + 동사원형」
일찍 일어나는 것은 어렵다.
5 보어로 쓰인 「to + 동사원형」
내 꿈은 수의사가 되는 것이다.

B

1 「refuse + to부정사」
그는 진찰 받는 것을 거부했다.
2 「want + to부정사」
Jessica는 여기에 머물고 싶어 한다.
3 「hope + to부정사」
나는 새 자전거를 사길 바란다.
4 「decide + to부정사」
그는 새로운 언어를 배우기로 결심했다.
5 「plan + to부정사」
우리는 축구 경기를 보려고 계획하고 있다.

UNIT 02

Check-up P. 084
1 to meet 2 something to do

1 부사적(목적)으로 쓰인 「to + 동사원형」
2 형용사적으로 쓰인 「something + to부정사」

: EXERCISES P. 085
A 1 to say 2 to sleep 3 to invite 4 to eat 5 to read
B 1 믿다니 2 통과해서 3 만나게 되어 4 읽으려고
C 1 to go 2 to buy 3 to give 4 to be
D 1 to, catch, the, bus 2 many, places, to, visit
3 to, see, the, picture

A

1 말할 것
나는 무언가 할 말이 있다.
2 잠잘 약간의 시간
나는 잠잘 시간이 좀 필요해.
3 초대할 많은 친구
우리는 초대할 친구가 많다.
4 먹을 약간의 사과
그는 먹을 사과를 좀 가져왔다.
5 읽을 잡지
그는 읽을 잡지를 샀다.

C

1 감정의 원인
그는 콘서트에 갈 것이다. 그는 행복하다.
→ 그는 콘서트에 가게 되어 행복하다.
2 목적
그녀는 가게에 갔다. 그녀는 우유를 좀 샀다.
→ 그녀는 우유를 좀 사러 가게에 갔다.
3 a tie를 수식하는 to give
나는 넥타이를 가지고 있다. 나는 그것을 아버지께 드릴 것이다.
→ 나는 아버지께 드릴 넥타이를 가지고 있다.
4 목적
그녀는 교사가 되고 싶었다. 그래서 열심히 공부했다.
→ 그녀는 교사가 되려고 열심히 공부했다.

UNIT 03

Check-up P. 086
1 smiling 2 Learning 3 helping

1 「keep + 동명사」

2 '~하는 것'이라는 의미가 되려면 주어 자리에 동명사나 to부정사가 와야 함

3 '하는 것'이라는 의미가 되려면 보어 자리에 동명사나 to부정사가 와야 함

: EXERCISES P. 087

Ⓐ 1 Riding 2 talking 3 baking 4 losing

Ⓑ 1 missing 2 cooking 3 buying 4 joining

Ⓒ 1 산책하는 것을 2 손톱을 물어뜯는 것
3 사람들을 돕는 데 4 열심히 공부하는 것은

Ⓓ 1 watching, musicals
2 Trying, new, food
3 changing, his, job
4 collecting, photos, of, movie, stars

1 '~하는 것'이라는 의미가 되려면 주어 자리에 동명사나 to부정사가 와야 함
자전거를 타는 것은 신 나는 일이다.

2 「love + 동명사 / to부정사」
나는 여동생에게 이야기하는 것을 매우 좋아한다.

3 「enjoy + 동명사」
우리 언니는 쿠키를 굽는 것을 좋아한다.

4 '하는 것'이라는 의미가 되려면 보어 자리에 동명사나 to부정사가 와야 함
Steve의 목표는 5킬로그램을 감량하는 것이다.

B

1 「be afraid of + 동명사」
나는 기차를 놓칠 까봐 걱정이다.

2 「enjoy + 동명사」
나는 이탈리아 음식을 요리하는 걸 즐긴다.

3 「give up + 동명사」
그녀는 새 신을 사는 걸 포기했다.

4 「talk about + 동명사」
그들은 댄스 동아리에 가입하는 것에 관해 이야기했다.

UNIT 04

Check-up P. 088
1 cooking 2 to do 3 to walk / walking

1 「enjoy + 동명사」

2 「want + to부정사」

3 「love + 동명사 / to부정사」

: EXERCISES P. 089

Ⓐ 1 to use 2 to cry / crying 3 reading 4 to have
5 to exercise / exercising

Ⓑ 1 to meet 2 going 3 to become 4 to study
5 traveling

Ⓒ 1 to meet 2 closing 3 to move 4 working

Ⓓ 1 enjoys, taking, a, nap
2 finished, checking, her, eyes
3 promised, to, come, back
4 Keep, walking, down

1 「want + to부정사」
나는 화장실을 사용하길 원해요.

2 「hate + 동명사 / to부정사」
그는 사람들 앞에서 우는 것을 매우 싫어한다.

3 「finish + 동명사」
Stella는 그 책 읽는 것을 마쳤다.

4 「would like + to부정사」
나는 햄버거를 하나 먹고 싶어요.

5 「start + 동명사 / to부정사」
그녀는 건강해지기 위해 운동을 시작했다.

B

1 「expect + to부정사」
우리는 당신을 곧 만나길 기대합니다.

2 「give up + 동명사」
Jessica는 다이어트를 포기했다.

3 「decide + to부정사」
Jack은 의사가 되기로 결심했다.

4 「plan + to부정사」
그들은 내년에 해외에서 공부를 하려고 계획했다.

5 「enjoy + 동명사」
그녀는 세계 곳곳을 여행하는 것을 즐긴다.

C

1 「promise + to부정사」
나는 오늘 밤에 그녀를 만나기로 약속했다.

2 「mind + 동명사」
창문을 닫아 주실래요?

3 「decide + to부정사」
Long 씨는 캐나다로 이주하기로 결정했다.

4 「quit + 동명사」
Kim 씨는 지난달에 회사를 그만두었다.

: Review Test

P. 090

01 ④	**02** ⑤	**03** ④	**04** ②	**05** ⑤
06 ③	**07** ⑤	**08** ①	**09** ③	**10** ③
11 ⑤	**12** ②	**13** ①	**14** ③	**15** ③

01 「want + to부정사」
그는 위대한 예술가가 되길 원한다.

02 「finish + 동명사」
너는 빨래를 끝냈니?

03 '~하는 것'이라는 의미가 되려면 주어 자리에 to부정사나 동명사가 와야 함
설탕을 너무 많이 먹는 것은 좋지 않다.

04 「enjoy + 동명사」, 「would like + to부정사」
그는 주말 마다 낚시하는 것을 즐긴다.
나는 기자가 되고 싶다.

05 '~하는 것'이라는 의미가 되려면 보어 자리에 to부정사나 동명사가 와야 함, 「finish + 동명사」
내 꿈은 기타 연주자가 되는 것이다.
Teddy는 시험공부를 끝냈다.

06 ③ 「anything + 형용사 + to부정사」
A 오늘 특별히 할 것이 있니?
B 사실, 여자 친구와 영화를 볼 거야.

07 보어 자리에는 to부정사와 동명사 모두 올 수 있지만, 동명사 앞에는 to를 쓰지 않음
A Kevin의 취미는 무엇이니?
B 그의 취미는 영화를 보는 것 / 온라인 게임을 하는 것 / 쇼핑을 가는 것 / 합창단에서 노래를 하는 것이야.

08 ② Run → Running / To run ③ happy see → happy to see ④ for invite → for inviting ⑤ to answering → to answer
① 그녀는 내년에 대학에 진학할 계획이다.
② 수영장 근처에서 뛰는 것은 위험하다.
③ Susan은 Michael을 봐서 행복했다.
④ 파티에 초대해 주셔서 감사합니다.
⑤ 이 질문은 너무 어려워서 대답할 수 없다.

09 「how + to부정사」 ~하는 방법, 「where + to부정사」 어디로 ~할 지
- Anna는 탁구 치는 법을 안다.
- 너는 이번 토요일에 어디로 갈지 아니?

10 ③ mind to go → mind going
① 중국 여행은 힘들었다.
② 그녀는 패스트푸드를 먹는 것을 그만두었다.
③ 나와 함께 가는 것이 싫으니?
④ 그들은 수영장에서 수영을 배웠다.
⑤ 나는 즐겁게 어린 남동생을 돌봐주었다.

11 ⑤ planned taking → planned to take
① 너는 그녀를 보기를 원하니?
② Peter는 아버지의 차 세차를 끝마쳤다.
③ 우리 형은 기타 연주하는 것을 좋아한다.
④ 그녀의 직업은 학교에서 음악을 가르치는 것이다.
⑤ 그녀는 런던으로 여행하는 것을 계획했다.

12 ② 부사적 쓰임(목적) ① ③ ④ ⑤ 명사적 쓰임(목적어)
① Jenny는 그 콘서트에 가기를 원한다.
② 우리는 물을 좀 사러 가게에 갔다.
③ Robert는 60세에 은퇴할 계획이다.
④ 그녀는 역사 보고서를 끝내기로 결심했다.
⑤ 나는 너를 곧 다시 만나기를 바라.

13 ① 명사적 쓰임(보어) ② ③ ④ ⑤ 형용사적 쓰임(명사 수식)
① 나의 취미는 모형 자동차를 만드는 것이다.
② 공연을 시작할 시간이다.
③ 내가 먹을 것을 좀 가져올게.
④ 나는 중요하게 할 말이 있어요.
⑤ 나는 그 셔츠를 살 약간의 돈을 가지고 있다.

[14-15]
나는 지난주에 동물원에 갔다. 볼 만한 동물들이 많았다. 내가 가장 좋아한 것은 원숭이에게 먹이를 주는 것이었다. 그들은 여기저기 뛰어다니며 재미난 소리를 냈다. 나는 또한 친구들과 사진을 많이 찍었다. 정말 재미있었다. 또 그곳에 가고 싶다.

14 ⓐ 「명사 + to부정사」 to부정사의 형용사적 쓰임(명사 수식)
ⓑ '~하는 것'이라는 의미로 쓰인 to부정사나 동명사 보어

15 ⓒ to부정사의 명사적 쓰임(목적어) ③ to부정사의 명사적 쓰임(목적어) ① to부정사의 형용사적 쓰임(명사 수식) ② to부정사의 형용사적 쓰임(명사 수식) ④ to부정사의 부사적 쓰임(목적) ⑤ to부정사의 부사적 쓰임(결과)
① 잠자리에 들 시간이다.
② 나는 할 일이 많다.
③ 우리는 할머니 댁 방문을 계획했다.
④ 나는 몸매를 유지하기 위해 건강에 좋은 음식을 먹는다.
⑤ Kelly는 자라서 대통령이 되었다.

: 서술형 평가

P. 092

01 to, use
02 seeing
03 to catch
04 to meet
05 winning → win
06 hold → holding
07 to meet
08 to talk
09 want to work for
10 (1) enjoys traveling and reading books
(2) enjoys exercising and reading books

01 「It(가주어) ~ to부정사(진주어)」

02 「look forward to + 동명사」 ~을 고대하다

03 to부정사의 부사적 쓰임(목적)
나는 기차를 잡고 싶었다. 그래서 열심히 뛰었다.
→ 나는 기차를 잡으려고 열심히 뛰었다.

04 to부정사의 부사적 쓰임(감정의 원인)
나는 옛 친구를 만났다. 그래서 나는 행복했다.
→ 나는 옛 친구를 만나서 행복했다.

05 「want + to부정사」: wanted to winning → wanted to win
그는 우승하기를 원했다.

06 「mind + 동명사」: mind hold → mind holding
나를 위해 문을 좀 잡아주시겠어요?

07 「plan + to부정사」 ~할 계획이다
A 네 시에 만나는 게 어때?
B 좋아.
→ 그들은 네 시에 만날 계획이다.

08 「want + to부정사」
A 여보세요?
B 여보세요. Alice와 통화할 수 있을까요?
→ 그 사람은 Alice와 통화하고 싶어 한다.

09 「want + to부정사」
Q: 장차 무엇을 하고 싶습니까?

10 「enjoy + 동명사」
[보기] Jessica는 운동과 여행을 즐긴다.
(1) David는 여행과 독서를 즐긴다.
(2) Steve는 운동과 독서를 즐긴다.

Chapter 09

UNIT 01

Check-up P. 094
1 strange **2** looks like

1 「look + 형용사」

2 「look like + 명사」

: EXERCISES P. 095

A **1** excited **2** fresh **3** great **4** warm **5** interesting

B **1** sounds **2** sounds like **3** look like **4** look

C **1** tastes sweet **2** smells like chocolate
3 feels like summer **4** sounds beautiful

D **1** don't, feel, good **2** smells, bad
3 sounds, like, an, angel's
4 looked, like, a, friendly, person

A

1 「feel + 형용사」
나는 오늘 신이 났다.

2 「taste + 형용사」
이 우유는 맛이 신선하다.

3 「smell + 형용사」
그 수프는 냄새가 좋다.

4 「look + 형용사」
그 스웨터는 따뜻해 보인다.

5 「sound + 형용사」
그 게임은 재미있을 것 같다.

B

1 「sound + 형용사」
그 노래는 소리가 익숙하다.

2 「sound like + 명사」
그 노래는 그녀가 가장 좋아하는 노래처럼 들린다.

3 「look like + 명사」
너는 네 아버지처럼 보이는구나.

4 「look + 형용사」
이 사진에서 너는 정말 잘생겨 보인다.

C

1 「taste + 형용사」
그 차는 맛이 달콤하다.

2 「smell like + 명사」
그 비누는 초콜릿 향이 난다.

3 「feel like + 명사」
여전히 덥구나. 여름처럼 느껴진다.

4 「sound + 형용사」
그의 노래는 아름답게 들리는구나.

UNIT 02

Check-up P. 096

1 me her pictures **2** to **3** a doll to me

1 「show + 간접목적어 + 직접목적어」

2 「send + 직접목적어 + to + 간접목적어」

3 「give + 직접목적어 + to + 간접목적어」

: EXERCISES P. 097

Ⓐ **1** for **2** of me **3** your secret to anybody
4 me a birthday gift

Ⓑ **1** for **2** of **3** to

Ⓒ **1** opera tickets for me **2** directions of me
3 the way to the station to us

Ⓓ **1** asked, him, his, name **2** show, me, your, ticket
3 lends, his, books, to, me
4 made, Korean, food, for, his, son

A

1 「buy + 직접목적어 + for + 간접목적어」
우리 선생님께서 학생들에게 아이스크림을 사주셨다.

2 「ask + 직접목적어 + of + 간접목적어」
Anne은 때때로 나에게 사적인 질문을 한다.

3 「tell + 직접목적어 + to + 간접목적어」
나는 누구에게도 네 비밀을 말하지 않을 거야.

4 「send + 간접목적어 + 직접목적어」
어제 나의 가장 친한 친구가 나에게 생일 선물을 보냈다.

B

1 「build + 직접목적어 + for + 간접목적어」
Ken은 부모님을 위해 집을 짓고 있다.

2 「ask + 직접목적어 + of + 간접목적어」
그 면접관은 나에게 많은 질문을 했다.

3 「write + 직접목적어 + to + 간접목적어」
Sidney는 종종 조부모님께 이메일을 쓴다.

C

1 「get + 간접목적어 + 직접목적어」(4문형)
→「get + 직접목적어 + for + 간접목적어」(3문형)
우리 아버지께서 나에게 오페라 표를 구해 주셨다.

2 「ask + 간접목적어 + 직접목적어」(4문형)
→「ask + 직접목적어 + of + 간접목적어」(3문형)
한 노인이 나에게 길을 물었다.

3 「show + 간접목적어 + 직접목적어」(4문형)
→「show + 직접목적어 + to + 간접목적어」(3문형)
한 친절한 소녀가 우리에게 역으로 가는 길을 알려주었다.

UNIT 03

Check-up P. 098

1 cute **2** to help

1 「find + 목적어 + 형용사」

2 「ask + 목적어 + to부정사」

: EXERCISES P. 099

Ⓐ **1** healthy **2** to be **3** a star **4** warm **5** to read

Ⓑ **1** a liar **2** boring **3** tidy **4** happy

Ⓒ **1** to wash **2** to join **3** to call **4** to sing
5 to make **6** to bring

Ⓓ **1** wants, you, to, come **2** made, people, upset
3 keep, the, classroom, clean
4 expected, him, to, pass

A

1 「find + 목적어 + 형용사」
나는 한국 음식이 건강에 좋다는 것을 알게 되었다.

2 「expect + 목적어 + to부정사」
우리는 그녀가 제시간에 오길 기대했다.

3 「make + 목적어 + 명사」
그 영화는 그를 스타로 만들었다.

4 「keep + 목적어 + 형용사」
뜨거운 커피가 당신을 따뜻하게 해줄 거예요.

5 「want + 목적어 + to부정사」
우리 아버지께서는 우리가 이 책들을 읽기를 원하신다.

B

1 「call + 목적어 + 명사」
그녀는 나를 거짓말쟁이라고 불렀다.

2 「find + 목적어 + 형용사」
그는 그 일이 지루하다는 것을 알아차렸다.

3 「keep + 목적어 + 형용사」
제발 네 방을 깨끗하게 유지해라.

4 「make + 목적어 + 형용사」
그 생일 선물이 나를 행복하게 했다.

C

1 「tell + 목적어 + to부정사」
우리 엄마가 나에게 손을 씻으라고 말했다.

2 「ask + 목적어 + to부정사」
Justin이 나에게 자신의 독서 동아리에 가입할 것을 부탁했다.

3 「want + 목적어 + to부정사」
그는 딸이 일주일에 한 번씩 전화해 주길 바랐다.

4 「expect + 목적어 + to부정사」
나는 새장 속의 새들이 노래하기를 기대했다.

5 「advise + 목적어 + to부정사」
부모들 대부분은 자녀들에게 친구를 많이 사귀라고 조언한다.

6 「order + 목적어 + to부정사」
선생님은 학생들에게 숙제를 가져오도록 시켰다.

: Review Test P. 100

01 ③	02 ①	03 ⑤	04 ②	05 ②
06 ④	07 ④	08 ②	09 ①	10 ②
11 ⑤	12 ①, ③	13 ①	14 ③	15 ①

01 「look + 형용사」
그녀의 그림은 좋아 보인다.

02 「ask + 직접목적어 + of + 간접목적어」
내가 너에게 뭐 하나 부탁해도 되겠니?

03 「be, look, smell, taste + 형용사」
그 호박파이는 맛있다 / 맛있어 보인다 / 맛있는 냄새가 난다 / 맛있다.

04 「make+ 목적어+동사원형」, 「tell, want, advise, expect + 목적어 + to부정사」
① 그의 어머니는 그에게 최선을 다하라고 말씀하셨다.
③ 그의 어머니는 그가 최선을 다하기를 원하셨다.
④ 그의 어머니는 그에게 최선을 다하라고 조언하셨다.
⑤ 그의 어머니는 그가 최선을 다할 것을 기대하셨다.

05 「give + 직접목적어 + to + 간접목적어」, 「buy, cook, make, get + 직접목적어 + for + 간접목적어」
우리 이모가 나를 위해 맛있는 피자를 샀다 / 요리했다 / 만들었다 / 가져왔다.

06 「pass + 직접목적어 + to + 간접목적어」, 「want + 목적어 + to부정사」
• 소금을 저에게 건네주시겠어요?
• 내가 너와 함께 가길 원하니?

07 ④ 「find + 목적어 + 형용사」: touchingly → touching
「주홍글자」를 읽는 것이 숙제였다. 처음에 그 책은 흥미롭게 보이지 않았다. 하지만 나중에 나는 그 책이 매우 감동적이라는 것을 알게 되었다. 나는 친구에게도 그 책을 읽으라고 말했다.

08 ② 「make + 직접목적어 + for + 간접목적어」 ① 「send + 직접목적어 + to + 간접목적어」 ③ 「lend + 직접목적어 + to+간접목적어」 ④ 「pass + 직접목적어 + to+간접목적어」 ⑤ 「tell + 직접목적어 + to + 간접목적어」
① 나는 영국에 있는 여동생에게 엽서를 보냈다.
② 우리 할머니께서는 우리를 위해 케이크를 만들어 주셨다.
③ Kendrick 씨가 우리에게 트럭을 빌려 줄 거야.
④ 그는 나에게 공을 넘기지 않았다.
⑤ 그녀는 가장 친한 친구에게 비밀을 말했다.

09 「look + 형용사」, 「ask + 목적어 + to부정사」, 「give + 직접목적어 + to + 간접목적어」
• 그 스커트는 그녀에게 잘 어울린다.
• James는 나에게 영화를 보러 가자고 했다.
• 우리 선생님은 나에게 몇 가지 조언을 해주셨다.

10 ② 「smell + 형용사」: smells like bad → smells bad
① 그건 어리석은 소리같이 들리는구나.
② 그 수프는 냄새가 안 좋아.
③ 그녀의 쿠키는 맛이 훌륭해.
④ Delaware 부인은 언제나 활기가 넘쳐 보인다.
⑤ 그 방에 있는 모든 사람들이 화가 났다.

11 ⑤ 「ask + 목적어 + to부정사」: asked Tom buy → asked Tom to buy
① Wanda는 그가 친절하다는 것을 알았다.
② 우리는 네가 정직하기를 기대해.
③ 그녀의 어머니는 그녀를 '백설공주'라고 불렀다.
④ 그들은 자리를 깨끗하게 유지해야 한다.
⑤ 나는 Tom에게 시장에서 꽃을 사오라고 부탁했다.

12 「send + 간접목적어 + 직접목적어」(4문형), 「send + 직접목적어 + to + 간접목적어」(3문형)

13 ① 「give + 간접목적어 + 직접목적어」 → 「give + 직접목적어 + to + 간접목적어」: for me → to me
① 나에게 그 공을 주세요.
② Cooper 씨가 우리에게 파이를 만들어주었다.
③ 우리 아빠가 그에게 많은 질문을 했다.
④ 그는 그녀에게 다이아몬드 반지를 사주었다.
⑤ 나는 그녀에게 꽃을 좀 보낼 것이다.

[14-15]
A 냄새가 좋구나! 뭐하고 있니?
B 엄마를 위한 아침을 만들고 있어요. 아시겠지만 엄마 생신이잖아요.
A 와. 넌 정말 좋은 아들이구나. 엄마가 정말 좋아할 거야.
B 고마워요. 나도 그것이 엄마를 행복하게 하길 바라요.
A 분명 그럴 거야.

14 ⓐ 「smell + 형용사」 ⓑ 「make + 직접목적어 + for + 간접목적어」

15 「make + 목적어 + 형용사」

: 서술형 평가 P. 102

01 send the document to you
02 bought a pair of glasses for me
03 want him to be a lawyer
04 doesn't look safe
05 told me to turn off the computer
06 told her children an interesting story
07 look upset
08 looks like a model
09 She teaches Korean to me
10 made delicious dishes for us / made us delicious dishes

01 「send + 간접목적어 + 직접목적어」
→「send + 직접목적어 + to + 간접목적어」
내가 내일 너에게 그 서류를 보낼게.

02 「buy + 간접목적어 + 직접목적어」
→「buy + 직접목적어 + for + 간접목적어」
우리 아버지께서 나에게 안경을 사주셨다.

03 「want + 목적어 + to부정사」: be → to be
Bob의 부모님은 그가 변호사가 되길 원한다.

04 「look + 형용사」: safely → safe
그 롤러코스터는 안전해 보이지 않는다.

[09-10]
안녕 Michael,
여기 내 생일 사진 몇 장 보내. 우리는 한식당에 가서 즐거운 시간을 보냈어. 사진에 있는 여자 분이 우리 선생님이야. 매주 월요일과 수요일에 나에게 한국어를 가르쳐 주셔. 내 옆에 있는 남자 분이 식당의 주방장이셔. 그가 우리에게 맛있는 음식을 만들어 주었어. 맛있어 보이지, 그렇지?

09 「teach + 간접목적어 + 직접목적어」
→「teach + 직접목적어 + to + 간접목적어」

10 「make + 간접목적어 + 직접목적어」, 「make + 직접목적어 + for + 간접목적어」

Chapter 10

UNIT 01

Check-up P. 104
1 good 2 wonderful

1 명사(teacher)를 수식하는 형용사 필요, good 좋은, well 건강한; 잘

2 명사(time)를 수식하는 형용사 필요, wonderful 멋진, 훌륭한, wonderfully 멋지게, 훌륭하게

: EXERCISES P. 105

Ⓐ 1 a little 2 a few 3 much 4 something exciting
Ⓑ 1 warm 2 tired 3 scary 4 interesting
Ⓒ 1 a little 2 little 3 few 4 a few
Ⓓ 1 many, animals 2 much, time 3 a, lot, of, participants

1 「a little + 셀 수 없는 명사(information)」
나는 그것에 관한 정보가 좀 필요해.

2 「a few + 셀 수 있는 명사의 복수형(girls)」
반에 여학생들이 몇 명 있었다.

3 「much + 셀 수 없는 명사(homework)」
우리는 오늘 숙제가 많지 않다.

4 「something + 형용사」
그는 뭔가 신 나는 일을 하기를 원한다.

1 약간이 있다는 뜻, 「a little + 셀 수 없는 명사(milk)」
냉장고에 우유가 좀 있어. 네가 마셔도 돼.

2 거의 없다는 뜻, 「little + 셀 수 없는 명사(coffee)」
찬장에 커피가 거의 없어. 좀 사야겠어.

3 거의 없다는 뜻, 「few + 셀 수 있는 명사의 복수형(friends)」
그는 아주 외롭다. 새 학교에 친구가 거의 없다.

4 약간 있다는 뜻, 「a few + 셀 수 있는 명사의 복수형(questions)」
나는 여전히 풀어야 할 문제가 좀 있어요. 시간을 좀 더 주세요.

UNIT 02

Check-up P. 106
1 carefully 2 heavily 3 comfortable

1 동사(Listen)를 수식하는 부사 필요, carefully 주의 깊게, careful 주의 깊은

2 동사(rain)를 수식하는 부사 필요, heavily 세게, 맹렬하게, heavy 맹렬한, 무거운

3 명사(chair)를 수식하는 형용사 필요, comfortable 편안한, comfortably 편안하게

: EXERCISES P. 107

Ⓐ **1** safe **2** high **3** happily **4** often takes

Ⓑ **1** drive **2** she passed the test **3** slowly **4** good

Ⓒ **1** well, good **2** quiet, quietly **3** fast, fast
4 happy, happily

Ⓓ **1** never, eats **2** a, highly, popular, singer
3 always, walks, very, fast

A

1 명사(neighborhood)를 수식하는 형용사 필요. safe 안전한, safely 안전하게
나는 안전한 동네에 산다.

2 high 높이, highly 매우, 상당히
나는 다리를 다쳤어. 높이 뛸 수가 없어.

3 동사(live)를 수식하는 부사 필요. happily 행복하게, happy 행복한
공주는 그 후로 행복하게 살았다.

4 빈도부사(often)는 일반동사(takes) 앞에 위치
그는 종종 강을 따라 산책을 한다.

B

1 부사(safely)는 동사(drive)를 수식
제발 안전하게 운전하세요.

2 부사(finally)는 문장 전체(she passed the test)를 수식
마침내, 그녀는 시험에 통과했다.

3 부사(very)는 다른 부사(slowly)를 수식
그녀는 매우 느리게 말하려고 노력했다.

4 부사(really)는 형용사(good)를 수식
그는 수학을 정말 잘한다.

C

1 동사(drive)를 수식하는 부사(well), 명사(driver)를 수식하는 형용사(good) 필요
Den은 운전을 아주 잘해. 그는 좋은 운전자야.

2 주어(Karen)를 보충 설명하는 주격 보어인 형용사(quiet), 동사(talk)를 수식하는 부사(quietly) 필요
Karen은 매우 조용하다. 그녀는 언제나 조용하게 말한다.

3 명사(runner)를 수식하는 형용사(fast), 동사(run)를 수식하는 부사(fast) 필요
Jim은 빠른 달리기 선수이다. 그는 매우 빠르게 달릴 수 있다.

4 명사(kid)를 수식하는 형용사(happy), 동사(play)를 수식하는 부사(happily) 필요
그는 행복한 아이야. 봐! 그가 행복하게 놀고 있어.

UNIT 03

Check-up P. 108
1 smarter **2** more interesting

1 smart – smarter – smartest

2 interesting – more interesting – most interesting

: EXERCISES P. 109

Ⓐ **1** well **2** more famous **3** brightest **4** most

Ⓑ **1** longer **2** loud **3** more **4** largest

Ⓒ **1** earlier, earliest **2** taller, tallest
3 better, best **4** bigger, biggest

Ⓓ **1** faster, than **2** more, difficult, than
3 the, highest, waterfall **4** as, new, as

A

1 「as + 원급 + as」
나는 엄마만큼 요리를 잘하지 못한다.

2 「비교급 + than」
Alison은 오빠보다 더 유명하다.

3 「the + 최상급」
시리우스는 밤하늘에서 가장 밝은 별이다.

4 「the + 최상급」
그는 그 영화에서 가장 잘생긴 배우였다.

B

1 「비교급 + than」
이 스카프는 내 것보다 길다.

2 「as + 원급 + as」
John의 목소리는 Ted의 목소리만큼 크다.

3 「비교급 + than」
나는 Andy보다 커피를 더 많이 마신다.

4 「the + 최상급」
세계에서 가장 큰 나라는 어느 나라입니까?

C

[1-4] 「비교급 + than」, 「the + 최상급」

1 Harold가 Bob보다 일찍 일어났지만 Mac이 그 중에서 가장 일찍 일어났다.

2 Wendy가 Mia보다 키가 크지만 Samuel이 우리 반에서 가장 큰 학생이다.

3 우리 엄마는 나보다 요리를 잘 하지만 우리 가족 중에서 우리 아빠가 요리를 가장 잘한다.

4 박물관이 은행보다 크지만 이 도시에서는 그 타워가 가장 크다.

: Review Test　P. 110

01 ⑤	02 ④	03 ④	04 ③	05 ①
06 ①	07 ④	08 ①	09 ④	10 ②, ④
11 ④	12 ②	13 ③	14 ①	15 ②

01 권유문에는 some을 이용, 「some + 셀 수 없는 명사」
뜨거운 물을 좀 드릴까요?

02 「비교급 + than」
내 친구 Jane은 나보다 바이올린 연주를 잘한다.

03 「much + 셀 수 없는 명사」
공원에 사람들이 많았다.

04 '약간'이라는 뜻으로 셀 수 있는 명사의 복수형과 함께 쓸 수 있는 수식어는 a few
[보기] 선생님은 학생들에게 몇 가지 질문을 했다.

05 '약간, 어떤, 아무것도'라는 뜻으로 의문문과 부정문에 쓰이는 수식어는 any
- 어떤 아이디어가 있나요?
- 고마워요, 하지만 나는 어떤 도움도 필요 없어요.

06 ① 의문문: any ② 긍정문: some ③ 권유문: some ④ 긍정문: some ⑤ 권유문: some
① 무슨 문제가 있나요?
② 나는 신을 운동화가 좀 필요해.
③ 뜨거운 초콜릿을 좀 드시겠어요?
④ 정원에 나무가 좀 있다.
⑤ 소풍을 위해 음식을 좀 가져가자.

07 ④ 「as + 원급 + as」 ① ② ③ ⑤ 「비교급 + than」
① Joshua는 Michael보다 나이가 많다.
② Andy는 John보다 유명하다.
③ 우리 형은 나보다 빨리 걷는다.
④ 이 머리핀은 저 머리핀만큼 비싸다.
⑤ Jimmy는 자신의 누나보다 돈을 많이 쓴다.

08 ② early - earlier - earliest ③ bad - worse - worst ④ long - longer - longest ⑤ famous - more famous - most famous

09 [보기] 어려운 ④ 어려운 ① 열심히 하는 ② 딱딱한 ③ ⑤ 열심히
[보기] 면접관은 그에게 어려운 질문을 했다.
① Jenny는 열심히 하는 직원이다.
② 그 돌은 매우 딱딱했다.
③ 목표가 있다면 열심히 노력하라.
④ 그 책은 이해하기 어렵다.
⑤ 그녀는 시험에 통과하기 위해 열심히 공부했다.

10 「A not as + 원급 + as B」 A는 B만큼 ~하지 않다
Ron은 Susan만큼 크지 않다.
① Ron은 Susan보다 크다.
② Susan은 Ron보다 크다.
③ Susan은 Ron만큼 크지 않다.
④ Ron은 Susan보다 작다.
⑤ Susan은 Ron보다 작다.

11 ① 「as + 원급 + as」: as faster as → as fast as ② 「비교급 + than」: early than → earlier than ③ 「as + 원급 + as」: as important than → as important as ⑤ 「the + 최상급」: the smarter → the smartest
① 나는 우리 엄마만큼 빨리 말하지 못한다.
② 나는 어제보다 일찍 일어났다.
③ 돈은 건강만큼 중요하지 않다.
④ Pam과 Dan은 가장 행복한 한 쌍이다.
⑤ Mary는 자기 반에서 가장 똑똑한 학생이다.

12 빈도부사는 일반동사 앞, be동사나 조동사 뒤에 위치:
② always is → is always
① Sarah는 가끔씩 산책을 한다.
② Jake는 항상 회사에 지각한다.
③ 나는 결코 당신의 친절을 잊지 않을 것입니다.
④ 우리 오빠는 보통 운동화를 신는다.
⑤ Rachel은 종종 친구들과 등산을 간다.

13 ① 「as + 원급 + as」: as much than → as much as ② 「the + 최상급」: the colder → the coldest ④ 「the + 최상급」: longer → the longest ⑤ expensivest → most expensive

[14-15]
A 안녕하세요, 도와드릴까요?
B 네, 오빠에게 줄 선물을 찾고 있어요. 등산에 유용한 것이 있나요?
A 그럼요, 등산화는 어때요? 이것이 우리 가게에서 가장 잘 팔리는 신발이에요.
B 좋아 보이네요. 그런데 오빠가 빨간색을 좋아할 것 같지는 않아요. 오빠는 항상 검은색 신발을 신어요.
A 그럼, 검은색이 낫겠네요. 사이즈가 어떻게 되나요?
B 275 아니면 280이에요.
A 그렇다면 큰 걸 추천해 드려요.
B 고마워요. 그걸로 할게요.

14 ① 「something + 형용사」: → something useful

15 빈도부사는 일반동사 앞, 조동사와 be동사 뒤에 위치

: 서술형 평가　P. 112

01 carefully
02 well
03 as tall as
04 heavier than
05 happier than
06 the biggest country
07 (1) often rains, never snows
(2) is usually, is sometimes
(3) is always, hardly rains
08 Chinese is more difficult than English.
09 Where is the smallest country in the world?
10 I always get up earlier than my sister.

01 동사(drive)를 수식하는 부사(carefully) 필요

Joe는 조심성 있는 운전자다.
→ Joe는 조심성 있게 운전한다.

02 동사(play)를 수식하는 부사(well) 필요

Janet은 매우 훌륭한 바이올린 연주자이다.
→ Janet은 바이올린 연주를 매우 잘한다.

[03-04]

03 「as + 원급 + as」

Andy는 Peter만큼 키가 크다.

04 「비교급 + than」

Andy는 Peter보다 몸무게가 더 나간다.

07 빈도부사는 일반동사 앞, be동사와 조동사 뒤에 위치

[보기] 봄에는 보통 시원하고, 때때로 비가 온다.
(1) 여름에는 종종 비가 오고, 눈은 결코 오지 않는다.
(2) 가을에는 보통 바람이 많이 불고, 가끔씩 덥다.
(3) 겨울에는 항상 춥고, 비가 거의 오지 않는다.

Chapter 11

UNIT 01

Check-up P. 114
1 and **2** but **3** so

1 and 그리고
2 but 하지만
3 so 그래서

: EXERCISES P. 115

Ⓐ **1** and **2** or **3** so **4** but
Ⓑ **1** or **2** and **3** so **4** but
Ⓒ **1** (d) **2** (b) **3** (a) **4** (c)
Ⓓ **1** tall, and, handsome **2** or, stay, here
3 but, doesn't, like, rock, music
4 so, I, opened, the, window

A

1 and ~와, 그리고
Eric은 머리와 눈이 갈색이다.

2 or 혹은, 또는
너는 고기 또는 생선 중 어떤 것을 원하니?

3 so 그래서
Karen은 모두에게 친절해서 다들 그녀를 좋아한다.

4 but 하지만
우리 할머니는 차를 많이 마시지만 커피는 마시지 않는다.

B

1 or 혹은, 또는
너는 아이스크림 또는 주스 중 어떤 것을 원하니?

2 and ~와, 그리고
내 남동생과 나는 같은 학교에 다닌다.

3 so 그래서
Dana는 감기에 걸려서 병원에 갔다.

4 but 하지만
Eugene은 일본어를 말할 수 있지만 쓰지는 못한다.

C

1 but 하지만
나는 매우 피곤하지만 일찍 자고 싶지는 않다.

2 so 그래서
Jane은 열차를 놓쳐서 회사에 지각했다.

3 or 혹은, 또는
Mark는 도서관에 있니 아니면 집에 갔니?

4 and ~와, 그리고
어제 나는 Emma를 만났고 우리는 차를 한 잔 했다.

UNIT 02

Check-up P. 116
1 When **2** until **3** before **4** After

1 when ~할 때
2 until ~할 때까지
3 before ~ 전에
4 after ~후에

: EXERCISES P. 117

Ⓐ **1** when **2** Before **3** after **4** stops
Ⓑ **1** when I arrive in London **2** before the movie starts
3 until I call your name **4** After they had breakfast
Ⓒ **1** (b) **2** (d) **3** (a) **4** (c)
Ⓓ **1** before, they, watched **2** after, he, graduated
3 When, she, met, him **4** until, their, teacher, told

A

1 when ~할 때
너는 여가가 있을 때 주로 뭘 하니?

2 before ~ 전에
그는 대학에 가기 전에 뉴욕으로 이사를 갔다.

3 after ~ 후에
나는 방 청소를 한 후에 너와 외출할 수 있어.

4 시간 부사절에서는 미래 시제 대신 현재 시제를 사용
Tim은 비가 그칠 때까지 집에 있을 거야.

B

1 when ~할 때
내가 런던에 도착하면 너에게 전화를 걸게.

2 before ~ 전에
우리 영화가 시작하기 전에 뭘 좀 먹자.

3 until ~할 때까지
제가 당신의 이름을 부를 때까지 여기서 기다려주세요.

4 after ~후에
그들은 아침을 먹은 후 산책을 갔다.

C

1 before ~ 전에
먹기 전에 손을 씻어라.

2 after ~후에
그는 집을 떠난 후 가족을 그리워했다.

3 when ~할 때
우리는 런던에 있을 때 여러 편의 연극을 보았다.

4 until ~할 때까지
그녀는 식사를 마칠 때까지 식탁을 떠날 수 없다.

UNIT 03

Check-up P. 118
1 that **2** if **3** because

1 that ~하는 것

2 if ~라면

3 because ~ 때문에

: EXERCISES P. 119

A **1** that **2** If **3** because **4** because

B **1** Because I didn't eat breakfast
2 that many children suffer from hunger in Africa
3 if you have questions

C **1** (b) **2** (c) **3** (a)

D **1** if, you, want **2** because, I, didn't, know
3 that, he, is, interested, in
4 Because, the, movie, was, boring

A

1 that ~하는 것
나는 언젠가는 비행기 조종사가 될 수 있을 거라고 믿는다.

2 if ~라면
내일 눈이 오면 나는 집에 있을 거야.

3 because ~ 때문에
James는 배가 아주 많이 고파서 햄버거를 두 개 먹었다.

4 because ~ 때문에
우리는 내일 시험이 있어서 지금 공부를 하고 있다.

B

1 because ~ 때문에
나는 아침을 먹지 않아서 지금 배가 매우 고프다.

2 that ~하는 것, hear의 목적어절을 이끄는 접속사 that
나는 아프리카에서 많은 어린이가 굶주림에 시달린다고 들었다.

3 if ~라면
만약 질문이 있으면 나에게 물어봐.

C

1 that ~하는 것, know의 목적어절을 이끄는 접속사 that
우리는 Cindy가 살이 많이 빠졌다는 것을 안다.

2 because ~ 때문에
밖이 너무 어둡기 때문에 너는 축구를 할 수 없어.

3 if ~라면
그는 원하면 우리와 함께 갈 수 있어.

: Review Test P. 120

01 ⑤	**02** ②	**03** ③	**04** ②	**05** ①
06 ③	**07** ②	**08** ⑤	**09** ②	**10** ③
11 ③	**12** ⑤	**13** ②	**14** ①	**15** ⑤

01 because ~ 때문에
Nathan은 어젯밤에 잠을 잘 못 자서 피곤하다.

02 if ~라면
서두르면 기차를 탈 수 있을 거야.

03 「both A and B」 A와 B 모두, 「either A or B」 A 또는 B
- Jane과 Mary 둘 다 스키 타러 가는 것을 좋아한다.
- 너는 컴퓨터를 사거나 돈을 은행에 저축할 수 있다.

04 before ~ 전에
- 그는 휴가를 떠나기 전에 보고서를 마쳤다.
- 저녁을 만들기 전에 쇼핑을 좀 하면 어때?

05 believe의 목적어절을 이끄는 접속사 that(~하는 것), 「It(가주어) ~ that절(진주어)」
- 나는 네가 약속을 지킬 거라고 믿어.
- 우리가 최선을 다했다는 것이 중요해.

06 ③ 지시형용사 that ①②④⑤ 목적어절을 이끄는 접속사 that
① 나는 그녀가 그와 사랑에 빠질 거라고 생각하지 않는다.
② Ken이 우리 오빠라는 것을 모두가 알고 있다.
③ 빨간 드레스를 입고 선글라스를 낀 저 소녀는 누구니?
④ 우리는 그녀가 86세라는 걸 믿을 수가 없다.
⑤ Ed는 안경을 찾을 수가 없다고 말했다.

07 ② 조건절에서 미래 대신 현재를 사용: will hurry → hurry
① 나는 여행을 가고 싶지만 시간이 없다.
② 서두르면 버스를 놓치지 않을 거야.
③ 떠나기 전에 가방을 다시 한 번 확인하렴.
④ 이 박사는 어렸을 때 책을 많이 읽었다.
⑤ Louis 씨는 교통 체증 때문에 늦게 왔다.

08 because ~ 때문에
나는 꿈에 그리던 차를 샀다. 나는 아주 행복하다.
→ 나는 꿈에 그리던 차를 사서 아주 행복하다.

09 when ~할 때
우리 아버지께서 나에게 전화하셨다. 나는 욕실에 있었다.
→ 우리 아버지께서 나에게 전화하셨을 때 나는 욕실에 있었다.

10 ③ 의문사 ①②④⑤ 접속사
① 나는 좋은 점수를 받고 매우 기뻤다.
② 집을 떠날 때 창문을 닫아주세요.
③ 너는 언제 Brian을 만날 거니?
④ 너는 커서 무엇이 되고 싶니?
⑤ 너는 잠자리에서 스마트폰을 가지고 노니?

11 ③ 시간 부사절에서는 미래 시제 대신 현재 시제를 사용: when I'll see → when I see
① **A** 너 어젯밤 파티에 왜 오지 않았니?
B 미안해. 너무 바빠서 갈 수가 없었어.
② **A** 비가 오기 전에 창문을 좀 닫아 주실래요?
B 물론이죠.
③ **A** John에게 동아리에 가입하라고 말해 주세요.
B 알았어요. 보면 얘기할게요.
④ **A** 휴가 동안 어딘가 갈 계획을 세우고 있니?
B 응. 나는 스페인과 독일에 갈 거야.
⑤ **A** 네가 그에게 전화를 했니, 아니면 그가 너에게 전화를 했니?
B 그가 나에게 전화했어.

12 so 그렇게, 그래서
A 왜 그렇게 열심히 공부하고 있니?
B 내일 시험이 있어서 공부해야 해.

13 ② 지시형용사 ①③④⑤ 접속사
① 나는 그녀가 실수를 했다고 생각하지 않는다.
② 나는 저 소녀가 매우 예쁘다고 생각한다.
③ 나는 그녀가 문을 잠그는 것을 보았다.
④ 너는 그녀가 친절하다고 생각하니?
⑤ 그녀는 그가 올 거라고 믿는다.

[14-15]
A 너 오늘 좋아 보이지 않는구나.
B 내 생각에 감기에 걸린 것 같아.
A 집에 가서 좀 쉬는 게 어때?
B 나도 그러고 싶지만 그럴 수 없어.
A 왜?
B 왜냐하면 플루트 수업이 있어. 만약 내가 한 번 더 수업에 빠지면 곤란을 겪게 될 거야. 벌써 몇 번 빠졌거든.
A 아, 안됐구나.

14 ⓐ and 그리고 ⓑ but 하지만 ⓒ because 왜냐하면

15 조건 부사절에서는 미래 시제 대신 현재 시제를 사용

: 서술형 평가 P. 122

01 after
02 but
03 If you eat less
04 after I see you at 1 pm
05 Because the movie was very sad
06 because you helped me
07 When Jake goes to school
08 (1) that the movie is not interesting
(2) that the movie is romantic
(3) that the movie is boring
09 I'm so excited because she is visiting me today.
10 When I see her, I'll give her a big hug.

03 if ~라면
적게 먹으려고 노력한다면 살이 빠질 거예요.

04 after ~ 후에
나는 한 시에 너를 만난 후, 세 시에 Mike를 만날 거야.

05 because ~ 때문에
나는 그 영화가 너무 슬퍼서 많이 울었다.

08 「think + 목적어절을 이끄는 접속사 that」
[보기] Tom 나는 그 영화가 슬프다고 생각해.
(1) Chris 나는 그 영화가 재미없다고 생각해.
(2) Anna 나는 그 영화가 로맨틱하다고 생각해.
(3) Wendy 나는 그 영화가 지루하다고 생각해.

[09-10]

Sarah는 나의 사촌이다. 그녀와 나는 5년 전에 그녀의 가족이 대도시로 이사할 때까지 같은 동네에 살았다. 그녀가 이사한 이후로 우리는 서로 만나지 못했다. 나는 몹시 설렌다. 그녀가 오늘 나를 보러 온다. 그녀를 만나면 꼭 안아 줄 것이다.

09 「because + 이유」
그녀가 오늘 나를 보러 오기 때문에 나는 몹시 설렌다.

10 시간 부사절에서는 미래 시제 대신 현재 시제를 사용

Chapter 12

UNIT 01

Check-up P. 124
1 at **2** on **3** in

1 at ~에 (장소의 한 지점)

2 on ~위에 (표면에 닿은 상태)

3 in ~안에 (장소의 내부)

: EXERCISES P. 125

Ⓐ **1** over **2** in **3** at **4** between

Ⓑ **1** in **2** on **3** at

Ⓒ **1** on **2** next to **3** under **4** between

Ⓓ **1** between, Seoul, and, Busan
2 across, from, the, post, office
3 in, front, of, the, house
4 from, your, school, to, the, train, station

A

1 over ~ 위에
그 다리는 강 위에 있다.

2 「in + 도시」
우리 조부모님은 부산에 산다.

3 해변의 내부가 아니므로 at이 적절
우리는 해변에서 비치발리볼을 했다.

4 「between A and B」 A와 B 사이에
그 방송국은 Powell 가와 King 가 사이에 있다.

B

1 in ~안에

2 on ~위에

3 at ~에(장소의 한 지점)

C

1 on ~위에
벽 위에 그림이 있다.

2 next to 옆에
의자 옆에 가방이 있다.

3 under ~ 아래에
책상 아래에 강아지가 누워 있다.

4 「between A and B」 A와 B 사이에
책상과 침대 사이에 의자가 있다.

UNIT 02

Check-up P. 126
1 at **2** on **3** in

1 「at + 구체적인 시점」

2 「on + 날짜」

3 「in + 월」

: EXERCISES P. 127

Ⓐ **1** at **2** on **3** on **4** in

Ⓑ **1** on **2** at **3** in

Ⓒ **1** for **2** during **3** during **4** until **5** by **6** until

Ⓓ **1** between, seven, and, eight
2 from, 2000, to, 2004
3 after, eleven, on, Fridays
4 before, nine, o'clock, in, the, morning

A

1 「at + 구체적인 시각」
나는 일곱 시에 약속이 있다.

2 「on + 날짜」
워크숍은 5월 13일에 있을 예정입니다.

3 「on + 요일」
Mandy는 토요일에 치과에 갔다.

4 「in + 오후」
그 교수님은 오후에 수업이 두 개 있다.

B

1 「on + 요일」
그 병원은 일요일마다 문을 닫니?

2 「at + 구체적인 시각」
당신은 세 시 정각에 예약되어 있습니다.

3 「in + 계절」
나는 가을 산의 색깔을 정말 좋아한다.

C

[1-3] 「for + 구체적인 숫자」, 「during + 특정 기간」

1 Larry는 일 년 동안 독일에서 공부할 것이다.

2 나는 겨울 방학 동안 이 그림을 그렸다.

3 밤사이에 누군가 유리창을 깼다.

[4-6] until: 계속되던 동작이나 상태가 완료, by: 일회성 동작이나 상태가 완료

4 나는 3월까지 여기에 머물 거야.

5 너는 월요일까지 과제를 마쳐야 해.

6 Luke는 자정까지 도서관에서 공부했다.

UNIT 03

Check-up P. 128
1 with 2 about

1 「with + 사물」 ~을 가지고

2 about ~에 대해

: EXERCISES P. 129

A 1 to 2 about 3 by 4 with
B 1 you 2 me 3 them 4 her
C 1 by 2 with 3 for 4 about
D 1 about, her, problem 2 like, his, father
3 by, fax 4 to, Italy, with, my, mother

1 to ~에게
나중에 이야기하자.

2 about ~에 대해
나의 과제는 한국 역사에 관한 것이다.

3 「by + 교통수단」 ~로
너는 보통 버스로 등교하니?

4 「with + 사람」 ~와 함께
너는 여자 친구와 뮤지컬을 보러 갈 거니?

B

[1-4] 「전치사 + 대명사의 목적격」

1 이것이 널 위한 나의 선물이야.

2 그 에세이는 내가 쓴 거야.

3 나는 그들과 함께 여행을 갈 것이다.

4 방학 동안 그녀에게 무슨 일이 있었니?

C

1 「by + 교통수단」 ~로
택시를 타고 그곳에 가는 것은 비싸다.

2 「with + 사물」 ~을 가지고
Tom은 접착제로 부서진 액자를 수리했다.

3 for ~을 위해
나는 내 딸을 위해 이 청바지를 샀다.

4 about ~에 대해
이 주제에 관해 질문 있니?

: Review Test P. 130

01 ①	02 ④	03 ③	04 ④	05 ④
06 ②	07 ④	08 ①	09 ④	10 ②
11 ⑤	12 ④, ⑤	13 ①	14 ⑤	15 ③

01 「in + 장소」 ~ 안에, 「in + 월」 ~에
• 선생님은 교실에 계신다.
• 여름 방학은 7월에 시작한다.

02 「at + 장소의 한 지점」 ~에, 「at + 구체적인 시각」 ~에
• 우리는 버스 정류장에서 버스를 기다리고 있다.
• 오후 두 시 정각에 만나자.

03 「on + 날짜」 ~에, 「on + 장소」 ~위에
• 결혼식은 4월 11일에 있을 예정입니다.
• 벽에 걸린 그림을 보아라.

04 ④ 「between A and B」, 「between+복수 명사」
그 높은 건물 옆에 / 뒤에 / 옆에 / 앞에 우체통이 있다.

05 「for + 구체적인 숫자」, 「during + 특정 기간」
• 나는 십 년 동안 요가 수업을 들었다. 지금 나는 요가 강사다.
• 나는 여름 동안 수영장에서 일했다.

06 by: 일회성 동작이나 상태가 완료, until: 계속되던 동작이나 상태가 완료
• 사장님은 오후 두 시까지는 돌아오실 겁니다.
• Brown 씨는 다음 주까지 여기 머물 것입니다.

07 ④ 장소를 나타내는 on ① ② ③ ⑤ 시간을 나타내는 on
① 콘서트는 5월 3일이다.
② 나는 생일에 친구들을 만났다.
③ 나는 목요일에 약속이 있다.
④ 탁자 위에 있는 모자는 우리 아버지께 받은 선물이다.
⑤ 그 식당은 크리스마스 당일에는 문을 닫는다.

08 ① 「on + 특정한 날」 ② 「in + 달」 ③ 「in + 장소」 ~안에
④ 「in + 오후」 ⑤ 「in + 장소」 ~안에
① 사람들은 부활절에 칠면조를 먹는다.
② 우리는 2월에 졸업할 것이다.

③ 우리 언니는 지금 호주에 산다.
④ 나는 아침에 차 마시는 것을 좋아한다.
⑤ 내 방에 큰 스피커가 두 개 있다.

09 ④ 「for + 구체적인 숫자」: during two weeks → for two weeks
① 나는 봄 날씨를 정말 좋아한다.
② 이 소포를 금요일까지 보내 주세요.
③ James는 지리에 관한 책을 한 권 샀다.
④ 나는 두 주 동안 시험공부를 했다.
⑤ 어린이날에 그 놀이동산은 아이들로 가득했다.

10 ② on은 표면에 닿은 위를 의미. 새가 나무에 붙어서 날아갈 수는 없으므로 on이 아니라 over가 적절
① 우리 집 앞에 나무가 한 그루 서 있다.
② 새들이 나무 위에서 날고 있다.
③ 너는 저녁 식사 전에 돌아와야 한다.
④ 그 영화는 음악과 사랑에 관한 것이다.
⑤ 우리는 여름에 많은 수중 스포츠를 즐긴다.

11 「from A to B」 A에서 B까지
본 여객기는 서울에서 상하이까지 비행합니다.

12 ④ 「by + 교통수단」: in bike → by bike ⑤ in front of ~ 앞에

13 「on + 요일」, 「from A to B」 A에서 B까지, 「by + 기한」(일회성 동작이 완료)
A 우리 금요일 밤에 파티 해. 놀러 와.
B 오, 몇 시?
A 저녁 여섯 시부터 열한 시까지야.
B 알았어. 일곱 시까지 그곳에 갈게. 그때 보자.

14 across from ~의 맞은편에
• 학교는 도서관 맞은편에 있다.
• 경찰서는 병원 맞은편에 있다.

15 ③ music store는 post office 옆에 있음
① 서점은 슈퍼마켓 옆에 있다.
② 슈퍼마켓은 은행 뒤에 있다.
③ 음반 가게는 서점 옆에 있다.
④ 꽃집은 음반 가게 맞은편에 있다.
⑤ 은행은 경찰서와 꽃집 사이에 있다.

: 서술형 평가 P. 132

01 in
02 during
03 with, on
04 under, on
05 at the bus stop at six
06 from 10 am to 9 pm
07 go to school by bus
08 on my desk at home
09 ⓐ for ⓑ at ⓒ in ⓓ in front of
10 for an hour, until 4 pm

01 「in + 월」 ~에, 「in + 장소」 ~ 안에
• 내 생일은 3월이다.
• 컵 안에 커피가 좀 있다.

02 「during + 특정 기간」 ~동안
• 밤 동안 눈이 엄청 내렸다.
• 수업 시간 동안 떠들지 마라.

[03-04] 「on + 장소」 (표면에 붙은) 위에, 「under + 장소」 (공간이 떨어진) 아래, with ~와 함께

03 강아지가 소녀와 함께 침대 위에서 자고 있다.

04 소녀가 나무 아래, 매트 위에 앉아 있다.

05 「at + 장소의 한 지점」, 「at + 구체적 시각」

06 「from A to B」 A에서 B까지

07 「by + 교통수단」 ~로
A 너는 어떻게 등교하니?
B 나는 보통 버스를 타고 학교에 가. 하지만 가끔은 학교까지 걸어가기도 해.

08 「on + 장소」 (표면에 닿은) ~위에, 「at + 장소」 ~에
A 네 휴대 전화는 어디 있니?
B 내 생각에 집 책상 위에 두고 온 것 같아.

[09-10]
10월 13일, 토요일
피곤한 하루였다. 나는 학교 과제를 위해 미술관에 가고 싶었다. 우리 반 친구 Sally에게 전화를 해서 오후 세 시에 만나기로 약속을 했다. 미술관 앞에서 그녀를 기다렸지만 그녀는 오지 않았다. 나는 한 시간 동안 그녀를 기다렸지만 그녀는 네 시까지 나타나지 않았다. 그녀가 늦은 것이 이번이 처음이 아니다. 그녀는 항상 늦는다!

09 ⓐ for ~을 위해 ⓑ 「at + 구체적 시각」 ~에 ⓒ 「in + 오후」 ~에 ⓓ in front of ~ 앞에서

10 「for + 구체적인 숫자」 ~동안, until ~까지(동작이나 상태가 그 시점까지 지속됨)

Workbook

Chapter 01

UNIT 01

A **1** I'm **2** He's **3** You're **4** It's **5** We're

B **1** is **2** are **3** is **4** are **5** are **6** was
7 were **8** was **9** were **10** were

C **1** was, is **2** was, am **3** were, are
4 were, are **5** was, is

D **1** I, was, at, home **2** We, were, very, tired
3 They, are, popular **4** You, are, creative
5 It, was, very, hot
6 You, were, at, the, amusement, park
7 He, is, in, the, restroom

E **1** She is a famous jazz singer.
2 I am in my room
3 He was hungry and thirsty
4 They are wild animals in Africa.
5 We were at the theater
6 You are troublemakers
7 He is my favorite classmate.

UNIT 02

A **1** wasn't **2** aren't **3** aren't **4** isn't **5** am not
6 wasn't **7** weren't

B **1** Am, I **2** Are, you **3** Is, a, potato **4** Is, she
5 Was, he **6** Were, my, books **7** Was, it
8 Were, you

C **1** I'm, not, a, little, child,
2 Is, that
3 They, weren't, happy
4 Was, he, on, holiday
5 The, final, tests, weren't
6 Are, the, bags, on, sale
7 We, aren't, in, the, library

D **1** Is this parking lot free?
2 The soup was not hot.
3 Are the paintings expensive?
4 Is your grandma healthy?
5 Was Beethoven a great musician?
6 I am not a member of a soccer club.
7 She was not hungry at that time.

UNIT 03

A

	주격 (~은, ~가)	소유격 (~의)	목적격 (~을)	소유대명사 (~의 것)
단수	I	my	me	mine
	You	your	you	yours
	He	his	him	his
	She	her	her	hers
	It	its	it	-
복수	We	our	us	ours
	You	your	you	yours
	They	their	them	theirs

B **1** your **2** She **3** its **4** mine **5** our **6** them
7 him

C **1** He is happy with his new shoes.
2 They are bored at the party.
3 She was not in her classroom.
4 This is their new computer. It is theirs.
5 We are her neighbors. She knows us.
6 You are very friendly. Everybody likes you.

D **1** There, is, a, mirror
2 Is, there, a, drugstore
3 There, are, ten, girls
4 There, were, three, pencils
5 Is, there, a, uniform
6 There, were, not, many, students
7 There, are, not, many, books

E **1** There is a scar on his face.
2 Was there a bear in the cave?
3 Are there girls at that school?
4 Are there many dishes in the sink?
5 There was not a fire in the building.
6 There is a mouse in his basement.
7 There was a rainbow in the sky this morning.

Chapter 02

UNIT 01

A **1** fixes **2** have **3** feels **4** tries **5** plays
6 likes **7** washes

B **1** speak, speaks **2** kisses, kiss **3** say, says

4 goes, go **5** eat, eats **6** watches, watch
7 study, studies

C **1** wears **2** plays **3** carries **4** has **5** do

D **1** flies, high **2** They, live, in **3** I, get, up
4 We, sing, a, song **5** He, catches, fish
6 He, drinks **7** She, walks, her, dog

E **1** I sweep the floor with a broom.
2 He plays the guitar for his girlfriend.
3 They finish their homework before bedtime.
4 He reads comic books during the break.
5 The bear sleeps in the cave during the winter.
6 We play musical instruments in music class.
7 He buys sports magazines at the bookstore every month.

UNIT 02

A **1** had **2** came **3** drove **4** broke **5** sat
6 lost **7** got **8** bought **9** shook **10** made
11 wore **12** ran **13** caught **14** ate **15** won
16 saw **17** held **18** hit **19** swam **20** cut
21 began **22** met **23** felt **24** cost **25** took
26 left **27** set **28** put **29** rode **30** rose

B **1** rang **2** dropped **3** did **4** changed **5** brought

C **1** cut **2** stayed **3** raised **4** paid **5** looked
6 worried **7** listened to **8** wore **9** took
10 heard

D **1** became, dark **2** the, sun, set
3 They, borrowed, a, book **4** I, gave, my, mother
5 She, waited, for, the, bus **6** broke, a, window
7 fell, down, on, the, street

E **1** My dad stopped his car at the traffic light.
2 She knocked on my door five minutes ago.
3 My brother broke his glasses this morning.
4 They moved to another city last month.
5 Her mother made a bag for her.
6 My hamster got out of its cage last night.
7 We learned a new song in music class today.

UNIT 03

A **1** don't share **2** don't run **3** doesn't smell
4 doesn't worry **5** doesn't remember
6 didn't bring **7** didn't answer **8** didn't say
9 didn't feel **10** didn't make

B **1** don't know **2** doesn't work **3** doesn't drink
4 don't like **5** don't wake up **6** didn't tell
7 didn't lose **8** didn't come **9** didn't hear
10 didn't eat

C **1** The cake doesn't taste delicious.
2 He doesn't have curly brown hair.
3 We didn't go on a trip last month.
4 My son doesn't believe in Santa Claus.
5 You didn't clean the milk off the floor.
6 She didn't visit her uncle in Canada.
7 I didn't study for the final test last week.

D **1** didn't, write, back **2** don't, watch, TV
3 didn't, tell, a, lie **4** didn't, meet, John
5 doesn't, eat, sweets
6 didn't, cheat, on, the, test
7 didn't, play, computer, games

UNIT 04

A **1** Do, I **2** Do, you **3** Does, it **4** Does, she
5 Did, he **6** Did, your, parents **7** Did, they
8 Did, you

B **1** Did, you, lose **2** Did, you, tell
3 Do, we, need **4** Does, he, play
5 Does, your, mother, drive

C **1** Did, rain, it, didn't **2** Does, raise, she, does
3 Does, live, he, doesn't **4** Do, have, we, do
5 Did, hear, I, did **6** Did, start, they, didn't
7 Did, fall, asleep, he, did

D **1** Did you order pizza?
2 Does she swim well?
3 Did he walk to school today?
4 Did you pass the audition?
5 Does the first class begin at nine o'clock?
6 Do you borrow books from the library?
7 Does she read newspapers every morning?

Chapter 03

UNIT 01

A **1** keys **2** mice **3** teeth **4** children **5** monkeys
6 men **7** toys **8** roofs **9** babies **10** knives
11 feet **12** people **13** zoos **14** deer **15** lives
16 geese **17** photos **18** leaves **19** boys

20 buses **21** oxen **22** sheep **23** women
24 radios **25** potatoes **26** cities **27** pianos
28 boxes **29** foxes **30** churches

B **1** sisters **2** mice **3** men **4** children **5** dishes

C **1** geese **2** tomatoes **3** knives **4** hobbies

D **1** three, minutes **2** many, horses
3 a, pair, of, sneakers **4** two, dictionaries
5 a, lot, of, roofs **6** many, lives
7 lots, of, heroes

E **1** He put three potatoes in the pot.
2 There are a lot of apartments
3 The brave man caught two thieves.
4 My teacher has six classes a day.
5 He saved his sheep from the wolves.
6 There were many men and women
7 Three foxes and two monkeys arrived at the zoo.

UNIT 02

A **1** 세모: Mike **2** 동그라미: coffee
3 세모: Harry, Jane, America **4** 네모: advice
5 네모: happiness

B **1** money **2** sugar **3** homework **4** salt
5 bottles

C **1** five pieces of paper **2** two glasses of milk
3 three bowls of soup **4** two cups of tea
5 six slices of pizza **6** three bottles of water

D **1** five, cups, of, green, tea
2 two, bowls, of, cereal
3 a, slice, of, bread
4 three, slices, of, cheese
5 two, glasses, of, lemonade.
6. five, pairs, of, socks
7 two, bowls, of, warm, soup

E **1** Drink two bottles of water a day.
2 We shared two slices of bread
3 ate three slices of pizza for dinner.
4 drinks two glasses of milk
5 moved five pieces of furniture
6 found information about Korea
7 has a lot of knowledge about computers.

UNIT 03

A **1** X **2** an **3** a **4** an, X **5** an

B **1** a **2** the **3** X, a **4** The **5** The

C **1** middle school **2** by bus **3** once an hour
4 plays the guitar **5** an MP3 player

D **1** The sun **2** an English teacher
3 plays the piano **4** went to bed
5 a teacher, an artist **6** play soccer, once a week
7 a nice dinner

E **1** She plays the piano as a hobby.
2 watched TV after dinner
3 They go on a vacation twice a year.
4 The student read an English novel
5 played baseball, went home by bike
6 two apples, a glass of milk
7 a horror movie, the movie was really scary

Chapter 04

UNIT 01

A **1** these **2** This **3** It **4** These **5** It **6** that
7 Those **8** those

B **1** What, time, is, it **2** What, is, the, date
3 What, day, is, it **4** How, is, the, weather
5 How, far, is, it **6** How, long, does, it, take

C **1** What, is, the, weather **2** These, cats, are
3 Those, kids, are **4** This, cell, phone, is
5 That, girl, is **6** It, is, Christmas, Eve
7 It, takes, about, an, hour

D **1** It's quite far from here.
2 It's already after ten.
3 It's very warm here.
4 It's summer in Hawaii.
5 I know that man very well.
6 This is my aunt Martha.
7 These are my favorite books.

UNIT 02

A **1** one **2** it **3** ones **4** it **5** ones **6** one
7 One, the others **8** One, the other
9 One, the other **10** One, the others
11 One, the others **12** One, the other

B 1 any 2 Some 3 any 4 some 5 any
6 some

C 1 some, hot, tea 2 any, good, ideas
3 a, new, one 4 I, borrow, one
5 It, is, very, funny
6 These, are, my favorite, ones
7 One, is, romance, the, other, is, science, fiction

D 1 you have any questions 2 Do you have one?
3 I lost it 4 gave me some advice
5 I'll order one online. 6 I'll lend it to you.
7 One is my father's, the other is mine

UNIT 03

A 1 myself 2 ourselves 3 yourself 4 itself
5 himself 6 herself 7 themselves
8 yourselves

B 1 itself 2 himself 3 herself 4 himself
5 yourself

C 1 introduce myself 2 cut yourself
3 talks to himself 4 by yourself

D 1 hurt, himself 2 enjoy, yourself
3 help, yourself, make, yourself, at, home
5 burn, yourself 6 take, care, of, myself
7 between, ourselves

E 1 eat lunch by myself
2 Talking to himself is
3 make yourself at home
4 yourself, clean your room
5 enjoyed ourselves at the exhibition
6 hurt herself last week
7 go in the pool by themselves

Chapter 05

UNIT 01

A 1 Did, leave, left 2 Do, like, like 3 Were, was
4 Does, ride, rides 5 Does, raise, raises
6 Did, live, lived 7 Do, read, read

B 1 are 2 goes 3 feeds 4 joined 5 started
6 wrote 7 visited

C 1 It is hot today. 2 Tom looks sad now.
3 We went skiing last winter.
4 We have lots of rain these days.
5 She and I are very busy these days.
6 She had a red car last year.
7 There are many people at the gym right now.

D 1 skips, dinner, every, day
2 didn't, go, off, this, morning
3 are, at, the, post, office, now
4 was, angry, with, me, this, morning
5 doesn't, work, on, weekends
6 played, soccer after, school
7 return, to, this, area, every, spring

UNIT 02

A 1 lying 2 riding 3 getting 4 cutting
5 planning 6 sitting 7 moving 8 making
9 smiling 10 driving 11 putting 12 hitting
13 taking 14 swimming 15 seeing 16 stopping
17 dying 18 having 19 running 20 leaving

B 1 is, sitting 2 Are, waiting, for 3 isn't, working
4 am, doing 5 are, chatting 6 were, lying
7 was, swimming 8 Were, looking, for
9 wasn't, watching 10 were, playing

C 1 was, reading 2 Is, watering 3 Is, fixing
4 am, writing

D 1 was, taking, a, nap, then
2 he, reading, a, fairy, tale
3 is, mopping, the, floor, now
4 were, collecting, shells
5 are, saving, money
6 wasn't, watching, the, movie
7 are, working, together

E 1 He isn't taking notes in his notebook.
2 Jason was wearing a pair of jeans then.
3 Two boys were arguing in the classroom.
4 Is she watching a weather report on TV?
5 They were traveling across the desert.
6 I'm not playing games with my cell phone.
7 The singers are singing a song on the stage.

Chapter 06

UNIT 01

A 1 데려와도 된다 2 아플지도 모른다 3 사용해도 된다

4 바꿀 지도 모른다 5 달릴 수 있다

B 1 can't, help 2 Can, sing 3 can, drive
4 Can, play 5 May, try 6 May, borrow
7 may, be 8 may, not, lift

C 1 is able to speak 2 Is, able to play
3 am not able to go 4 were able to dive
5 wasn't able to play

D 1 can't, be, a, student
2 May[Can], I, open
3 may[can], take, the, chair
4 is, able, to, dance
5 Can, you, solve, the, problem
6 wasn't, able, to, find
7 may, go, to

E 1 may move to London
2 may not show up on time
3 Will Kate be able to get a job
4 cannot borrow the book
5 May I check my email
6 can play the guitar very well
7 was not able to fix the computer

UNIT 02

A 1 청소해야 한다 2 참가야 한다 3 피곤함이 틀림없다
4 먹지 말아야 한다 5 거짓말을 하지 말아야 한다
6 서두를 필요가 없다

B 1 must not run 2 don't have to go
3 don't have to knock 4 must not drive
5 shouldn't eat 6 should see 7 should be
8 shouldn't drink

C 1 has to be home by twelve o'clock
2 Do. have to finish my work today
3 have to eat the vegetables on your plate

D 1 Should, I, go, now
2 must, be, hungry
3 You, should, say
4 must, not, watch, TV
5 must, be, back, home
6 has, to, do, his, homework
7 should, not, leave, your, belongings

E 1 should visit Korea
2 must stop at the red light
3 must not play computer games
4 have to wear a swimming cap
5 don't have to answer all the questions
6 should not talk to strangers
7 must not be at home

UNIT 03

A 1 won't tell 2 won't do 3 will go 4 will be
5 am not going to send 6 is going to snow
7 am going to buy 8 aren't going to work

B 1 will answer 2 won't forgive 3 won't eat
4 Are, going to buy 5 am going to meet
6 Is, going to come

C 1 Will, you, buy, a, new, car
2 are, going, to, arrive, in, London
3 is, going, to, do, yoga
4 isn't, going, to, graduate
5 will, go, fishing
6 won't, stay, in, New, York
7 Are, they, going, to, talk, about

D 1 Will you be at home
2 will buy some
3 Is Harry going to call me
4 will not work late
5 is going to see a musical
6 Are they going to get married
7 isn't going to join our club.

Chapter 07

UNIT 01

A 1 Who 2 What 3 Which

B 1 He is my brother. 2 Doing jigsaw puzzles.
3 Diana did. 4 I think black is better.

C 1 Which is 2 What is 3 Who(m) did you visit
4 What does he do

D 1 Who, will, you, meet
2 Which, do, you, like
3 Who, are, the, people
4 Which, do, you, want
5 What, subject, are, you, studying
6 What, did, your, mother, say
7 What, plans, do, you, have

E 1 Who is the president of your class?
2 Who did you talk with on the phone?
3 What kind of music do you like?
4 What color will you wear for the party?
5 What did your grandfather do?
6 Which do you speak better, English or French?
7 Which way did they go, this way or that way?

UNIT 02

A 1 When 2 How often 3 Where 4 Why

B 1 In North America. 2 Because of heavy traffic.
3 The first of January. 4 Every 15 minutes.

C 1 When did she first see
2 Where do pink dolphins live
3 How much was the shirt
4 Why did you cry

D 1 Why, was, he
2 How, do, you, get
3 Why, are, you
4 When, do, you, get, up
5 Where, did, you, meet
6 How, often, do, you, wash
7 When, is, your, appointment

E 1 Why do we dream?
2 When can I see you?
3 How tall is that building?
4 When does the concert start?
5 Where did he go last night?
6 Where did you find the book?
7 How many CDs do you have?

UNIT 03

A 1 isn't it 2 were you 3 can you 4 will he
5 did you 6 did I 7 isn't she 8 didn't you
9 does he 10 are you

B 1 Doesn't he wear 2 Weren't they
3 Didn't you hear 4 Isn't she 5 Can't you see
6 Aren't they

C 1 Is this ball yours or hers?
2 Which is cheaper, this or that?
3 Which do you want, donuts or cookies?
4 Is your sister a doctor or a teacher?
5 Which would you like, coffee or tea?
6 Do you go to school by bus or by subway?
7 Which season do you like more, summer or winter?

D 1 Can't, you, find 2 Aren't, you 3 isn't, she
4 won't, you 5 will, you
6 Which, does, he, like, better
7. go, shopping, or, go, home

UNIT 04

A 1 How 2 How 3 What 4 How 5 How
6 What 7 What 8 What

B 1 well you cook 2 a tall guy he is
3 a nice car she has 4 fresh the apples are
5 interesting the news is
6 beautiful eyes you have
7 expensive shoes you wore

C 1 What, a, nice, day 2 How, cute
3 How, boring 4 What, long, hair
5 What, a, great, teacher
6 What, an, exciting, trip
7 How, beautifully

D 1 How sweet you are!
2 How beautiful life is!
3 How big that elephant is!
4 What an amazing story it is!
5 What a wonderful time you had!
6 What tasty cakes they sell!
7 What an exciting game it was!

UNIT 05

A 1 Be 2 Don't give up. 3 Go 4 Stay
5 Turn off 6 Clean 7 Don't worry 8 Don't make

B 1 Let's not eat 2 Let's not sit 3 Let's not run
4 Let's have 5 Let's order 6 Let's clean
7 Let's exercise 8 Let's not take

C 1 Let's, take, a, trip 2 Don't, pick, flowers
3 Go, out, play 4 Don't talk to me
5 Let's, go, to, the, movies
6 Let's, not, eat, fast, food
7 Don't, play, computer, games

D 1 Let's meet in front of the museum.
2 Cut the cake into pieces.
3 Let's go to the beach

4 Let's not throw trash
5 Don't make the same mistake
6 Put your hands on your waist.
7 Don't use your cell phone

Chapter 08

UNIT 01

A 1 to learn 2 to read 3 To collect
4 to exercise 5 to be

B 1 to eat 2 to ride 3 to learn 4 to help
5 how to play 6 what to do 7 where to go
8 when to leave

C 1 It, to learn Chinese 2 It, to read this novel
3 It, to cross the street here
4 It, to find a perfect gift for her
5 It, to keep a diary every day

D 1 wish, to, take, a, break 2 need, to, go
3 hopes, to, see, you 4 to, make, friends
5 to, learn, new, things
6 likes, to, bake, cakes
7 plan, to, visit, the, museum

E 1 is fun to ride a horse
2 would like to take a walk
3 likes to go to the movies
4 They decided to go camping
5 It can be dangerous to swim
6 is to become a soccer player
7 is to go to the art gallery

UNIT 02

A 1 work to do 2 money to buy
3 people to invite 4 bread to eat
5 magazine to read 6 anything to wear
7 water to drink

B 1 to see me 2 to believe Jessica's lies
3 to have you here 4 to hear the bad news
5 to borrow some books 6 to take a walk

C 1 sad, to, hear 2 to, buy, books
3 money, to, buy 4 sorry, to, say
5 to, make, jam 6 many, friends, to, help
7 to, get, into, university

D 1 something to tell me 2 time to stay here
3 have something to do 4 To lose weight
5 came here to meet you
6 was surprised to hear the news
7 went to Vancouver to study English

UNIT 03

A 1 being 2 selling 3 Speaking 4 chatting

B 1 playing 2 opening 3 looking 4 cleaning

C 1 Talking with him 2 sailing 3 riding horses
4 Swimming in the sea 5 singing together

D 1 is, good, at, throwing, balls
2 for, inviting, us
3 Eating, fast, food, is
4 is, going, to, Jejudo
5 Having, a, true, friend, is
6 is, fixing, computers.
7 Speaking, in, front, of, people, is

E 1 sorry for being late
2 How about having a cup of tea
3 Driving a car is
4 is good at drawing
5 is making home movies
6 Singing a song makes
7 enjoy taking pictures of pets

UNIT 04

A 1 working 2 to go 3 swimming 4 to listen
5 to write 6 playing

B 1 walking 2 opening 3 to meet 4 to get
5 going 6 to ask 7 to study 8 eating

C 1 crying 2 raining 3 trying 4 listening

D 1 Stop talking 2 wants to know 3 kept walking
4 enjoyed talking 5 hope to see 6 mind driving
7 need to send

E 1 want to have a cat
2 hopes to go on a trip
3 finished painting the house
4 started jumping with delight
5 mind turning down the volume
6 enjoys spending time with his friends
7 promised to finish the project

Chapter 09

UNIT 01

Ⓐ **1** looks, sad **2** look, nice **3** tastes, spicy **4** tastes, fresh **5** feels, soft **6** smells, great

Ⓑ **1** strong **2** a strong man **3** warm **4** a rock star **5** babies **6** so cute **7** honey **8** sour

Ⓒ **1** I, feel, happy
2 felt, like, winter
3 tastes, like, chicken
4 tastes, very, sweet
5 looked, tired, today
6 looked, like, a, real, princess
7 sounds, wonderful
8 sound, like, your, mom

Ⓓ **1** looks happy with him
2 I feel lonely
3 it smells like coffee
4 The game sounds interesting.
5 Jane looked very angry

UNIT 02

Ⓐ **1** to **2** to **3** of **4** for **5** to **6** to **7** for

Ⓑ **1** some flowers to me **2** a house for her cat **3** the list to me **4** wine to me **5** many questions of her **6** a fax to them **7** an expensive suit for her husband

Ⓒ **1** lent, a, book, to, me
2 buy, my, mother, a, scarf.
3 asked, me, some, questions.
4 gave, me, a, lot, of, information
5 sent, her, friend, a, postcard
6 showed, her, report, card, to, her, mother
7 made, a, sweater, for, me

Ⓓ **1** send you a package
2 teaches me English
3 asked me a few questions
4 lent his tent to us
5 gave Christmas gift to us
6 brought my mother a cup of coffee
7 made me a beautiful dress

UNIT 03

Ⓐ **1** to marry **2** to go **3** to get out **4** to sit down **5** to become **6** to come **7** to read

Ⓑ **1** calm **2** cold **3** happy **4** a bookworm **5** interesting **6** a great swimmer **7** warm

Ⓒ **1** keep, your, room, clean
2 want, you, to, come **3** named, her, Sally
4 advise, you, to, find **5** expect, him, to, win
6 found, the, soccer, game, exciting
7 told, me, to, study

Ⓓ **1** found him guilty **2** named the bird Dodo
3 found his jokes funny **4** expect him to stay
5 ordered her son to play
6 advised me to exercise
7 told me to take care of my brother

Chapter 10

UNIT 01

Ⓐ **1** happy **2** clean **3** wrong **4** new **5** boring **6** old **7** salty **8** beautiful

Ⓑ **1** many **2** much **3** little **4** few **5** a few **6** a little

Ⓒ **1** a, lot, of, jobs **2** a, little, sugar
3 little, money **4** few, things
5 many, stars **6** a, lot, of, water
7 a, few, books

Ⓓ **1** There were a few chairs
2 There is nothing wrong
3 keep the children safe
4 don't do anything dangerous
5 looks really beautiful
6 asked me some difficult questions
7 He told me something new

UNIT 02

Ⓐ **1** quietly **2** happily **3** simply **4** carefully **5** nicely **6** really **7** mainly **8** newly **9** terribly **10** comfortably **11** well **12** fast **13** heavily **14** slowly **15** possibly **16** badly **17** early **18** specially **19** necessarily **20** luckily

Ⓑ **1** late **2** late **3** lately **4** hardly **5** hard

6 hard 7 highly 8 high 9 high

C 1 will never let 2 is always kind
3 is usually at home
4 sometimes goes to the movies

D 1 easy, easily 2 clearly, clear
3 carelessly, careless 4 quickly, quick
5 beautifully, beautiful 6 fluently, fluent

E 1 tried to answer honestly
2 always go to work by subway
3 sometimes plays tennis after school
4 Luckily, solved the difficult problem

UNIT 03

A 1 happier, happiest 2 more serious, most serious
3 dirtier, dirtiest 4 easier, easiest
5 simpler, simplest 6 luckier, luckiest
7 better, best 8 more, most 9 older, oldest
10 later, latest 11 more expensive, most expensive
12 thinner, thinnest 13 more colorful, most colorful
14 hotter, hottest 15 larger, largest
16 more famous, most famous 17 worse, worst
18 less, least 19 elder, eldest 20 latter, last

B 1 sweeter than 2 heavier than
3 more carefully than 4 less than
5 better than 6 the hottest 7 the oldest
8 the best 9 the strongest 10 the most famous

C 1 bigger than 2 cleaner than
3 more quickly than 4 fresher than
5 harder than

D 1 as cheap as 2 as old as 3 as expensive as
4 as comfortable as 5 as high as

E 1 as, heavy, as 2 fatter, than 3 more, than
4 the, fastest, way 5 the, most, popular, song

Chapter 11

UNIT 01

A 1 and 2 but 3 so 4 or 5 but 6 or 7 and
8 so

B 1 or, baseball 2 Jack, and, Gale 3 so, I, went, to, bed, early 4 but, I, can't, remember, it

C 1 or send me a text message
2 and won first prizo 3 but you didn't answer
4 so we went on a picnic 5 but he couldn't
6 so I took a taxi 7 or chocolate cake
8 and writing children's books

D 1 sweet, and, sour 2 and, go, shopping
3 so, he, took, a, pill 4 or, having, dinner
5 yesterday, or, the, day, before, yesterday
6 so, I, was, late, for, school
7 but, an, F, in, math

UNIT 02

A 1 before 2 when 3 after 4 before 5 When
6 until 7 after

B 1 When I go jogging
2 before you come in
3 After it stopped snowing
4 When Carol smiled at me
5 after I finish reading it
6 until I found it
7 before she sang a song

C 1 when he was in the USA
2 after she gets the message
3 until the dough is golden brown
4 Before it gets dark
5 Until she sends me an email
6 After Daniel left home
7 before you go back to Korea
8 When winter vacation comes

D 1 before, you, go, out
2 After, I, had, dinner
3 until, I, went, to, university
4 When, we, lived, in, Paris
5 After, you, watch, the, DVD

UNIT 03

A 1 if 2 that 3 that 4 If 5 because
6 because

B 1 that you can finish the work on time
2 if you have any questions about that
3 because she was very busy

C 1 if you wear this suit 2 because he was sick
3 that people always want to be happy

D **1** if, you, want
2 because, he, was, tired
3 that, he, came, from, England
4 that, she, is, good, at
5 because, I didn't, know, your, phone, number
6 If, you, work, together

E **1** that the picture is very nice
2 because he told a lie again
3 that today is my brother's birthday
4 If you didn't bring your textbook
5 If you don't arrive on time
6 Because she is my best friend

Chapter 12

UNIT 01

A **1** in **2** at **3** on

B **1** over, under
2 in front of, behind
3 between, next to, across from

C **1** at, the, party **2** next, to, you
3 in, Los, Angeles **4** on, the, floor
5 over, the, fence **6** behind, the, teacher
7 under, the, big, tree.

D **1** a huge hole in front of you
2 put the lamp beside the bed
3 sleeping next to me
4 from top to toe
5 at the park across from the library
6 between the black van and the sports car
7 a restaurant near the downtown area

UNIT 02

A **1** in **2** at **3** at **4** on **5** on **6** at **7** in **8** in
9 on

B **1** until **2** by **3** by **4** until

C **1** for **2** during **3** during **4** for

D **1** until, Friday **2** after, four, o'clock
3 before, nine **4** in, summer
5 from, April, to, October
6 on, Thanksgiving, Day
7 between, Christmas, and, New, Year

E **1** play soccer after school
2 until nine o'clock at night
3 at two in the afternoon
4 at 8 pm on Wednesday
5 from June to August
6 During the class, for 15 minutes
7 wash my father's car before dinner

UNIT 03

A **1** to **2** for **3** with **4** by **5** for **6** with **7** by
8 about

B **1** about **2** by **3** with **4** to

C **1** from, Chris **2** smells, like, roses
3 to, Busan, by, the, KTX **4** to, her
5 for, his, queen **6** about, her, dream
7 with, chopsticks

D **1** is in a red sweater
2 don't know anything about him
3 a birthday gift for my mother
4 sent a present to Charlie
5 lives with a roommate in a dormitory
6 pay by credit card in this restaurant
7 dressed like Snow White for Halloween

새 교과서 반영
중등 내신 완벽 대비서
GRAMMAR 공감

- 최신 교과서의 학습 내용을 반영한 **체계적인 문법 설명**
- 2,500여 개의 전국 중학교 기출 문제 완전 분석 후 **문법 포인트, 문제 반영**
- 공부감각을 업그레이드 시켜주는 다양한 **서술형 평가 코너 수록 및 워크북 제공**
- 놓치기 쉬운 문법 포인트를 잡아 주는 **Plus α, Tips 코너 수록**
- 말하기, 쓰기, 읽기의 실용적 쓰임을 생각한 **통합형 문법 학습**
- 2,000여 개 이상의 충분한 문제풀이를 통한 **문법 감각 향상**

넥서스 중등 영어
공감시리즈로
공부감각을
키우세요!

NEXUS makes your next day
www.nexusEDU.kr | 책에 대해 궁금한 사항은 넥서스에듀 홈페이지 **1:1 고객상담 게시판**을 이용하세요.